# BALCONY EMPIRE

# BALCONY EMPIRE

## FASCIST ITALY AT WAR

REYNOLDS (and ELEANOR) PACKARD

New York OXFORD UNIVERSITY PRESS Toronto
1942

42 - 25891

# BALCONY EMPIRE

# I

## PROLOGUE

An old, ramshackle office building on the Via della Mercede, 54, was some years ago remodeled and ornamented with stucco walls, plaster-of-Paris pillars, and an imitation dome, studded with tiny circular windows that looked like misplaced portholes. Chromium fittings added a modern, Fascist touch. Under the dome a bar was set up where excellent drinks were served cheaper than those to be had at any *bottiglicria* in Italy. An efficient, fast long-distance telephone service with soundproof booths was inaugurated on the mezzanine floor above the bar. Newspapers from all over Italy and many parts of Europe were carefully kept on file. There were a ping-pong table, a piano, a reception room, a bridge room, and a vine-covered garden. There were also two large and several small writing rooms, outfitted with desks and lamps, where those without private offices on the floors above could work.

There were dances on frequent occasions — even after Italy went to war and such social pleasures were banned elsewhere. Real coffee was served here, even though the Fascist clubs could not obtain more than a *surrogato*, made from roasted barley and peanuts. Eggs fried in butter could be bought at the bar every morning for breakfast, although the Italian ration for ordinary people was one egg a week and one quarter of a pound of butter a month. There were free tickets to the opera from time to time. Seventy per cent reduction on the price of all Italian railway tickets was to be had for the asking.

Here were issued the latest news bulletins, communiqués, and official announcements. There was a reference library (Fascist). And the price of membership to this philanthropic institution was only one hundred lire — about five dollars — a year.

If you were a foreign correspondent stationed in Rome, you had to belong whether or not you wanted to. This was Mussolini's idea of the best way to deal with foreign correspondents. In it was a Black Shirt version of the Machiavellian touch. Mussolini, once a newspaperman himself, always believed that newspapermen could be bought, or at least cajoled, into serving the purposes of Fascism.

Thus Il Duce established, as a Fascist-subsidized institution, this Foreign Press Club known as the Associazione della Stampa Estera. Besides pampering the correspondents with the object of keeping them in a good humor, the club served another purpose: it greatly simplified the work of the OVRA — the Fascist Secret Police — whose duty it was to check on the activities of the correspondents. Many news facilities were offered the correspondent as an inducement to him to work in the building, and every possible obstruction was placed in his way if he insisted on doing his work elsewhere. Phone calls to foreign cities went through faster from the Stampa Estera than from the homes of the correspondents or from any other outside point. The reason was simple: the OVRA, with the aid of expert linguists, had carefully tapped all the phones in the Foreign Press Club building and was prepared to listen in at a moment's notice.

The OVRA had established a setup which worked efficiently only from this one point. A call, say to Zurich, from some other part of Rome would catch the telephone operator unprepared.

She would be afraid to let the call go through until she could arrange for a censor who knew the language. And if she were in doubt as to the language to be used in the forthcoming conversation, she would check back with seemingly stupid questions until she had ascertained whether it would be in English, French, or some other tongue. If she made a mistake, the censor merely cut the line.

The Foreign Press Club also offered the Fascist Press Ministry — whose pompous official title was the Ministry of Popular Culture — an opportunity to plant propaganda news, over the bar, on the foreign correspondents. One must admit that it was cleverly done and that it was often difficult to distinguish between a Fascist handout and genuine information.

On the other hand, once one learned how to utilize it, the Press Club became a valuable market place for news tips. American correspondents used it as a sort of stock exchange where one had to be wary of wildcat shares, but where there were many good "buys" for those who knew how to judge values. We both used it to its utmost — not, however, without making a few blunders at first — and became so well acquainted with the different foreign correspondents, the Swiss, Swedish, Spanish, Germans, Greeks, and Yugoslavs, and their individual and national prejudices, that we could tell fairly accurately the value of a given piece of information. Actually, anti-Fascist news occupied most of the correspondents' gossip, as many of them tried to draw each other out in an effort to get inside information for their own embassy or legation. Most of the European correspondents were virtually government envoys.

It was in the Stampa Estera at 8:05 P.M., December 10, 1941, that we had the first definite indication, amounting almost to official confirmation, that Mussolini would line up with Japan and declare war against the United States the following day.

The correspondents gathered round the bar had all been discussing the probabilities for and against the Axis' coming to the aid of Japan under the Tripartite Pact and most of the correspondents, including ourselves, fully believed the Axis would soon be at war with America. For one thing, it was rather reliably reported that Mussolini would speak from the balcony of the Palazzo Venezia to the Roman Fascists the next day, and this was such a rare occurrence that it usually presaged an announcement of great importance.

While the talk was going on, the Japanese correspondents sat at a table a few feet away, drinking *americanos* and pretending not to listen. The frank discussion of whether or not Japan needed help and whether it would be to the advantage of the Axis to live up to the provisions of the Tripartite Pact did not please them. If they listened openly, they might hear Japan insulted and be forced to take some action. One of them, Maida of the *Asahi Shimbum*, had already once been expelled from Italy for striking an employee of the Stampa Estera. It was better to seem not to hear.

As the pros and cons flew back and forth, the Nazi *Gauleiter* of all the German correspondents in Italy, Baron Wolfgang von Langen, came up to the bar and ordered a beer. When he heard the conversation, he turned to us with that half-joking, half-hostile manner he always used with Americans (after each new Roosevelt pronouncement against Hitler, he always stopped speaking to Americans for exactly three days), and said, "If we do not declare war I think the Americans will be greatly disappointed. They seem to want it. They have already arrested all our German correspondents in America."

We knew they had also arrested the Italian correspondents a few hours later, but did not say so. No use letting these people, few of them real friends, know that we ourselves were perhaps in imminent danger of arrest. Instead we replied:

"The Germans have also arrested all the American correspondents in Berlin."

"Only as a reprisal," von Langen declared belligerently. "Herr Doktor Schmidt expressly stated at the press conference that there was no personal ill-will toward any of them."

How often we were to hear that same phrase during the next

few months. The Italians who eventually arrested and interned us certainly overworked Herr Doktor Schmidt's statement for all it was worth.

At this point, a pro-Italian Swiss journalist spoke up and said: "If the Americans have arrested the German but not the Italian journalists, perhaps they hope to keep Italy out of the war. Another attempt to divide the Axis, perhaps. But I do not think Mussolini will stay out if Hitler goes in."

Just then an usher came up and said, "Signor Direttore Packard is wanted on the telephone." The *direttore* merely meant manager of the Rome Bureau of the United Press. Italians are very punctilious about using all one's titles, if any.

Reynolds went to the phone and emitted such grunts and groans as usually characterize a correspondent's telephone conversation when he knows that several of his colleagues are listening and hoping to find out something. When he came back, there was a certain suppressed excitement in his step. He didn't keep his news to himself, however, but announced to everyone present:

"One of my staff has just informed me that the Ministry of Popular Culture has phoned to say that American correspondents cannot send any more cables or make any long-distance calls. We are incommunicado. The Ministry says that the same restrictions have been placed on all the other American correspondents in Rome."

"That means they have decided on war," a Hungarian correspondent said somberly. The only Finnish correspondent in Rome, Miss Liizi Karttunin, sobbed.

"That means you are going to side with the enemies of my country. And once you were our best friends. How terrible."

We soothed her as best we could.

She was sixty-eight, but young-looking; strong, hard-working, and courageous in the traditional Finnish manner, and with an added sense of humor her countrymen usually lacked. Her home had been in the Isthmus of Karelia, occupied by the Russians in 1940.

As soon as we could get away, we hastened to the office and telephoned the American Embassy. When we informed Chargé d'Affaires George Wadsworth, who was still hard at work at his desk at 8:15 P.M., that our office had been closed down, he replied:

"That fits in with all the other indications we've had. Looks as though the lid is going to blow off tomorrow." He added that the report that the Duce was speaking next day appeared to be confirmed on all sides.

In the office we tore up the three news dispatches we had been waiting for the censor to pass and threw them into the air like confetti. We felt suddenly imbued with a holiday spirit. It was the end of our work in Italy. For the first time in three years we were free from the tyranny of the telephone. All during that time we had never gone anywhere or done anything without leaving word at the office as to where we were and how we could be reached by telephone. It was the indispensable precaution against being beaten on a big news story. We determined to leave the office early and make the most of these few remaining hours between peace and war. But before we could leave we had to destroy all our files and documents dealing with the nonofficial news we obtained from secret sources. We carefully burned all these papers in a tin wastebasket behind the locked doors of Reynolds' private office. We had kept them in one single bundle so that in case of just such an emergency we could dispose of them quickly.

As we were throwing the ashes out the window, there was a knock on the door. Eleanor opened it, and two of our staffers, Eddie Laura and Gino Zaccardi — Italo-Americans — filed in, looking both embarrassed and defiant. They said they had something important to tell us. What they had to say was that, faced with a declaration of war, they had chosen to become Italian citizens and had turned in their American passports to the police, at the same time signing a statement that they considered themselves Italians henceforth.

We thought they had made a poor choice and said so, but

we knew they were both in a position which made it hard for them to leave Italy. Eddie was the sole support of a widowed Italian mother, while Gino had an Italian fiancée. What was hardest to forgive, however, was the surrender of the passports. They were the new green ones, of which only a limited number had been issued, as most Americans had been evacuated from Europe before the color of the passports had been changed. We foresaw correctly that the Embassy was going to be very upset about two such passports falling into Fascist hands. With a little alteration they could be used to get Axis agents into the United States.

However, it was too late to do anything, and in silence we returned to the outer office, where our Italian employees were standing around looking forlorn and lost. For some reason we felt much more hostile toward Eddie and Gino than we did toward the ones who had always been Italian. For the most part we had got along well with our Italian staff. Most of them weren't Fascists, and all of them were friendly to Americans and American ways. Now the coming war had cost them their jobs, and it might not be so easy to find new ones, for previous service with an American firm would be no recommendation.

Our two one hundred per cent American staffers, Livingstone Pomeroy and Robert Allen-Tuska, were also waiting impatiently for instructions, as they had last-minute personal affairs they wanted to attend to before the actual declaration of war. We told everyone we were taking the evening off but would be in next morning to wind up office business, as the Duce wasn't to speak until 2:30 P.M.

Feeling more and more excited every moment with the sense of tremendous events rushing toward us, we hurried downstairs and had farewell drinks at the Stampa Estera bar with Swiss, Spanish, and Scandinavian friends and the mystery man, Prince Popoff. The Prince called himself a White Russian, but he was from that part of czarist Russia which subsequently became Estonia, and no one knew exactly why he was an exile from that non-Bolshevist state. He had lived in Rome many years, working for a Swiss newspaper. The manner of the Germans had changed perceptibly in the hour that had passed since we left the bar. They accorded us that cold courtesy with which the Heidelberg student faces his opponent with bared saber the moment before the seconds give the duelists the signal to start. The Japanese giggled foolishly in the background.

We gathered up the companions with whom we had previously arranged to have dinner — John Goshie, an Embassy secretary, and Camille Cianfarra, New York Times correspondent, and went to one of our favorite restaurants in Rome.

The headwaiter, who knew us, showed surprise as we entered. He quickly recovered himself, however, and led us to a corner alcove where we were hidden from the general view.

"This has the advantage," he said in stilted English, "of not being too conspicuous. Tomorrow the Fascists may come and remember that you were here tonight and that we were friendly to you."

He wore the party badge himself, yet he talked about the Fascists as though he were no part of them.

After he finished taking our order and the silver ice bucket containing the Orvieto had been placed on the table, he said: "You, too, have heard that the Duce will declare war on America tomorrow? It is terrible. It is the end of business for us. It is the end of everything for Italy."

He quickly hurried away and beamed upon General Cavallero, chief of the General Staff, who had just come in, garbed in mufti, with his wife. The General had apparently come to Rome for a conference with Mussolini about the forthcoming war against the United States. Despite the presence of this professional Black Shirt, we were nevertheless objects of interest. Four different Italians who had seen us enter came over to shake hands with us and wish us luck. Two were Italian journalists, the third a banker, and the fourth the manager of one of the best-known hotels in Italy. Two of them asked us to relay greetings to their relatives in the United States. At the end of the meal the headwaiter came over to us and whispered, "Will you have a bottle of champagne on the house? A sort of farewell present to our American friends."

We told him we would rather have Strega, as it was more fitting that we should drink farewell to Rome with *liquore italiano*. He personally served us the drinks and then, clinking glasses all around, said in a low voice:

"Here's to America! May you return soon."

Here again was Italian charm oozing through the mail of Fascism. And yet, just how far could such friendliness be trusted? Certainly these people were risking their positions, even their careers, to be so friendly with us. Or were they thinking ahead, thinking of the day when Americans would return to Italy and they would be able to recall with pride that gesture of friendliness on the eve of war against the United States? That undoubtedly is the enigma of the Italians. No other people can be so sincerely friendly and yet make such effective use of friendliness as a means to an end.

Goshie, as the diplomat, made Cianfarra and ourselves extremely conscious that we were only newspapermen when, with an attempt at humor, he asked us: "What is the difference between a diplomat and a foreign correspondent?"

His answer was, "The diplomat is sure to get home."

It was true, and it occurred to us not for the first time that we might spend the entire war as prisoners in Italy. With this grim thought in mind, we broke up and went to our respective homes. We spent part of the night burning letters from friendly anti-Fascists, for fear the house might be searched and incriminating evidence be found against them.

The next morning we had breakfast served to us with tears. The Italian cook and maid, as well as the *portiera* of the apartment house in which we lived, came into our bedroom with coffee and bootleg eggs. They wanted to know if it were true that Mussolini was going to declare war on the United States.

Why did he want to do that? Americans were such sympathetic people, and America was where all good Italians went when they left Italy. How would they ever find such generous people to work for after the Americans were gone? They had learned of the forthcoming declaration of war through the omniscient, ever-functioning gossip radio system of the Italian people, whose commentators as well as listeners range from the humblest to the highest, from the servants to their masters.

We went to the office, and Reynolds paid the salaries to date of all the employees. Many of the Italian staffers and office boys turned their heads away as they shook hands with us. They were embarrassed at the tears that welled in their eyes. It was the last of the U.P. in Rome for all the unknown number of war years to come.

Out in the street, people were already beginning to converge upon the Palazzo Venezia. At one P.M. we locked up the office and went out to see what was taking place. Thousands upon thousands of people, many of them in Black Shirt uniforms, were walking in groups down the middle of the Corso Umberto, on which all vehicular traffic had been suspended.

Besides banners and standards, many of them carried obscene cartoons of President Roosevelt and our First Lady of the land. Some were so mean and scurrilous that they cannot even be mentioned. One of the more refined ones depicted Mrs. Roosevelt wearing a toilet seat for a necklace. Another had crossed canes on a field of dollar signs. The President was also depicted in scores of ways as a gourmand eating up little countries. The favorite Fascist phrase, "Down with Pluto-Democracy," was emblazoned on hundreds of banners. Only people wearing black shirts, however, carried these insults.

We slipped down a side street to reach the rear of Venice Square, so we would not get caught in the press of the fifty thousand people gathered there. The balcony was already prepared for the occasion, being draped with the Italian and Fascist flags and equipped with a microphone.

Soon Mussolini, dressed in the uniform of a corporal of honor of the Black Shirt Militia and a field cap that covered his baldness, popped out on the balcony, and the paid Fascist claques

let out a roar of "Duce! Duce! Duce!" The German Ambassador
to the Quirinal, Hans Georg von Mackensen, towering above Mussolini, then appeared on the balcony, followed by the tiny Japanese Ambassador, Zembei Horikiri. Mussolini, who had decreed
that all press photographers must photograph him from below
knee-high level in order to give the impression of height, looked
smaller than ever. And like a little man suffering from a dwarf complex, he tried to look fierce and mimicked his own conception of
a war lord.

It was one of the briefest speeches the Duce had ever made —
less than three hundred words long. Between each sentence, he
paused lengthily and gave the professional cheering squad an opportunity to arouse the people. In front of each group of claques
was a loud-speaker that amplified the applause and cheering ten-
fold. Over the radio, it must have made an impressive sound; but
to us, who could see motionless hands and lips on all sides, the
noise seemed as unreal as offstage sound effects breaking in at the
wrong time. Certainly, most of the people we saw didn't find anything in the speech that warranted acclamation.

It was war against the United States, where most of them had
relatives, and it was a glorification of the Japanese, whom the
Fascist press some years before had, on Mussolini's orders, referred to as a menace to the white race.

The professional applause and cheers came like irreverent laugh-
ter at a funeral when Il Duce roared: "The powers of the Steel
Pact — Fascist Italy and Nazi Germany — participate in this war
as from today on the side of the heroic Japanese against the United
States. . . . I say to you that it is a privilege to fight with them.

". . . The Tripartite Pact becomes a military alliance which
draws around its colors two hundred and fifty million men, determined to do all in order to win.

". . . Italians, once more arise and be worthy of this historic
hour. We will win."

The fifty thousand people started dispersing before the prearranged applause and shouts of "Duce! Duce! Duce!" had come

to an end. We estimated that of those fifty thousand people, at least forty thousand refrained from any show of approval. Here, beyond doubt, was a silent protest — the first open protest against an act by the Duce that we had ever seen during our three years in Fascist Italy.

But, we agreed, it was not the sort of protest that would overthrow the Fascist regime. It was a passive, voiceless protest of silence, eloquent in its way, but certainly futile. Here was Fascism in the Italy of today: one man telling fifty thousand people amidst a theatrical setting that he is doing the very thing they object to, and they listen in silence and return to their homes or their offices and grumble cautiously among themselves.

Suddenly it came upon us that we were at war with all these people around us. We didn't know where to go next. We noticed that people stared at us as they overheard us talking in English.

Already the kiosks we passed were displaying newspapers that contained the Duce's speech. It had been given to the press before he spoke, so that the editors could have it put in type and ready for circulation the moment Mussolini finished speaking. We could see the banner line: DUCE DECLARES WAR AGAINST THE UNITED STATES. It was like a nightmare — hearing a speech and then almost simultaneously reading it in the newspapers. We turned automatically toward the office and accidentally bumped into Popoff from the Foreign Press Club. He always had spoken to us in his most excellent Oxford English, but this time he resorted to Italian.

"You have heard," he said in a most impersonal tone, "that the Italian police are arresting all the American correspondents. It's in reciprocity, of course, for the arrest of Italian correspondents in America."

"Grazie," we chorused, and dived into a taxicab that was cruising slowly down the street.

"To the American Embassy. Presto," we directed, and sat back to grope for our bearings.

They were difficult to find. The Italians were such a likable people. Anybody who had ever lived in Italy had found them so. Yet here they were being lined up against the United States, the land of their prosperous relatives, and this, apparently, against their own will. Somewhere along the line of modern history, Mussolini had run off the track and dragged Italy into a wreckage of war.

As the cab weaved its way slowly through a tangle of streets without sidewalks, the chauffeur banging on the side of the car to urge people out of the way — the Duce had forbidden the use of horns as unaesthetic — we thought back on the early days of Fascism. There were domestic reforms, many of them, that Mussolini had made which were not to be passed over lightly by the student of sociology. There was no doubt that he had cleaned up the big cities of Italy so that they shone like polished mirrors and had undertaken an agricultural program which had already increased national production and was tending to improve the lot of many farmers. Yet he was responsible for the present debacle.

He was the one who had declared war on England and stabbed France in the back. Yet even before then, Fascist action had been cast into a definite military line by the Steel Pact of 1939; and that, too, was merely a follow-up of the Italo-German co-operation in Spain.

When he decided to help Franco, Mussolini abandoned one of the principles of his earlier days as dictator — Fascism is not for export. During that conflict, which marked the beginning of the military collaboration of Germany and Italy on the actual field of battle, the Duce imparted to Fascism an international character by announcing to the world that Italy would not tolerate a Bolshevik power in the Mediterranean.

But Italian participation in Spain was a direct aftermath of the Black Shirt campaign in Ethiopia. Yes, we agreed, as the cab turned into the Via Boncompagni and we could see the entrance to the United States Embassy guarded by *carabinieri*, it all went back to the days when Mussolini decided to invade Ethiopia. Then and there, it seemed to us in retrospect, he had set a course which inevitably carried him right through six years of history into the war against the United States. The Fascist victory in Ethiopia had been a victory of airplanes and artillery over carbines and spears; but it was enough to make Mussolini think that he had tweaked the British lion's tail and that he could henceforth pull it at will. He immediately conceived the idea of building up an anti-British bloc in Europe with the hope of extending the Fascist Empire overseas and of developing Fascist influence in Europe. There was only one other person in the world at that moment who fitted in with his plans. He was Hitler. Hitler had already shown his friendship by giving Italy economic aid during the League of Nations sanctions period. And thus the Axis was born, like some horror child, out of the womb of the Ethiopian war.

The cab came to a halt and we made a run for it, through the line of *carabinieri*, who were garbed in the same greenish-gray uniforms with steel helmets that they wore when they took over the patrolling of the streets of Addis Ababa, following Badoglio's triumphal entry. Only this time they were patrolling outside the United States Embassy in Rome.

# II

WE WERE IN PARIS WHEN MUSSOLINI BEGAN TO PAVE THE WAY FOR a military thrust at Ethiopia. He started with a political campaign on December 9, 1934, when he pounced upon the clash at Ualual, in southern Abyssinia, between an Ethiopian camel corps and Italian Dubats. There may or may not have been a few casualties as Mussolini claimed, but it was enough to start balcony speeches. Mussolini immediately demanded reparations for the alleged attack on his troops, but refused to arbitrate. On January 3, 1935, Ethiopia embarrassed everybody except Mussolini by invoking Article II of the Covenant to request the League to take "every measure effectively to safeguard peace."

From then on, until the late summer of 1935, the League of Nations adroitly avoided taking any stand or even investigating the incident. It kept urging Ethiopia to arbitrate, although it was Italy and not Ethiopia which had refused to do so. The embarrassing dispute was passed from committee to commission and back to subcommittee, the one aim of all these bodies being to pass it on to someone else as soon as possible.

The League's inability to act was much more serious than any dispute between Italy and Ethiopia. It meant the collapse of the whole postwar political system. Part of the trouble arose because the practical permanent and nonpolitical functionaries of the Foreign Offices of London and Paris urged the sacrifice of Ethiopia as a cheap way to keep Mussolini happy and on the Allied side, while at the same time the public statesmen, who depended on getting votes to stay in office, did not dare to take this attitude publicly.

A compromise between the idealistic and realistic attitudes was attempted when Eden went to Rome in June, 1935. He suggested that Italy accept part of the Ogaden and advantageous frontier rectifications on the Sudanese-Eritrean border, plus economic concessions in Ethiopia as a compromise.

Mussolini curtly replied: "Mr. Eden, Fascist Italy is not interested in collecting deserts."

Meanwhile, Mussolini had been steadily mobilizing his forces and shipping them to the Italian East African colonies of Eritrea, adjacent to northern Ethiopia, and Italian Somaliland, on Ethiopia's southern frontier. The first troops sailed for Africa on February 16, and four days later General Emilio de Bono was appointed supreme commander of Italian forces in East Africa. From then on a steady stream of Italian soldiers and military supplies flowed to East Africa through the Suez Canal, with the tacit consent of the British and French, who, had they dared, could have closed the canal to Italian transports and thus frustrated Mussolini's Ethiopian adventure from the very beginning.

But Mussolini had carefully studied the world reaction to the Japanese invasion of Manchuria — an invasion which had exposed the incapacity of the League to check a determined power bent on conquest. It revealed that the two most powerful nations in the League, Britain and France, were in no position to take a strong stand against aggression. With the rise of Hitler, France and England had even more reason for conciliating Italy. Mussolini was confident that with a little diplomatic maneuvering he could hog-tie the League.

By the summer of 1935, it was clear that war was inevitable, and while the League procrastinated, news organizations prepared for war coverage. The U.P. sent Ed Beattie to Addis Ababa, Bud Ekins was next rushed to Harar, and, finally, Webb Miller flew to Asmara. We were envious and wanted to get in on the coming war. Hugh Baillie, President of the U.P., came to Paris in September. Reynolds hinted that we were both fairly good.

"Are you both good enough to catch the *Porthos* out of Marseilles day after tomorrow?" he asked.

"Isn't there anything sooner?" Eleanor asked, trying to make an impression.

Baillie laughed. "Just catch that boat. I want you to backstop from French Somaliland when the war starts. And cover the Red Sea as well. You will also be in a position to pinch-hit quickly if any of the boys get sick and have to leave."

We caught the *Porthos*, which proved to be a virtual transport, it was so full of French soldiers being sent to Djibouti.

On the evening of October 2, her wireless picked up a French newscast, containing Mussolini's speech delivered from the balcony of the Palazzo Venezia that same afternoon. The Duce said:

"When, in 1915, Italy threw her fate with the Allies, how many cries of admiration there were, how many promises. But after the common victory, which cost Italy six hundred thousand dead, four hundred thousand lost, one million wounded, when peace was being discussed around the table, only the crumbs of the rich colonial booty were left for us to pick up. . . .

"We have been patient with Ethiopia for forty years — it is enough now. Instead of recognizing the rights of Italy, the League of Nations dares to talk of sanctions. . . . To acts of war, we shall answer with acts of war.

"Let me repeat, in the most categorical manner, the sacred pledge which I make at this moment before all the Italians

gathered together today, that I shall do everything in my power
to prevent a colonial conflict from taking on the aspect and
weight of a European war. . . ."

It was a plain warning to the British that any attempt to
interfere with Fascist Italy's plans at that late date would plunge
Europe into war. Mussolini was willing to gamble Fascist Italy's
very national existence rather than turn back.

Next day, October 3, we received a wireless message from the
U.P. saying that Italian troops had invaded Ethiopia at five A.M.
and that our European boss, Webb Miller, had scored a world-
shaking scoop on the news.

The French soldiers and officers aboard the ship were visibly
shaken by the event. Their universal comment on the Italians
was: "Les salauds!"

On October 6 we arrived in Djibouti, a small, sleepy, blisteringly
hot colonial town of native huts and a few whitewashed plaster
hotels, that had boomed overnight, like a bonanza mining camp,
as a result of the war. It was crowded with correspondents, ad-
venturers, spies, and armament salesmen who were hoping that
the Anglo-French embargo on arms to Ethiopia would eventually
be lifted. The town was so crowded that the first night we had
to sleep in the back yard of the Continental Hotel on the folding
cots we had brought with us. Practically everyone in Djibouti, from
the little native boys who offered to fan flies away from customers
on the café terraces to the French colonial authorities, regarded
the war as a means to make money. Black girls were brought in
from the desert hinterlands by enterprising Armenian impresarios
as dancers in cabarets hastily set up under the palm trees outside
of the town.

But in all this helter-skelter, one thing was clear — the Anglo-
French embargo on arms to Ethiopia was airtight. Even newspaper
correspondents, boarding the Djibouti-Addis Ababa train, were not
permitted by the French authorities to take revolvers that they had
brought with them for personal protection. Tecle Hawariat, the
Ethiopian Minister to France, whom we had known personally in

Paris, was greatly upset when the French refused to accord him diplomatic immunity and confiscated a score of cases of rifles and ammunition which he was taking to his own tribesmen. He told Eleanor from his train window:

"This embargo is the most unfair action that has been taken against Ethiopia. In Geneva, I was told by almost all the League members — with the exception of Italy, of course — that they wanted to see my country win. And this is what they are doing to us. I am heartbroken. It is true that the embargo also applies to Italy, but that is merely a trick which favors the Italians. The Italians have been preparing many years for this invasion, and they already have more than enough artillery, aviation, machine guns, and hand grenades which they can ship to their front lines through Eritrea. Why isn't this embargo applied to the Italians at Port Said?"

The British authorities were as strict as the French. Reynolds made a trip through the desert to Zeila, one of the main British Somaliland ports on the Red Sea, and discussed the arms-embargo regulations at lunch with the British Resident General in his home. He stated with great pride that no arms were reaching the Ethiopians through his area. The Negus was being strangled by his own friends.

Eleanor made a trip to Aden, on the other side of the Red Sea, and found that the British there were prepared for an attack by the Italians. On an automobile trip around the Crown Colony, she saw new consignments of antiaircraft guns, both land and seaplanes, and that the harbor had a big detachment of the British fleet, including a battleship, cruisers, and destroyers. There was no doubt that the British believed Italy might go to war against England if any incidents broke out which Mussolini might interpret as British intervention. In a way, these defense measures on the part of the British showed the extent to which Mussolini had been successful in his bluff threats.

The possibility of such a war was used by Mussolini to keep the British from really taking any stronger measures than they did against his Ethiopian invasion. Italians disseminated rumors that they had shipped large quantities of Mas boats to Massawa and Assab, where they were hidden in secret harbors, and that several hundred more were strategically scattered in different parts of the Mediterranean.

From what we had seen at first hand, Mussolini had been extremely successful in the political manipulation of his campaign, and we were anxious to see how the military part of the program was working out. This opportunity came to Reynolds when he was suddenly transferred to Asmara in November as a war correspondent with the Italian army. Eleanor was simultaneously transferred to Cairo. We made the trip from Djibouti to Massawa together aboard an Italian freighter en route to Egypt and spent our last evening before separating in Massawa, where we had dinner at the only hotel. All the men wore shorts, polo shirts, and sun helmets and went out of their way to make our acquaintance, the sole reason being that white women were rare events in East Africa.

Before it got dark, we tried to walk down the main street, which ran along the docks, but soon abandoned the effort as thousands of soldiers and dock hands gathered around us to catch a glimpse of la donna bianca. During this short walk, however, we ran across plenty of evidence of the inefficiency of the Italian supply services. We saw at least six smashed tanks that had been dropped while being unloaded as a result of using cranes that were too light for the work. Bags of sugar and flour had been left uncovered on the docks and rained upon. Huge packages of spaghetti had spilled their contents on one of the wharves. The ships in the harbor were jammed, and we could see one boat that was ready to depart but couldn't leave because it was so hemmed in by other vessels.

Eleanor left during the night aboard the freighter, and Reynolds went out to the airfield in the morning for a scheduled departure at nine o'clock. But there was a delay. The plane from Asmara had not yet landed, although it could be heard in the dense cloud banks overhead, circling around in search of a patch of visibility. It finally landed safely an hour and a half overdue. Airport officials calmly explained that there was no direct phone, cable, or wireless communication between the Asmara and Massawa airports and that each plane, when it took off, had to risk finding visibility on arrival.

"It is rather dangerous, flying up to Asmara," one official told Reynolds, "because it is a straight climb of more than three thousand meters. The pilots fly out to sea until they reach half of the altitude and then turn back toward Asmara."

When Reynolds arrived in Asmara, feeling as though he had just come off an aerial roller-coaster, he was met by Webb Miller. In the ride into town, Webb said: "If de Bono is not removed soon, the Italians, instead of taking Ethiopia, will lose Eritrea."

He said that de Bono had been put in charge because he was a veteran Black Shirt, member of the Quadrumvirate, and a personal friend of Il Duce. He was making a mess of things. After six weeks of fighting, he had not succeeded in penetrating into Ethiopia more than seventy-five miles at any point. It was true, Webb said, that de Bono had taken Aduwa, Aksum and Adigrat, but those cities had fallen during the first few days of the war, when the Ethiopians retired with virtually no fighting to more tenable positions in the interior. After that, his flying columns which went in pursuit of the native warriors suffered severe casualties and were seldom able to engage the enemy in pitched combat. The Ethiopians, few of whom had uniforms, took their white shammas and dirtied them with black mud so that they could not be seen in the dark and under cover of night would sneak up on the Italian encampments, killing and castrating many Italian soldiers with their hooked knives.

It was so bad, in fact, despite the reassuring communiqués issued by Rome, that Mussolini had to call upon an anti-Fascist and his worst enemy to come out of military retirement and make order out of chaos. He was General Pietro Badoglio, who, at the time of the Black Shirt March on Rome, said to King Victor Emmanuel: "Give me a battalion of Royal Carabinieri and I will sweep away these Fascist upstarts. At the first shot fired, all Fascism will crumble."

Badoglio had started World War I as a lieutenant colonel but so distinguished himself that by the end of the conflict in 1918, he had risen to the rank of general and become assistant Chief of Staff of the Italian army. Badoglio was not enthusiastic about taking over the arduous Ethiopian post, being already sixty-four years of age and definitely anti-Mussolini in sentiment, but he accepted the offer — albeit reluctantly. He said to friends: "I feel it my duty to come to the aid of Italy, even a Fascist Italy, at this critical moment. I dread to think of the conditions I shall find in Asmara."

His apprehensions were not dissipated by his arrival in East Africa. As he went ashore at Massawa in a naval cutter on November 17, de Bono, on his way home, passed him in another. There was a formal exchange of salutes across a span of twenty yards, but not a single word was spoken between them. There was no conference between the outgoing and incoming commanders of the Italian Expeditionary Force.

Badoglio, after a brief ceremony in Massawa, went straight to the station and took his place in the cable train known as the *littorina*. Halfway up to Asmara, the train broke down and Badoglio found himself stranded midway, a victim of de Bono's inefficiency. An automobile was sent to him after several hours' delay, and he continued his trip by highway. Finally, in Asmara, Badoglio called in all of de Bono's former staff and reviewed Italy's war effort to date. He found the situation so black that the next day he summoned the press, both Italian and foreign correspondents, and told them abruptly:

"There have been too many picnic excursions by correspondents. You have been sending stories which have been damaging to the military efforts of Italy. From now on you will be confined to Asmara and you will write your stories on the communiqués issued to you. There is going to be a long period of reconstruction and road building in which there will be little of news value to send. That is all."

Without a smile, he turned his back on us and left the room. Before the week was up, the two hundred foreign correspondents who had been attached to the Italian army at Asmara, many of them free-lance writers and European free-lunch seekers, had dwindled to less than twenty. A number of correspondents representing important American newspapers or news agencies, such as John Whitaker, who at that time was with the *New York Herald Tribune*, and Bill Chapin of I.N.S., went to Italian Somaliland to try their luck at reporting under General Graziani. He was known as "the Breaker of Natives" because, while he was in charge of the pacification of Libya, he took dissident chieftains, bound hand and foot, up in airplanes and dropped them from a height of several thousand feet upon tribal encampments.

The day after Badoglio took over command from de Bono, the League of Nations imposed sanctions on Italy. It sounded a much more impressive performance than it actually was, since, to be effective, sanctions should have been applied months before. For one thing, Italy had had plenty of warning that sanctions were coming, so that she had been able to get in some huge reserves of supplies against what Mussolini called "the economic siege"; for another, many of the League nations did not apply the sanctions in good faith. The blockade was leaky from the start.

During the military doldrums, while Badoglio was reorganizing his army for a major offensive, political operations ordered by Mussolini were undertaken. These consisted mainly in the use, for the first time in modern warfare, of parachute fifth columnists — this phrase, however, was not coined until the Spanish Civil War. All dispatches regarding these operations were killed by the Italian censors and little, if anything, ever trickled through about them. The most successful of these fifth columnists was a young Italian captain whose name was not revealed. Accompanied by a trusted askari, who acted as interpreter, he was dropped in the Azabu Galla country with a bag of Menelik gold pieces, with which he bribed the native chieftains of this area to turn traitor. Their treachery cost the Negus' soldiers many thousands of lives after the battle of Amba Aradam.

This battle, which started at the end of February, 1936, inaugurated Badoglio's tactics of mass combat, in which Italian artillery and aviation were brought into full play against native warriors equipped with nothing heavier than outmoded machine guns and trench mortars.

The correspondents were taken to the Italian positions facing the saddle-shaped Amba Aradam two weeks before the battle started. Herbert Matthews, of *The New York Times*, and Reynolds went to Badoglio's main observation post the day after their arrival in camp and, looking through a giant telescope, could clearly see the Ethiopians preparing their pathetic defenses only about five miles away.

Badoglio estimated on the basis of intelligence reports that there were about forty thousand of them. Through the telescope, Reynolds saw the chieftains' tents, which were all shaped like beach cabins, and the goings and comings of the soldiers under the command of Ras Mulugeta, Minister of War.

"In another two weeks there will be at least eighty thousand of them there, possibly more," one of the staff officers said.

"Why are you waiting?" Reynolds asked. "Wouldn't it be easier for you to attack now before they get forty thousand more reinforcements?"

The officer laughed and replied, "We are waiting until they all get there and then we will surround them and break the backbone of Ethiopian resistance."

The day before the battle started, Badoglio called us into his tent and said in his tense, jerky way of speaking: "Tomorrow we are going to launch my first major offensive against the Ethiopians. Motorized units will start out at dawn on both the left and the right flank to make an encircling movement. The next day we will occupy three major points which you can see on this map," and he pointed to two escarpments on the left and the right flank and to a valley in the center.

"The third day, our artillery and aviation will let loose from dawn until dusk," he continued. "On the fourth day, our infantry will attack, gaining the key positions at all points. On the fifth day, the infantry will charge from all sides and practically win the battle. On the sixth day, the final charges will be made, the battle will be over, and the Italian flag will wave from the top of Amba Aradam.

"You can start writing your dispatches now if you wish, but I don't advise you to do so, because not a word will be permitted to be sent until the battle is over. You are incommunicado. You are under army orders, and if any of you should send so much as a single word of what I have told you, you will be treated as spies. I am giving you this information so that as war correspondents you can follow more intelligently the battle as it progresses. I will receive you on the night of the sixth day."

And on the evening of the sixth day he received us. He looked like a tired football coach in the turtleneck sweater he was wearing. His eyes were bleary, but through his grim expression there flashed from time to time a smile of satisfaction. He said briefly:

"The battle has gone according to plan. The Italian flag flies on the summit of Aradam. You yourselves have seen how it developed. There is nothing more for me to say. Go to your typewriters and write what you want."

He did not tell us, however, that at that moment the Azabu Galla traitors, bought by the Menelik gold pieces of the Italian fifth columnists, were attacking from the rear the surviving remnants of Ras Mulugeta's routed army. Later we learned that they had killed Ras Mulugeta as he tried to escape through their country on a mule.

After the victory of Amba Aradam, the Italians relaxed their restrictions on correspondents, and the United Press, which had been trying to send Eleanor to Ethiopia, was finally granted permission to do so, despite the Latin prejudice against women doing a man's work. Eleanor arrived at Badoglio's headquarters at Enda Jesus just outside of Makale, shortly after the battle of Amba Alagi, which ended on February 27 with the massacre of the armies of Ras Kassa and Ras Seyum.

Badoglio paused for mopping up and consolidation of his positions while he waited for the Ethiopians to mass once more before unleashing another attack. Haile Selassie obliged him by rallying all the remnants of the Abyssinian forces in the north. Italian officers told us quite frankly that the next big battle would take place somewhere between Amba Alagi and Lake Ashangi, the exact place and date to be determined by the action of the Ethiopians themselves. It was clear to us that it was to be another Amba Aradam blood bath, with the Ethiopians, always equipped with inadequate weapons only, stupidly massing so that they could be mowed down more readily by Fascist artillery, aviation, and machine guns. They did everything possible to end the war quickly for Mussolini.

We often asked ourselves at this time how it was that Badoglio, an artillery expert in the World War, seemed to know more about native psychology than de Bono, who had also made a name for himself as an authority on colonial warfare. According to staff officers, Badoglio was a great believer in military brain trusts, whereas de Bono wanted to plan all the strategy himself. They told us that for the battle of Amba Aradam, the battle of Amba Alagi, and for the forthcoming battle in front of Lake Ashangi, Badoglio had assigned, in each case, twelve promising young officers to draft, individually and without consultation with each other or anyone else, twelve different battle plans.

"Badoglio studied all of them," one of the staff officers said, "and then sat down and drafted his own plans, selecting the best ideas of the lot. He is a master strategist himself, but he believes younger officers have fresher ideas."

Eleanor asked why Badoglio was so sure that the Ethiopians would always conveniently mass into targets for Italian aviation and artillery.

"His younger officers convinced him," the officer said, and, inferring that he was one of them, proudly added, "and most of us knew about them because we were in Ethiopia before. Their guerrilla tactics are only used against smaller numbers."

By the end of March, the Negus had massed in front of Lake

Ashangi sixty thousand men, including his Imperial Guard, which numbered twenty thousand and which were the best-equipped soldiers he possessed. On April 1, the uneven battle started and continued for four days, the Italians gradually pushing the Negus' troops back to Quoram at the southern tip of the lake. This battle resulted in the complete annihilation of the Lion of Judah's forces in the north, and the road to Dessye lay open to the Fascist army. The Negus himself barely escaped capture and succeeded in returning to his capital only with the greatest difficulty, traveling part of the way on muleback, disguised as a minor chieftain for fear of native traitors bought over by the Fascists.

The Italians sent their flying columns in pursuit and quickly reached Dessye on April 15, without having encountered any serious resistance en route. So fast was this advance over one bad road and through forest and mountainous terrain on each side of it that sufficient supplies could be sent forward only by planes and mules. Marking the first time that an army in the field had ever been fed on a large scale by transport planes, Badoglio sent out trimotored Savoias laden with spaghetti, hay, flour, bread, casks of wine, and live goats. The hay, flour, and bread were dropped in burlap bags from the planes as they swooped down low, while the spaghetti, wine, and goats were lowered by parachute.

In the meantime, Achille Starace, Secretary of the Fascist party, headed a motorized column of five thousand picked troops, mainly Black Shirts, which was moving on Gondar and Lake Tana in western Ethiopia, within the sphere of British influence. On April 15, we took off in an airplane with General Aimone Cat, head of all Italian aviation under Badoglio, from Enda Jesus airfield to have a look at the advance. It was quite an adventure. First, Aimone-Cat made Eleanor pilot the plane and next he tried landing in a millet field covered with rocks, which the Ethiopians used to keep the ground moist, and broke off the rear wheel. The whole purpose of the dangerous exploit was merely to enable Aimone-Cat to say *buon giorno* to a column of askaris. The mechanic replaced the broken wheel with a piece of wood which was attached by bits of wire so that it acted as a ski. The General then had us all crowd into the cockpit to remove all possible weight from the tail. The plane ricocheted over the uneven ground, barely skimmed a hilltop, and gained altitude.

We then flew over Lake Tana, where Aimone-Cat came down to a few hundred feet aboveground so we could see Starace's soldiers on the shore. They were taking off their uniforms and swimming in the lake. We also flew over Gondar, where we could see the Italians moving into the medieval Portuguese palaces there. It was the first confirmation any foreign correspondent had had that Italy had further challenged Britain by taking over a British sphere of influence, the headwaters of the Blue Nile.

The correspondents accompanied the General Staff when it transferred from Enda Jesus to Dessye. It took us five days to make the trip. Matthews traveled in the same car with us, which was driven by a sergeant named Sergio. It was the most enlightening excursion that any of the journalists on the Italian side made throughout the entire war. The Fascist-press officers did not have time to prepare any stage effects for our benefit. We saw the Italian army as it really was, without any dressing up for the benefit of the press. We saw the good and the bad qualities of Italians as soldiers.

Their best quality was their ability to endure monotony and hardships. All along the road, which taped around mountain peaks, along precipices and across barren plains, we passed groups of soldiers chipping rocks. They were covered with white dust kicked up in this rainless season by the thousands of trucks and vehicles passing by. They looked like clowns with their red eyes and lips making holes in the dust masks over their faces. They acted like clowns, too, whenever they saw Eleanor.

"Una donna bianca," they would cry, and pretend to drop dead from surprise or else turn somersaults of delight, for they had not seen a white woman for many months. Whenever our car was held up by a traffic tangle, which it was every fifteen minutes, the soldiers would crowd around and peer at Eleanor as though she were a museum piece. They offered her wine, hardtack, Ethiopian castrating knives, or any other souvenirs they had collected during their fighting.

At one camp, which had not moved for three months, we were surprised to see that the Italian soldiers and even officers had become as indifferent to flies as the Ethiopians. They were horrible, slow-moving flies that fastened onto the eyes and mouth. They wouldn't budge if swished at, but had to be brushed off by hand. The Italians didn't even bother to do that.

We had a wonderful tent, at the U.P.'s expense, equipped with oilskin floor and windows with mosquito netting. So we didn't mind spending the night there. But the other correspondents went almost crazy and could never believe it possible for any white person to stay in such a place for three months.

Matthews said, "Any other army would revolt under such conditions."

No effort had been made to alleviate the situation. There was no mosquito netting for the soldiers. Only a few of the officers had brought along their own.

The colonel in charge caused Eleanor to break out laughing when he said: "There were not many flies when we first got here. They get worse all the time."

The reason for her laugh was that it was quite evident they had not done anything about sanitation. There were a few latrines, but the Italian soldiers were not keen about using them; as a result, human excrement was to be seen all over the camp. Rubbish piles had not been burned. But the Italians took it all with songs.

A score of them came to the officers' mess tent where we were dining and asked if they could serenade *la donna bianca*. Permission was granted, and without any accompanying music they sang popular Italian airs like *Santa Lucia* and *Funiculi, Funicula* and their own regimental songs.

Reynolds asked the colonel if the soldiers were given any entertainment, such as moving pictures, to keep them contented. He looked as though he thought Reynolds mad.

"They enjoy singing like this," he said, "and you can see they are quite happy and have good morale."

The next night, we pitched camp alongside a shallow river close to a regiment of soldiers. It was still light, and Eleanor and Reynolds decided to take a bath. Eleanor cautiously donned her bathing suit in our tent and put on a bathrobe. We slipped through the woods to a spot where we thought we would not run into any soldiers, but coming out of a thicket we suddenly found ourselves on the riverbank in front of some two hundred naked soldiers, standing knee-deep in the river, soaping themselves under the command of an Italian captain in uniform who stood on the opposite bank. More cries of *donna bianca* broke out. The captain quickly took charge of the situation and bellowed out a series of orders.

"About face. March to shore. Don drawers. Return to your bathing."

He then called to us, "I hope *la signora* now finds everything satisfactory and will enjoy the water."

The traffic tangles were incredible. Although the Italians had done a wonderful job of building the road, they had made no attempt to widen it at intervals, so that when a truck broke down it wouldn't hold up the hundreds of trucks behind it. Finally, Badoglio dispatched a motorcyclist bearing an order to push trucks over the precipices as soon as they were immobilized.

At one spot near Dessye, where the road corkscrewed down to a plain, we drove across the flat land for miles before we realized we were not on the tenuous road at all, but completely lost. It was dark by this time, and there was no moon. Except for packs of hyenas that were roving about, their eyes gleaming in the headlights, there was no sign of life. For half an hour Sergio drove around looking for the road. Finally we saw a campfire. Then we debated what to do about it. If Ethiopians were there, we would have a hard time explaining to them in Amharic that three of us were not Italians, but Americans. And even if we could explain that, Sergio wanted to know: what about him? We finally decided to take a chance and found Italian soldiers there who directed us to the road. No attempt had been made to mark it, and, as we learned later, a number of trucks had lost their way and their drivers had been caught by Ethiopian guerrillas. We arrived in Dessye late that night, too tired even to put up our tent, and just slept in the car.

In Dessye, we saw the Italians introduce Trieste-minted thalers into native circulation. They were exact replicas of the Maria Theresa thalers of Ethiopia except that they had a bit more silver in them. The Italians did not want to be accused of cheating. Despite their slightly greater silver content, the natives were suspicious of their shininess and refused to accept them. The Italians then resorted to the tricks of antique fakers and dirtied them with chemicals.

We stayed in Dessye only a few days. Following the destruction of the Negus' northern armies in the Lake Ashangi sector, Badoglio decided to make a dash for Addis Ababa. We rode with him on that wild dash. He led the procession himself in a Studebaker car, followed by six other staff cars and a half-dozen other automobiles containing journalists. Several nights on this eight-day trip from Dessye to Addis Ababa, we encamped along the highway virtually unprotected, there being only a few hundred askaris on either flank of us. We could see, on near-by mountaintops, the campfires of all that was left of the Negus' northern army. If five hundred of them had banded together and under cover of darkness made a surprise attack, Badoglio and his entire staff would have been wiped out, to say nothing of the correspondents, including ourselves. But again Italian luck held. Badoglio on May 5 marched into Addis Ababa, where many houses were still in flames and shooting was still going on following the rioting of drink-maddened Ethiopians, which broke out after Haile Selassie's unexpected departure four days before. This really ended the war, which had lasted seven months and three days, although there was still fighting in progress in a number of sectors.

Although the Italian press announced that Badoglio had speeded up his entry into Addis Ababa to protect the lives of the foreign colony there, Fascist officers gave us quite another version. A major told us at supper one night:

"Badoglio was determined to get here before his rival, Graziani."

"And is he pleased!" a captain added. "Graziani was a poor second."

It was true. Graziani also had been racing toward Addis, following his victory over Ras Nasibu at Sasa Baneh, on April 30, but was not able en route to occupy Harar, the second biggest city in Ethiopia, until May 9. He remained there, disgruntled, and did not go to Addis until after Badoglio left.

The night of Badoglio's entry into Addis was bad. The Ethiopians were still on a looting rampage induced by the liquor they had consumed during their raiding of foreign shops. The correspondents were quartered in tents in the yard of the Italian Legation. We heard bullets pinging against the Legation walls and near-by buildings. But the worst attack by the Ethiopian marauders that night was against the American Legation. It was in the very center of the native quarter, four and one half miles away from the so-called diplomatic district where all other legations were located.

United States Minister Cornelius van H. Engert, his wife, small children, and all the members of the Legation staff had, on orders from the State Department, gone that morning to the British Legation, which was protected by barbed-wire entanglements and machine guns and garrisoned by fifty Sikhs. As soon as the Italians arrived, however, William Cramp, American Vice-Consul, and three United States Marines returned to the American Legation. Eddie Neal, of the A.P., who was later killed in the Spanish Civil War, joined them. Everything was quiet until 10:20 P.M. Then an attack in force on the compound started. Cramp and the marines returned fire. As the attackers gained ground, Cramp decided to send a message to the Italian headquarters asking for aid. Eddie volunteered to carry it and slipped out into the darkness, with bullets sprinkling around him, to the Italian Command. He came back with a detachment of fifty soldiers, headed by a captain. The next morning, forty-odd bodies of would-be looters were found outside the Legation walls, grim testimony to the marksmanship of its American defenders.

When we met the Engerts on their return to the American Legation later that day, we found them extremely dejected. They both said, with diplomatic caution, that they had never wanted to leave and had hoped that the British would lend them a few Sikhs to help them defend themselves as was done in the case of the French Legation.

After spending the first three nights in tents, the correspondents attached to the Italian army were given rooms in the Imperial Hotel, which was owned by a Greek. A number of Black Shirt politicians, including Ciano, who had been playing at war, were also lodged there. Most of them regarded the trip to Addis Ababa at that time as having the same political importance as the March on Rome back in 1922. They came by airplane and stayed only a few days, during which they carefully had themselves photographed on the abandoned throne of the Negus. It was a milestone for them in their Fascist careers. Ciano, whom we had met on several occasions in Asmara, where he was stationed as a captain of aviation, had the room next to ours. Hearing the tinkle of ice against glasses one evening, he came in and joined us for a drink. He was bubbling over with enthusiasm.

"England is through," he said, "or she would have taken a stronger stand against us. We have not only won this campaign; we are ready for the future. We have the only experienced army in Europe as a result of our Ethiopian training."

Although we found him possessed of great personal charm, and knew that he was a master linguist, we must confess that we didn't see in him any of the potential qualities of a foreign minister.

Back in Rome, Mussolini, on May 9, came out on the balcony of the Palazzo Venezia and announced that the second Roman Empire had been created, fifteen centuries after the fall of the ancient Roman Empire, by the acquisition of Ethiopia. He said that King Victor Emmanuel III had assumed the title of Emperor of Ethiopia and that Marshal Pietro Badoglio had been named Viceroy over the conquered land.

On the radio in the Imperial Hotel in Addis Ababa, we heard the Duce say:

"Italy at last has her empire. . . .

"It is an empire of peace because Italy wants peace for herself and for everyone and decided on war only when she was driven to it by the imperious necessities of life.

"The Italian people have created with their blood an empire. They will render it fertile and fruitful with their work. They will defend it against anyone with their weapons."

The Duce's speech hinted at an era of peace to come as far as Italians were concerned. But scarcely had the reconstruction work in Ethiopia started before Mussolini, already overproud of his newly discovered military might, found an opportunity to send his Black Shirts into battle once again. This time it was not a colonial, but a European, power that was involved. As soon as the Franco revolt started, Mussolini sent aid to the insurgents, thus belying the very words he had spoken just a few months earlier, at the conclusion of the Ethiopian campaign.

# III

AN ENGLISH D. H. RAPIDS CABIN PLANE CIRCLED AROUND THE AIR-
field at Santa Cruz de la Palma as the sun was sinking behind the
corrugated-iron hangar. It made a perfect landing and taxied up to
the customs shed. Two pretty young girls in light summer prints descended from the airplane, followed by a soldierly-looking middle-
aged man in a linen suit, who immediately reached into his pocket,
pulled out a pipe, and lighted up. Shortly afterwards, an English
pilot climbed out of the cockpit and joined them. It was hardly the
season for tourists to arrive in a winter resort like the Canaries,
being July 14 and very hot, but the pipe-smoking Englishman, dis-
daining to make any attempt at speaking Spanish, asked the Civil
Guards:

"Is there a good hotel along the beach here? We want to get in
some bathing."

The Civil Guards muttered some answer in Spanish which none
of the English group appeared to understand. A customs official,
anxious to be helpful, rushed to their assistance. Once again the
Englishman explained that they were looking for a hotel on the

beach. The customs official told him in English that it was not the season in the Canaries but they would find accommodations at one of the smaller hotels which he recommended.

Examination of their passports, which were perfectly in order, showed that their itinerary had been: Croyden, from where they took off on July 11, Biarritz, Oporto, Lisbon, Casablanca, and Cape Juby, in the Spanish colony of Rio de Oro. While the pilot garaged his plane, the rest of the party passed through the customs without any difficulty and took a cab to the hotel. The crowd of Spanish mechanics, fliers, and customs officials who had gathered around to admire the two girls never dreamed of the role this innocent-looking party was to play in the destiny of Spain.

At the hotel, using their right names, they registered as Major Hugh Pollard, retired army officer, his daughter, Diana Pollard, and Miss Dorothy Watson. The pilot gave his name as Captain Cecil Bebb. That night, over a bottle of sherry in the hotel lobby, the Major and the two girls, with the aid of a tourist guidebook, and a road map of the islands, began to plan their sight-seeing for the next few days. The following morning the three of them took a passenger steamer and went to Santa Cruz de Tenerife, another Canary island across the bay. After a stroll during which they visited a number of curio shops where they bought appropriate souvenirs, they turned down a side street and stopped at the house of a lawyer. A Spanish servant ushered them into a living room, where they were soon joined by the lawyer.

The Major, speaking Spanish with a British accent, said to him: "Viva la muerte."

The lawyer turned pale, tugged at his black tie, and asked, "What did you say?"

"Long live death," the Major replied, this time in English.

The lawyer assured him that there must be some mistake, but the Major insisted that the phrase was a password. The Spaniard, still distrustful, told him to return within an hour when a friend of his who might be able to establish contact would be present. The three English people went to a café, where they had some of the inevitable sherry. Returning at the appointed hour, they met the lawyer's friend who, though suspicious, was much calmer than the lawyer.

After great difficulty, the Major finally convinced the two Spaniards he was the envoy that General Francisco Franco had been expecting. They advised him to return to his hotel at Santa Cruz de la Palma and await developments.

It was quite an adventure for the Major, who since his days as an intelligence officer during the World War, had done nothing more exciting than collect ancient firearms and edit the sports section of Country Life. An ardent Catholic, he had become interested in the situation of the Church in Spain following the advent of the Republic.

In the middle of the next night, the Major heard a knock on his bedroom door. There stood the second Spaniard. He admitted this time that he was General Franco's aide-de-camp and said that everything was in readiness. He wanted Pollard to arrange for immediate departure of his private plane.

The Major called the pilot, who hastily dressed, and the two of them, accompanied by the Spaniard, left the hotel and scrambled into a closed Cadillac. A short, chubby man and a rather tall, distinguished-looking woman were already in the car. They exchanged greetings in Spanish, and the car moved off. The woman was tearful and constantly called upon the Virgin Mary to protect her husband on the adventure he was about to undertake.

At the airfield, the Major was surprised at the ease with which Captain Bebb, who had been told nothing of the plot, obtained permission to leave in the private plane with Franco and his aide-de-camp. The Major and Franco's wife remained behind.

Later that day, Captain Bebb arrived at Casablanca, in French Morocco, some seven hundred miles away, where his two passengers hurried to a small hotel. They were greeted in a back room by a group of Spaniards who saluted their leader with great deference. They included the Marquis Pepe del Mérito, the Spanish sherry producer, who, along with Juan de la Cierva, the inventor of the autogiro, had bought the plane and financed the Pollard expedition, and Luis Bolin, London correspondent of the Madrid newspaper *ABC*, who as a personal friend had prevailed on Pollard to make the trip to the Canaries. They told Franco that the revolution had started at dawn in Spanish Morocco but that they had not as yet heard how it fared. It was July 17, 1936.

After a sleepless night, Franco took off the following morning for Ceuta, not knowing whether he would be shot as a traitor or acclaimed as a leader upon his arrival. He was acclaimed as a leader. In Spanish Morocco the revolution had succeeded. Blue-shirted Falangistas, red-bereted Carlistas, and green-bereted Alfonsistas were rising up on the mainland along with the army. The so-called Nationalist movement was underway. General Queipo de Llano, Military Governor of Seville, had turned against the Republican government, which he had once stanchly supported. Other cities in the south of Spain which immediately joined the revolution were Cádiz, Algeciras, Granada, Córdoba. In the north, where General Emilio Mola became the rebel leader, Burgos, Valladolid, Pamplona, Saragossa, Salamanca, Vitoria, Ávila, Segovia, and Vigo followed suit. In Madrid, Barcelona, and San Sebastián, small groups of revolutionaries, mostly army, were fighting losing battles from behind the walls of the buildings they had seized. The Canaries and the Balearic Islands, with the exception of Minorca, joined the revolt. Insurgent officers also took over the Spanish colonies and protectorates of Ifni, Rio de Oro, and Fernando Po.

Almost all of the naval officers joined the uprising, but in most cases, as aboard the battleship *Jaime 1* and the cruisers *Cervantes* and *Libertad*, the crews remained loyal and, overpowering their officers, threw them overboard. On the battleship *Espana* and the cruiser *Almirante Cervera*, the loyal crews were overpowered by the officers with the aid of land forces of El Ferrol, where they were being repaired.

The assassination in Madrid on July 13, 1936, of Calvo Sotelo, leader of the Monarchist party in the Cortes and Minister of Finance under Primo de Rivera in 1925, has frequently been cited as the cause of the revolt. But the fact that Major Pollard had taken off from Croyden two days before to deliver a plane to Franco proved that the uprising had been hatched previously. As a matter of fact, during the time we were in Franco Spain, we were told on all sides that the Sotelo assassination had harmed rather than helped the army plot. A number of Franco followers explained to us that it had, by whipping up political sentiment to such a pitch, forced the army to start the movement ahead of schedule — the original date having been set at July 22. General José Sanjurjo, who was to have been the leader of the entire movement, was, as a result, left behind in Portugal. It was not until July 20 that he was able to arrange for a private plane to take him to Spain. En route the plane crashed and he was killed, leaving the leadership open to Mola and Franco.

Queipo de Llano, most colorful, eccentric, and unpredictable of all Spanish generals, held the fate of the revolution in his hands. Without his support, Franco could never have brought over his Moors and Spanish Legionaries of the famed El Tercio to the mainland. Well known as a Socialist, and as a leader of the anti-Monarchist movement which had forced Alfonso to go into exile, Queipo had been entrusted by the Republican Cabinet to govern Seville. His change-over was made all the more difficult by the fact that the population under him was predominantly Socialist.

Not above tricking the people, Queipo de Llano used the small garrison of two hundred and fifty soldiers that he had at his disposal to convince the people of Seville that thousands of reinforcements were arriving hourly. He dressed them, in turn, in the uniforms of all the armed branches of Spain, which he took from the commissary storehouse, and rushed them in trucks through the principal streets of the town. For the final display, he made his two hundred and fifty soldiers stain their faces with walnut juice so that they looked like Moors beneath the turbans and baggy trousers with which he had masqueraded them. Over the radio he lied glibly, announcing that the revolution had succeeded throughout Spain, that Madrid and Barcelona had joined the movement. Through this

ruse, he prevented hundreds of small towns that might have op-
posd the revolt on the first day from taking action. This gave the
revolutionaries just enough time to take over many of these towns
before the truth was known.

Early the same morning that Franco arrived at Ceuta, Mussolini, who habitually rises at six A.M., was at the Palazzo Venezia
studying the reports that were pouring onto his desk from his
agents in Tangiers and Gibraltar. He was especially interested in
the news about the progress of the revolution in Spanish Morocco,
Cádiz, and Seville, for that was where his next role was to be
played. He pressed a button and soon was in communication with
an airfield in southern Italy. He gave the order and, within twenty
minutes, the first dozen Savoia transport planes began taking off
for Ceuta and by nightfall they had carried several hundred of the
crack Legionaries and Moors in Spanish Morocco to Cádiz and
Seville.

Franco also used the navy units that he had at his disposal on
the second day of the revolution to transport still greater numbers
of reinforcements to the mainland, and even they had aerial escort
which included Italian chaser planes, most of them piloted by
Italians. But the first African contingents to reach southern Spain,
to bolster the flimsy control that Queipo had of the situation, were
borne on Italian wings.

We confirmed while we were in Italy that during the day of
July 18 Ciano, who by then had become Foreign Minister — a post
previously held by Mussolini himself — left his office in the Chigi
Palace and was in constant conference with Il Duce. The reason
was that Italian participation in the Franco revolt was a Ciano
brainchild which Mussolini immediately took unto himself. Ciano
had been approached by Spanish army representatives soon after
he returned from Ethiopia. It was the very moment that Fascist
Italy was feeling its strength, and Ciano was looking for some international coup with which to inaugurate his career as Foreign
Minister. He grabbed at this opportunity and within a few days
had drawn up an impressive memorandum which he submitted to

Il Duce. It fitted well into Mussolini's plan for Italian supremacy in the Mediterranean that was being developed at that very moment under the slogan of *Mare Nostrum*.

The negotiations which Ciano had with Spanish rebel representatives, ending in Mussolini's agreement to support the revolution, were carried out with the greatest secrecy and without the Ambassador from Republican Spain in Rome having the slightest inkling of them. They were also kept secret from Alfonso, who was in exile in Rome, lest the movement be compromised by his knowledge of it. They were afraid that if the ex-King were taken into the plot, the Carlistas, who were so strong in northern Spain, might not be so eager to join in the uprising. As it was, the monarchists generally — both Carlistas and Alfonsistas — revolted with the tacit understanding that the choice of a king to reoccupy the Spanish throne would be made only after the war was over.

Thus Mussolini was committed to take an active part in the Spanish revolution even before it started. The story in Rome was that his willingness to help was so apparent that the Spanish revolutionaries were wary of him from the very beginning. After the war got under way, Franco asked Rome for some heavy artillery and fifty thousand rifles. Mussolini quickly answered:

"The artillery and rifles will be on their way shortly and there will be a man with every rifle and a crew with every gun."

Mussolini had intended to send regular Italian army infantry, but Badoglio opposed the idea. The hero of Ethiopia feared such a move might precipitate a general European war — a war in which he felt Italy was not prepared to defend herself.

"If you go into the Spanish adventure," Badoglio told Mussolini, "please do not expect me to come in at the last minute and save the situation. I am one hundred per cent against it."

Mussolini, of course, could have gone over Badoglio's head and sent army units anyway, but he was reluctant to oppose the man who at that moment enjoyed the reputation of being the best strategist in Italy. Ciano solved the dilemma by opening the enlistment of sixty thousand men to go to Spain as "volunteers." They were for the most part unemployed men whom the Fascists collected from all over Italy. They were volunteers in the sense that if they didn't join up they wouldn't be able to eat. They were given a short period of military training. Naturally, they were inferior to regular troops, and a few veteran Black Shirt militiamen, including officers, had to be sent along to strengthen them.

Badoglio did not fall into the bad graces of Mussolini as a result of the stand he took, because both Il Duce and Ciano were rather proud of the compromise they finally devised, feeling that they were in a position to contend that Italy was not intervening officially in the Spanish war.

On July 18, 1936, we arrived in Paris, returning from vacation in New York after our Ethiopian assignment. There was a cable awaiting us. It was from Hugh Baillie, instructing us to proceed immediately to Hendaye on the Spanish-French border, from where we were to try to get into rebel Spain, for the United Press had no correspondents there. The Loyalist side was being well covered by the regular Madrid bureau.

Without unpacking, we took the train that same night and arrived the following morning at Hendaye, which, within the next twenty-four hours, became one of the greatest news centers in the world. Practically all of the correspondents stayed in the Basque Hotel Imatz, where newspaper ethics reached a new low. Rival reporters eavesdropped outside the lone telephone booth in the hotel, taking notes on what was being dictated. Over drinks, correspondents pumped each other for news tips and gave mendacious accounts of what they themselves had sent.

Within three days of our arrival, we succeeded in entering Spain by way of Dancharinéa, one of the two passes joining Spain and France which the rebels held, and continued to Burgos, where the last knot of Loyalists was being machine-gunned to death in a barricaded house. We were received by General Mola, who told us:

"We are encountering some resistance at the present moment because the Socialist government in Madrid is using its power to prevent the people from rising up and joining the Nationalist movement in which they heartily believe. You can be sure that the fighting will be over within the next three weeks. I tell you this because if I were not sure that this revolution would succeed quickly and without much bloodshed, I never would have taken part in it.

"We are winning in the north, and General Franco is pushing up from the south. We will effect a junction in a few days, and then the final push on Madrid will begin."

There was no doubt that Mola was sincere in what he was saying. A tall, homely man who peered through tortoise shell glasses and groped for words to express himself, he struck us as incapable of political hypocrisy. He was a pure strategist, an army man who had little if any conception of the passions and aspirations of the different classes in Spain. His mistaken belief in a short, almost bloodless revolution was held by practically all the rebel leaders, who otherwise would probably never have dared to start the revolt, with the resultant stalemate that led to Spain's becoming an international battlefield. The fact that all the countries of Europe regarded Spain as a microcosm of the world struggle that was just beginning to crystallize between Leftists and Rightists, between democracy and totalitarianism — the struggle that had its counterpart on a less violent scale within almost every country — made intervention almost inevitable.

The controversy over the chronological order of foreign intervention in Spain will probably never be absolutely cleared up. But to us, who were in Hendaye during the first days of the war, it would seem that following the Italians, the French were next to meddle in Spain. We saw, during those first war days, truckloads of French rifles and cartridges being sent over the Hendaye-Irún bridge to the Basque army. During the battle for Irún, for example, which was the first of the pitched battles in the north between the Rebels and the Loyalists, we saw Frenchmen at the French frontier town of Biriatou, standing on a rocky summit overlooking both sides of the battlefield, making semaphore signals to the Basque Loyalists, telling them how to correct their artillery fire.

It was to halt this French aid that Franco and Mola, once they had effected a junction between the northern and southern armies, decided it was imperative to concentrate on taking an otherwise unimportant town like Irún before attempting to push on to Madrid.

To the best of our knowledge, German and Russian intervention in the Spanish skies occurred more or less at the same time — during the Franco drive on Madrid, immediately after the fall of Toledo, September 27, 1936. Both followed up their aerial aid with land forces shortly afterward, the Germans contributing mainly technicians.

The British played both sides politically. English Parliamentarians in large numbers, headed by the Duchess of Atholl, visited the Republican sectors and encouraged Loyalist war efforts with their presence and speeches. Later, English Leftists formed the Walter Brigade, which became a part of the International Brigade and fought in some of the most important battles of the war.

The Franco side, on the other hand, was visited by General Fuller and General Groves, as well as Randolph Churchill, son of Winston Churchill, who made the trip in the guise of a *Daily Mail* correspondent. A smaller group of Parliamentarians also trekked through Franco Spain, and half a dozen English lords, including one who was decorated under the *nom de guerre* of Peter Kemp, accepted commissions in the Franco army.

Franco did not count on only his own troops and foreign allies, but also on Spanish Rightists in Madrid and other cities he was trying to take. During the first siege of Madrid, which failed, Franco surprised everybody by saying in a public speech in Salamanca:

"I have four columns marching on Madrid — and a fifth column inside Madrid which will rise up and fight for us at the opportune moment."

Franco must therefore be given credit for having coined the phrase that has become a part of every language in the world today to describe an enemy working from within.

Reynolds went to Salamanca in the early winter of 1936 to try to interview Franco, shortly after El Generalissimo had established headquarters there. Reynolds was not very successful from the standpoint of American newspaper enterprise because of the scores of intermediaries, political and military, who kept Franco practically isolated from the rest of the world. Luis Bolin, the ABC correspondent who had induced Pollard to take the plane to Franco in the Canaries, was in charge of the press with the rank of captain. He was horrified at the idea of anybody's interviewing Franco. Reynolds insisted, however, and Bolin finally promised that he would see what could be done.

"He is in no position to give an interview at this time," Bolin said, "and if he did, I'm sure he would give it to a Spaniard."

The next day, however, Bolin told Reynolds to write out a list of questions. Reynolds was bubbling over with them and made out the list immediately, on Bolin's typewriter. Two days later, Bolin said half of the questions had been thrown out and that the remaining five had been answered by one of the staff officers. He hoped within the next forty-eight hours it would be possible for Franco to read the answers and approve them. The approval was duly given, and Reynolds was returned the answers which bore Franco's initials, F. F. B. Reynolds was then permitted, after being searched for weapons, to see the rebel chief in his private office for two minutes, but was not allowed to ask any questions. Reynolds found that Franco was more closely guarded than either Mussolini or Hitler. The Generalissimo depended almost exclusively on Moorish soldiers, whom he trusted more than the Spaniards — any one of whom might have been a Republican fifth columnist. In close-up, Franco was about as unlike a dictator as anybody could be. He was a small, paunchy man with a rather sweet smile that lightened up an otherwise drab but aristocratic face. His gray hair was sparse but wispy. His general's red sash made Reynolds nervous, as it appeared on the point of slipping off the rotundity of his waist and falling to the floor. He seemed nervous and bashful. Conversation was brief and stilted.

"Good day," Franco said, rising and extending his hand, which

Reynolds took. Reynolds thanked him for having answered the questions, and Franco replied:

"*No hay de que.*"

A staff officer then hurriedly escorted Reynolds out in a way that could be described only as a rather polished bum's rush.

While waiting in Salamanca to see Franco, Reynolds met Miguel de Unamuno, the greatest of modern Spanish philosophers. Although nobody knew whether or not he approved of Franco — the general opinion was that he didn't — Unamuno, nevertheless, still held the chair of philosophy at the University of Salamanca. This was at the time that everyone in Franco Spain was wearing a button to show that he belonged to one of the half-dozen Rightist parties or groups. Foreign correspondents wore the insignia of their own country, which in those days was unusual, so as not to be stopped every ten steps by Falangistas and asked questions. Unamuno had stuck into the buttonhole of his left lapel a piece of tinfoil that had been molded into the shape of a bird's head. The Spaniard with Reynolds asked the philosopher: "*Por Dios,* what party does that insignia represent?"

"It is my own party. I founded it myself," Unamuno replied. "I am the only member of it, and if anybody else joins I shall resign."

This was Unamuno, the individualist, whom the Spaniards loved. He felt that philosophically there was no such thing as absolute right on one side or the other of the two warring factions in Spain. He criticized and praised them both. But little that he ever said was published; it was generally so cryptic that the Franco press censors feared even his expressions of approval of their movement might carry a hidden condemnation that would be brought to light at some future date. He died in his home a few weeks later, on New Year's Eve, — apparently of heart failure — while talking to a friend.

No foreign correspondents were permitted to make a trip to southern Spain until the last of January, 1937, when an excursion was organized by the official Oficina de la Prensa to the Malaga front for the impending victory of the southern army, nominally under Queipo de Llano.

"No wonder we couldn't come here before," George Axelsson, of The New York Times, exclaimed when he saw the troops marching on Malaga. "There's spaghetti in them thar Spanish omelets."

At least half of the Rebel forces were Italians, who were wearing the regular Fascist militia uniforms, except for their headgear. Instead of the usual khaki trench caps, the Italians wore black berets to match their black shirts. They numbered about forty thousand and were completely equipped, having artillery, tanks, and machine guns brought from Italy. But even then we were not permitted by the Spanish censorship to make any reference to the participation of the Italians.

After encountering only slight resistance, the Insurgents paraded into Malaga on February 7. But the Italians, on reaching the city limits, carefully marched around the town in order not to give the population of the fallen city the impression that foreign troops had won the battle. All correspondents who were in Franco Spain from the beginning of the war are unanimously agreed that this was the first time that Italian infantry had been used in the Civil War.

Mussolini, who was still pleased with himself as a result of the Ethiopian campaign, was anxious to throw his troops into more important battles. He thought it would be quite a feather in his black cap if Fascist forces could take Madrid after the Moors, Foreign Legionaries, Falangistas, and Royalists had failed. Franco was reluctant to give any such opportunity to the Italians. He was already suspicious of aid from Rome and Berlin and feared what it might cost him later. But owing to the shortage of trained Spanish man power at his disposal, Franco finally acceded to Fascist pressure.

The Black Shirts who had helped to take Malaga were then brought up from the south and concentrated at the snow-covered pass just north of Sigüenza in preparation for an exclusively Italian offensive. It was the beginning of March. The drive started on the ninth, when they advanced twelve miles in a single day over the Guadalajara road. They met little resistance, and the advance was so easy for the first few days that the Italians became careless. The deep snow on either side of the road made it hard for the flanking troops to march over the rough, mountainous terrain, and since these troops met no Republican forces in the mountains, they were pulled back to the main highway to make their marching less arduous. By the time they reached Brihuega, about fifteen miles from their immediate objective, Guadalajara, they were lined up in trainlike formation, making no attempt to protect the fields on either side.

Meanwhile, the Spanish general, Juan Orgaz, commanding the Moors and Foreign Legionaries in the Toledo sector of the Madrid front, was also supposed to start an offensive. The plan was to squeeze Madrid from two sides, but General Orgaz did not move on schedule. The Spanish Rebels unofficially claimed afterward that the Italians themselves had not started their offensive on the date they were supposed to, that General Orgaz had moved his troops for the offensive into the trenches on the southern Madrid front only to have them suffer heavy casualties from Republican shelling while awaiting the signal to go over the top. Annoyed at this, General Orgaz again withdrew the bulk of his troops to safer positions and, consequently, was not ready to attack when the Italians wanted him to.

The Republican army in Madrid, knowing nothing of the potential trap in the soutn, however, had rushed up reinforcements to meet the Italians on the Guadalajara road. The Italian troops, confident in their superior equipment, which included light tanks, fought at first when they encountered the Republicans, but were not able to make any headway. It had been raining throughout most of the drive, but now the storm turned into a terrific downpour, grounding the planes on whose support the Italian commanding officers had counted. The Republican planes were able to take off from their concrete runways on the Madrid airfields and encountered no resistance whatever in the air. The Italian infantry, bunched together on the road, instead of deployed in the fields and woods as it should have been, made a target impossible to miss, and the Republican pilots mowed them down by the hundreds. The Fascists tried to withdraw, and in the confusion of the retreat the Republican infantry closed in on all sides and took thousands of prisoners as well as enormous amounts of war booty.

We were both in Salamanca at the time. We were having dinner in the Gran Hotel when we were joined by an English-speaking major with a blue sash around his waist — meaning he was a member of the General Staff. He was obviously delighted about something. Eleanor asked him if he had fallen in love.

"Almost — with those bloody Reds," he said in a low voice. "They have given those obnoxious Eye-ties a terrific trouncing."

This was the first we had heard of the Italian disaster at Guadalajara. He then went on to give us details about how Franco learned of it.

"An Italian colonel who had been leading one of the Black Shirt regiments on the Guadalajara front," the major said, "was dispatched to the Generalissimo's headquarters to report to him how well the advance was going. I suppose it took him over twenty-four hours to reach Salamanca from the front line. His information was certainly old when he arrived. Because even while he was talking to *El Caudillo*, word was received from our own headquarters at Sigüenza of their defeat. Was he embarrassed!"

He refused to divulge the name of the Italian colonel. This major was far from being the only one to be outspoken about the Italian setback. Even Franco and his generals did not conceal their satisfaction. They had long been chafing under the patronizing attitude of the Italian military leaders and consequently were pleased at this blow to Fascist prestige. Spanish Rebel officers in the bars of Salamanca and Burgos, San Sebastián and Seville, toasted the valor of the Spanish Republicans and declared that the defeat at Guadalajara would show Mussolini that Spaniards — even though Republican Spaniards — were not to be so easily annihilated as Ethiopians.

The Italian officers whom we met in Salamanca at the time were just as full of national pride and declared that the real reason they had suffered such a disaster was because they were fighting not Spaniards, but Italians. They gave credit for the Republican victory to the anti-Fascist Garibaldi Battalion of the International Brigade. They also said that it was hard for them to fight wholeheartedly against other Italians. Still another alibi for Guadalajara was that the vanguard of the Black Shirts was confused when it established contact with the Republicans and heard Italian being spoken. But the more intelligent of the Italian officers realized that there had been a disgraceful defeat and were definitely broken up over it.

Nothing more was seen or heard of Italian troops for a while after Guadalajara. It would naturally take Mussolini some time to reorganize his forces. But he went further than that. He withdrew most of the Black Shirt troops and many of the high officers concerned in the Guadalajara battle in great anger and, in defiance of Badoglio, subsequently replaced them with better-trained soldiers of the regular Italian army. Anyway, he was determined not to be driven out of Spain by a defeat, and during April new Italian troops reappeared with orders to restore Italian prestige during the Nationalist offensive on the Basque coast, scheduled for the summer of 1937.

Meanwhile, the Germans were also lending a hand. We had first seen German fliers in Avila during Franco's early and unsuccessful attack on Madrid and, later, great numbers of German ground troops in mustard-colored uniforms and knee-length boots in Salamanca. Nobody seemed to know what they were doing at Franco's headquarters. They were apparently specialists, because the Germans never sent any infantry, though they did contribute technicians of all kinds, including antiaircraft, antitank, and artillery crews, field-radio operators, wire layers, repair outfits and other types of subsidiary service men in which Franco was gravely lacking.

When we went to Vitoria in April, 1937, to report the Mola offensive against Bilbao, we found the Germans, for once, almost as prominent as the Italians. The German communications command was installed in the hotel where we stayed. The whole mezzanine floor was reserved for them and all the signs on the doors were in German. Outside in the street were enormous trucks containing powerful generating dynamos for powering radio senders. Besides communicating with Nazi fliers and specialists at the front, this command also sent direct to Berlin. The Nazis considered the Spanish telephone system in northern Spain so unreliable that they installed a complete duplicate system of their own which no one else was allowed to use. It was an example of the importance the Nazis always attributed to fast, efficient communications.

During the Bilbao campaign, the Italians and Germans took over most of the artillery work, and there were reports of many disputes between the Italo-German and Spanish commands because the former claimed that when they had shelled a position to prepare it for an infantry attack, the Spanish infantry failed to advance, the Spanish officers having changed their minds at the last minute about the day of the attack and having failed to inform the artillery.

The Italian infantry, aided by whippet tanks, also participated on a large scale. The number of Italian soldiers actually fighting in the Spanish war probably reached its peak during the 1937 summer campaign against the Basque country and the Asturias. Four divisions of infantry were used: the Black Arrows, the Black Flames, the Littorio, and the Twenty-third of March, which, with the supporting units of tanks, aircraft, and so on, totaled around eighty thousand men.

The rift between the Spanish Rebels and the Italians was quite apparent to us as correspondents. Anxious to wipe out the bad name they had gained at Guadalajara, the Italian military authorities invited many of the foreign correspondents, including Reynolds, to visit the Italian sectors on the Bilbao front. Reynolds made one of these trips and was shown a greatly reorganized Black Shirt army, one that was far superior in equipment and numbers to that which had lost at Guadalajara. The Fascist press officials, who were all in Black Shirt uniform, operated a special courier service for dispatches between the front lines and Saint-Jean de Luz, in France. It enabled messages sent by this route to reach the outside world at least eight hours and frequently twelve hours before those filed by cable through slower Spanish censorship.

Reynolds availed himself of this service. Returning to Vitoria, where the Spanish press headquarters for this offensive were located, he was severely reprimanded by Major Lambari — in peacetime, a designer for Vogue — who was at the head of the foreign section of the Spanish Oficina de la Prensa, for having had anything to do with the Italians. Lambari said that any future excursions made by non-Italian correspondents to the front in the company of Fascist officials would be punished by immediate expulsion. He added:

"It's about time you fellows realize this is a Spanish war. We can't help it if we have to have some outside help. The other side has it, too. But we are determined that you are going to see this war through Spanish eyes."

Even so, the Spaniards had a difficult time dislocating Bill Carney, of The New York Times, and Pembroke Stevens (later killed in China) of the London Daily Telegraph. They were among the first to have seen the journalistic advantages of reporting the war with the help of Italian press officers as compared to working only through the Spanish Press Bureau and, as a result, had established connections which were difficult for the Spaniards to break. Nevertheless, even these two were eventually compelled to sever their relations with the Italians.

One of the chief Fascist press officers was Piero Saporiti, who, when the war ended, came to the United States as correspondent for Virginio Gayda's Giornale d'Italia and proceeded to send the most virulent attacks upon President Roosevelt and the United States' attitude toward World War II.

As in Malaga, the Fascist columns which helped to take Bilbao did not enter the city itself when it fell on June 19, but circled around through the outskirts where they encamped. In a few days, they moved on, joining the mopping-up operations northward and participated in the offensive against Santander. By the time that Santander was ready to surrender, the Black Shirt officers were determined not to make any more back-door entrances. And when Santander fell on August 26, the Italians marched in through the suburbs and continued down all the principal streets of the city.

It reminded us of a Roman holiday. The Italian tanks were decorated with ivy leaves and plaster plaques of the heads of Mussolini and Franco, while the Black Shirt soldiers had stuck daisies and bluebells into the muzzles of their guns and behind their ears. This time even the Spanish newspapers were compelled to pay them tribute for the part they had played in this campaign.

During this fighting, the Italians also occupied innumerable small towns on their own, and not until the next day would groups of Falangistas arrive to take charge of the administration of the towns and mete out "summary justice," generally meaning wholesale deaths in front of firing squads before the army officers would arrive and establish military tribunals.

While the Spaniards displayed contempt for the Italians, the Italians in turn were openly disapproving of the mass executions. Compelled to accept foreign aid against their will, the Spaniards, as a form of Freudian self-defense, became haughtier and more arrogant. They would often make fun of the ill-kempt appearance of the Black Shirts, who made a poor sartorial showing in contrast to the more smartly garbed Spaniards, who went in for flowing capes, wide cowboy belts, jaunty caps, and open collars which, with Byronic flare, folded back over the necklines of their uniforms. The Germans and the Italians all this time had little personal or social contact. Even the Fascist chaser pilots, who collaborated with the German bombers, had their separate encampments, always far removed from the Germans. We had the impression that the Spaniards were much more friendly and got along much better in every way with the Germans than they did with the Italians. Most of us agreed that this was because the Germans sent a much smaller contingent — probably no more than ten thousand men at any one time — composed exclusively of experts. Also, it was quite obvious that the Germans had been carefully instructed on how to behave in Spain, and, contrary to their Teutonic character, remained very much in the background. Besides, the Germans didn't have a Guadalajara to live down.

The greatest tragedy that befell the foreign correspondents on the Franco side during the war occurred outside of Teruel. Major Lambari led a string of six cars of newspapermen up to the Teruel front while it was under heavy shell fire from the Republicans. As soon as the cavalcade halted at the field headquarters in a small town, the Republicans increased their artillery fire. One shell landed just in front of a car occupied by Eddie Neal, of the A.P.; Bradish Johnson, of Newsweek; Kim Philby, of the London Times; and William Sheepshanks, of Reuter's. They were all peppered with shell splinters and, with the exception of Philby, who miraculously suffered only a minor head wound, were killed. The death of Johnson, who was on his first trip to the front, made us all more fatalistic than ever. He had been riding in another automobile when the halt was made, and he changed places with the Spanish driver in order to talk with Eddie Neal. The shell came less than a minute later.

As the nonintervention movement developed, Mussolini was forced to put less and less of his men in the fighting field. Even during the push on Barcelona, the Black Shirts were reduced to almost half of what they had been in the Bilbao offensive. And in the victory parade down the main streets of Barcelona, following its fall on January 26, 1939, only twenty thousand Italians appeared. He recognized that from the point of view of European diplomacy it was desirable that Franco in the future use more Spanish troops and fewer Italians. The most critical phase of the war for Franco, however, was over, because in the preceding year Franco had been able to train a considerable number of Spanish troops.

The Fascist Twenty-third of March Division took part in the decisive battle of the Ebro in 1938, which ended with Franco driving a Rebel wedge to the Mediterranean, dividing Catalonia from Madrid and Valencia, and that was the last important activity of Italian infantry in Spain. The fight for Madrid, which fell on March 28, 1939, was virtually a Spanish affair on both sides, as far as land forces were concerned. Franco, of course, continued to rely on Axis aviation until the war ended.

Both Mussolini and Hitler often changed the personnel of their aviation corps in Spain so that the maximum number of their pilots could get training under real war conditions. Most of the ones we saw were very young and stayed in Spain only about three months before being replaced by a fresh batch of recruits. For the most part, Italian aviation was confined to chaser planes, except in the Balearics, where several squadrons of Italian bombers were based. Many of the Italian fliers in the Balearics were Fascist career men who came to Spain in much the same way as they had gone to Ethiopia; it was another steppingstone in Fascist promotion. Among the more notable of these were Ettore Muti, who later became Secretary General of the Fascist party, and the Duce's sons, Bruno and Vittorio.

All the international grievances on the Franco side were patched up in time for the final victory parade in Madrid on May 11, 1939. We sat in the press gallery in front of Franco's reviewing stand, which was carefully surrounded by his trusted Moorish guard. For five hours the troops marched by in the rain. All the Italians in Spain, including those reserve troops that had been sitting on farm fences back in Miranda de Ebro and Palencia, took part. All their heavy artillery and many of their tanks were paraded forth. It was all right because the word had gone around that all this matériel was being left behind and all the men were leaving. Overhead, Italian and German planes maneuvered in trick formations. They, too, were to be left behind, but the pilots were to go.

The keynote of the parade was Spanish strength, but to the foreign correspondents it was a menacing display of Italo-German solidarity. It was the manifest culmination of how Mussolini and Hitler had grown closer than ever as a result of the Spanish Civil War. From a simultaneous recognition by Rome and Berlin of the Franco government, the Italo-German collaboration increased to a general agreement regarding European problems outside of Spain. This agreement, born during the Spanish Civil War, turned the Axis from a newspaper phrase into a concrete political entity with military overtones.

Franco had succeeded in winning the war with the aid of Axis men and matériel. He had succeeded, despite predictions to the contrary, in arranging for the departure of his military guests, all of whom actually left within the next three months.

Both Italy and Germany were charging merely secondhand prices for the matériel, but the real payment was to be made on a politico-military basis in the future: Spain was to aid the Axis in the war to come. Actually, Franco proved a tougher bargainer than either Mussolini or Hitler, as he shaved down the first installments to nothing more than moral support, despite Axis efforts to drag Spain into the war shortly after Italy's entry.

Major Pollard, in his capacity as a sporting editor, sat next to us in the press tribune. As the Victory Parade came to an end, he turned to Eleanor and said:

"No more airplane trips to the Canaries for me."

# IV

THE NEXT PHASE OF THE FASCIST IMPERIALIST PROGRAM WAS initiated November 30, 1938, more than two months after the Munich "appeasement" conference, when Mussolini convened the Italian Chamber of Deputies for the ostensible purpose of permitting Foreign Minister Ciano to inform its meek members what Italy's foreign policy had been during the Czech crisis. Ciano revealed to the Chamber in considerable detail the extent of Italy's secret mobilization on September 27, the disposition of the troops, and the measures taken by the Italian navy in preparation for possible action. Ciano then assured the dummy Chamber what everyone already knew: that the Duce thoroughly endorsed both Hitler's annexation of Austria and his policy in Czechoslovakia.

The foreign correspondents in the press gallery nodded sleepily. Czechoslovakia was "old stuff" by now. The newspaper-reading public didn't want to hear about it any more. Most of the chief correspondents in Rome hadn't even bothered to come to this meeting of the Chamber, since the published agenda of the meeting mentioned only a review of the Italian part in the Czech crisis. Some organizations, indeed, had only Italian tipsters there to give them "protective" coverage.

But Count Ciano had more up his sleeve than that. Suddenly, as he droned through his speech, which he read from typewritten sheets in front of him, he looked up, raised his voice — perhaps as a signal — and said:

"Italy will pursue the consolidation of peace with tenacity and realism, not unmingled with that circumspection which is indispensable if we wish to safeguard with inflexible resolution the interests and natural aspirations of the Italian people."

It was a jaw-breaking sentence and vague enough not to mean anything in particular. But it meant something to certain members of the Chamber who, beyond any shadow of doubt, had been instructed what to do. Several score leaped to their feet simultaneously and shouted: "Tunisia! Tunisia! Tunisia!" The handpicked Black Shirts in the spectators' gallery immediately took up the cry and added shouts for "Nizza" and "Savoia" on their own account. One deputy who either was not in on the plot or who was perhaps acting a part then leaped to his feet and, pretending indignation that the Foreign Minister's speech had been interrupted, waved his hands and cried, "Per cortesia! Per cortesia!" (Please! Please!) In the noise and confusion, the audience in the spectators' gallery misunderstood cortesia for "Corsica" and willingly added shouts for this additional piece of French territory to their demands.

The press gallery had, of course, wakened to life at the first shout, but the Italian correspondents were in a considerable quandary. Could they be positive this was a staged performance? Because if it was not, they should, as well-trained Fascist journalists, first get permission from the Press Ministry before passing the news on to any foreign employers. Genuinely spontaneous demonstrations were subject to censorship. They glanced across the room at the diplomatic gallery. The prominently placed chair usually occupied by the French Ambassador to Rome, Monsieur

André François-Poncet, was vacant. Evidently he had taken the demonstration seriously.

It took quite a while for the cheering to die down and for order to be restored so that Ciano could go on with his speech — which contained no mention whatsoever of Tunisia, Nice, Savoy, or Corsica. Long before that, however, those foreign correspondents who had been present had phoned their accounts of the demonstration to their offices in Paris, London, Berlin, and so on. Soon frantic queries came pouring into the Rome bureaus of those unfortunate organizations who had had only Italian newsmen in the Chamber. The Italian Press Ministry had, as usual, muzzled the local men working for foreign organizations until it later received instructions from the Foreign Office to release the story. There were many hard words exchanged in newspaper offices and in the Stampa Estera that evening. Although the foreign correspondents could not say so without risk of expulsion from Italy, it became all the more obvious that the scene was staged when word got around that the demonstration had been led by Achille Starace, Secretary General of the Fascist party, and Roberto Farinacci, ex-Secretary General and, after Mussolini and Balbo, the third most influential leader in the party.

The following day the students of Rome University, always glad of an excuse for a holiday, turned their backs on their classrooms and, gathering in groups of one hundred or more, paraded through the main streets of Rome shouting about Italian rights to Tunisia, Corsica, Nice, Savoy. In their zeal, they added another claim on French territory — Djibouti. Some of them marched past the United States Consulate, on the Via Vittorio Veneto, but didn't stop there, and in the end they all converged on the French Embassy, the approaches to which, however, had been safely cordoned off by squads of carabinieri who had received warning of the impending demonstration well in advance. Most of the students were dressed in their black shirts and black tunics with bright-blue silk scarfs — a costume not worn on ordinary schooldays, indicating they had had the demonstration in mind when they dressed that morning. Many of them also wore the bright-colored hats, Pied Piper in shape and trimmed with dozens of small pins and insignia, which peculiarly distinguishes the GUF (Gruppo Universitario Fascista). Similar student demonstrations took place in the streets and in front of the French Consulates in Naples, Milan, and other large cities.

The French did not take this challenge meekly. Of course, no official demand had been made, so no official reply could be given; but French students quickly counterdemonstrated, marching through Paris and several other French cities, sometimes laying facetious claims to Milan and Turin, sometimes getting really angry enough to shout, "Down with Mussolini! Down with Fascism! Down with Italy!" At the same time, more serious and still angrier mass meetings were held in Corsica, where the population, mostly of Italian race, affirmed their very positive desire to remain a part of France. This was particularly galling to the Fascists, since it was part of their propaganda that all people of Italian race wish themselves and their lands to be a part of Italy.

Some of the Italians in Tunisia reacted more to the Black Shirts' satisfaction. The Italians there were always in a special position, because by the Italo-French treaty of 1896 they retained their Italian citizenship, and for years they had been subjected to intensive Fascist propaganda. Enough of them approved the idea of Italian domination of Tunisia to try to stage some demonstrations. The French population of Tunisia retaliated, and in the ensuing street clashes there were many broken windows and quite a few broken heads.

The Chamber demonstration to voice Italian claims on Tunisia and other French lands apparently came as a great surprise to French officials, who thought that the Tunisian question, at least, had been settled by the Laval-Mussolini negotiations in 1935. French politicians also thought Il Duce was too deeply involved in Spain to be able to undertake any other adventures elsewhere. But the Tunisia manifestations were really a sign that a Franco victory in Spain was already a foregone conclusion and that Mussolini knew it. Despite assertions made later by Virginio Gayda in the *Giornale d'Italia* that Italian troops would remain in Spain until a political as well as a military victory was achieved, Mussolini realized by this time that an alliance with Spain and economic concessions were about all the profit he was going to get out of the Spanish war. Franco plainly was not going to tolerate Italian intervention in his internal affairs or concede any naval or air bases. The results to Italy of the Spanish war were, therefore, more political than military, though certainly not unimportant in the general European picture.

The rapid crumbling of the Spanish Loyalists' resistance about this time left Il Duce with his hands free to make mischief elsewhere. He had two successful enterprises under his belt now, Ethiopia and Spain, and the ease with which he had engineered them was making him bold — bold enough to tackle France, generally considered a much stronger military power than Italy. Not that Mussolini had any idea of going to war with France. Not yet, anyway. There was a great deal of diplomatic groundwork to be done first. For one thing, British friendship for France had to be alienated and the effectiveness of the Soviet-French treaty of alliance somehow nullified. In view of the indecision, weakness, and disunity that had been manifest among the French in the preceding years, Mussolini undoubtedly convinced himself that if he could isolate France politically, the vacillating French government would yield him some of his claims rather than go to war. The demonstration in the Italian Chamber was only the opening shot, as the Ualual incident had been in the Ethiopian affair. Indeed, it seems probable that at that time Mussolini did not at all envisage the outbreak of World War II, nine months later, and that the Führer upset the Duce's French applecart when he precipitated the present war. Diplomatic maneuvers of the kind Mussolini was planning take a long time to work out.

When news of rioting in Tunis was received in our Rome bureau, we were in Rome on the tail end of a vacation following the winding up of our assignment in Prague, where we had been throughout the German-Czech crisis. We were, in fact, waiting for instructions from the head office about where to go next. On the evening of the day of the Tunis demonstrations, we received orders to fly to Tunis the next morning.

By luck, there were two seats left in an Ala Littoria plane, and we took off in the morning from Ostia. It was a seaplane, operated with the usual Fascist efficiency. As we rose off the water, gaining altitude, we tried to check our watches with the plane's clock, only to notice that it wasn't running. An hour later, when we had reached a height of more than ten thousand feet and it seemed a good idea to make use of the air tubes intended to facilitate breathing, Eleanor picked one up, only to have it break off in her hand. When we had really got out to sea and were just about halfway between the mainlands of Europe and Africa, a feed pipe sprung a leak and spouted oil over some of the passengers. One of the crew of three, the mechanic, came over to fix it but could find no proper material to make the necessary repairs. After mumbling *porca miseria* a few times, he pulled out his shirttail and, with his handkerchief, made a tourniquet around the pipe. We asked him if he thought it would hold until we reached Tunis, and he replied, "I hope so. Otherwise I'll lose my shirt." The only Italian we knew on the trip was Gino Tomaselli, roving correspondent for the important Milan newspaper, *Corriere della Sera.* He spoke to us, as he remembered us from the Ethiopian days when we all drove into Addis Ababa with the Badoglio column. He said that he was going to write a series of articles on how the French were mistreating the Italians. Eleanor told him that he seemed to have a pretty good idea of what he was going to write in advance. He laughed and said, "Yes, but I need a Tunis date line."

At the airfield, Tomaselli was greeted by three Fascists who were wearing the party insignia despite the fact that they were on French soil, and he went away with them immediately in an automobile so as to get off his first dispatch. We rode into Tunis in the autobus of the airline. At the office in town, our bags were taken out of the car and placed inside, awaiting our instructions as to which hotel to send them. The clerks in the office called our attention to a small hole in the plate-glass window where a stone had gone through. They then told us how badly the French had acted and claimed that the French police had given the anti-Italian French demonstrators a free hand. They also recommended to us the Fascist hotel as the best place to stay. We told them that we were going to make a tour of the city and that later in the day we would send around for our luggage. We were determined not to have any Fascist guides on this trip. Not knowing the town, we rambled around and entered several of the more attractive cafés. All the waiters were Italian. In each place we discreetly asked the waiters how they were being treated by the French, and they all reacted the same — they didn't react at all and very carefully refused to commit themselves. As time went on, we could see the anomalous position of the Italians in Tunisia: virtually all of them retained their citizenship but worked for French employers. If they protested against the French, they were apt to lose their jobs, and if they sided with the French, they were bound to find themselves in still graver difficulties with the Fascist party, which had set up a sort of state-within-a-state in Tunisia.

That evening, just after we had installed ourselves comfortably in a French hotel, anti-Italian demonstrations broke out in the streets. We dashed out and followed the crowds that were converging on the Italian Consulate building. It was of white stone and made a perfect background for a patriotic French display. They threw large bottles of red and blue ink against the Consulate so that it became striped with the colors of the French flag — red, white, and blue. After they had decorated the Italian Consulate to their satisfaction, they marched down the streets singing La Marseillaise. Hundreds of Arabs also participated in the demonstration.

As we were still lingering outside the Consulate, waiting for the possibility of further activity, Tomaselli came out and, spotting us, said, "Did you see what they have done? I want you to come into the Consulate and let me show you something. It is really terrible. I am writing about it tonight, and I am sure it's a good story for you, too."

We followed him, and after a certain amount of formality, we were ushered into the office of the Consul General, M. Silimbani, and there shown a picture on the wall of Victor Emmanuel III, whose face had been blued out by a blob of ink. Miraculously, the ink had not splattered on the wall itself in any way. It looked like another plant to us. It was just too much of a coincidence that ink, in or out of a bottle, could have come in through a window and splattered itself on the one object there that could make for an international incident and leave no other trace of its trajectory. Sensing our skepticism, the Italian Consulate officials showered us with assurances that it had really happened. They even told us that the French might exercise surreptitious censorship of our dispatches if we tried to send the incident and that therefore they would be delighted to give us facilities for sending via Rome. We assured them in turn that we did not think there was any French censorship and, besides, we weren't sure we could even use the incident. During the next few days we soon became aware of how highly organized were the Fascists in Tunisia. Having just come from Czechoslovakia, it reminded us of the Sudeten German organization under Konrad Henlein, which was merely a subsidiary of Berlin. In Czechoslovakia, we discovered, as time went on, that most of the experts in the movement to have the Sudeten areas break away from Czechoslovakia were actually Reich Germans who had no claim to Czechoslovak citizenship in any way. And so it was in Tunisia. The anti-French Italians, who were in control of the Tunisia movement, were all imported from Italy. Every morning we received unasked-for pamphlets from this organization, which listed Italian grievances and set forth the juridical claims of the Italians. Just to make sure that we wouldn't miss anything, Italians constantly called upon us, quite unsolicited, and expounded the Fascist thesis. One was the party lawyer, who wouldn't let us leave until he had explained that the Italian claims dated back to about the fifteenth century. Many of the Italian city-states, particularly Genoa and Naples, he said, had had treaties with the beys of Tunis whereunder they had not only trade concessions, but extraterritorial rights as well. These individual treaties with Italian city-states had been carried over to beyond 1870, when Italy was unified, and the Italian nation continued to enjoy the same privileges in Tunisia as had formerly been exercised by its component parts. These Italian privileges had been abruptly terminated by the French invasion of Tunisia in 1881, after which France had established a protectorate over this Arab state. The lawyer added that Italy had protested the French armed nullification of her rights at the time and refused to recognize the protectorate until 1896, when, as he smartly put it, a particularly weak Italian democratic cabinet had allowed itself to be browbeaten into an official acquiescence to France's domination of Tunisia.

The Italian organization — a vaguer setup than the Henlein party, for it had no definite headquarters, officers, or specific program — had as its mouthpiece the Italian-language daily newspaper *L'Unione*, whose editor in chief was Enrico Santamaria. As far as we could run down any nominal head of the movement, it was Santamaria. The Italian Consulate officers were much too identified with the government at Rome for Mussolini to use them in carrying out his tricky policy and could not have any official roles in the movement. Both the French and the Arabs — and that included journalists as well as members of the Residence General staff — assured us that Santamaria was the only leader, at least the only one you could put your finger on and still not arrest. A number of the other lieutenants had been arrested. These included Ubaldo Rey, head of the Italian war veterans in Tunis, who had been sentenced to three months' imprisonment for starting anti-French riots, and a Fascist named Antonio Larosa, who had confessed under police questioning that he had set fire to the Italian Dopo Lavoro (After-Work) Club in an effort to make the French authorities appear responsible for the incendiarism. Another of the Italians to be arrested was Vestri Luginio, a clerk in the Italian Consulate.

We had no trouble in interviewing Santamaria, who received us in his office in *L'Unione*. He was a rather good-looking, curly-haired, swarthy Italian in his early thirties, who spoke to us in perfect French. He immediately disclaimed the French-newspaper reports that he was a veritable Henlein and kept repeating that he was "just another newspaperman," trying to give his Italian readers in Tunisia all the news that would interest them. He also gave us the official contention of the Italian Consulate that the French police, who had already called in one hundred mobile guards from Algeria, were not giving Italian residents the proper protection. He countercharged in his interview with us that the French were falsifying statistics with regard to the number of Italians in Tunisia. He said that there were 120,000 Italians, whereas the French only credited them with 94,289.

"The French tried to claim 108,068 in their 1936 census, which is the basis of the present argument," he told us. "But in doing this, they had the nerve to include transients, especially French soldiers who are sent here, and also Italians who have been forced to become naturalized French in order to keep their jobs. Why, the protectorate would not be able to function if it were not for Italian labor! It is Italian labor that has been used in building up the cities, ports, and roads of Tunisia. Some idea as to how little the French have contributed in this respect can be had when you realize that in 1881, when the French protectorate was established, there were only seven hundred French here as compared to ten thousand Italians."

Taking advantage of the fact that he had said he was just another newspaperman, we asked him to tell us just exactly what were the Italian claims regarding Tunisia, so we could write a dispatch describing them in detail. He frowned, and it was quite clear that he thought we were hitting below the belt in asking such a question. We told him that Italian claims on France to date, as far as we could see, were being disseminated and publicized in the world press by non-Italian correspondents who still weren't able to say whether Mussolini wanted to take over Tunisia as a colony or merely improve the welfare of Italian residents there. We added that the Italian claims seemed to be based entirely on supposedly unofficial shouts of "Tunisia! Tunisia! Tunisia!" and nothing else. This request of ours for clarification brought the interview to a sudden end, and he politely escorted us to the door, saying that he hoped he had been instrumental in helping us understand the Italian point of view.

In contrast to the Fascist willingness to feed the press Italian history, figures, and grievances, the French were extremely stand-offish. Their attitude, and rightly so, was that every story written about revindications and incidents was just so much propaganda for the Fascist claims — whatever they might be. The French Residence General had a press bureau, but its staff concentrated mainly on telling foreign correspondents who had gathered in Tunis in great numbers at this time not to bother to send any stories. They gave us little, if anything, in the way of French history, figures, and grievances to refute the Italians. We had been there nearly a week before the French Governor General, Eirik Labonne, was free to see us. Our conversation — he made it quite clear that it was not to be an interview — took place in his private office. He was tall, thin, and extremely dignified. If it were not known that he was French, he might easily have been taken, at first, for a New Englander. But he was, once the conversation became animated, extremely French. He shrugged his shoulders from time to time as though the entire Italian affair were an awful bore and the Italians themselves the sort of people that, socially, one does not talk about.

"Haven't you noticed," he asked us, "that the Italians look just like the Arabs? I find it so embarrassing whenever I am called on to address any gathering of workers here to make out whether I'm talking to Arabs or Italians. It's quite annoying. In a way, though, it's rather amusing, because the Italians' great claim to supplying labor to our protectorate is the very thing that has done more than anything else to make the Arabs dislike them. Mussolini's effort to play the role of the Protector of Islam is not succeeding here. Every Arab knows that the freer hand the Italians are given here, the more unemployment there will be in Islam. The Italians who come over here think nothing of sitting down beside an Arab and chipping stone."

M. Labonne became indignant when we asked him about what the French were doing for the Italians living in Tunisia and gave us a scholarly review of the reforms and treaties since recognition by Italy of the French protectorate in 1896. At that time a treaty was drawn up wherein persons professing Italian nationality retained their Italian citizenship, although residing in Tunisia. Their descendants would also retain Italian citizenship in complete accordance with Italian law. Italian hospitals and Italian schools already established in the protectorate were to be maintained; there was also a commercial clause whereby Italy received "most-favored-nation" treatment after France, and it was specified that Italian citizens and property would be treated exactly as if they were French. In 1919 France gave notice of her desire to terminate the treaty, but never did so, and it was automatically renewed every three months during the ensuing years. In 1935, the Laval-Mussolini negotiations resulted in a new treaty being signed on January 6, wherein the Duce dropped most of his claims on Tunisia and received in exchange a rectification of the Libyan-Tunisian border which favored Italy. The 1935 agreement provided that children born of Italian parents in Tunisia before 1945 were to remain Italian; those born between 1945 and 1965 would have the right to adopt Italian citizenship, if they should so desire, at the age of twenty-one; all born after 1965 would be French. (A few days after our interview with M. Labonne, December 17, 1938, the French Foreign Office announced that Italy had notified Ambassador François-Poncet that Italy considered the Franco-Italian agreement of 1935 to be null and void. The status of Italian nationals, therefore, reverted to the 1896 convention, which, being renewed every three months, continued to govern the situation until the outbreak of World War II.)

Although M. Labonne and his press bureau were inclined to be inarticulate about the political angle of Tunisia, they were willing to be more than liberal about informing all the correspondents as to France's determination to fight, if necessary, to maintain its protectorate over Tunisia. As a result, we had no trouble whatsoever in obtaining permission to visit France's "Tunisian Maginot Line," its "Tunisian Gibraltar," and to attend maneuvers of the French forces, including thousands of black-faced Senegalese, in the field. It was quite the story of the day — whether or not France was able to defend Tunisia against the Italians who had so quickly taken over Ethiopia and assured Franco of victory in Spain. Reynolds joined up with Max Easterman, of the London Daily Herald, Geoffrey Cox, of the London Daily Express, and Frank Smothers, of the Chicago Daily News, and they jointly hired a car to make the excursion. Eleanor stayed in Tunis to cover the demonstrations. There were probably too many in the large Buick to make a trip of this nature. Each of us had his own idea as to where we should go first and how long we should stay at any one place when we did get there. Our reporting was still further complicated when we arrived at the so-called Tunisian Maginot Line — actually the Berthome Line, as it was General Philippe Berthome who had directed its construction. There the French military authorities discovered that our chauffeur, whom Cox had hired back in Tunis, was an Italian suspected of Fascist intelligence work. As a result, we had to leave the car several times at some point distant from fortifications and travel overland for miles either on foot or on muleback. The French officers were less embarrassed about the presence of the chauffeur than we. One colonel with whom we had lunch at Médenine told us that it probably wouldn't make any difference anyway if he did accompany us up to the secret fortifications, as he was quite sure that the Italians had already documented themselves very thoroughly about them. "However," he said with a shrug of his shoulders, "there's no reason to make it easy for them."

We had a chance to see that the Berthome Line was located between the Libyan frontier and Médenine and consisted mostly of elaborate underground works where whole battalions could hide. There were tank traps and miles of barbed wire, intended specifically to halt cavalry and camel corps which Mussolini had stationed just on the other side of the border. Every oasis was a fortress in itself, complete with machine-gun nests, concrete redoubts, subterranean air-raid shelters, and still more barbed-wire entanglements. A French captain, who was escorting us on a tour of one of the oases, described them as the "green corpuscles of the Berthome Line" — green because they were all protected against the African sun by palm trees, which shot up in the air as high as forty feet, and verdant foliage. He emphasized that in the event of a siege, each oasis was self-sufficient, being a natural storehouse of figs, dates, and spring water. At Gabès, situated in the Little Sirte in the middle of the Gulf of Gabès, we were shown sunken artillery emplacements all pointing seaward in case of a naval attack. We also saw a review of many thousands of Senegalese who were stationed there. On the way back, we halted at Sfax and Sousse, both important ports, and found the French unloading great quantities of military supplies. Italian workmen, however, as well as Arabs, were being used to do most of the dock work and undoubtedly were keeping Mussolini well informed as to the bills of lading of the different ships. At Sousse, Smothers insisted that we halt for a moment in front of an Italian school in which the children were singing. We did, and easily recognized what they were singing. It was the Fascist anthem, Giovinezza.

The only place we encountered real secrecy was at Bizerta, where we were shown only part of that important naval base. The one-hour conducted tour that we had at this base was quite sufficient to show why Italy was fostering its claims upon Tunisia. It was rightly called the "Tunisian Gibraltar." It was less than one hundred and fifty miles from Italy's big, fortified islands of Sardinia, on the northwest, and Sicily, on the northeast. Rome was only three hundred and fifty miles away. Bizerta could always be a threat to the Italian supply line to Mussolini's empire in East Africa. Second only to Toulon at the time as a French naval base, it had drydocks, machine and repair shops, underground cisterns for fuel, blown out of the rock and safe against naval or aerial bombardments, coaling facilities, arsenals, barracks, and a hospital, all protected by vast fortifications. It was large enough to hold all the fleets of continental Europe. There was even a lake, well stocked with edible fish, to say nothing of a productive hinterland which could be called upon for necessary food supplies. In this way, it was even superior to Gibraltar, which has always had to import all its supplies. We also saw a big seaplane port and an airfield, as well as a special dock for submarines. Nature had taken a hand in making it well-nigh invincible. In order to reach the inner bay, ships had to pass through a mile-long canal which had just been dredged at the time to a depth of forty feet and was wide enough for the new, 35,000-ton French line ships to pass through.

By the time we got back to Tunis after our four-day trip, we found that the French, as a result of a series of arrests and the bringing up of still further reinforcements of mounted Mobile Guards from Algeria, had put an end to demonstrations. The most the Italians could do in the way of manifestation was to refuse to repair damages or replace broken windows resulting from previous riots, so that there would still be evidence of "French disorders." In fact, the Italians didn't clean up until after Daladier himself, weeks later, made a tour of Tunisia. He arrived in Tunis on January 3, after a stop at Corsica en route, and was given an enthusiastic reception by the French and Arabs, who mingled their cries of "Vive Daladier" and "Vive France" with "Yalia Duladia" and "Yalia Francia." He was presented to Sidi Ahmed, Bey of Tunis, ruler of the 2,335,000 Arabs in Tunisia, amidst great ceremony, and later spoke at a banquet attended by French officials and Arab leaders. Without making any specific mention of Italian revindications, he said:

"France will never permit your efforts to be turned from your goal, which is to create here on African soil a great, human community, comparable to the French.

"France has the power to guarantee your security. . . . Her power is invincible."

To give his visit a military significance that would not be lost on Mussolini, he proceeded the next day on an inspection tour of the desert fortifications along the Libyan frontier.

Hardly had Daladier returned to Paris from Tunisia, on January 8, than Chamberlain visited Rome and had several days of conferences with Mussolini. It looked like an important meeting, and the U.P. as well as the other new organizations bolstered its Rome staff. Eleanor was called to Rome to help out. But the best that foreign correspondents could make of the meeting was:

There were no new developments in Anglo-Italian relations; there was no improvement in French-Italian relations, and Mussolini did not expect any until the Spanish Civil War was settled, because of the great divergence of views between France and Italy over the Spanish question. The conferences were mainly an exchange of views, with Chamberlain emphasizing the importance the British government attached to the friendly relations between London and Paris, and the Duce stressing that the Rome-Berlin Axis would remain the basis of Italian foreign policy. Within these very restricted limits, Mussolini and Chamberlain apparently discussed what might be done to ease European tension by arriving at an agreement between France and Italy.

As a result of this conference, the Fascists were greatly elated when, on January 28, Prime Minister Chamberlain in a speech declared that Britain was willing to discuss on a basis of equality the aspirations of other nations so long as they did not conflict with the vital interests of others. Italian officials quoted Chamberlain's speech as proof of the "sympathetic understanding" that their claims were receiving in British official quarters. The Fascists also interpreted the speech as a rebuke to the French government, which, they asserted, by taking an intransigent attitude, was preventing the opening of negotiations between Rome and Paris and was therefore aggravating European tension.

Mussolini undoubtedly saw in Chamberlain's visit to Rome at

least a faint tendency on the part of the British to show sympathy toward Italian revindications on France, and he was anxious to develop that tendency diplomatically while at the same time keeping Italian aspirations in the news. One of his tricks was to make vague references to them on unimportant occasions. Italian tipsters would then point out to the foreign correspondents at the Stampa Estera bar the hidden international significance contained in his words. It meant that Mussolini could always step out from under the interpretation given by the foreign press of what he had said, yet every foreign correspondent felt it his bounden duty to explain these speeches. Shortly after Chamberlain had left Rome, Mussolini, while awarding prizes in the Adriano Theater in Rome to Italian farmers for wheat production, seized the opportunity to deliver another of his cryptic statements. He said:

"I have just learned that, according to a French prelate, the Vatican is supposed to have advised France to stand firm. I am absolutely convinced that this is utter nonsense. To stand firm is an excellent expression, but what will happen tomorrow if the man is found — as he certainly will be — to tell the Italians they must stand even firmer."

Virtually every dispatch that went out of Rome that night regarding the speech explained that it must refer to Italian claims on Tunisia. And once again Mussolini had his cause headlined throughout the world. Four days later, the Duce, speaking from his balcony at the Palazzo Venezia, told cheering thousands who had gathered there in celebration of the fall of Barcelona: "Their motto was 'No Paseran.' But we did pass, and I tell you that we will continue to do so." The Fascist screech leaders had received their instructions and proceeded to make his words apply to France. They started yelling "Tunisia! Tunisia! Tunisia!" and "Corsica! Corsica! Corsica!" and "Down with France." Mussolini could still say to Chamberlain that he had not tried to whip up anti-French sentiment, that this was just spontaneous outburst by the Italian people and in no way connected, as far as he was concerned, with his speech.

Carrying out his war of nerves, Mussolini sent Marshal Badoglio, Chief of the General Staff, to Libya on February 20. The brief communiqué announcing the Marshal's arrival in Tripoli gave no explanation of the reasons for his visit. But in view of the state of Italo-French relations, the commentators were ready to hint that he was going to inspect the Italian fortifications along the Libyan-Tunisian frontier and intended to reorganize the military setup to meet any contingency. At the same time, foreign correspondents were privately tipped by authoritative quarters that the Italian garrison in Libya had been more than doubled. The situation was alarming enough for the Earl of Perth (Sir Eric Drummond), the British Ambassador, to call on Ciano three times in a fortnight. British Embassy officials indicated that Lord Perth was trying to find out what was happening in Libya, justifying his inquiries by reference to the Anglo-Italian agreement of April 16, 1938, whereby Italy undertook not to disturb the *status quo* in the Mediterranean.

At this time, Ciano went to Warsaw (February 23) in order to have a series of conversations with Foreign Minister Joseph Beck, where, the correspondents were given to understand, he put out feelers as to the scope and solidity of the French-Polish alliance and sounded out what the Polish attitude would be in the event of an Italo-French war in the Mediterranean. It was Fascist diplomacy used once again to intimidate France.

Still playing the diplomatic game, Mussolini selected King Victor Emmanuel, as the least offensive of all his collaborators, to announce to the world that he had secretly submitted on the previous December 17 a statement of issues between France and Italy which he considered required discussion and solution. It was attached to the note wherein the Italian Foreign Office informed the French Foreign Office that it regarded the 1935 Mussolini-Laval agreement on Tunisia as no longer binding. The announcement was made by the King on March 23, when he spoke in the Palazzo Montecitorio before representatives of the Senate and the newly formed Chamber of Fasces and Corporations. Mussolini and all members of the Cabinet attended the ceremony, which lasted less than half an hour. The fact that the King merely mentioned the statement without revealing the nature of the French-Italian problems listed therein was interpreted by Italian press officers as proof that Italy wished to avoid any embitterment that might result from public discussion, and implied that Il Duce considered a settlement possible through ordinary diplomatic channels. At the same time, they tried to show that Italy had left all doors wide open to France. English and American correspondents in Rome were unanimously agreed, however, that both the King's speech and the note to which it referred were merely a wily maneuver to place the onus for any widening of the Italo-French breach solely upon France. It was hardly clear how France could walk through the doors that had been opened to her without diplomatic or territorial loss.

Having prepared the way by the King's speech, Mussolini, on March 26 — the twentieth anniversary of the foundation of the Fascist party — came out more bluntly and, speaking to crowds in front of the Palazzo Venezia, virtually invited France to discuss Italo-French problems, which, this time, he extended to embrace Djibouti and the Suez Canal as well as Tunisia. Corsica, Nice, and Savoy, on the other hand, were dropped. Without saying what Italy aspired to in connection with these issues, Il Duce said that France was at perfect liberty to reject the proposal for discussion, but that if she did, she would have only herself to blame if the breach between the two nations became too wide to bridge. He thundered that Italy certainly would refuse to make any contribution to European appeasement until her "sacred rights" were recognized. Meanwhile, he said, Italy would arm to the utmost possible limits, even to the point "of wiping out all that is called civil life." The international applause for the speech was led by Hitler, and the German press expressed pleasure at the emphasis which Mussolini had cunningly placed during the course of the speech on the increasing unity of the Rome-Berlin Axis. Even London and Moscow were not too critical and tried to find encouragement in the fact that he had not taken a more drastic stand. The French press admitted that it was less peremptory than had been expected. From shouts in the Chamber of Deputies and cries of students parading the streets of Rome, Mussolini had managed to set forth his claims upon France to the entire world in such a way that he was now gaining, if not approval, at least passive consent, and France found herself placed on the defensive and in the position of being held responsible for any eventual breaking of the peace. This was all done within a span of less than four months. It was *diplomazia lampa*, the Italian brother of *Blitzkrieg*.

The Italian press added a little saber rattling as an aftermath to the Duce's speech, with *Il Resto del Carlino* editorially declaring:

"If France does not grant immediately the minimum that Mussolini demanded, tomorrow she will have to cede the maximum which is far more than is foreseen beyond the Alps. Therefore, the intransigent Frenchmen are our natural allies and deserve our gratitude. They believe themselves strong; instead they are weak. They believe themselves dignified; they are vainglorious and are headed for the most scorching humiliation."

Mussolini had carefully prepared world opinion for trouble between France and Italy over Tunisia. And then his fine Italian hand struck out — and caught the chancellories of Europe unprepared. For the blow was not struck, as expected, against France, but against Albania. This surprise coup left the world indignant but resulted in Mussolini's successfully taking still more territory unto himself for his empire, without in any way interfering with the continued prosecution of his claims on France.

ON APRIL 3, WHILE ITALO-FRENCH RELATIONS REMAINED IN MID-
crisis, we learned, not over the Foreign Press bar as was usually the
case, but at a bridge game where an Albanian friend of ours was
trying to play Culbertson, that King Zog was in difficulties once
again with Il Duce. She said that Colonel Zef Sereggi, Zog's aide-
de-camp and Minister to Italy, accompanied by the Italian Minister
to Tirana, Francesco Jacomoni, had flown to Rome two days before
and, after a hurried conference with Count Ciano, had flown back
to Tirana to get a reply from Zog that would appease Mussolini,
whom she described as being in "a towering rage." As far as we
could make out from other sources during the next day, the OVRA
(Italian Secret Police) had informed Mussolini that Zog was flirt-
ing with the British and, as a show of force, twenty thousand
Italian troops along with a naval squadron and a considerable
number of planes had been concentrated at Bari and Brindisi, the
two Adriatic ports closest to Albania. The Italian Press Bureau,
when queried about these reports, denied their truth, while their
undercover tipsters at the Stampa Estera bar intimated that, if the

reports were true, they merely meant that Italy was anxious to bring a salutary influence to bear upon King Zog, who, they said, had been misusing Italian money. They assured us that there was no question of any military move against Albania. The whole thing was just another bit of political melodrama.

Nevertheless, the situation was sufficiently threatening to us to agree that Eleanor should fly to Tirana immediately. It was already late, the banks were closed, and the next day's plane left at six A.M. Lire were useless in Albania, even if they could be smuggled out of Italy, and the amount of foreign currency in the Packards' home savings bank, filed under "Money" in *The Encyclopaedia Britannica*, amounted to less than seventy dollars. By law, no one was permitted to take even the smallest fraction of this amount out of Italy without first going through a fortnight of red tape to obtain the necessary permission from the Italian Ministero di Scambi e Valuta. Eleanor, however, undertook to carry this money in her brassière, and Reynolds wired the London office to send funds direct to Tirana. The next morning, Eleanor boarded an Ala Littoria passenger plane which was only half filled. This lack of passengers seemed surprising in view of the reported break between Mussolini and Zog, which might be expected to result in much official flying back and forth between the two capitals. When the plane landed at the Tirana airport at noon, the explanation was soon found. The airfield was jammed with big Italian passenger planes while great crowds of people churned about in the Ala Littoria offices and outside the wire fencing around the field itself. Italian officials were dashing about and gesticulating. Gradually it became clear what was happening: all the Italians in Albania were being repatriated upon urgent orders from Rome, and since there was neither the means nor time to transport them all to Durazzo, where they could take boats, a whole fleet of cabin planes had been sent from Italy to speed up the evacuation. Many of the Italians were looking bewildered and apprehensive; they had been forced to leave with but a small suitcase apiece, abandoning all their household as well as business possessions.

At this point, Eleanor found herself the victim of a commonplace Italian trick. The camera which she had been obliged to hand over to airline officials in Rome for safekeeping during the trip had been carefully left behind when she changed planes at Brindisi. Airline officials in Tirana were apologetic, abjectly so — the camera would be forwarded at once on the next plane; they already knew there would be no "next plane" for days to come. It was part of Italian policy to prevent the taking of any pictures by outsiders during the next few days.

Eleanor then proceeded to the Italian-owned Hotel Carlton, which had been recommended by all tourist agencies in Rome as the cleanest hostelry in Tirana. (Albanian hotels had the reputation of being rather bedbuggy, but perhaps that was only another form of Fascist propaganda.) At the entrance to the Carlton, she found the proprietor and the assistant manager, garbed in overcoats and hats, superintending the removal by Albanian porters of five large trunks. Other trunks, boxes, and bundles wrapped in multicolored tablecloths were piled on the sidewalk. The proprietor, obviously astonished that anyone was arriving in Tirana, explained that he had no rooms to rent because he was closing down his hotel, that everybody was leaving, that he was already late in arriving at the airfield, and, Madonna mia, he couldn't spare another moment for explanations.

Even a new arrival could see by this time that important international developments were under way, so Eleanor, entrusting her luggage, with appropriate indications in sign language, to an Albanian porter, set off on her own to find a horse and buggy (there were no taxis in Albania) to take her to the telegraph office. After sending several prepaid dispatches describing all she had seen, she inquired of the telegraph clerks, who spoke both Italian and French, the location of the Bank of Albania, where the United Press money was to have been sent. The clerks gave the disconcerting answer that Queen Geraldine, half-American wife of King Zog, had given birth to an heir to the Albanian throne early that morning and as a result the banks of Tirana would be closed for three days as a sign of rejoicing. The price of telegrams being what it was, this was disastrous news for a correspondent who had started out with only sixty-eight dollars — a sum already depleted by the telegrams sent.

Toma Lorusso, an Italian in Tirana who acted as string correspondent for practically all the news agencies and newspapers in Rome, including the United Press, was finally located. Lorusso, one of the few Italians remaining behind, said, "It's lucky for you that you have arrived, because I am no longer in a position to send news." It was surprising to find him, in view of the Italian hegira from Albania. A short, dynamic, twitchy man who reminded one of an exposed ganglion, he jumped about and said: "I can't send anything or tell you anything because I'm an Italian. You will just have to do the best you can until it's over, and then I can tell you plenty."

Continuing in the horse-drawn buggy, Eleanor next went to the American Legation on the outskirts of town, where she called on the Minister, Hugh G. Grant. He kept her waiting fifteen minutes, explaining when he came out that he had just finished coding a long message to the State Department. He was pleasant and informal and said that in view of the rumors of a crisis in Albania's relations with Italy, he had asked for an audience with King Zog and had talked with him that morning. He said the King had assured him that difficulties with Italy were in the process of settlement by diplomatic negotiations and that reports of a possible Italian invasion of Albania were sheer sensationalism. This version hardly fitted into the Italian activity at the Tirana airfield, but Grant attributed this wholesale departure of Italians to Mussolini's histrionic diplomacy, which had no other purpose than to force a revision of Italo-Albanian treaties in favor of Italy. Grant was rather pleased that he had been able to talk to Zog in the middle of the crisis and so give the State Department some valuable background on the events that were taking place. He was therefore extremely perturbed when he found out ten days later that his dispatch had never been sent, having been held up by Italian agents in the telegraph office who, though they naturally could not read the code, concluded that it was just as well if nothing from the American Minister got through.

Later in the afternoon, the Albanian Minister of Foreign Affairs, Ekrem Lobohova, told Eleanor that there was no crisis between Italy and Albania and that the foreign press was completely misrepresenting the state of affairs. "Italy and Albania have always been friendly since the last war, and are friendly now. The issues being discussed between us are unimportant and will easily be settled by ordinary diplomatic negotiations. There is no reason whatsoever to speak of a rupture in Italo-Albanian relations."

At the Rockefeller Foundation Anti-Malaria Clinic, which was headed by the American research bacteriologist, Dr. Lewis Hackett, there was much more plain speaking that evening. Dr. Hackett and his assistant, Dr. Marston Bates, of Fort Lauderdale, Florida, said they expected the Italians to walk in any minute. They said that Italo-Albanian relations had long been strained to an extent far greater than was realized by either diplomats or correspondents. Some of Dr. Hackett's Albanian assistants, who had been educated in Paris, Rome, and Vienna, since Albania had no university, were very bitter against the Italians but at the same time did not approve of Zog, whom they regarded as a kind of royal racketeer who thought more of his personal profit than of the social welfare of the people. These young intellectuals, mostly Left wing, declared that Albania would never prosper until both the Italians and Zog's ruling clique were ousted. They all said that if the Italians dared to invade Albania, they would seek rifles and go out to fight. (However, when the time came they didn't.)

Next day many shops in Tirana were closed, and people gathered in little knots on the sidewalk and talked excitedly, as reports circulated through the capital that the Italian demands on Zog included permanent use of Albania's harbors for the Italian navy and the establishment of Italian garrisons at several points along the coast and in all the oil regions. By early afternoon, groups of people began forming into parades and marched up and down the streets,

shouting: "Down with Italy! Down with Mussolini!" Finally the
demonstrators marched on the royal palace, where the men
shouted: "Give us arms! Give us arms!" Thousands milled around
the courtyard for several hours, calling on the King to come out and
speak to them. Zog did not appear, but later made a radio broadcast
to the nation, telling the people to be calm as he was still negotiating with Rome, but that Albania would resist in the event of
attack. While all these demonstrations were going on, the doors
and windows of the Italian Legation, which was situated just
opposite the palace gates, were being quietly and systematically
shuttered and barred so that it looked as if the Legation was being
closed down — or else being converted into a fortress. Actually,
forty Italians were locking themselves in there and, with rifles and
machine guns, were preparing for a siege. As the afternoon wore on
and Zog refused to appear, the shouting throngs moved away from
the palace and massed in the main square around which were
located most of the ministries and government buildings. The
shouts of "Down with Italy! Down with Mussolini!" were changed
to "Give us arms! We are being sold out! Give us arms! We are
being betrayed!" The Albanian personnel at the telegraph office
had already gone over to the Italians. They refused to send any
press messages by any other route than via Rome, although there
were lines operating to London via Belgrade and Athens. They
were not going to jeopardize their posts in the future by allowing
any news to get out which didn't pass through Fascist censorship.

The Albanian reserves in the meantime were being called up,
but at best Zog could not put in the field more than thirty thousand
rifles. It was a toy army, without any means of transportation other
than its feet, and with a few hundred mules to carry some ancient
field artillery and machine guns. Its aviation consisted of two
planes.

The next day, Good Friday, Eleanor was awakened at six A.M.
by a knock at her hotel-room door. It was a clerk of the American
Legation, who said that he had instructions from Minister Grant
to tell all the Americans in town to proceed immediately to the

United States Legation, as word had been received that the Italians
had already landed at Durazzo and fighting had broken out. He
said there could be no doubt about the authenticity of the news, as
it came direct from the British Legation in Durazzo. The British
Minister had personally phoned and given Grant an eyewitness
account of the invasion. As Eleanor rushed to the telegraph office
to send the news — although it looked hopeless that any dispatch
would ever get out — twenty-one Italian bombers, flying in formations of three, appeared high overhead and then dived down, their
motors roaring. When they reached as low as six hundred feet,
they straightened out and circled above the city, scattering leaflets
which snowed down the populace, who, strangely enough, didn't
take fright but merely stood in the streets and gaped skyward. The
leaflets were written in Albanian and called upon the people not
to resist.

"Albanians!" the leaflets said, "Italian troops landing today in
your country belong to a people who have been your friends
throughout centuries and have often demonstrated this friendship
to you.

"Do not oppose them with useless resistance. It will be wiped
out.

"Do not listen to the government or the men who have impover-
ished you and now would lead you to futile bloodshed. Soldiers of
His Majesty the King-Emperor of Italy have come and will remain
only for the time necessary to restore order, justice, and peace."

Even as the leaflets were still fluttering in the breeze, King Zog
was again at the microphone. This time, he was talking war and
was speaking to London and Paris as well as to his own cities.

"Italian demands violated Albanian sovereignty," he said. "The
Albanian people will never accept such demands. They will fight
the invader with all their force, even to the last man.

"Do not lose courage. Defend the honor of your nation.

"I appeal to France, Great Britain, and the civilized world for
aid. Help the Albanian people. They are only one million strong
and must defend their country against a nation of forty-four million.

"I deny that there is the slightest modicum of truth in the Italians' charges that their nationals have been mistreated in Albania. No one has been mistreated. There has been during my regime justice for everyone."

Queen Geraldine, with her two-day-old baby, was already making her escape in an ambulance over the inland, mountain road to Greece. She had changed her mind. At first she had planned to seek refuge in the American Legation and had sent one of her ladies-in-waiting to ask Minister Grant if he would take her in. He agreed to give her sanctuary during the invasion, on the grounds that she had an American mother.

At the American Legation, reports of the progress of the Italian invasion were being received by phone, radio, and by word of mouth as all the legations in Tirana pooled their information. The invasion had started simultaneously at four ports — Durazzo, connected by direct highway with Tirana; Valona, shipping center of the Albanian oil fields; San Giovanni di Medua, the port for the commercial center of Scutari; and Port Edda, in the south, near the Greek frontier. These ports were virtually undefended, for King Zog had dispatched the Albanian army to the mountains, and the only real show of resistance was at Durazzo, where the local gendarmes and a group of civilian patriots fought the Italians as best they could with rifles and machine guns. The first Italian landing party was repulsed and sent scuttling back to its ships. Then the Italian naval guns opened fire and drove the Albanian fighters from their strongholds in buildings on the water front. The shelling shattered the windows of the British Legation. The Italians made another attempt, using more men this time, and succeeded in gaining vantage points in the city. But it was not until after five hours of fighting that the Italians were actually in possession of Durazzo. In the meantime, the defenders, their numbers already greatly lessened by casualties, were trying to make a stand on the Durazzo-Tirana highway, but their resistance faded away as their ammunition gave out and their few machine guns began to crack up.

The Italians safely barricaded in their Legation began working from within in an effort to break the morale of the Albanian people. More effective than trying to snipe from behind shuttered windows, they used the telephone. One of them called up a personal friend in the Greek Legation and told him as "one pal to another" that the Greek should not venture out of the Legation quarter because the rest of the town was to be severely bombed from the air, beginning at three P.M. Unwittingly, the Greek played the Italian game. In good faith, he and his colleagues phoned the other legations, including the American, what the Italian had said. The word spread in no time, and an hour later Tirana was a caldron of excitement. Thousands of people began pouring out of the city and scores of German-Jewish refugees besieged the American Legation, asking for shelter. Minister Grant explained to them, first nicely and then more insistently, as they clamored for admittance, that the only way he could assure Americans protection in any eventuality was to give refuge to American citizens only. When they refused to understand, Grant shut the gates against them, but phoned to the German Minister and told him that even though these refugees were Jews they were still German citizens and as such were entitled to protection in the German Legation. The German Minister suavely replied that of course the German Jews could come into the German Legation, where he would personally welcome them. Grant then sent word to the Jews that arrangements had been made for them to go to the German Legation. Not a single one moved. They preferred to stand outside the walls of the American Legation than accept protection in any form from the Reich.

Meanwhile, Zog sent an envoy to parley with the Italians for suspension of hostilities and when he returned late in the afternoon and reported that it was impossible to arrange any terms for even a temporary truce, Zog announced that he was leaving for the mountains to lead his troops. He said it would be impossible to defend Tirana, which was on a plain and devoid of any defenses, natural or otherwise. That evening he slipped quietly out of the capital in a big American sedan whose curtains were drawn. But instead of joining his troops, he sped over the same road that his wife and newborn son had traveled earlier and joined them the next morning at Florina, Greece. The Albanians had been abandoned by their sovereigns. The members of the government also disappeared about the same time as Zog, most of them taking the road to Elbasan, which also led to Greece.

The promised bombing of Tirana, however, never occurred.

By sundown the Italian troops had not yet arrived, and Minister Grant insisted that all the Americans spend the night in the Legation, fearing there might be fighting in the streets when the invading soldiers tried to enter the city, despite the fact that the regular Albanian army had been withdrawn into the mountains. Dr. Hackett and Dr. and Mrs. Bates were loath to leave their comfortable quarters in the Rockefeller Foundation, where they were sure they would be safe, but finally yielded to the Minister's persuasions. Dr. Hackett decided to drive back to the Foundation to get some mattresses and blankets, as the Legation hardly had enough to accommodate all the refugees, and Eleanor went with him to make her fourth and final trip to the telegraph office, always in the hope that something might get through. She had finished writing her dispatches and was just paying for them (having managed to borrow some money in the meantime) when there was a burst of rifle fire a few streets away. The Albanian telegraph officials, who hadn't turned a hair that morning when Italian bombing planes roared overhead, quickly dodged away from the windows. Rifle fire was something they were more familiar with than bombs. As the firing continued, Eleanor said, "The Italians must have arrived." The Italophile telegraph clerk shook his head and said, "No, it is the Albanians shooting. We heard there was going to be trouble when the government left."

"But what are they shooting at?"

"Into the air, or, possibly, at each other," the clerk replied.

As Eleanor stood within the shelter of the doorway, waiting for Dr. Hackett to return and pick her up (and worrying about

whether he would be able to with all the firing going on), the
shooting began to grow in volume and come closer. Rifles were
crackling in all directions, and occasionally bullets would cause
plaster to fall in flakes from the walls of the telegraph office. The
shooters were not visible, however, and most of the bullets were
fairly high, so that a person in a crouching position was unlikely
to be hit. A car suddenly tore down an adjacent side street, and Dr.
Hackett paused a couple of seconds while Eleanor got in before
speeding down another back street in the hope of avoiding the
shooting. After reaching the general vicinity of the King's palace,
the doctor approached the American Legation through a pasture,
as he could see the usual road was blocked by mobs looting the
palace.

Back at the Legation, Hackett and Eleanor found the men there
already organizing a sentry system and cleaning up and oiling what
few old revolvers and army pistols they happened to have on hand.
There was no reason why the Albanians should have a grudge
against the Americans, and no one really believed they would attack the Legation; but it was just as well to be prepared for any
emergency. One never knew what might come into the heads of a
mob — particularly if its members started drinking that green, fiery
Albanian liquor called "raki." An American engineer employed by
the Italian company exploiting the Albanian oil fields inspected
the sentries every half-hour. He had left the oil fields near Valona
when his Italian employers were peremptorily evacuated by the
Duce. He said the Albanians in the district planned to sabotage the
wells, but it was learned later that the Italians' advance in that
region had been so rapid that the wells were still undamaged when
the invaders took possession of them.

As the evening wore on, the shooting came closer to the Legation
quarter, and suddenly there was a burst of machine-gun fire. Several
Americans rushed out of the Legation to look down the road. They
could see the machine gun spitting from the gateway of the
Italian Legation. A few moments later, one of the Albanian
servants of the American Legation came running up and said that

a crowd of several hundred Albanians had decided to attack the Italian Legation in revenge for the invasion of their country, but had been driven off by machine-gun fire. After that, the Italian gun crackled at more or less regular intervals — apparently as a warning — but the Albanians made no further attempts to rush the Legation. Rifle shooting in the city died down soon after midnight; many of the Albanians got sleepy and went to bed, while others were dispersed by a citizens' committee organized by one of the Albanian police officers who had not fled the city. If any Albanians were killed in the rioting, the volunteer committee removed the bodies during the night, because none were visible in the streets at eight o'clock the next morning.

At nine-thirty A.M. Saturday, the vanguard of the Italian troops — motorcycle-mounted Bersaglieri wearing steel helmets bedecked with coq plumes — roared into the main square of Tirana from the direction of the airfield and the Durazzo road. They had taken possession of the airfield on the way in, and within half an hour over a thousand Italian Grenadiers had been landed in Tirana by transport planes. The first troops immediately took over the government buildings, the radio station, and the telegraph office. A few Italophile Albanians feebly cheered the Bersaglieri, but the great mass watched in sullen silence. One Albanian workman caused a moment's intense excitement when a good-sized mirror slipped from beneath his blue denim work smock and broke on the pavement with the noise of a bursting bomb. He was immediately arrested for looting.

An hour later — eleven A.M. — Count Ciano arrived at the airfield and descended from his plane, his face beaming with smiles, a trench cap perched jauntily on the side of his head, a swagger stick in his hand. He was dressed in a natty Black Shirt uniform and greeted with an air of great condescension the group of Albanian Quislings who had come out to the airfield to welcome him. After a few brief ceremonies, he got into an automobile and drove through the main streets of the town, bowing and smiling affably whenever a few friendly Albanians would cheer and applaud. The

welcoming committee had already put up pictures of King Victor
Emmanuel and the Duce in the streets, along with banners which
said in Albanian such things as LONG LIVE THE KING OF ITALY and
WE SALUTE OUR ITALIAN DELIVERERS and OUR HEARTS OVERFLOW
WITH GRATITUDE TO THE ITALIAN NATION, WHICH HAS RESCUED US
FROM THE HANDS OF A TYRANT. The committee had not had time,
however, to take down the streamers in Albanian national colors
that decorated every street and lamppost, put up in celebration of
the birth of King Zog's son. There they remained, forlorn pennants
of a three-day-old baby boy who had already lost his heritage.

After heading a military parade through the streets, Ciano went
to the Italian Legation, where he held quite a reception. In her
capacity as correspondent, Eleanor was admitted to this and sought
a few moments' private conversation with Ciano by way of an interview on this important occasion for Italy. Ciano, who incidentally
has a remarkable memory, remembered her from Ethiopia and was
in an expansive mood. He talked as if Italy had done the Albanians
a great favor by coming over and invading their country.

"Resistance has practically ceased already, and in a day or two we
will have practically the entire country," he said. "We do not
anticipate that Zog's army will give us much trouble even if they
try guerrilla tactics. The country is disgusted with Zog, and I don't
think even the army will remain faithful to him."

Even Ciano himself did not yet know that it was Zog who was
unfaithful to the army instead of vice versa. Ciano continued, "Of
course, there will have to be a great deal of reorganization done
here before our big reforms can be started. Probably we will
establish an Albanian Fascist party so that the country and its
growth can be governed by sound Fascist principles that will put it
in harmony with Italy. This is the end of Zog and all that he stood
for in Albania."

It was also the end of the independence of Albania and its existence as a nation.

Italian domination of Albania dated back to pre-Mussolini days
but had since then been greatly reinforced by Il Duce's machina-

tions. When World War I ended in 1918, Albania, which had been overrun in turn by Austrians, Serbs, and Greeks, was almost completely occupied by Italian troops. As a result of the peace negotiations, however, they withdrew from everywhere except the island of Saseno, which gave them command of the Straits of Otranto, gateway to the Adriatic. Italy's special interests in Albania were officially recognized in 1921 by Great Britain, France, and Japan. By 1924, two years after Mussolini came to power, Zog, then Ahmed Zogu, had made himself de facto ruler of the country. A year later he legitimatized his position by being elected President of Albania, and in 1928 changed his title from President to King.

Mussolini, ever dabbling in Albanian affairs, had for many years backed Zog, both politically and financially. Rightly or wrongly, Zog at first most feared the newly formed state of Yugoslavia, with its intense nationalist feeling resulting from its recent liberation from the Austrian Empire. Zog therefore signed a friendship treaty with Italy, in 1926, wherein the two countries engaged to give each other mutual support and cordial collaboration. This treaty was supplemented in 1927 by a defensive military alliance wherein each country promised, in case of war, to support the other "with all its military, financial, and other resources." By 1931 the Albanians in general and Zog in particular had begun to grow restive under Italian management and economic penetration. Zog balked at renewing the friendship treaty which had expired, but was soon in a difficult position owing to his inability to meet current government expenses. (As a modern state, Albania had never been a going concern financially. Under the old Turkish rule which only ended in 1912, local government had been in the hands of the Moslem tribal chiefs who ruled their clans autocratically and levied taxes in kind — i.e., sheep, goats, pigs, and farm produce such as corn, milk, and wheat.) Mussolini then attempted to bribe the Zog government into complacency with Italian suzerainty by offering a loan of ten million gold francs annually. This worked until 1933, when the Fascists tried to increase the number of their schools in Albania: Zog packed up the Italian teachers and sent them home. In 1935, negotiations were reopened, and the following year Italy agreed to lend forty million gold francs in five annual installments, the money to be spent for public works, construction of which was to be supervised by Italy. As a guarantee of her investment, Italy got a monopoly of tobacco and oil production and took over control of Albanian finance, customs, revenues, exports, and imports. Altogether, the Fascists claimed they had advanced Albania, through Zog, about $100,000,000.

As the Albanian crisis rapidly came to a head, Italian tipsters, whose duty it was to keep foreign correspondents "on the right track" (from the Fascist point of view), told us that the Duce was angry with Zog for two reasons: first, they charged, the members of the Albanian government had not spent the money advanced by Italy in improving and developing the country, such as by the construction of military roads, so that it would be an asset instead of a liability to Italy; and, second, Zog had put out diplomatic feelers in anti-Axis countries, notably Britain, Yugoslavia, Rumania, Turkey, and Greece. The Fascist journalists made it plain that Il Duce found the second offense much harder to forgive than the first. It was at this period that England and France were negotiating those treaties with eastern European countries which Rome and Berlin constantly referred to as attempts to encircle the Axis.

In other words, Zog and his government would have been entitled to a goodly share of the Italian loans if the Albanian King had not shown a willingness to be friendly with non-Axis countries. Motto: never borrow from Mussolini.

Ciano's forecast that Italian troops would meet with little armed resistance, even in the mountains, proved correct. The Albanian army, left leaderless and uncertain what to do, soon melted away. Within three days the Italians had occupied the whole of Albania, and ex-King Zog's soldiers came drifting back to Tirana in ones, twos, and small groups. But the Fascists did not wait for this to get their projects started. A provisional government of Albanian leaders friendly to Italy was formed to carry on for a few days while a Constituent Assembly was being summoned. On April 12, the ten

Albanian provinces sent one hundred and twenty delegates (all hand-picked by the Black Shirts) to Tirana, where Ciano and his satellites could tell them what they were going to decide to do with Albania. The Assembly met in the tiny opera house, and Eleanor procured an interpreter and attended. It was the first time in her life she was ever frisked. After carefully inspecting her pass, the Albanian attendants searched the pockets of her camel's-hair coat, looked at her armpits for a shoulder holster, carefully appraised her silk-dress-clad silhouette, and pawed through her handbag. All the men were even more carefully searched. Evidently Zhafer Ypi, the Italophile Albanian who headed the provisional government and who was going to preside at the Assembly, was not taking a chance on any Albanian wolf in Black Shirt's clothing sneaking in and taking a pot shot at him.

When the Assembly had convened, Zhafer Ypi got up and spoke some honeyed words about Italy. He said, in part: "The power of Italy is the surest defense of Albania's borders. Thus we shall be assured of our general defense, national union, and sovereignty. Albania will retain her national flag, which will wave with the Italian flag. We shall have a modern country with the aid of the great Italian government. We shall have public works, moral and material benefits, and, above all, proper schools which will eradicate illiteracy and assure the necessary culture to all people."

After speaking for about half an hour, Ypi proposed that the Assembly offer the Albanian crown to King Victor Emmanuel and asked the dummy delegates to discuss the subject. Of course, no one was supposed to say anything except to express enthusiastic approval, but one old sportsman, in long white felt drawers trimmed with black braid and a black Eton jacket trimmed with pom-poms, got up and spoke at great length in Albanian. He was apparently from some backwoods mountain district where the men still had the habit of carrying guns around with them, for he wore a cowboy type of holster in which the revolver was conspicuously missing, having been checked at the door. One could tell from the frowns and uneasy movements of the other delegates that he wasn't saying any of the right things. Eleanor's interpreter was afraid to tell her what the speaker was saying and tried to put her off with vague generalities — that the delegate thought that after having got rid of one bad king the Assembly should not rush hastily into choosing another, but should give the matter lengthy consideration. Fascist organization had slipped up somewhere when this delegate was chosen! After this momentary embarrassment had been got over, however, the Assembly without a dissenting vote adopted the motion to offer the crown to the Italian King. After the motion was passed, Ciano was supposed to appear and give the Assembly a few words of congratulation and appreciation, but he never turned up. No one seemed to know why.

Next day the Fascist Grand Council expressed its approval of Albania's decision to seek union with Italy, and after the Council had adjourned, Mussolini appeared on his Palazzo Venezia balcony to take his usual round of applause after this latest coup. Some of the crowd in Venice Square, after cheering Albania, did not forget to shout "Down with France" and even "On to Paris." This was just to let the world know that, despite the annexation of Albania, Mussolini considered that the claims on France were still on the agenda.

On April 15, the Chamber of Fasces and Corporations and the Italian Senate kindly gave their approval in Rome of the Albanians' choice of sovereign and empowered King Victor Emmanuel, already Emperor of Ethiopia, to become, also, King of Albania. There was now nothing left to do except to have the King officially accept the (nonexistent) crown, which he did on June 3. Some Albanians got a kind of sour satisfaction out of the fact that if King Victor Emmanuel wanted a real Albanian crown, he would have to get the Fascists to give up some of their microscopic gold reserve to make him one. A real Albanian crown hadn't existed since before the Turkish invasion, during the days of Skanderbeg, many centuries ago. Zog had always claimed he couldn't afford one. At the time King Victor Emmanuel received the crown-offering Albanian delegation, he presented them in turn with a statute, drawn up by

Mussolini, of fifty-four articles outlining the future government of Albania. Under it, the King had almost despotic powers, having only an Albanian Fascist council which could advise him but could not take any action without his consent. The King's powers were, of course, actually to be wielded by Mussolini. Albanian affairs in practice became a department of the Italian Foreign Office, just as the French protectorate of Tunisia was ruled by the Quai d'Orsay. Francesco Jacomoni, former Italian Minister to the court of King Zog, was appointed Rome's governor at Tirana, with the title of Lieutenant General.

In view of subsequent developments, one side light on the Albanian affair should be mentioned. The Greeks had been extremely apprehensive that the Black Shirt troops would not pause at the Albano-Greek frontier, but would march straight on. Such a move would have caught the Greeks totally unprepared, much more so than they were later on. In this connection, the Italian Chargé d'Affaires in Athens, three days after the invasion, assured the Greek Premier, General Metaxas, he had nothing to worry about. A summary of the Italian note on the subject was published in Greek papers. It read:

"All rumors regarding an alleged Italian action against Greece are false. Such rumors could only have been circulated by agents provocateurs. Fascist Italy confirms her intention to respect absolutely the territorial integrity of Greece. Fascist Italy wishes to maintain and further develop the cordial relations which bind the two countries. She is also willing to give concrete proof of this desire."

It was the Mussolini way of preparing for the invasion of Greece eighteen months later.

# VI

Bud Ekins established an all-time speed record for expulsion from Italy. One of the best-known correspondents in the U.P. foreign service, with long experience in the Far East, he was sent to Rome as bureau manager at the beginning of July, 1939, and before the middle of August, the same summer, he was escorted out of the country by two secret-service men who made sure he crossed the border. Altogether, he remained less than five weeks. What had he done? He had tipped his New York office about a persistent report in Rome that Il Duce was sick. It was an informative (FYI) message, couched in baseball slang, that Bud discreetly phoned from his own home in the suburbs of Rome at two A.M. to the private residence of one of the U.P. news editors in London. It was a practice generally followed by foreign correspondents — i.e., to inform the main office of a report in their bailiwick that cannot be sent as news but might possibly be checked by correspondents in other capitals of Europe. The only trouble was that Ekins, being new in Rome, didn't realize that every outgoing call, no matter how innocent it appeared, was recorded on a special phonograph record and played off later in the foreign-language audition room of the OVRA headquarters, and that the more cryptic the message, the more suspicious were the OVRA listeners; also, and most important of all, he didn't realize that it was a Fascist dictum that Mussolini could not be sick. The first intimation that Bud had that he was in difficulty with Mussolini was later the same day when plain-clothes men from the Questura arrived at the United Press, took him into custody, and locked up the office, sealing both doors and windows. At the Questura, Bud was ordered to leave the country within the next forty-eight hours and to designate the train on which he planned to travel, so that he would have a police escort. Meanwhile, the U.P. was to be kept closed indefinitely.

Reynolds, who was reorganizing the office in post-Civil War Madrid, and Eleanor, who was covering the Franco government in Burgos, were both ordered to Rome. E. L. Keen, European general manager, and Virgil Pinkley, European business manager, hastened to Rome to bring pressure to bear, with the aid of the United States Embassy, upon both the Press and Foreign Ministries, in the hope of having the closing-down order rescinded. Reynolds was to replace Ekins, and Eleanor was to take the place of Hugo Speck, a member of the Rome staff, who was to be transferred to Turkey. The day we arrived, August 15, the office was still shut, and Keen and Pinkley were calling on Ciano at the Chigi Palace. We decided to drop in at the Foreign Press Club and pick up what informative gossip we could about the situation. There we found Don Minifie, of the *New York Herald Tribune*, Betsy Mackenzie, of the *London News Chronicle*, and Maxwell Macartney, of *The Times*, London, who were all effervescent with suggestions of how not to be expelled from Italy.

"There are three sacrosanct rules here," Macartney said, in his clipped, Scotch way. "And if you break any one of them, out you go. You never write anything that hints the lira isn't sound. You never write anything that might cast doubts upon the valor of the Italian army. And certainly, at no time, do you dare hint that the Duck is not a Gibraltar of good health."

Both Betsy and Don agreed that these three points were the formula for the continued stay of a newspaperman in Italy.

Betsy told us that she had learned from diplomatic sources — which is the vague way an English correspondent refers to the British Embassy — that Ekins had been expelled on the personal order of Mussolini himself. He had not even consulted Ciano or Dino Alfieri, then the Press Minister. The first Ciano heard of it was when Ambassador William Phillips called on him at the Chigi Palace about the matter. Ciano then went to the Duce to see what could be done. Mussolini was in bad humor that morning and was reported to have said to Ciano, "You worry about your Salzburg trip, and I'll handle this myself."

Alfieri never even dared to speak to the Duce about it.

A few days after Ciano returned from Salzburg, where he conferred with Ribbentrop and Hitler about the impending Russo-German Pact, the U.P. office was reopened and U.P. cables started to flow once again from Rome. That evening, we met Ciano, by accident, on the terrace of the Ambasciatori Hotel, where he was having dinner alone. He was sitting in the usual corner reserved for him. His table was so located that he could be struck at only from the front, but there was always a table in front of him at which were seated two burly plain-clothes men with bulging hip pockets. He saw us as we came in and called us over to his table, asking us to sit down, which we did.

After the usual exchange of social amenities, we ventured to ask him about his recent trip to Salzburg. His habitual smile immediately soured into a frown, and he replied, "It was a most cordial meeting that I had with the Führer and Herr von Ribbentrop. Naturally, it is impossible for me to say anything about what was discussed."

Somehow, the conversation from then on became patchy with awkward silences and we felt that we had committed a faux pas mentioning Salzburg. We excused ourselves and went over to another table, as he had not invited us to dine with him. The next day, at the Foreign Press Club, we learned how tactless we had been in asking Ciano about Salzburg. According to reports from the English correspondents in Rome, who had undoubtedly got them from the Embassy, Ciano had had a terrible scene with Hitler. Ciano's greatest value to Mussolini was said to be that he never exceeded instructions, and he arrived at Salzburg with orders from Il Duce to concede far less during the negotiations than Hitler wanted. The result was that Hitler had flown into one of his hysterical rages in which he screamed, banged fists on the table, and threw things on the floor. Ciano was said not to have had even a chance to explain the Italian point of view. All he could do was to listen and say, "No," until he could finally escape from the room and tell Ribbentrop that it was useless to insist on the matter as only the Duce could make such concessions. Nevertheless, in the face of this scene, the German Press Bureau issued a statement on the Salzburg consultations which included the following sentence: "The discussion resulted in one hundred per cent agreement on all questions, and not a single problem remains unsettled."

The nature of the conversations was secret, although Ciano's newspaper, *Il Telegrafo*, of Leghorn, admitted that among the subjects discussed were the problems of the Franco regime in Spain, the alleged desire of the Japanese militarists for an alliance with the Axis, and the Danzig situation. Afterward, it was taken for granted that the "Danzig situation" included the forthcoming Russo-German Pact and the German invasion of Poland. That was the real secret. It was probably on that matter that Ciano and Hitler disagreed, since Mussolini did not see any advantage or necessity in going to war with England and France at that moment. In fact, he was far from prepared, and at the same time he saw all his plans for pressing his claims on France ruined.

Refusing to heed Mussolini, for the first time since the formation of the Axis, Hitler went ahead with his plans to invade Poland and announced the first preliminary steps thereto on August 24 — the signing of the Russo-German Pact. Also, for the first time, Hitler ran counter to the feelings of not only the Italian people but also of many of the Fascist leaders. If there had been one idea that

Mussolini had succeeded in selling to his country, it was that Communist Russia stood for all the evils, especially social, in Europe. It was difficult suddenly to explain to the Italian people that Italy's ally, Germany, had lined itself up with Italy's bugaboo — Communist Russia. Nevertheless, Mussolini, possibly even against his own wishes, tried to make the Moscow-Berlin alliance popular. He ordered Virginio Gayda and Giovanni Ansaldo to lead the press campaign on behalf of Germany's new alliance. The Italian press, in chorus, declared that the accord between Nazism and Communism broke up England's encirclement of the Axis countries. Mussolini's own newspaper, the *Popolo d'Italia*, said that the accord would also have an effect on "certain zones in the Balkans and the Near East which interest Italy," and warned Turkey, Greece, and Rumania, which had received military guarantees from England and France, that it would be difficult for France and England to back up their guarantees as a result of the signing of the pact. Gayda recalled that Italy had concluded a treaty of friendship and nonaggression with Moscow ten years before and added that the German-Russian agreement "completed the system already begun by Italy." Other newspapers referred to the Soviet decision to ally itself with Germany as "Soviet perfidy," but stressed their satisfaction that Italy's potential enemies would be the sufferers.

At the same time, Mussolini started calling more men to the colors. The classes of 1902 and 1910 were called up on August 21, followed by the classes of 1903 and 1913, on August 25, making a total of 1,800,000 men under arms. Mussolini apparently wanted to create the impression that if Germany did invade Poland, and England and France came in, Italy would take up arms then and there on behalf of Germany. It was a bluff aimed to restrain England and France, as were other warlike measures taken almost simultaneously.

On August 25 and 26, Mussolini and Hitler held long telephone conferences, and on the twenty-seventh Hitler sent Mussolini a special message by airplane courier. Two days later, measures for civilian defense were put into operation: street lights were dimmed in Rome and other large cities, while air-raid drills were also carried out. Suspension of motor traffic was announced for September 3, and those who could were advised to leave big cities. Cafés were ordered to close at eleven P.M., and railroad passenger traffic was to be reduced by one half beginning September 5. A ban on coffee was announced with the explanation that all supplies were to be reserved for the army. Italian shipping to both North and South America, as well as to the Far East, was suspended, and all Italian vessels outside of home waters were ordered to return immediately.

Mussolini made one last effort, however, to prevent Germany's invasion of Poland when, on August 31, he offered to mediate in the Polish-German dispute, suggesting the calling of a conference of the five-power-pact signatories for September 5.

With the signing of the Russo-German Pact, it had become so clear in the Foreign Press Club that the invasion of Poland was inevitable that everyone had made bets at the bar as to the exact date it would start. Reynolds, who believed it was more imminent than anyone else, lost a bottle of Vat 69 to Herbert Matthews, of *The New York Times*, by five hours. Reynolds had wagered that Germany would invade Poland before midnight of August 31. Herbert, who was upset at winning by such a small number of hours, only accepted the bottle after great insistence and then carefully forgot to take it with him and left it behind in our office.

It was a sad-looking Rome that confronted us when we emerged from the Ambasciatori Hotel at nine o'clock on Friday, September 1. As we went down in the elevator, passed through the hotel lobby, and got into a taxi, we could see that the great mass of Italian people were worried. The elevator boy, the desk clerks, the doorman, and even the taxicab driver all bombarded us with the same question: "Do you think Italy will get into the war?" The morning papers in Rome hadn't carried a word about the invasion of Poland, but the Rome radio had announced it in its early broadcast, and the news had spread by word of mouth as only it can spread in Italy. On every street corner that we passed on the way to the office, we saw groups of men, looking dejected and excited,

discussing the news. Women paused in their marketing to stand
and talk. The great cause of anxiety was the Pact of Steel, signed
by Italy and Germany on the previous May 22, converting the Axis
into a military alliance in which each signatory undertook to come
to the aid of the other "in case of an ideological war." Could the
invasion of Poland be construed as an ideological war? The funereal
aspect of Rome was not relieved until late in the afternoon, when
the last editions of the newspapers appeared. They published the
telegram which Hitler had sent Mussolini that same afternoon.
It read:

"I thank you cordially for the diplomatic and political aid which
you recently have accorded to Germany. I am convinced that with
Germany's military might, I will be able to accomplish the mission
that we have to fill. I think, therefore, that in these circumstances
I will not have need of military aid from Italy. I thank you, Duce,
for all that I know you will do in the future for the common Axis
of Fascism and National Socialism."

A Rome communiqué was also published in the last editions. It
said:

"The Council of Ministers having examined the situation
brought about in Europe as a consequence of the German-Polish
conflict, whose origin goes back to the Versailles Treaty,

"Gives its full approval to the military measures adopted to date
which have purely a precautionary character, and

"Announces to the people that Italy will take no initiative whatever toward military operations."

These two announcements were the signal for nation-wide rejoicing. Since that day, there has never been manifest a Roman-
holiday spirit of like magnitude by the Italian people. The newspaper kiosks were rocked by the throngs who wanted to see with
their own eyes the telegram and communiqué that meant Italy
was remaining out of the fighting. It meant to every one of them
that the expected entrance of England and France into the conflict within the next few days would not drag Italy into war for
the time being. Students did not dare to stage any of their "spon-

taneous demonstrations," but the smile on the face of every passer-by was a public manifestation of how the people felt. In the
cafés and shops the people were joking and laughing once again.

The best proof of Italy's intention to remain nonbelligerent for
a while was seen in the resumption of Italian shipping. The Rex,
which sailed for New York from Genoa on September 8, was followed by the Conte di Savoia, which left Genoa on September 15.
The Italian line announced that there would be a total of twelve
departures of Italian passenger vessels for the United States up
until at least January. Both diplomats and newspapermen were
agreed that Italy would not declare war or allow itself to become
involved in war as long as its crack ships were liable to capture by
the British.

Reports were current in Rome during September and October
that Mussolini had even accepted orders for war supplies from the
British, including forty thousand pairs of army boots and many
thousands of woolen army shirts and blankets for which the raw
materials were to be supplied by the British themselves. This was
a period in which Mussolini undoubtedly attained his greatest
height as a master of duplicity. In the press, he saw to it that the
editorials were definitely pro-German and that all dispatches from
the front were tinctured with Axis partisanship. On the basis of
the printed word in Italy, the Rome-Berlin Axis was still as firm
as ever. But under cover, Mussolini definitely took in the English.
Because of his inability ever to speak English better than an organ-
grinder, despite years of private tutoring, Mussolini called upon the
polished and suave linguist, Ciano, to play the role of liaison officer with the British. Ciano, all smiles and personal friendliness, did
much to convince Ambassador Sir Percy Loraine (Lord Perth's successor) and Ambassador William Phillips that Italy was certainly
far from sure of wishing to continue being a partner of Nazi Germany. Several British correspondents told us that on one occasion,
when Sir Percy Loraine called at the Chigi Palace and complained
about the bitter editorials against England written by Gayda and
Ansaldo, Ciano said to him, with tears welling in his eyes, "But,

my dear Sir Percy, you must surely realize that these editorials are merely the cover under which it is possible for us to work out better and more friendly relations with England. I give you my word of honor that Italy could never go to war against its dear friend, Britain, whose ally we were in the last war."

Sir Noel Charles, who was Counselor to the British Embassy, with ministerial rank, was one of the best golf players in Rome, and somehow he and Ciano always seemed to meet at the country club outside of Rome. They would frequently make up a twosome and, while going around the links together, would discuss Italo-British relations. Always, Ciano gave Sir Noel repeated assurances of the great feeling of amity that Italy had for England. The German correspondents — and it should be stated here that the Nazis had learned much of diplomatic chicanery from the Italians — pretended to be upset at what at worst could only be described as social friendliness on the links. This show of anxiety on the part of the German correspondents in the Foreign Press Club was immediately reported to both the British and American Embassies by the Anglo-American correspondents, thus strengthening the impression that there was a possibility of splitting the Axis. Even then, many of us were suspicious of all this diplomatic byplay, and now that those suspicions have been confirmed by history, there can be no doubt that the Nazis and Fascists were putting on an act that had but one purpose — the purpose that has always characterized Hitler's war policy — to have but one front. By Italy's remaining on the fence, at this critical time of World War II, Germany had only one front to worry about along the Maginot Line. Italy, as the weaker half of the Axis, not only protected herself, but also protected the Italo-German border from attack by the French.

So clever was this Fascist subterfuge that Sir Percy Loraine became worried that publicity being given in the American press to his visits to the Chigi Palace might hamper the work of Italo-British rapprochement. He called upon Ambassador Phillips to intercede on his behalf. The first we knew of this was one day at the end of October when John Whitaker, of the *Chicago Daily News*, dropped in our office and informed us that Ambassador Phillips was anxious to receive the heads of all the newspaper bureaus at luncheon the next day at the Ambassador's private residence, the palatial Villa Taverna. Besides Reynolds and Whitaker, there gathered around the luncheon table: Don Minifie, of the *New York Herald Tribune*; Dick Massock, of the Associated Press; Camille Cianfarra, in the absence of Herbert Matthews, who was out of Rome, of *The New York Times*; Norton, of the *Chicago Tribune*; and Cecil Brown, then of International News Service. From the Embassy, there were Ambassador Phillips, William Reed, Counselor, and Alan Rogers, Second Secretary, who was also the Embassy Press Officer.

Over the coffee and liqueurs, the Ambassador said it was a rather delicate subject that he wanted to broach and that he had requested Whitaker to arrange for the heads of the bureaus to come to luncheon with him and discuss the matter. He then pointed out that the British correspondents in Rome were careful as to the international repercussions that their dispatches might cause and that they, on the instructions of their Embassy, never sent anything which might embarrass British diplomacy. "It has been suggested to me," the Ambassador continued, "that it might be helpful to British diplomacy at this moment if the American correspondents would, as the British correspondents are doing, refrain from making any mention in their dispatches of the meetings which occur from time to time between Sir Percy Loraine or Sir Noel Charles and Count Ciano. Great importance is given these meetings not only in the American press, where they are first published, but also in other parts of the world to which they are relayed. Do you think that you, as American correspondents, could co-operate in this matter?"

(These words of the Ambassador are reproduced from notes which Reynolds made during the luncheon.)

The reaction was definitely a shock to the Ambassador. Correspondents interrupted each other in their efforts to explain to him that American journalism, when the United States was not at war, was based entirely on the principle of freedom of the press: He was told that the greatness of American journalism rested on the fact that it had never become an instrument of diplomacy except in wartime, that American journalism was respected throughout the world because of this, and that if we became involved in diplomacy, we would no longer be good newspapermen.

"Mr. Ambassador, do you not think it would be possible for such meetings to be held secretly so that the press does not learn about them?" Reynolds asked.

"How does the press learn about them?" the Ambassador wanted to know.

"Mainly from Italian tipsters," Reynolds answered. "And besides, the Italians have made no effort to prevent our sending such news, although they are strict enough about other things. If Ciano really wanted to stop the news leaking out, the Italian tipsters wouldn't dare to tell us and the Italian censors wouldn't pass these messages. The whole matter of publicity certainly goes right back to Ciano."

The Ambassador's usually enigmatic countenance revealed for once his disappointment.

"It has been a most interesting discussion," he said, "and at least I have learned how you feel about the matter. From this discussion, I can see that there is nothing else for me to say except to thank you for coming here today and talking the whole thing over with me so frankly and honestly."

The Ambassador then rose, and after shaking hands with him we walked out in groups. We all felt rather depressed at this latest example of the age-old friction between diplomacy and journalism.

A number of us went to the Ambasciatori bar and talked about the anomalous position in which we found ourselves. Norton, of the *Chicago Tribune*, was all for sending a story about the luncheon, as he thought it was just the sort of thing Colonel McCormick would like to expose — an effort on the part of American diplomacy to muzzle the press. He agreed, however, after considerable debate, that the luncheon had been off the record and was not for newspaper publication at the time.

"You can write it in your reminiscences," he was told.

Further indication that the Italians were not in agreement with Germany was seen in the attitude of the Italian press toward the Russian invasion of Finland, which started on November 30, 1939. A few days later, thousands of Italian students, who never demonstrated except on orders from the Fascist party, paraded through the main streets of Rome, carrying banners inscribed with, LONG LIVE FINLAND and PLUCKY FINLAND, and marched to the Finnish Legation, where they shouted, "Viva Finlandia, Viva Finlandia!" After the Finnish Minister had thanked them for their gesture of friendliness, they reassembled and marched across town to the Russian Embassy, a block from which they were dispersed by cordons of Italian infantry, equipped with rifles and full war kit. That, too, was part of the diplomatic melodrama. These manifestations, with practically the same words and banners, were repeated for several days. In the meantime, a half-dozen prominent Italian correspondents had flown to Helsinki and were sending dispatches to the Italian press, glorifying Finnish resistance as "heroism of which even Fascists would be proud."

Nikolai Gorelkin, newly appointed Soviet Ambassador to Rome who had arrived only a fortnight before, as a direct result of the Russo-German alliance, but who had not yet presented his credentials to King Victor Emmanuel III, quietly slipped out of Rome and returned to Moscow as a protest against the friendly attitude that Italy was displaying toward Finland. The Italian Ambassador to Moscow, Augusto Rosso, was reciprocally recalled to Rome. On the surface, it looked as though Italy, despite its first forced approval of the Russo-German alliance, was now taking an independent stand and there was greater chance than ever that British diplomacy would woo Italy away from Germany. It was at this point that the Italian press bureau was more lenient than ever as to what American correspondents could send, providing it was not too overt in the way of hints that the Axis was cracking.

With the British already lured into a state of hopefulness, Mussolini perpetrated another strategem. Sir Percy Loraine was informed by Ciano that one of the obstacles to Anglo-Italian *rapprochement* was the British blockade. Ciano said that the navicert system was operating quite satisfactorily, except for the delay that it occasioned Italian ships at Gibraltar. He suggested that it would be a grand thing for friendly relations between Britain and Italy if all the merchandise aboard Italian ships, coming from all parts of the world, could be checked in Genoa and Naples by British blockade officials, instead of at Gibraltar. The Ciano thesis was that the British, who by this time — as he put it — should realize they could trust Italy, would be given storehouses in Naples and Genoa in which they could lock up all Italian imports until properly passed upon by the British blockade officials on the spot, and this would save Italian ships weeks and even months of delay. To the British, it seemed a feasible plan, and they agreed. More than two hundred British blockade experts were stationed in Genoa and Naples, and forty-two others worked in tents and sheds erected in the British Embassy grounds in Rome. Thus more and more spurious cargo was permitted to pass through Gibraltar and reach these two Italian ports. We doubt if the most astute observers realized what was taking place. It was simply this: when war was finally declared by Mussolini against France and England, all the contraband merchandise which should have been stored in Gibraltar was conveniently at hand in efficiently packed storehouses in Genoa and Naples. The British blockade experts were evacuated, and the contraband was immediately taken over by the Italians and sent to the front or to war factories.

The Italo-British courtship experienced its first serious quarrel in the first week of March, 1940, when the British contraband control halted thirteen Italian ships in the English Channel, which were carrying German coal from Rotterdam to Italy. The Anglo-French blockade on German exports had gone into operation on December 4, but in conformity with the trend of Italo-British diplomacy, the British had made an exception in favor of Italy whereby Italy could continue to carry German coal by sea until March 1. The Italians ignored the fact that March 1 had already passed and directed the flotilla of thirteen ships to put to sea. The British took the ships into custody, displaying, however, a willingness to negotiate the matter. When news of the British move reached Berlin, German Foreign Minister von Ribbentrop immediately jumped on the Rome Express. Before he arrived, however, the British had already released the ships. But if there had ever been the remotest chance of winning Italy away from Hitler, the British seizure of the coal ships ended it. Mussolini felt that he had been personally insulted and made to look ridiculous — a *bruta figura* — and this he could never forgive. The British in Rome laughed jubilantly about the way they had spiked Ribbentrop's plans while he was still on the train en route to Rome, but the fact of the matter was that he and Ciano came to a secret agreement whereby Italy was to import twelve million tons of coal yearly from Germany to be shipped by train.

But if this March 10–11 visit of Ribbentrop to Ciano and Mussolini was to prove remarkably fruitful in the development of Italo-German relations, despite the fact that it was almost unanimously branded as a failure by the Anglo-American press, Ribbentrop did undoubtedly get a decidedly cold shoulder when he went out of his accustomed power-diplomacy field and paid a visit to the Pope. The Vatican, which had had plenty of reason to complain about Nazi treatment of Catholics, took this opportunity to show its displeasure and disapproval of Nazi methods. Before Ribbentrop even arrived at the Vatican the coolness of the reception to be accorded him was made plain by the publication of an official announcement in the Vatican newspaper *Osservatore Romano* to the effect that Ribbentrop had asked for an audience through the German Minister to the Holy See — the implication being that Pius XII would never have sought such an interview. Other small slights were administered by the Vatican. According to custom, anyone having a private audience with the Pope is called for in a Vatican car bearing the flag of the visitor's country, but in Ribbentrop's case the

Nazi flag was conspicuously absent. Also, Monsignor Aborio Nella, Master of the Papal Chamber, and official "greeter" to all the Pope's guests, avoided being photographed with Ribbentrop, contrary to invariable Vatican custom. Ribbentrop, who is not noted for having a thin skin, bore all these pinpricks with cool indifference; he even made a concession to Vatican feelings by not wearing any Nazi insignia.

What kind of proposal Hitler was offering the Pope at this meeting has never been definitely established, but there were detailed reports emanating from high Vatican Secretariat of State quarters that Hitler wanted Vatican backing in a peace plan — the last chance to make peace (although he naturally did not tell the Pope so) before he smashed at France, taking in Norway, Denmark, Holland, and Belgium on his way. As inducements to the Holy See to support him in this peace move, Hitler offered, through Ribbentrop, complete and unhampered exercise of the Catholic religion both in Germany and occupied Poland, and a German political lining up with the other Western powers, France, England, and Italy, to free Russia from atheism. Pius XII is said to have rejected this embryo peace plan because it did not conform with his precepts of peace based on justice, particularly with regard to Poland. Nevertheless, Ribbentrop remained closeted in private audience with the Pope for one hour and five minutes. Furthermore, when he made his courtesy call on Secretary of State Cardinal Maglione afterward — with most visitors merely a perfunctory greeting call lasting only two or three minutes — he stayed three quarters of an hour. Whatever he said to Maglione, it was sufficiently important to send that dignified prelate hurrying immediately across the Vatican courtyards to the Pope's private apartments.

Had Ribbentrop succeeded in convincing the Pope, Mussolini would undoubtedly also have been willing to lend a hand in launching peace proposals. Ribbentrop saw Mussolini again after his interview with the Pope and probably then gave the Duce a hint of Germany's plans for the future prosecution of the war, failing peace, and intimated that the Führer would like to talk with his Axis partner again. At any rate, it was less than a week later that Mussolini went to Brenner Pass to meet Hitler. Without actually saying so, the Italian newspapers went out of their way, at the Duce's orders, to give everyone, including the foreign correspondents, the impression that Ribbentrop had accomplished nothing during his visit by insisting that his conversations had consisted of merely a routine exchange of information.

Ciano tendered Ribbentrop one of his impish dinners at Rome's exclusive Hunting Club on the eve of the German Foreign Minister's departure. It was remarkable for the array of feminine beauty present. Although the ladies were all of the upper crust, they had been chosen with an eye to their physical charms. Over the champagne, Ribbentrop is said to have whispered to Ciano, "What beautiful women you have invited here tonight!" To which, the story goes, Ciano replied, "I may not be much of a foreign minister, but I am an expert on the kind of women foreign ministers like."

Four days after Ribbentrop's departure, American Undersecretary of State Sumner Welles arrived in Rome for his second visit following his swing around the capitals of the belligerent countries. Welles had made his first visit to Rome when he arrived on the Italian liner Rex on February 25. At that time, he had talked with Ciano and Mussolini and had also received American correspondents in Rome in Ambassador Phillips' private office at the American Embassy. Eleanor attended this press conference and found that although Welles asked if the correspondents had any questions they would like to ask (they had several dozen), Welles would only reply again and again, like a phonograph record being repeatedly played, "I am sorry, but I cannot make any comment whatever on that subject. I am not at liberty to tell you anything about my conversations with Mussolini or Ciano." Welles would not even take the correspondents a little bit into his confidence by making a few remarks "off the record," and the whole reception of the press seemed rather pointless.

On his return visit to Rome, however, something happened to crack the usual frigid calm of his exterior. After an hour and eight minutes' stay with Ciano on March 16, Welles strode out of the Chigi Palace red-faced and angry. What had transpired during the interview to cause this phenomenon was never revealed to the press, but it did not prevent Welles from completing his day's program by seeing Mussolini that afternoon. Despite the eyewitness evidence of bystanders that Welles was extremely annoyed when he left the Chigi Palace, this did not prevent the Fascist Press Ministry from issuing a communiqué in which it was blandly announced that Welles' talk with Ciano had been "long and cordial." Earlier in the day, Welles had had another "cordial" forty-five-minute talk with King Victor Emmanuel. Although Welles was no more communicative about this than about any of his other conversations, the British correspondents circulated the report that the Italian King had beseeched Welles to urge Roosevelt to make some peace move that would end the European conflict.

This concluded Welles' official program, and he was preparing to enjoy himself in Rome for a day or two while awaiting the departure of his boat, when the tranquillity of a Roman Sunday was shattered by the news that Mussolini was suddenly departing for a meeting with Hitler. Luckily, the United Press got a tip-off on the meeting in time for Eleanor to confirm it by rushing down to the station, where she saw the Duce's bulletproof car dash up to the side entrance and Mussolini, most unusually clad in mufti, hurry to the platform for what was supposed to be a secret departure. All that was known about his destination, however, was that he was going north. This meant elaborate checking of his route by telephoning railroad stations on the way. We would have one of our Italian-language experts call up a stationmaster and say, "This is Rome speaking. Has the presidential train passed through yet?" (Mussolini's official title was President of the Council of Ministers.) Most stationmasters would innocently assume it was the Rome police watching over the Duce's well-being and give the desired information. We confirmed the destination around mid-

night by the excited rural stationmaster of the tiny town of Bren-
nero. He said between gurgles of excitement that Mussolini's train
was on a siding and his party already asleep. When Aldo Forte, of
our Rome staff, whom Reynolds had already dispatched northward,
phoned from Bolzano we told him to rush to Brenner Pass, less
than fifty miles away.

Next day, March 18, the first Hitler-Mussolini meeting since the
beginning of war occurred. The meeting must have been hastily
arranged, as there was no adequate police protection for the two
dictators and, in fact, any smart assassin could have snuffed out
their lives easily, as it was possible to approach to within a few
feet of them. Aldo phoned that Hitler looked pale and worn. The
reason for this was soon afterward apparent — his efforts to arrange
an advantageous peace having failed, Hitler was about to take the
irrevocable step of spreading the war to Norway, Denmark, Holland, and Belgium in his effort to smash France.

Correctly sensing the historic importance of the meeting, Sumner Welles loitered in Rome and allowed unofficial hints to be con-
veyed to the Chigi Palace that he would like another interview
with Mussolini, or at least with Ciano, in order to learn something
about the Brenner conversations. His hints were ignored, however;
the most Ciano would do was to indicate that if Welles went to
the golf club for lunch he would probably meet someone from
Ciano's Cabinet, who, however, either did not know anything or
had been carefully instructed to say that he didn't. One hint as to
how the wind was blowing was contributed to the American Embassy and Welles by Eleanor, who managed to get hold of a copy
of the Press Ministry's secret instructions to the Italian newspapers
concerning the recent events. The instructions were to play up the
great importance of the Brenner meeting, to emphasize the firm-
ness and fidelity of Italo-German friendship, and to omit any reference whatsoever to Welles and his mission. Another hint on the
probable course of events was given by Gayda, who wrote in the
Giornale d'Italia, "The Brenner talks had a double aim: firstly, the
construction of a just Europe based on equality of rights and, sec-

ondly, the protection of Italian interests in this new Europe alongside the protection of German interests."

The chronological juxtaposition of Ribbentrop's visit to the
Pope, Welles' talks to the King, Duce, Ciano, and the Pope
(whom he saw after his other official visits had ended), and Mussolini's conference with Hitler, caused such a fantastic crop of
rumors that Welles was finally moved to quash some of them on
the eve of his departure from Rome. He said, "In order to allay
the flood of rumors about my mission, I wish to state categorically
that I have not received any peace plan or proposal from any belligerent or from any other government; nor am I bringing back to
the President any such proposals. My mission has been solely one
of gathering information for the President and the Secretary of
State as to present conditions in Europe." Welles' statement is
certainly literally true, since he did not receive any formal proposals as such and definitely did not bring any back to America
with him, but there are grounds for believing that he discussed
with Pius XII, in the light of his own and the Pope's individual
and separate talks with Ribbentrop, what constituted Germany's
minimum peace demands and decided that these could not form
the basis of a peace plan that would be acceptable to Britain and
France — or, indeed, to the Vatican and the United States.

Little by little it became apparent to those correspondents who
had no Axis to grind, like the Swedish and the Swiss, that Italy was
beginning to turn a cold shoulder to England. As the German
armies smashed through to victory after victory in Norway, and
German coal trains began rolling down the Brenner Pass, the general Fascist atmosphere changed in an intangible way, and less and
less did Sir Noel Charles accidentally run into Ciano on the golf
links. Anti-British and anti-French posters, showing Black Shirts
breaking symbolic chains at Gibraltar and Suez, and representing
Tunisia as a pistol pointed at the heart of Sicily, began to appear,
first in the provinces, then in the outskirts of Rome, finally in the
center of the capital itself. Others less gentlemanly depicted John
Bull and Marianne riding a kind of plutocratic juggernaut over the

poverty-stricken working peoples of Europe (including, of course, Italy), or indulging in cannibal banquets wherein they were eating corpses representing various countries of Europe.

One night toward the end of May, we went to the Caffè Greco, on the Via Condotti, which was the rendezvous of Italian artists and writers, almost all of whom were anti-Fascist, to meet some English friends of ours for an after-supper round of Strega. They were Maxwell Macartney, of the London *Times*, Scott Watson, of the *London Daily Herald*, and Mr. and Mrs. Bernard Wall, of the British Institute. After much talk about the international situation, we decided to go to the Florida and have a glimpse of its floor show. "A bit of amusement in a war-dulled world," Macartney said. As we turned down the Via Condotti toward the Piazza di Spagna, we noticed the anti-British posters that had been plastered on the sides of houses there for the past several days. There were two particularly nasty posters. One depicted a Falstaffian John Bull gorging himself with chunks of the Mediterranean, and another portrayed a caricatured Neville Chamberlain, with umbrella in hand, splashing in the water as he tried to swim to a departing ferry. The caption was: "England Misses the Boat." It may have been the conversation we had had in the Caffè Greco about the Italians' intrigue regarding England, plus possibly that second round of Strega, that imbued us with a patriotic spirit of devil-may-care. In any event, Mrs. Wall said: "I think we should remove these offensive atrocities. They just aren't aesthetic." She proceeded to scratch at one of them with her scarlet, mandarin nails. Eleanor decided Mrs. Wall needed some assistance and started tearing down the other poster. Out of the dark, a stocky Italian wearing the Fascist badge came running toward us. He pulled Mrs. Wall and Eleanor away from the posters.

"E *vietato*, è *vietato*," he cried, and shoved Mrs. Wall and Eleanor away.

Reynolds grabbed him by the lapel. He broke away and swung, knocking Reynolds down with a blow to the chin. Groggy, Reynolds staggered to his feet and knocked down his assailant. Two more Italians sprang out unexpectedly from the Piazza di Spagna and jumped upon Reynolds, bowling him over with blows about the face and body. As the three Italians and Reynolds writhed about in the street like a snake ball, Eleanor joined in the fray, kicking the Fascists in the face. Her intervention was so effective that they released Reynolds long enough to knock her down. Gendarmes then magically appeared and took us all into custody. Our English friends, who had so far kept out of the melee, which they told us later was the sort of physical exhibition they didn't approve of, became worried about the fate of Mrs. Wall and Eleanor.

"This isn't the sort of thing that ladies should be involved in, you know," said Macartney. "Let's see if we can't do something to protect their names. There's no telling what sort of street brawl the Fascist press will make of this trivial episode."

We could talk freely among ourselves, as it was evident that neither the three Fascist brawlers nor the gendarmes could speak a word of English.

"I have it," Scott Watson said. "We can start another scrum, and the ladies can dash away in the confusion."

Both Macartney and Reynolds agreed.

"Here we go," said Reynolds, and cracked one of the assailants on the jaw. Macartney and Watson took care of the other two Fascists. It was a real free-for-all, and the gendarmes were at least three minutes in separating them. When the three Anglo-Saxon men were picked up, almost unconscious, and the party resumed its march in the direction of the Questura, it was discovered that the two Amazons were missing.

At the Questura, the three Fascist assailants were particularly bitter about a woman who had kicked them, but the gendarmes, who felt ashamed of themselves for allowing two of their prisoners to escape, concentrated on accusing Reynolds as the one responsible for everything.

Oddly enough, the night prefect merely took the documentation of the men involved in the fracas and dismissed the case. It was obvious that the police had received their orders. Mussolini did not want any international incidents to speed up the effects of his poster campaign.

Almost the next day, it was announced that the Germans had struck at France through neutral Belgium. The next night, Sir Noel Charles became the protagonist of a diplomatic incident. Informed by phone that three Britishers were being held in custody in the lobby of the Albergo Excelsior as a result of a poster scuffle, he automobiled to the hotel and succeeded in preventing any arrests. As he returned to his car, he found it covered with anti-British posters. He refused, however, to budge until the police had removed them.

A few days later a really full-dress demonstration took place when students carrying a coffin draped with the French and British flags demonstrated as close as they could get to the French Embassy, which was guarded by hundreds of troops. Besides the coffin, the students carried a figurine representing France as "Chamberlain's fishwife," and another of England as "her lover." After shouting "Down with France," and frequently punctuating this with obscene abuse, the thousands of students re-formed into marching lines and proceeded to the British Embassy, which was also heavily guarded. Here they burned the British and French flags and coffin, throwing their Fascist *squadristi* clubs on the blaze to make a bigger fire. Mussolini drove by to have a look at how his demonstration was going and was wildly cheered by the students. Similar manifestations were staged in Milan, Naples, and other large cities.

The burning of the British flag was far too serious an insult for the British to let pass unnoticed, but rather than make just a routine protest, the newly appointed British Prime Minister, Winston Churchill, decided to take a hand in the matter himself. On May 16, Churchill wrote a personal letter to Mussolini in which he said, in part:

"We can, no doubt, inflict grievous injuries upon one another and maul each other cruelly and darken the Mediterranean with our strife. If you so decree, it must be so. But I declare that I have never been the enemy of Italian greatness, nor ever, at heart, the foe of the Italian lawgiver. . . . I beg you to believe that it is in no spirit of weakness or of fear that I make this solemn appeal, which will remain on record. Down the ages, above all other calls, comes the cry that the joint heirs of Latin and Christian civilization must not be ranged against one another in mortal strife. Hearken to it, I beseech you in all honor and respect, before the dread signal is given. It will never be given by us."

But the course of destiny was flowing at breakneck speed, and Mussolini, beguiled by the Nazi victories in the Low Countries and France, had already turned his eyes toward another vision — a false mirage wherein he thought he saw a second Roman Empire truly great and powerful. His reply to Churchill was brief and cool, reminding the British Prime Minister of Britain's part in the League of Nations sanctions against Italy and of the British domination of Italian accesses to the ocean. In one sense, it was a remarkably frank and un-Mussolinilike letter, in that it stated the Duce's grievances plainly and only reverted to the usual Black Shirt alibiing in the last sentence, which said:

"If it was to honor your signature that your government declared war on Germany, you will understand that the same sense of honor and respect for engagements assumed in the Italian-German treaty guides Italian policy today and tomorrow in the face of any event whatsoever."

After dispatching his answer to Churchill, the Duce speeded up his campaign to prepare Italian sentiment for the climax he had planned for it — his declaration of war against England and France.

# VII

WHEN WE ARRIVED AT THE UNION CLUB AND FOUND LADIES IN THE bar, we knew things were bad. This was the first time in half a century that women had ever invaded the male precincts of the Union Club, which was probably the most staid of all British social organizations on the continent. Giuseppe, who had grown gray and bald behind the bar, was visibly disturbed at the sudden departure from tradition, or perhaps he realized his career was through. The bar was crowded with not only newspaper people, but also with bankers from Barclay's, Imperial Airways executives, British Institute officials, members of the Embassy, and those ubiquitous retired British colonels who make the most of their pensions in foreign capitals throughout the world. Everybody was drinking and laughing, but there was an undercurrent of tensity in all the gaiety.

Betsy Mackenzie grabbed us and said, "You must have a drink on me. This is the first time I've ever been able to buy a drink in this bar. And to think it's taking a declaration of war to make that possible!"

"It's a bit thick," Macartney said, "to think that the Duck has the bloody cheek to make them come around and collect it."

"Half a mo', half a mo'," Ian Munro, who was the British Press Attaché, said. "They don't know what this is all about."

He then explained to us that, only half an hour before, Sir Percy Loraine as well as François-Poncet had received notification to appear at the Chigi Palace at four-thirty in the afternoon. "There's no doubt about it, now — Ciano is going to hand them notification of war. And the Duck is going to speak from the balcony at six this afternoon."

"And that means," Betsy said, turning to us, "that you two will have to take over our apartment."

"You mean those barracks with a farm on the roof?" Macartney asked. "Why, they don't want a place like that."

"Maybe they don't," Betsy said, "but I haven't been giving them news beats for the past year without their helping us out now."

In another corner of the bar, Spud Murphy, of Reuter's, was handing his apartment over to a Dane, and like transactions were being made on all sides of us. In most cases the matter had already been discussed weeks before, and this was just the last oral formality. Nothing could be put in writing that the Italians would consider legal, because it was war between Italy and England. We agreed to take over the Mackenzie household, servants and all, and see what we could salvage for them.

Reynolds sent Eleanor scurrying over to the office to try to get something out in the way of a story on the impending declaration of war. To Eleanor's surprise, she was able to send on the telephone to our office in Zurich a circuitously worded dispatch in which she said that Mussolini was going to speak at six P.M. from the balcony of the Palazzo Venezia, and that the speech, which would be broadcast over a nation-wide radio hookup, would contain the announcement of war against England and France. By some strange quirk of Italian mentality, the telephone censors let the message pass.

Back in the Union Club, Reynolds was getting his story from Munro, who was trying to make up for the past. Munro, before becoming British Press Attaché, had been correspondent for the conservative *Morning Post*, and when that folded up, he became correspondent for the *Daily Mail*. As a newspaperman, he had few equals in Rome. He had collaborated with the United Press bureau managers one after another, including Reynolds, and always gave as much, if not more, than he received. When England went to war against Germany, and he was appointed Press Attaché, all the newspapermen rubbed their hands and said to themselves, "At last we've got an inside track in the British Embassy." How wrong we all were. Because as a press officer, Munro suddenly transformed himself into the most noncommittal diplomat that any foreign correspondent ever encountered. He knew only too well what newspapermen could make out of the slightest hint. But that day, June 10, 1940, the lid was off, and he was trying to make amends. He told Reynolds that the diplomatic list, which included the journalists and all those representatives of English companies and institutions considered essential by the British government, had been approved two months before by the Italian Foreign Office, and that a similar list of Italian diplomats, headed by Giuseppe Bastianini, Ambassador to the Court of St. James's, had been approved by Whitehall. He said that the diplomatic train would leave Rome probably within the next forty-eight hours and would proceed to Ancona, where the Italian passenger ship *Conte Rosso* would take the British évacués to Lisbon, and that the British ship *Monarch of Bermuda* would transport Italian évacués in like manner to Lisbon. He admitted that there must have been several thousand English who could not be included on the diplomatic list and who would have to be left behind.

"But we think the Italians will treat them all right," Munro said. "They'd better, as we will have more Italians staying in England."

Scott Watson, of the *Daily Herald*, told Munro that he was not going out on the diplomatic train on which a post had been reserved for him.

"I've just come from the Press Ministry, and Capomazza [he

referred to the Marchese di Capomazza, who, while he was Second Secretary in the Italian Embassy in Washington, married an American girl and had since become second in command of the Foreign Press] has given me a pass that will permit me to travel through Italy and cross the Yugoslav border. Once in Yugoslavia, I can go on to Athens, where my paper has assigned me."

Munro pointed out that he was taking a risk, inasmuch as England and Italy would be at war and such passes might lose their validity. Nevertheless, Scott Watson remained firm in his decision and, as a matter of fact, encountered no difficulty when, three days later, after England and Italy were at war, he traveled alone and unescorted through Italy and crossed the frontier. This was all the more amazing inasmuch as Scott Watson was a correspondent of an English Labour paper which had long been opposed to Fascism. It was just one of those gestures that the Italians would often make.

At four in the afternoon, gendarmes and Italian infantry were stationed in strategic, out-of-the-way places around Venice Square. Most of them were hidden in back yards and basements, as a precautionary measure in case the crowd should get out of hand. At five P.M., thousands of uniformed Fascists, including students, began to converge from all parts of Rome upon the Palazzo Venezia. They carried placards, most of them scurrilous, caricaturing John Bull and Churchill. By six, one hundred thousand people must have squeezed themselves into Venice Square and adjacent streets. At 6:01, Mussolini, dressed in his uniform of a corporal of honor, bounced up like a jack-in-the-box on the balcony. He was greeted with probably the greatest applause he had ever received since he announced the end of the Ethiopian War. This acclamation was the result of the fickleness of the Italian people. Little did they know the tragedy they were applauding. They thought they were acclaiming the end of a conflict and that the war would be over a few weeks after Italy's entry. It looked as though Mussolini was making a "smart move" to realize his revindications upon France with a minimum spilling of blood.

They thought France was already beaten and England left in a hopeless position. It was money for jam. The Duce interrupted the applause and started speaking. Throwing his arms about as never before, to emphasize each point, he said:

"Fighters of land, sea, and air, Black Shirts of the Revolution and of the Legions, men and women of Italy, of the Italian Empire, and the Kingdom of Albania, listen. The hour destined by fate is sounding for us. A declaration of war already has been handed to the Ambassadors of Great Britain and France.

"Several decades of recent history may be summarized in these words: phrases, promises, threats of blackmail, and, finally, the League of Nations.

"Our conscience is absolutely clear.

"If today we have decided to take the risk and make the sacrifices of war, it is because we do not avoid the supreme test that will determine the course of history. We want to break the territorial and military chains that confine us in our sea, because a country of forty-five million souls is not truly free if it has not free access to the ocean. . . .

"It is a conflict between two ages, two ideas. . . .

"I solemnly declare that Italy does not intend to drag other people, bordering on her, by sea or land, into the conflict. Switzerland, Yugoslavia, Greece, Turkey, and Egypt, take note of these words of mine. It depends on them and only on them if these words of mine are rigorously confirmed or not. . . .

"Proletarian, Fascist Italy has arisen for the third time, strong, proud, compact as never before."

Eleanor, who was at Venice Square to describe the reaction of the people, counted seven times that the Duce was called back for curtain bows after he had finished his speech. There was little doubt that the Italian public had been taken in by the Fascist propaganda and that they believed that Italy was merely, to use a bullfighter's term, giving the coup de grâce to France, political enemy since the risorgimento. Few of them thought of it as actually involving Italy in a war of blood with England. It would

all be over within a few weeks. Many women in the crowd, however, cried as they paused to think that even in that short space of
time their menfolk might be killed on French battlefields.

Before the crowds dispersed, Black Shirts could be seen pasting
up announcements that Italy, beginning that very night, would
be plunged into blackouts until the war was over. Thousands of
workers also started bluing the bulbs of the street lights.

After we had sent all there was to send on the speech and
reaction of the populace to it, we called at the Mackenzie apartment to take over our new home. Betsy and her sister, Phyllis, secretary to the British Air Attaché, had heard the speech over the
radio. But on orders of the British Embassy, they had not ventured to Venice Square. Their cook and maid were in tears.

Phyllis gave us a good news tip. She said that the note Ciano
had coldly handed Sir Percy without any personal comment stated
that the war was not to go into effect until midnight. We later
confirmed this on the phone with our border string correspondent,
who said that hours after the Duce had spoken, declaring war
upon England and France, the train service between Italy and
France continued normally. Hundreds of French and English
were permitted to pass through customs without any unusual delay
and continue into France, while the same freedom of movement
held true for Italians returning to their homeland from across
the French border. It was the last of the old-fashioned style of
declaring war in advance.

Before midnight, however, American Embassy officials, reinforced by volunteers from the American colony, moved into the
British Embassy as part of the arrangements for the United States
to take over British interests. The American Embassy later took
over the interests of most of Britain's allies including Holland,
Belgium, Norway and Poland.

Two days later, the diplomatic train bearing the British official
party left from the Rome Termini Station at ten P.M., in the midst
of a blackout. Scores of Italians, many of them wearing the Fascist
badge, risked their positions by going to the station to say farewell

to their English friends. The only incident was when a flash of powder flared and *Life* photographer McAvoy took a picture of Sir Percy Loraine and Sir Noel Charles. He was immediately collared by Italian secret police and rushed out of the station to the Questura, where he received an expulsion order. The Duce did not want the Italian public to whom he had been feeding such virulent anti-British propaganda to know how well he was treating the British on their departure. They were all given comfortable accommodations in sleepers and first-class compartments, according to their diplomatic rank.

Most of the fighting during the first week after Mussolini's declaration of war was done by the foreign correspondents in Rome, who resorted to all known tricks to keep a long-distance telephone line open daily at one P.M. to Berne or Zurich in Switzerland, which were relay points for America and other parts of Europe. There were only three lines connecting Italy and Switzerland, and there were about twenty-five correspondents — Americans, Germans, Swedes, Danes, Spaniards, and Swiss — who were determined to be first in getting off the Italian war communiqués when they were issued at one P.M. For the first week, we succeeded in holding a line by putting a call in to Zurich at 12:30 P.M. and then holding it a whole half-hour by talking idle chitchat until the communiqué arrived. Other correspondents would try to take the line away by booking lightning calls that cost ten times the normal rate, resulting in three-cornered arguments with the operator, the party trying to break in, and the party already holding the line. But all this mad scramble was useless at first because the communiqués never contained any news, the reason being that for the first ten days nothing happened.

One of the great mysteries of the war will be why the Italians, who entered the war at the moment they deemed the most propitious, did not from the very beginning start an attack. With the French armies in the north of France collapsing everywhere, the French soldiers on the Italian frontier were without reserves and undoubtedly becoming demoralized at the way the Germans were advancing. Probably the explanation was typical Italian mismanagement. At any rate, the Italians missed the bus, because when their large-scale offensive under the nominal command of Humbert, Prince of Piedmont, finally started, there only remained four days before the signing of the French armistice in which to penetrate French territory. They were just beginning to move when they were called to a halt, with the result that they failed even to reach one of Italy's primary revindications on France — Nice, only forty miles across the border. They also failed to grab Corsica, Savoy, Djibouti, and Tunisia, which formed the remainder of their oft-voiced claims on France. If Mussolini had seized Tunisia, with its powerful naval base at Bizerta, all possibility of the British sending convoys through the Mediterranean would have been ended, and the British Mediterranean fleet, one half of it based at Gibraltar and the other half based at Alexandria, would have been divided by the Italian domination of the narrow stretch of water between Tunisia and Sicily. Mussolini, because of the slowness with which his armies moved, only advanced at one point. And that was a bare ten miles along the French Riviera, resulting in the fall of Menton. Even this small gain resulted in proportionately terrific Italian losses, which most correspondents placed at between twenty and twenty-five thousand killed and wounded. Geographically, everything favored France, and the Fascists were obliged to pour in regiment after regiment of soldiers to gain even a few hundred feet or a small peak in one of the mountain passes.

There was so much café grumbling about the Riviera fiasco that Mussolini tried to justify the smallness of the advance and the heavy losses by publishing a letter which he sent to Prince Humbert. The letter was written on July 2, the very day that Il Duce returned from an inspection tour of the Menton area.

"Italians and foreigners should know," the Duce wrote, "that the battle of the western Alpine front was fought on a 120-mile front in mountains 7000 to 9000 feet above sea level during heavy snowstorms on June 21, 22, 23, and 24, and that the Italians broke through the French Alpine 'Maginot Line' against stubborn resistance. Italians and foreigners should know that the French themselves were astonished at the contempt for danger shown by Italian soldiers of every corps.

"Italians and foreigners should know that the battle was hard-fought and sanguinary. Thousands of men rendered *hors de combat* gave witness to that."

The letter revealed that the French had such a momentum of hate that they continued fighting for several hours after the armistice was supposed to go into effect. The French apparently were anxious to get one last opportunity to hit at the Italians, whom they regarded as "stabbers in the back" because of Mussolini's last-minute declaration of war.

The personal ill-will between the Italians and the French was also manifest at the arrival of the French Armistice Commission at the Ala Littoria airfield on the outskirts of Rome. As soon as the French had signed the armistice with Germany, the Nazis lent them a plane to fly to Italy. The French delegates were in a desperate hurry because the German armistice was not to operate until the Italian one was signed, when the two would go into effect simultaneously, and meanwhile the advancing German troops were eating up mile after mile of French territory, causing unoccupied France to grow smaller and smaller. Eleanor was out at the airfield to watch the arrival of the French Commission on the afternoon of June 24.

It was a sunny, breezy day of the kind that used to delight the hearts of tourists in Italy. The Roman countryside looked fresh and green — the intense, wilting heat of summer had not yet touched it. As the time of the plane's arrival was not known exactly, most of the correspondents got there early and shuffled aimlessly around, causing considerable anxiety to the three press officers who tried vainly to herd them all together, apparently fearing, for some reason, that the correspondents would get out of control. The reception committee arrived, and here Italian ill-will showed itself, for the highest-ranking officer was an army captain. There was also a naval lieutenant and one or two army lieutenants. They likewise stood uneasily around, repeatedly scanning the skies. The plane was overdue, and the reporters began to wonder if there had been a crack-up or a forced landing. Finally, a speck appeared which the airport officials could tell was not an Italian plane from the sound of its motors. As soon as the ugly, black, snub-nosed plane, emblazoned with two swastikas, landed, the French Commission stepped wearily out and glanced around. They looked dejected, but the set of their shoulders was almost defiant, as if they expected and were prepared for slights and sneers. The Commission was composed of General Charles Huntzinger, Admiral Maurice Leluc, Air General Jean Marie Bergeret, General Parisot, and M. Léon Noël. There was also a chic, slender girl with them — probably the Commission's confidential secretary. General Huntzinger and General Bergeret, both of whom were in uniform, snapped out smart military salutes to the reception committee, while the others shook hands. The Italian officers were courteous enough, but their respective ranks were a snub in themselves, and they could not conceal a certain exultation of manner.

The official party got into cars and drove away to the Villa Incisa, twelve miles outside of Rome, where Count Ciano, Marshal Badoglio, Admiral Domenico Cavagnari, and Air General Francesco Pricolo were waiting for them, while the correspondents returned to town to await the announcement of the armistice terms, which were expected to be stiff. Many of the correspondents expected Mussolini would demand to be allowed to occupy Nice and Tunisia; it was not until later that we realized that Hitler had insisted that the Italians must not bring up their territorial claims upon France. The Duce acquiesced to the Führer's wishes and doubtless regretted it many times later.

Once the Italian and French armistice delegates met, little time was lost. The document was signed at 7:15 P.M., Italian summer time, that same evening. The German government was notified twenty minutes later, and the cessation of hostilities was fixed at

1:35 A.M. the next morning, in order to give six hours' time in which to notify all the German, Italian, and French military commands on land, sea, and air that fighting was to cease.

The French government was simultaneously informed in accordance with the provisions of the armistice by Rome radio. We luckily had an open line to Zurich at the time and flashed the signing as it was being announced on the air. The armistice contained twenty-five clauses, the majority of a technical nature, describing rather specifically how French demilitarization was to be carried out, but the interesting thing was that the Duce was not empowered to occupy a single one of the French territories he had been claiming for Italy before the war.

The three clauses of the armistice which were to have the most important bearing on future war developments were Articles II, XII, and XX. Article II stated:

"When the armistice comes into force and for the duration of the armistice, Italian troops will stand on their advanced lines in all theaters of operation."

Article XII dealt in detail with the French navy, which was disposed of as follows:

"Units of the French fleet shall be concentrated in ports to be indicated, and demobilized and disarmed under the control of Italy and Germany, except for such units as the Italian and German governments shall agree upon for the safeguarding of French colonial territories.

"The determining factor in the selection of the ports referred to above shall be the assignment of naval units in peacetime.

"All warships not in French metropolitan waters, except those which shall be recognized as necessary to safeguard French colonial interests, shall be brought back to metropolitan ports." (The French weren't able to fulfill that section because the British wouldn't permit the French naval units in their ports to leave.)

"The Italian government declares that it does not intend to use, in the present war, units of the French fleet placed under its control, and that on conclusion of peace it does not intend to lay claim to the French fleet.

"For the duration of the armistice, the Italian government may ask French ships to sweep mines."

Article XX was to prove very useful in Libya. It said:

"Goods shall be freely transported between Germany and Italy through nonoccupied French territories." Under this clause, if enforced, the Axis could route supplies to the Libyan army by way of Tunisia, which meant a much shorter trip by sea, where Axis convoys were exposed to attack by the British fleet.

We all wondered why the Duce had been content to ask such comparatively lenient terms and came to the conclusion that Hitler had made some observations about people who came in at the last minute not deserving to get more than the Germans, who had done all the conquering. We thought it was merely Hitler's way of showing Mussolini that if he wanted to profit from the war, he would have to get busy and do some fighting against the remaining enemy, the British. Only later did we realize that the Nazis were already thinking of obtaining France's aid and support in the war against England and that, in pursuit of that policy, they were willing to sacrifice the Italian claims in an effort to conciliate the French. It was the beginning of a policy which was to be diligently carried out with all Nazi weapons: terrorism, force, and oppression on the one hand, and propaganda, limited concessions, and political wirepulling on the other. This policy finally brought about the appointment of the Germanophile Pierre Laval as Premier of France in the summer of 1942 — a move calculated by Berlin to get active French co-operation with the German war effort. To achieve that desired end, Hitler undoubtedly told Laval that France could keep Nice, Savoy, Corsica, and Tunisia. There was no enthusiasm in the Italian press over the appointment of Laval and his subsequent activities. But this is getting ahead of the story.

During the first three months of Italy's participation in the war, we were constantly being surprised at the number of English whom we ran into in Rome. During this period, they continued for the most part quite unmolested and without surveillance by the Italian police. Eleanor's masseuse, who was an elderly English-woman, was among those left behind. She told Eleanor that she had gone to the British Consulate in Rome ten days before war was declared and had been informed that there was no immediate danger of war and that if she kept a close watch on the newspapers she could see for herself when it would be time to leave.

"But I find Italian newspapers such a bore," she said, "that I didn't bother to read them, and here I am. All my Italian clients continue to have me as though nothing has happened."

Eleanor made a trip to Florence, about this time, to write a story on the wealthier English people who were still residing in their villas there. She found that they were living normal, prewar lives except that their social relations with Italian friends had been somewhat curtailed. One English lady told Eleanor, "It is not that there's any rule against our visiting or receiving Italians, but we don't want to involve them in difficulties with the police. We have noticed that whenever we do have contact with Italians, they are immediately summoned to the Questura."

But when Mussolini saw, toward the middle of September, that England was going to fight on despite the French armistice, he tightened up restrictions upon English nationals and immediately launched a systematic campaign to round them up. The first we heard of it was one morning when Eleanor's masseuse failed to keep her appointment. Telephoning to her apartment, Eleanor was informed by the *portiera* that the Englishwoman had been taken away to *confino* the day before by two plain-clothes men.

Another English acquaintance of ours who next disappeared was Dr. Edward Strutt. He was a quaint, gray-haired old codger with a nose as bulbous and red as a beet, who was a great Latin scholar and drinker. He had worked at odd jobs for all the American and British newspaper organizations in Rome for the past two-score years and was a duly qualified member of the Foreign Press Club. He was especially useful at helping to translate the Pope's

Latin speeches. His great failing was his desire to impress people with his scholarly and literary attainments. He was constantly dedicating sonnets to Eleanor, which he would bring to the office and deliver to Reynolds, who would then find occasion to pay him for some imaginary assignment which he hadn't had. It must have been a little more than three months after Italy's declaration of war against England and France that there was a meeting of the Foreign Press Club. And Strutt, whom the Italian press officers had always liked, was still an active member. The Italians winked their eyes and accepted his explanation that he was now an American correspondent, working for the *Baltimore Sun*, and therefore was not to be regarded as an alien Englishman. It seems that once he had sent the *Baltimore Sun* an article about Italian beaches. The Italians felt sorry for him and let him continue, not only unmolested at first but also as an active member of the Stampa Estera. Everything would have been fine if Strutt had not decided he had to speak. It was the occasion of a reception for Press Minister Alessandro Pavolini. The German correspondents, who numbered more than three fourths of the members of the organization, had decided that their *Gauleiter*, Baron Wolfgang von Langen, was to make a speech welcoming Pavolini. It was a chance for them to pay a few Teutonic tributes to Italy. But as von Langen arose to his feet to speak, Strutt popped up and beat him to the spoken word. In perfect Italian, Strutt made a long peroration which included almost everything from Greek poetry to Roman gynecology. The Italians, it must be said, thought it was a rather absurd but amusing incident, and Pavolini made a pleasant reply. But the Germans were furious, and the following morning von Langen demanded that the Italians arrest him.

The next we heard of him was a week later when we received a letter in Italian from him. It didn't give the name of the town, but said that he was confined in a tiny village at an altitude of six thousand feet, with the result that he suffered from the cold at night. He said the streets were unpaved and the cobblestones hurt his feet. That was about all, except for a few Latin phrases. The local censor, however, had written a postscript in red ink in which he said: "The altitude is less than three thousand feet, and it is not true that the streets are unpaved."

Strutt in turn had written a post-postscript, saying: "Do not believe the censor, he has had too much Chianti."

The censor then appended still another remark: "That is also untrue."

It is doubtful that in any country at war there ever existed a more fantastic censorship than in Italy before the Germans made them tighten up their restrictions. Most of the censors, like the local one who handled Strutt's letter, took the whole thing as a joke and were constantly making whimsical notes on the margins of letters that we received.

One of our best friends in Rome was a Danish correspondent, Jorgen Bast, of the Copenhagen *Berlingske Tidende*. He showed us some of the correspondence which he had with his wife. For nearly two months they had been writing back and forth about her coming to Rome on a visit. Finally, everything was arranged, and she wrote to tell Bast that she was leaving on the following day. The Italian censor wrote in red ink: "Congratulations. It certainly took a long time."

Newspaper interest in the fate of the several thousand English who remained behind in Italy became so keen when they were eventually rounded up and placed in concentration camps or tiny villages that Reynolds sought permission to visit one of the concentration camps. Finally, Marchese di Capomazza, after the usual several weeks' delay, handed him a pass to visit the one at Parma. It enabled Reynolds to pass twenty-four hours inside the camp, eating, drinking, and sleeping with the English inmates as one of them. This particular group, numbering about forty men, was housed in an old castle, built around a central courtyard in which they exercised and played games. Most of the men, Reynolds found, were married. The wives of some had been confined to small towns in other parts of Italy, while other wives — and there seemed to be no especial reason for this privilege — were permitted to live in the town of Parma and see their husbands three or four times a week. Again, it was Fascist ineptitude rather than Italian meanness. One of the Englishmen with whom Reynolds became friendly had been the representative in Italy for the Walt Disney color films. He said they were treated all right but the food was not so good. The dining room was divided into two groups: those who had money and those who didn't. Those who had no money were given the food of a humble Italian worker, while those who had means to buy supplementary fare sat at a separate table and were waited on by an Italian cameriere in a dirty white coat. They were permitted to buy wine from the camp bar and even send out into the city for supplementary delicacies that were available in the local stores. Reynolds ate at the no-money table. But the ever-present police lieutenant who had escorted him was there. It made frank conversation impossible. The lunch at the no money tables consisted of spaghetti with tomato sauce, potatoes, and an apple each for dessert. The evening meal comprised soup, tripe with seaweedlike spinach, and potatoes, and a dessert made of chestnuts. There was no coffee except for those at the paying table. They slept on army cots which had sheets and blankets, from four to six in a room.

When Reynolds left in the morning, the police lieutenant called all the people together and told them that he appreciated the kind reception they had given him. One wizened old Englishman, with false teeth that interfered with an Oxford accent, who had sat across the table from Reynolds in the dining room, took this as a signal for a speech. He had come to Italy on a holiday and was caught by the war the day he was leaving. Traveling on the vacation budget of a small private income, he had soon gone through his funds on hand. He said, "Don't you believe, old chap, that everything here is roses and honeysuckle. We haven't eaten any English food since we've been here. And spaghetti, old man, is rough going as a steady diet. Also . . ."

The police lieutenant, who spoke perfect English, interrupted at this point and said, "You see how ungrateful people can be. They always complain no matter what you do for them. It's getting late, and we'll miss the train if you don't come now."

Returning to Rome from Parma, Reynolds had to change trains at Bologna. As he got into a first-class compartment, he found himself alone with a distinguished, Junoesque lady who was talking in English out the window to a friend on the platform. The conversation was of such a nature that Reynolds felt compelled to inform his unknown train companion that he spoke English and mumbled something about would she like the door closed or open. Immediately, she changed the subject matter to horses and crops. After the train had started, she asked Reynolds if he would mind closing the window as it made a *courant d'air*. This started the conversation, and soon she was asking what people thought of the recent arrest of Prince Torlonia and Prince Doria, who had been accused of anti-Fascist sentiment. Reynolds said that all the American correspondents had sent the story and that the New York papers had asked for more. Prince Torlonia was released shortly afterward.

"Well," she said, "it's getting to be a pretty pass when people are being arrested just because they are of the aristocracy. I am a member of the Fascist party. In fact, I was one of the first women ever to join it, and I must say that what is taking place now doesn't make sense. The trouble started when he began to have ideas about empire. I do hope you aren't a newspaperman."

Reynolds told her that he was a newspaperman, but that correspondents were not quite so bad as she believed.

"I think I should tell you, nevertheless," she said, "that I am the mother of Prince Torlonia. I know that he was only arrested because servants whom he had upbraided for stealing my jewelry denounced him. I am returning to Rome now to take up this matter with Mussolini."

At lunch, in the *carrozza ristorante*, she said that although she was a member of the Fascist party, she was determined to leave

Italy and return to her home in America "if only to die there," as she felt Italy, since Mussolini's ambitions for empire had taken control of him, was no longer the same. It proved to be a prophetic statement, because Princess Torlonia, née Elsie Moore, returned to America and died within a few days before Mussolini declared war on the United States. Her son, Prince Torlonia, who was at her deathbed, barely had time to catch a plane for Europe and rejoin his wife, Princess Beatrice, daughter of the King of Spain, who had remained in Rome.

This incident is recorded because it was a typical example of how Italian aristocracy of foreign connections first accepted Fascism and then became alienated from it when Mussolini embarked on an anti-British and inevitably anti-American policy.

Pro-British and pro-American sentiment, however, was not confined exclusively to the upper classes — it permeated many strata of the middle and proletariat classes too, particularly those who had been familiar with and profited from the visits of Anglo-Saxon tourists to Italy. But this feeling was not as yet sufficiently widespread to make the majority of Italians regret their plunge into war. The Italians did not conceal their disappointment that the Italo-French armistice hadn't placed large sections of French territory in their possession, but they consoled themselves with the conviction that the Germans would go on to conquer England that summer and that there would then be a general peace conference in which all Italy's imperial ambitions would be satisfied. Perhaps the tide of Mussolini's popularity turned just at this point and slowly began to ebb away.

Meanwhile, the far-reaching effects of the French collapse were beginning to be felt throughout Europe. A week before the armistice, when the Germans had their hands full sweeping over France, the Russians took over Latvia, Lithuania, and Estonia, and the ink was scarcely dry on the armistice signatures before the Soviets were presenting an ultimatum to Rumania's King Carol, demanding the transfer of Bessarabia and Bukovina. As a matter of policy, following the Russo-German Pact, the Nazis urged Carol to yield to the Soviet ultimatum, but the Germans were privately worried about Bolshevik expansionism, and when Mussolini urged upon Hitler the undesirability of a Russian domination of the Balkans, he found a sympathetic listener.

# VIII

To counteract the enormous prestige that Germany had built up in central and Balkan Europe as a result of the Reichswehr's victories in Poland, the Low Countries, and France, the Fascists caused a startling rumor to be circulated to the effect that Hungary was about to offer the vacant Hapsburg throne to King Victor Emmanuel. A Hungarian delegation was supposed to be staying incognito at one of Rome's leading hotels while they carried on clandestine negotiations regarding the conditions under which the Italian King could accept this additional crown. We first heard about it from the *Corriere della Sera* correspondent, Luigi Barzini, Jr. — a Columbia University graduate and the son of a member of the Italian Senate. We had met him in Ethiopia, where he frequently acted as a substitute correspondent for American newspapers. He demonstrated his mastery of English when he wrote a delicately worded story, published in *Esquire*, about the extraordinary house of ill-fame which the Fascist government operated in Asmara for the biological convenience of its soldiers, going and coming from the Abyssinian fronts. Until he was finally sent to *confino* on suspicion of being pro-Anglo-Saxon, Barzini was friendly to most American correspondents and gladly contributed tidbits that rarely fell to foreigners.

We were lunching in the Albergo Excelsior Grill when Barzini strolled in and sat down at our table. Before long, he burst out with the report. Obviously, he was very excited about it. So were we — if true, we didn't want to be beaten on it. Barzini said, "The Press Ministry claims to know nothing about it and of course the Italian newspapers don't even dare hint at it until they get permission, but," and here he leaned across the table and lowered his voice to a conspiratorial whisper, "I hear the Hungarian mission may be staying in this very hotel."

We called up one of our staffers who spoke Italian like a native and instructed him to sound out the porters, valets, and floor waiters of the Excelsior to see if he could run down any Hungarian delegation. He reported a couple of hours later that although there was a stray Hungarian or two in the hotel, there was nothing that could possibly constitute a mission. To make a similar investigation of all possible hotels in Rome would have required an army of legmen, so we started working through diplomatic channels but were unable to pin anything down. Within the next two days we had at least a dozen more tips on it, and so did all the other correspondents in the Stampa Estera. The Hungarian correspondents were indignant about the story, insisting that Hungarians would never be satisfied with a foreign king — if they couldn't have their own king back, they wouldn't have any. But these same Hungarians admitted that it was inconceivable such reports would be persistently circulated if they were not backed by some important political motive.

In some ways, such a move on Hungary's part seemed plausible enough. The peace conferences of 1919 had left the remains of Austria and Hungary ringed around by succession states that regarded them still as enemies. Mussolini, ever a diplomatic opportunist, had been the first to champion these former enemies, with whom he made numerous friendship pacts and treaties. The

Duce had been obliged to bow to Hitler on the question of Austria, but Hungary was still very much his protégé.

With all Europe now in turmoil, this relationship was becoming daily more important to both Italy and Hungary. It was important for Italy because it was her best guarantee against having her influence in southeastern Europe wiped out by Germany and Russia. For Hungary it was important because Italy's backing enabled her to resist Nazi penetration and too-pressing Nazi demands for "co-operation." To be sure, Hungarians did not want an Italian king, but European peoples had often waived their personal desires when it was a question of self-preservation.

We spent several uneasy days and nights for fear one of our rivals would be able to confirm the story and we would be beaten on it. But finally it faded away from sheer lack of nourishment, and we came to realize it was a trial balloon aimed at publicizing Hungary's friendship for Italy. It never saw the light of print in a newspaper, although it undoubtedly formed the subject of long reports to a good many foreign offices from a good many ambassadors and ministers in Rome. It was just the kind of thing calculated to give the governments of all Hungary's small neighbors a fine case of jitters. Perhaps it may even have given the Wilhelmstrasse a slight headache. Whether the Hungarian government was in on the plot, it is impossible to say, but, at any rate, Italy was back into the Balkan picture with a bang.

Part of the European diplomatic game was that if you couldn't get something for yourself, you tried to get it for a protégé. If Mussolini was upset by the Soviet occupation of Bessarabia and Bukovina and apprehensive that the Russians might encroach still further into Rumania, he was probably very little less concerned over the tales his Bucharest Legation was telling him about Nazi salesmen and tourists in Rumania. Germany was Italy's ally, but that did not mean that Mussolini was willing to have Italy left out in any division of Balkan spoils. At the same time, however, Italy didn't have the necessary industrial output to compete with Germany in any economic penetration, so the Duce put forward the claims — which he had long kept on ice — of his two chief protégés, Hungary and Bulgaria. (Bulgaria was another nation defeated in World War I that Mussolini had taken under his protection when it was forlorn and friendless. He had also arranged a match between Bulgaria's King Boris and one of King Victor Emmanuel's daughters.)

This time Mussolini's plans did not run counter to Hitler's. The Führer didn't want to start a war in the Balkans, because he was concentrating all his fighting forces on England, whom he still hoped to conquer that year. At the same time, he wanted to spike once and for all any Balkan ambitions that Russia might have. On the basis of their World War I performance, the Rumanians did not look like such good fighters as the Hungarians, whom Hitler thought could be relied on to resist by force any Soviet attempt to extend her borders. Besides, Hitler felt Rumania should be punished for accepting an Anglo-French guarantee contrary to his warnings.

King Carol of Rumania consequently found himself in a hopeless position. France had been humbled to the dust and was completely incapable of carrying out her part of the guarantee, while Britain was going through such a critical period that her help was bound to be negligible, if she could send any at all. Carol felt that he had no choice but to yield when the two Axis dictators intimated they thought Bulgaria had been waiting for southern Dobruja long enough. From Mussolini's and Hitler's point of view, Dobruja was a bribe to induce the Bulgarian people, who were racially close to the Russians, to stay snug in the Axis camp and not get too chummy with the Soviets. Bulgaria was also important as a bulwark against Turkey should Turkey decide to do something about her thus far unfunctioning alliance with England.

We knew something was in the air when we learned July 26, 1940, that Rumanian Premier John Gigurtu and Foreign Minister Manolescu had been summoned to see Hitler and Ribbentrop at Berchtesgaden. Another indication that the carving of Dobruja from Rumania was really under way was when, for the first time, a genuine Bulgarian correspondent arrived in Rome and took up headquarters at the Stampa Estera. He was duly cautious, but, in execrable French, he confided that the Bulgarians thought it advisable to have a correspondent in Rome because Italo-Bulgarian relations had become "very close." Less than a month afterward, it was announced in Bucharest that Rumania had agreed to cede southern Dobruja to Bulgaria and that there would be an exchange of populations at the same time to rid both countries of each other's minorities. Thus Bulgaria regained her 1912 borders.

Meanwhile Hungarian-Rumanian negotiations were going on, but advanced nowhere because Hungary was demanding much more of Transylvania than Rumania was willing to give. The Hungarians claimed that Transylvania, which belonged to them before World War I, was predominantly Hungarian-populated throughout, while the Rumanians claimed that only small parts of it had more Hungarians than Rumanians. Hitler and Mussolini soon settled this squabble, however. On August 30, 1940, Ciano and Ribbentrop met in Vienna and parceled out Transylvania, giving two thirds of it to Hungary. The Rumanians protested that they lost over a million Rumanian nationals by this transfer, but all that interested the Axis dictators was that the strategic Carpathian mountain frontier bordering on Russia was now in the hands of the Hungarians who had been bitterly anti-Bolshevik ever since they had experienced a Red government under Bela Kun in their own country in 1920. Hitler and Mussolini felt that, with the aid of some German war materials, the Hungarians were capable of defending this frontier in any crisis. The helpless Rumanians were given an Axis guarantee of the integrity of what remained of their country, and the Germans restricted themselves thereafter to boring from within, until they attained a completely pro-Nazi Rumanian government, which proceeded to oust King Carol.

This result was the best that Mussolini could hope for. He had considerably strengthened his two protégés in the Danubian bloc, and it was to be expected that they would be sufficiently grateful to repay him when and if they could, but the economic exploitation of Rumania he was compelled to leave to Hitler. The situation when the general reshuffle had finished, however, distinctly favored the Axis — of the Danubian and Balkan nations, only Yugoslavia and Greece remained outside the Axis orbit.

With all the Rome correspondents fed up with writing stories about the Balkans which the foreign news editors in New York were relegating to the real-estate section of the newspapers, we welcomed the announcement at the daily press conference that Mussolini would receive the heads of bureaus the next morning at seven A.M. at the Villa Torlonia, an armed citadel in the heart of Rome. Guido Rocco, head of the foreign press, who had the title but not the post of Ambassador, made the announcement and smilingly added:

"It will probably be difficult for the American correspondents who are not accustomed to the rigors of Fascist living to get up so early."

He said he was sorry but that women correspondents were not invited.

After the meeting was over, Capomazza told Herbert Matthews, Dick Massock, and Reynolds that the idea of the reception was to show how Mussolini kept fit in wartime. He said we would have a chance to see him do his early-morning calisthenics before he went to his desk in the Palazzo Venezia and that later in the afternoon we would see him take more exercise before resuming work in the evening.

Dick Massock was furious and told Capomazza that he thought the whole thing was unfair.

"That was my idea," Dick said. "I wrote Ambassador Rocco a formal letter last week, asking him if it wouldn't be possible for the Associated Press to have an exclusive story on how the Duce keeps fit during wartime. And now what happens? Everybody is getting in on it, including the United Press."

"You should be flattered," Capomazza answered suavely, "that your idea was so good that His Excellency Pavolini decided to let all the other correspondents profit by it. After all, if it's good propaganda, why should we give it exclusively to one organization and not everybody else?"

Herbert and Reynolds consoled Dick at the Ambasciatori bar with a drink, and Reynolds said maliciously, "That'll teach you to go to the Press Ministry with an enterprise story. Hereafter you had better do what the U.P. does: ferret it out for yourself."

The next morning, twenty-three correspondents gathered in front of the Ministry of Popular Culture — the official title of the Press Ministry, which the American correspondents generally dubbed the Ministry of Unpopular Culture — and were herded into three busses by more than a dozen press officers, Foreign Office representatives, and secret-service men. Arriving at the Via Nomentana entrance of the Villa Torlonia, whose high walls were guarded by plain-clothes men stationed at twenty-yard intervals, the correspondents waited around in groups for at least ten minutes. Then, one by one, as Rocco called out the names in alphabetical order, we were permitted to pass through the half-open iron gates. Actually, each one of the correspondents filed through a gantlet of three secret-service police on either side, who looked us over carefully to make sure we had no concealed firearms. Reynolds, who happened to have a pipe and tobacco pouch in his coat pocket, felt one of the detectives adroitly, almost as if by accident, touch the suspicious bulge with a practiced hand. It was the Fascist way of frisking Mussolini's guests.

Rocco, whose retinue had grown to about twenty Italians by this time, led us down a gravel walk, past the white-pillared, centuries-old villa that had a Southern colonial touch about its architecture, through a wooded grove to a good-sized paddock. Here we were lined up in groups, the Germans, Japanese, Hungarians, and other Europeans being given positions closer to the riding range than the Americans. It was also curious to note that most of the plain-clothes men formed a semicircle around the American group. We waited for ten minutes and then out galloped the Duce on a finely trained chestnut mare, a Hanoverian cavalry horse, which was a gift from Hitler. Its name was Thiene. Bare-armed, Mussolini wore a white cotton singlet, a white Fascist cap, and the gray militia breeches which were tucked into carefully polished boots. He was followed by his riding master and fencing instructor, Camillo Ridolfi, in the uniform of a Black Shirt captain, and two grooms in khaki uniforms. After making the Fascist salute, he proceeded to gallop around the paddock with the two grooms. Ridolfi looked on from his horse. As soon as he had warmed up, the Duce began to take the various jumps — brush jumps, fences, and hurdles. Altogether, he cleared the bars eighteen times. The two grooms, who followed twenty yards behind, carefully knocked down three of the highest hurdles which, of course, the Duce had cleared without difficulty. The Duce was always good by contrast.

Sweating and smiling, the Duce rode over to the German group and said: *"Bin Ich muede? Bin Ich krank? Schwach?"*

*"Nein, nein,"* chorused the German correspondents.

It was clear to most of the Americans present that Mussolini was still brooding over Bud Ekins' message about his reported illness. Now that Italy was at war, more than ever did he want people to believe that he was not sick, tired, or weak.

Then came the worst ordeal of the morning's visit. Everybody's name was called off alphabetically by groups. Rocco started with the Europeans first, and each time a name was called, the Duce gave the Fascist salute, which was smartly returned by the person presented in accordance with the recognized protocol. When he came to the American group, it was an awkward moment because each one of us salved his conscience by raising a droopy arm in a way which was a cross between a schoolboy asking permission to leave the classroom and a paralytic trying to scratch his head.

The Duce then rode off, and we were escorted to a long table, set in picnic style, in another part of the grove. The table was arrayed with sandwiches of all kinds and bottles of liquor, ranging from Scotch whisky and Courvoisier to Italian Strega. Ridolfi, who was having a drink at the table, was immediately surrounded by the American correspondents. He was plied with questions about the Duce's horsemanship, his early rising habits, and even diet. It was the first opportunity to get some firsthand information about Mussolini's personal habits since Italy entered the war. With apprehensive press officers moving closer, ready to interrupt if he made any slip, Ridolfi rattled on, obviously pleased at the chance to talk to visitors.

"I have been with Il Duce as his equerry and fencing instructor for more than twenty years," Ridolfi said. "He never drinks coffee nor anything stronger than orange juice. He is a vegetarian and eats very little. I can assure you I have never known him for years now to eat any meat."

"Oh, yes, he eats a lot of spaghetti, but only with butter and cheese sauce," he continued. "No meat sauce. His favorite vegetables are broccoli and zucchini. But he likes fruit more than anything else, especially grapes, which he eats at both lunch and supper. Oh, and he likes peaches, too."

Allen Raymond, who had just replaced Minifie as the *Herald Tribune* correspondent in Rome, whispered, "It looks as though the Axis isn't a steel pact after all, but just a vegetable compound."

When Rocco judged we had been given enough of the right kind of Fascist propaganda with our drinks, he took us back to the gate, where we were carefully checked out, one by one. The police were taking no chances that anyone might be left behind. Rocco said that the same correspondents were to meet at the Press Ministry at three P.M. for the afternoon visit.

At noon, Capomazza telephoned the U.P. office and said that Eleanor was invited to join the party in the afternoon. When we reached the Press Ministry at the appointed hour, we found the number of busses had been doubled. The assembled throng this time included, besides the women correspondents, at least fifteen girls, mainly young stenographers who worked in the different newspaper offices. Only the prettiest stenographers, however, had been invited. Later we learned what had happened. The Duce had reprimanded Rocco for bringing only men in the morning and added that he expected the afternoon gathering to be bedizened by a certain amount of femininity. These girls, however, were to be connected with the press; how remotely didn't matter.

It was the tennis game more than anything else that turned us against Mussolini as a man. We had long been opposed to his political ideas and foreign policy, but we had somehow thought that he must possess certain personal qualities in order to remain dictator of forty-four million people. As we were being conducted to the old jousting field which had been converted into an excellent tennis court, Eleanor, Reynolds, and Allen Raymond saw Mussolini slip out of the back door of the villa and bicycle through a sylvan patch toward the tennis court, only three hundred yards away. We were not supposed to see him. Five minutes later we arrived by a more roundabout way at the tennis court. The game was in full progress and the umpire, who was Press Minister Pavolini, insisted the Duce had been playing for more than half an hour.

The dictator, garbed in a beige polo shirt and shorts which revealed the scar of the wound he had received on the thigh during World War I, was playing doubles. He was serving underhand like a novice, and he violated every tennis rule and tradition by walking at least two steps beyond the base line to serve. Even so, the two athletes who were playing against him — Mario Delardinelli, Rome's leading professional tennis player, and Erlado Monzogoio, a member of Italy's national soccer team — had difficulty in returning his soap-bubble serves. Whenever the ball was returned, it floated slowly up so that a lame man with a broken arm could have hit it. Il Duce lobbed, smashed, and smiled, pleased with his triumph. His partner, Lucio Savorgnan, former university champion, covered three quarters of the court.

After five games, Mussolini stopped playing and received from the Fascist Black Shirts in the gallery fawning congratulations.

"Thanks," he responded, "I am proud to have won."

We gasped, for we had seen him leave his house and knew he

had played five games only, three of which he lost, despite the efforts of his opponents to force victory upon him. Pavolini joined the correspondents and announced that the official score was 7–5.

That night in a faraway corner of the Press Club, Matthews and Raymond discussed with us the spectacle we had seen. If Mussolini could not afford to lose even a tennis game for fear of suffering loss of prestige, it was evident to what ends he was going in World War II to keep the Italians from learning how much he was losing. Needless to say, we didn't try to send our personal reactions.

When Hitler and Mussolini realized that Britain was not going to be conquered as they had hoped, they decided they must do something to restrain the activities of the United States, whose growing friendship and helpfulness to England and increasing hostility to the Axis were becoming a nuisance to the two dictators. They therefore brought to a boil a diplomatic brew which had been simmering on the back of the stove for a long time, and the result was the Tripartite Pact. Hints of a possible alliance with Japan had appeared in the Axis press as far back as the summer of 1939, when Ciano was supposed to have talked the matter over with Ribbentrop and Hitler during his Salzburg trip. The Axis had been inclined, however, to avoid an alliance with an Asiatic power as long as it had seemed possible to conclude the war within a year and to keep it restricted to the European continent.

The Tripartite Pact was signed in Berlin September 27, 1940, by Ciano, Ribbentrop, and the Japanese Ambassador to Germany, Saburo Kurusu — the same Saburo Kurusu who came to Washington more than a year later to beguile the American government with protestations of peaceful intentions while the Japanese leaders in Tokyo were preparing a blitz attack on Pearl Harbor. The day that the pact was signed in Berlin, Rocco held a full-dress press conference, attended by practically every employee of the Ministry of Unpopular Culture and, for the first time, the full quota of the Japanese correspondents. The little Nipponese devils, as a rule, didn't attend these conferences and instead sent pretty Italian stenographers who took shorthand notes of all that was said. Rocco pompously explained that the pact provided for Japanese recognition of the leadership of Italy and Germany in the establishment of a new order in Europe, while the Axis gave similar recognition to Japan's position in the future Asiatic setup.

"I want to emphasize that although the three countries will give each other all military and economic aid in the event of a new power entering the conflict," Rocco said, "the pact cannot be interpreted as being directed against Russia. In fact, clause five specifically states that Russia is to be excepted."

The Tass correspondent, who was a member of the staff of the Soviet Embassy, was not present to receive this polite reassurance.

All the American correspondents in Rome immediately tapped Foreign Office contacts as to how the pact might apply to the United States. Checking with Matthews and Raymond, we found they had the same Chigi Palace answers as ourselves: the pact as far as Italy was concerned was not designed to come into operation, but merely to keep America sufficiently worried about the Pacific so that she would not interfere in Europe.

"Italy doesn't like the Japs any better than you do," one Foreign Office official told Eleanor, "but we don't want the United States butting in over here. After all, big and great as your country is, you will think twice about fighting a war both in Asia and Europe at the same time."

The pact was another shock to the Italian people, who found themselves with another ally whom they disliked and distrusted as much as Germany. There were soon a lot of Japanese journalists, new diplomatic attachés, and military missions running around Italy, but all they could ever get from the Italians was chilly politeness. No unofficial Italians fraternized with the Japs — not even at the country club where they went to play golf and meet members of the Foreign Office in the restaurant and bar. Both at the country club and in the Foreign Press Club, where the Japanese became more and more obnoxious, they surprised everyone with their hard drinking, frequently consuming a bottle of whisky each in an evening. There were frequent reports of drunken brawls in the Japanese Club, and now and then a Nipponese would appear with a black eye.

With the Tripartite Pact a *fait accompli*, Mussolini took the attitude that the United States would keep out of the war in Europe, and began to prepare for an annexation of Greece. He had already, as only an ex-newspaperman could have done, made a legendary figure out of an Albanian hill-billy named Daut Hoggia. In reality, a local drunkard and mountain bandit, Daut Hoggia, who had had his head chopped off, was suddenly glorified in the Italian press as an Albanian nationalist leader. According to Mussolini's own newspaper, the *Popolo d'Italia*, Hoggia had been executed by an interborder organization led by Greeks, which decapitated him while he slept on the Albanian side of the Greco-Albanian border and took his head to Greek police officials to collect the reward for his death. According to the Greeks, a price had been put on his head because he was a murderer, while the Italians claimed it was because he was an Albanian patriot who had agitated for the return to Albania of the Greek province of Ciamuria. The Italian press described him with a whole paintbox of color — a forty-five-year-old Moslem, measuring six feet tall, weighing one hundred and ninety-five pounds, who thought only of Albania's greatness.

Reports began to emanate from Belgrade that there were serious disorders in Albania and that the Italians were having great difficulty in controlling tribal chieftains. Leon Kay, who was then the U.P. bureau manager of Yugoslavia, sent many of these reports, which he credited to their source Yugoslav newspapers and diplomatic quarters. Ciano was so incensed over these reports that he insisted that Reynolds go to Albania immediately and see for himself whether or not they were true. Reynolds pleaded that as bureau manager in Rome, he had too much administrative work to absent himself from his office. But there was nothing to do about it. Ciano made quite clear to Reynolds that he had to go to Albania or else have a serious black mark registered against him in his dossier. The whole thing was absurd as Reynolds couldn't speak a word of Albanian and he was to be escorted throughout the trip by an Italian press officer. Furthermore, it was quite obvious that the Italians were by this time, with all their soldiers and machine guns, well in control of the situation. Nevertheless, Reynolds took off in an Ala Littoria airplane, equipped with a three months' pass for Albania, personally signed by Ciano, and arrived at Tirana airfield at noon. As he got out of the airplane he was greeted by Paolo Veronese, an Italian member of the Albanian press bureau. From then on, like a sticker bur, Veronese never left Reynolds. He drove Reynolds to the Albanian press bureau, where Lorusso, the small, nervous Italian correspondent whom Eleanor had met just before the Italian invasion of Albania, was now the director of Albanian propaganda. Lorusso and Veronese took Reynolds out to lunch at the Hotel Foresteria, the new Italian hotel in Tirana where a comfortable room had been reserved for him. Lorusso outlined the itinerary to be followed, which included the Burelli district, birthplace of King Zog, where the massacre of Italian soldiers was reported to have occurred.

During the next four days Reynolds was taken throughout the breadth of Albania by automobile and muleback. Needless to say, there was no sign of disorder of any kind. Veronese would speak to Albanian peasants, mountaineers, and businessmen in pidgin Albanian and then translate, saying:

"He says everything has been quiet and normal here ever since the arrival of the Italians."

But the best trick that Veronese unfolded was an apparently chance meeting with Madame Daut Hoggia, the widow of the Albanian patriot or brigand, according to which version one accepted. Arriving at the village of Konispoli on the Greek-Albanian frontier, Reynolds and Veronese ran into an Albanian horse doctor, Muhri Timos, who had studied veterinary science in Paris.

"A newspaperman?" he said. "Then you should have an interview with Madame Daut Hoggia. She is staying in a house just down the street. She is a personal friend of mine, and I am sure I can arrange for her to receive you."

As we arrived at her door, the Albanian prefect of Konispoli, wearing an Albanian Fascist badge, chanced to come along. We entered the rickety whitewashed house which seemed ready to topple down the mountainside on which it was perched. Madame Daut Hoggia was expectantly and uncomfortably sitting on the edge of a chair. She was dressed in Moslem fashion with pantaloons as voluminous as those of the traditional Dutch boy, and a red-embroidered shirtwaist. The horse doctor, who spoke the dialect of the region, talked to her for about fifteen minutes and then translated into French what he claimed she had said. His version was:

"I think the Greeks poisoned him because he was too big and strong to be attacked even if asleep. They probably put poison into a watermelon, of which he was very fond, and then cut off his head. I cannot forgive the Greeks for putting his handsome head into a potato sack and selling it to their police for money.

"I'm convinced that the plot was organized in Greece and carried out with the aid of Albanians with Greek sympathies. I hope Italy will see that the assassination of my husband is paid for by the Greeks."

Throughout the interview Madame Hoggia looked longingly at the cushions spread on the wooden floor on which, in Albanian fashion, she was accustomed to squat. As she talked, her four bare-footed sons and two pigtailed daughters stared open-mouthed at Reynolds.

After completing the controlled tour of Albania, which included stops at Scutari, Durazzo, Argirokastron, and Koritza, Reynolds returned to Tirana and was invited to lunch at the home of Lieutenant-General Francesco Jacomoni, whose wife was the daughter of General Cavallero. She was a brilliant hostess who spoke perfect French and was a militant Fascist. Despite her femininity, during the meal both Jacomoni and his wife boasted about how well the Italians were preparing the Albanians politically for "greater things." In the afternoon, they took Reynolds to see a gymnastic show by Albanian Fascist schoolteachers. "These teachers are already instructing Albanian children,"

Jacomoni said, "in the principles of Fascism. They will grow up to be good Fascists because they are young enough to learn, without preconceived ideas, what we are trying to teach them."

This entire Albanian trip was a journalistic failure, since the truth about it could not be sent, but it gave Reynolds a valuable background in connection with the political character of the impending attack on Greece. One thing that impressed Reynolds the most was that in all the local party headquarters to which Veronese unfailingly took him in every town, there was an Albanian presiding over an impressive desk in an impressive office, while off in the corner was a small table at which an Italian Fascist held forth. The Italians were unobtrusively pulling the strings through Albanian ward leaders whose greatest weakness was personal vanity. Reynolds was also surprised at the small number of Italian troops, probably not more than twenty thousand in all, which he encountered during the tour. The whole setup was more political than military, with Italian domination achieved through Albanian chieftains whom the Fascists had bought out with money and flattery.

Shortly after Reynolds' return to Rome, the Italian press launched a campaign against Greece, claiming that Albanians in the Greek province of Ciamuria were being mistreated. It was reminiscent of the Mussolini method in Tunisia and the system Hitler had used in the Sudeten districts of Czechoslovakia. It was old, familiar Axis technique.

The second phase of Mussolini's preparatory work was the publication of stories in a number of Italian newspapers, including the ultra-Fascist *Tevere* and the more conservative *Popolo di Roma*, that the Greeks, "under the influence of their Anglophile King George II," were giving surreptitious aid to Britain and that great sectors of Greek public opinion were consequently demanding the abdication of their King in favor of his brother, Prince Paul, who had married the German Princess Frederika Luise of Brunswick, a granddaughter of the Kaiser. The culmination of the Italian press campaign against Greece came October 26, when the official Fascist news agency, Stefani, announced that Greek troops had attacked an Albanian frontier post, resulting in a number of Albanian casualties. With Greece doing everything it could to maintain an unprovocative attitude, the Stefani announcement was generally discredited abroad. The next day Greek official circles hastened to deny the report, but it was useless, as Mussolini was already intent on another *casus belli*.

And on October 28, at three o'clock in the morning, the Italian Minister in Athens, Emmanuele Grazzi, handed Premier John Metaxas an ultimatum making the following accusations:

(1) That Greece was tolerating the use of her territorial waters and ports by the British navy for the prosecution of the war against Italy;

(2) That Greece was permitting the organization of the British secret service in the Greek islands;

(3) That Greece was guilty of terrorism against the Albanian population of Ciamuria and of persistent attempts to create disorders along the Greek-Albanian frontier.

"These provocations," the ultimatum declared, "can no longer be tolerated by Italy."

The ultimatum then demanded that Italy be given the right to occupy certain strategic points — Corfu, Crete, Epirus, and the Peiraeus — "for the duration of the war in the Mediterranean."

"The Italian government asks that the Greek government give immediate orders to military authorities that this occupation may take place in a peaceful manner. Wherever the Italian troops may meet resistance, this resistance will be broken by armed force, and the Greek government would have the responsibility for the resultant consequences."

Metaxas rejected the ultimatum, informing Grazzi that he considered it tantamount to a declaration of war.

The ultimatum was supposed to expire at 5:30 A.M., two and one-half hours after presented, but actually the Italian troops started crossing the Greek border at five A.M. and the Italo-Greek War had started — on the very day that Italy celebrated its eighteenth anniversary of the March on Rome.

# IX

THE GREEK WAR HAD BEEN IN PROGRESS BARELY ONE DAY WHEN ALL
the American correspondents began receiving instructions from
New York to proceed to the Greco-Albanian front. But how to get
there? The Italians were not issuing passes for Albania to anyone,
not even the Germans. The European correspondents, who were
more like diplomats than newspapermen, just sat back and waited
for the time, perhaps months hence, when the Italians might
eventually get around to organizing an official trip. Not so the
Americans, who all began studying every possibility, from stowing
away on a transport ship to bribing some government official going
to Tirana to sell his ticket. It looked well-nigh impossible, and for
two nights, Matthews, Raymond, Whitaker, Cianfarra, Eleanor,
and Reynolds gathered at the bar of the Foreign Press Club for
the sole purpose of pumping each other as to what each one had
accomplished in the way of individual enterprise. Massock and
Whitaker, we discovered, were working on their Press Ministry
and Foreign Office contacts, while Raymond and Matthews were
studying, although independently of each other, possibilities of
hiring a private plane or boat to cross the Adriatic. It looked bad

for the United Press, but the Packards' attitude was that if any official permission was to be granted, it would be all-inclusive and every office would have the same opportunity to send at least one representative. We were mainly worried about Matthews and Raymond. They might by chance find some devil-may-care, do-anything-for-a-good-fee sort of flier or skipper who would undertake such an adventure. But once in Albania, we didn't see how either Raymond or Matthews could ever work his way to the front. There were scores of military posts to be passed.

On the third night of the war, Eleanor suddenly remembered. It seemed a crazy idea, a bit risky, but, as she pointed out, the most serious consequence would probably be arrest, followed by expulsion. What she remembered was that Reynolds still had tucked away in a bureau drawer an old Albanian *lascia-passare* signed by Ciano that would have been good for another three weeks if all such passes had not been automatically canceled at the outbreak of the Italo-Greek hostilities.

"If you doctor up that old permit you used on your last trip," Eleanor said, "you could make it look like new."

"Wait a moment," Reynolds said. "I'm the one that's going to use it."

Eleanor, however, took the worthless pass and rejuvenated it. We had some impressive rubber stamps in the U.P. office, bearing such words as *Autorizzato* and *Valido*, as well as a printing machine for reproducing any date of the year. By stamping the old permit with the Italian phrase for "Authorized" and "Valid, October 31, 1940," Eleanor made it look quite fresh and awe-inspiring. The next day, Reynolds, with the all-important paper in his wallet, called at the office of the Ala Littoria airline and asked for a ticket to Tirana. The airline official said, "Have you got permission from the Air Ministry to make such a trip?"

Reynolds showed him the pass. He looked at it and said, "That's all right, only you need a stamp on it from the Air Ministry. If you run up there and come back in the next two hours, I'll keep a seat on the plane for you."

At the Air Ministry, a colonel inspected the paper and, seeing Ciano's signature on it, plus the counterfeit renewal, said, "Most unusual, most unusual. But I guess Count Ciano knows what he's doing." He then stamped it, and half an hour later, Reynolds had the ticket in his pocket.

Reynolds took off the next morning at seven and encountered no trouble until he reached Brindisi, where the plane landed for inspection of passengers and cargo by the maritime customs and police. Each passenger was called into the police office at the airfield and questioned, unless a uniformed Black Shirt, with regard to his credentials. The police officer was a professional tough and growled that the pass could not possibly be in order. He told Reynolds he would be arrested. The argument that ensued soon degenerated into a yelling contest in which there was much banging on the table and mutual threats.

"And wait until Count Ciano hears what little respect you have for his signature," Reynolds said.

That did it, and Reynolds was permitted to continue his trip to Tirana.

In Tirana, luck was with him, because Lorusso, head of the Albanian Propaganda Ministry, had left an hour before for the front, with a dozen Italian correspondents. Only Veronese was in the office. He was most apologetic that he had not been informed of Reynolds' arrival, as otherwise he would have been at the airfield. He just assumed that Reynolds' papers must have been in order or otherwise he wouldn't be there. Also, he knew that Reynolds had been authorized to make a previous trip through Albania, which he himself had personally conducted.

"But you must have a military pass," he said, still apologetically. "I'll get it for you right away. I'm so sorry I didn't have a chance to get it in advance."

Two hours later, he called on Reynolds at the Hotel Foresteria, with the pass duly signed by Lieutenant-General Jacomoni. It was complete with red seal and blue ribbon.

"I've also arranged for you to go to Argirokastron, where the

Italian army press headquarters are located, tomorrow. You must be at the Bureau of Albanian Tourism at six in the morning. There's a captain there who is driving to Argirokastron, and he will be glad to take you. It's all arranged."

The least Reynolds could do was to buy Veronese a drink. All the time they were at the bar, Veronese reiterated how sorry he was everything had not been arranged in advance. The next morning, Reynolds met the captain at the appointed time, but the departure was delayed for an hour as a result of a Greek air raid over Tirana. As they stood out in the street, watching the Greek planes drop bombs on the airfield less than a mile away, the captain said that the tourist trade, which had never existed since the occupation of Albania by the Italians, was no longer even a fiction. The office was being closed down and he was helping out with the press. The back of the car was loaded with typewriters, mimeographed sheets of propaganda in Greek, and odds and ends that the Italian correspondents had left behind. Several Albanian trucks sequestered for the purpose were transporting several tons of heavy luggage and foodstuffs for the Italian correspondents. The captain, whose name was Roberto Martinelli, was a wild driver. His recklessness seemed all the more frightening in view of the number of automobiles and trucks that had slithered off the muddy Tirana-Argirokastron road at hairpin turns. The dead bodies of soldiers spilled out of several of these overturned trucks that Reynolds could see a few hundred feet below, where they had finally ended their fall against a rock or a tree on the precipitous mountainside. It was a gruesome indication of how fast the Italians were attempting to rush all reinforcements they had in Albania to the Greek front. There was not even time to take away the dead.

At Argirokastron, Lorusso greeted Reynolds coldly. He couldn't believe that any foreign correspondent, let alone an American, could have received permission to come to the front. Reynolds casually pulled out the Albanian permit signed by Jacomoni, and Lorusso broke into smiles and said, "Amico mio, how glad I am to see you. We're going to the Janina front tomorrow, and I have a place in my car for you."

The next day, Reynolds entered Greek territory with Lorusso and was impressed by the small number of Italian soldiers in evidence. Rain was coming down in torrents. He found all the bridges blown up and all strategic points on the Argirokastron-Janina road dynamited. All along the route were traffic jams, where the Italians had sent up scores of truckloads of reinforcements before the bridges and gaps had been repaired. Reynolds passed at least twelve villages, which he inspected with the Italian correspondents. They had all been evacuated except for a few sick and aged who, for physical reasons, were unable to leave. Even they were admirably surly. It was impossible to reach the front that night, owing to the traffic snarls, and the party returned to Argirokastron around nine. After supper, the Italian correspondents sat down at their typewriters in an improvised press room. Lorusso announced before they started to type that the theme of the day was that the populace of every Greek town through which the Italians passed had stayed behind and greeted the soldiers with flowers, bread, and wine.

"The keynote tonight is the friendliness of the Greek people," Lorusso said. "They greet us as liberators who are freeing them from a tyrannical government."

As Reynolds watched the Italian correspondents industriously type out such falsehoods, Lorusso came over and said, "You don't seem to be writing anything tonight. It's a grand story about the way the Greeks are welcoming the Italian army."

Reynolds said he was going to write war stories only and he was waiting to get to the front. Sometimes we thought that Fascists, after making up their propaganda out of sheer fantasy, read it and then believed it themselves.

The next day, however, Lorusso insisted on conducting a tour to Ciamuria, just across the Albanian frontier. But owing to a two-hour picnic lunch consisting of canned *minestrone*, *cotechino*, great chunks of Gorgonzola, and fiascos of Chianti, the party did not reach farther than Konispoli, inside the Albanian frontier. Outside of the fact that "a good time was had by all," the whole trip was pointless. Again, Reynolds was surprised at the absence of soldiers. He didn't see more than two hundred altogether that day, whereas for any sort of major push it would be reasonable to find tens of thousands of reserves behind the lines of any active sector. When they returned to the press headquarters in Argirokastron and a spaghetti supper was finished, Lorusso informed the Italian correspondents that the theme of the day was: "The heroism of the Albanians."

"You might mention how when these Albanians were wounded, they all cried 'Viva il Duce.' It's good color stuff too, to talk about their white, flowerpot fezzes. You know, the idea of the Catholic Moslem world fighting side by side. Don't forget that Mussolini is the Defender of Islam."

More discouraged than ever, Reynolds retired to the bedroom that had been given him and, after drowning one by one in a porcelain washbasin all the bedbugs that speckled his sheets, went to sleep. Early in the morning, he was awakened by an air-raid siren and, slipping on his boots, trousers, and sweater, ran out into the street to see what was happening. Eight Greek planes were dropping bombs on the airfield two miles away. Reynolds was soon bowled over by hundreds of Albanians who were tearing panic-stricken down the streets, seeking refuge in air shelters that had been dug out of the neighboring mountainside. When he was able to pick himself up, Reynolds saw that everything in the street had been flattened to the ground. It was as though a hurricane had passed over. Vegetable stalls, huckster wagons, and mule carts were strewn together in a jigsaw puzzle of wreckage. These were the heroic Albanians that Lorusso had told Italian correspondents to describe as fighting so bravely for the Italians. After the air raid ended, Reynolds found Lorusso in his room, shaving. Reynolds said that the air raid seemed to have been rather effective.

"Yes," Lorusso said. "They went right for the barracks. And you know why? Because the entire Greek Consulate staff in Argirokastron was a bunch of spies. When they left just an hour before the war started, they took with them all the plans of this town. But we managed to bring down four of the eight planes."

Reynolds said he would like to motor out and see a few of them.

"What a waste of time!" Lorusso said. "You have a story. Four out of eight shot down. They all crashed in the mountains, and it would take hours on muleback to reach them."

Fortunately, Lorusso was not shaving to go to the front. He had just learned by telephone from Tirana that His Excellency Benini, Foreign Office Undersecretary for Albanian Affairs, had arrived in Tirana.

"I am leaving right away," Lorusso said. "I must see His Excellency and tell him how well we are doing. You will have to look after yourselves for the next few days."

It was welcome news to the Italian correspondents, who all wanted to see some fighting. Immediately, a trip without Lorusso was jubilantly organized to the Janina sector. We made faster time than before. The rain had stopped. Most of the blown-up bridges had been replaced by military pontoons, and the dynamited gaps in the road had been filled in with stones and bricks from the walls of Greek farmhouses which had been torn down for that purpose.

General Sebastiano Visconte Prasca, in charge of all operations in Greece, was returning from the front. He halted his car and spoke to the Italian correspondents, who, as usual, didn't ask any questions. He said:

"We are going much faster now that the rain has cleared up. We were delayed by the Greeks' blowing up their bridges and roads, but we have repaired all the damages done. Naturally, there is still much to be done. I am confident there is nothing to cause worry."

Reynolds thought that he detected expressions of surprise on the faces of the Italian correspondents. They had interpreted Prasca's few words as meaning that the campaign was not running smoothly. Only Italians can realize the dire import that is contained in the efflorescence of Italian diction.

As the party approached the front, Reynolds was again baffled by the lack of soldiers on all sides. There were only groups of a few hundreds each gathered here and there. The number of soldiers was even less as they came within range of Greek artillery fire, which got heavier as the afternoon wore on, and all the correspondents had to seek cover in roadside ditches. One shell landed close to Reynolds and took off the arm of an Italian soldier lying a few yards away. Reynolds could see three soldiers with white, flowerpot fezzes running to the rear. They were shouting something in Albanian. Reynolds asked the Italian correspondent next to him what they were saying. The Italian replied, "They're crazy. They say the Greeks are coming." He jumped up and tried to intercept them. He knocked down the leading one, saying in Italian, "You pigs of misery, it's only artillery fire. Get back to your posts." They just kept on running.

As though trying to counteract the bad impression that Reynolds must have received, the Italian said that he was going to drive his automobile down the road to a point where it was possible to see the Greek soldiers defending Janina from its mountain ramparts. Reynolds, who was certainly not keen on any such expedition, nevertheless felt compelled, as a result of national pride, not to appear afraid and accepted the invitation. Driving at maximum speed, the Italian correspondent suddenly brought the automobile to a stop. A machine-gun bullet had crashed through the engine. In two seconds, Reynolds and the Italian were out of the car and serpentining themselves to a shell hole. Abandoning the car, they crawled back more than two miles to where the main group of Italian journalists had been left.

The trip was a revelation. It showed that the Italians had launched an attack without adequate preparation. The entire advance had been stopped by a bit of artillery fire and a few machine guns. It seemed ridiculous that Mussolini would have attempted to invade a country like Greece without bringing up at least several hundred thousand troops. And yet Reynolds was convinced from what he saw that there could not have been more than thirty thousand Italian troops on the Greek front. Perhaps the explanation was to be found in the false statement of Lorusso that nonexistent Greek villagers of occupied towns greeted their Italian invaders with flowers, bread, and wine. Eleanor, back in Rome, in the meantime had unearthed the real story but couldn't send it.

The Greek invasion was a Ciano idea. In collusion with Jacomoni, one of his favorite yes-men, Ciano had worked out a plan that appeared logical on paper. He had already successfully convinced Mussolini that Italian intervention in Spain would win the war for Franco and lower Anglo-French prestige. Now the plan that he submitted to the Duce was that the Greeks could be bought as easily as street peddlers. Mussolini checked with Grazzi, Italian Minister in Athens, who agreed that a lot of money and few troops would be sufficient for an Italian parade into Athens. Members of the Chigi Palace told Eleanor that Greek government leaders had accepted the bribe, but didn't carry out their part of the bargain. One Foreign Office official said, "The Greeks accepted many millions of lire and then used the money to fight us."

This and similar statements may have been mere Fascist alibis, but there was no doubt that Reynolds, as the only non-Italian correspondent in Greece with the Italian army at the beginning of the war, could see that Mussolini was counting on some sort of diplomatic coup for the annexation of Greece. Certainly, he could never have expected to conquer Greece with thirty thousand soldiers. The only advance that the Italians made was over territory abandoned by the Greeks as untenable — between the Metaxas Line and the Albanian border. Once the Italians approached that line, they ceased advancing and, after a brief pause, began retreating. The Ciano plot had failed.

After his baptism of fire on the Greek front, Reynolds wrote a series of articles which he sent to Eleanor by an Italian correspondent who returned to Rome from Argirokastron. Immediately after these dispatches appeared in the New York papers, the American correspondents in Rome were sent nasty messages demanding to know why they too were not at the front. A number of them immediately went to Rocco and protested that they were being discriminated against. But their protests were nothing compared to those of the German correspondents, who, as we learned later, took the matter up with their Embassy. Ambassador von Mackensen then protested to Ciano, stating that it was most embarrassing that correspondents of Italy's Axis partner should not be at the Greek front while the correspondent of a potential enemy, America, was there. That was enough, and six days after arriving at Argirokastron, Reynolds was expelled from Albania and Greece on Foreign Office orders transmitted to Lorusso, who had returned from his conference in Tirana with Benini.

"That's all very well," Reynolds told Lorusso, "but how do I leave? On foot?"

"That's your problem," Lorusso said.

Reynolds then proceeded not to find any means of transportation away from the Greek front. Two days after the order of expulsion, and Reynolds was still in Argirokastron, Lorusso received a Foreign Office order saying, "Get Packard back to Rome tomorrow. This is imperative."

Lorusso got busy. A special car was given to Reynolds to take him to Tirana, where a place on the daily airplane was found for him by canceling the reservation of a Black Shirt general. The Italians couldn't afford to offend the Germans.

On the return journey to Italy, Reynolds found that the Greeks were already taking the initiative. They were not only bombing by airplane points in Albania, but also Italian Adriatic ports through which Fascist reinforcements and supplies were being dispatched to the Greek front. As the plane in which Reynolds traveled arrived over Brindisi, Greek planes appeared in the sky. Reynolds could see three of them dropping bombs on the Brindisi railway station. Even as he looked, two Greek chasers, or maybe they were English, began machine-gunning his plane. It was a queer sensation: wishing the Greeks or English success, yet at the same time hoping to escape alive. The Italian pilot power-dived and hovered around the airfield at an altitude of less than one hundred feet, skimming treetops and chimney pots in order not to be a target for the raiding planes. It was impossible to land for at least another half-hour because Italian chasers were constantly taking off and returning. Reynolds was delayed a day in Brindisi until the railway could resume traffic.

As soon as Reynolds arrived in Rome, he was summoned before Rocco for what looked like certain expulsion. Rocco assumed his most austere manner and reprimanded Reynolds for having violated military regulations by going to Albania. He himself hadn't yet learned the ruse that was used and tried to get out of Reynolds how he managed to do it. Reynolds refused to give any information, and the incident was closed. Obviously, the Italians did not want to expel Reynolds, for he would then have been free to send the real story, unhampered by Italian censorship, of the puny forces which the Italians had in the field. Never in his life had Reynolds so wished to be expelled from any country.

It wasn't long before the tenacity of Greek resistance and the energy of Greek raids into the Italian lines made the Fascist fables about Greek villagers and their gifts of bread, wine, and flowers, welcoming Italian soldiers as "liberators" who were going to free the country from "British tyranny," look absurd. The propagandists floundered about uncertainly, looking for a way out, until November 18, three weeks after the war started, when Mussolini made another speech from his Palazzo Venezia balcony and gave a new twist to the official Italian attitude toward the Greeks. Said the Duce:

"After a long period of patience, we have finally torn the mask from a country guaranteed by Great Britain — our subtle enemy, Greece. One thing must be said, and it may surprise certain Italians who are not mentally living in our times. It is this: that the Greeks hate Italians as they hate no other people. It is a hatred that appears at first inexplicable, but it is a genuine, deep, and incurable hate common to all classes in cities and villages, in the higher and lower classes everywhere in Greece. Its reasons are mysterious.

"On this hatred, which may be called grotesque, the policy of Greece has been based throughout recent years. It consisted of complete political complicity with Great Britain. Nor could it have been otherwise, seeing that the King is English, the political caste is English, the stock exchange and the national purse are English."

From then on, Fascist propaganda was on the right track — the Greeks cordially hated the Italians and the Italians hated them in return.

It was significant that the Duce, contrary to his invariable custom when declaring war, made no speech about the Greek invasion until three weeks after it had started. It was the strongest tangible evidence that the Fascists had tried to bribe the Greeks and believed that they had succeeded. That was why the Duce did not speak when the war first started; he did not want to commit himself. Had the Greek government acceded to the Italian ultimatum after only a protest or a weak show of resistance, as they were supposed to, then Mussolini would have made a speech about the noble Greeks being a sister Mediterranean nation and consequently recognizing the justice of the Italian contention that the Mediterranean must be rid of British domination. The Duce couldn't risk speaking about a secret political plot.

Although, when the Italians realized the Greeks intended to fight, they rushed reinforcements to their token army of thirty thousand which had started the campaign, it was already too late, and by December 6 the Italian retreat had become such a military disgrace that somebody's political head had to fall. Logically, it should have been Ciano's, since he was the author of the plot to buy over Greece. But the Duce was still fond of his son-in-law and was not disposed to sacrifice a political collaborator on whose loyalty he felt he could rely more than on anyone else's.

It was a good opportunity to get rid of one whose disapproval of the Duce's military adventures and general hostility to Fascism had long been an irritation to Mussolini. Consequently, on December 6, it was announced that Marshal Pietro Badoglio, Chief of the General Staff, had resigned "at his own request." Two days later, the Chief of the Naval Staff, Admiral Cavagnari, and two other prominent admirals also resigned.

Badoglio was replaced by General Ugo Cavallero, a soldier of small military reputation but large political pull — he was the father-in-law of Jacomoni. Even with all the troops Mussolini was willing to put at his disposal, it was some time before Cavallero was able to stem the tide of Greek invasion, and by that time the Greeks held nearly a quarter of southern and eastern Albania, including Koritza, Argirokastron, Elbasan, and Port Edda. The furious Fascists, seeking to alibi themselves, heaped further blame on Badoglio and for the first time in years allowed a hint of internal disunity to appear in the Italian press. This was when Farinacci, powerful Fascist political boss of Cremona, printed an attack on Badoglio in his newspaper, *Regime Fascista*. The editorial said:

"The new Chief of the General Staff, General Ugo Cavallero, is re-establishing the situation in Albania. The enemy attacks have been broken by our heroic resistance, and there is every hope of an imminent recovery.

"A certain person [Badoglio] is frequenting salons and hunting preserves of groups who accepted favors from him, saying he did not support the undertaking and that he demanded more divisions to do it. It should be known that this person actually undertook the task with the forces already existing in Albania and made no qualification. Everything else is contrary to the truth.

"It is infantile to put the responsibility on the political command when it is more than clear that the military conduct of the war solely concerns technical organization.

"The government did not hold back money from the army. It provided 170 billion lire for preparations. Hence, it had the right to expect the armed forces to be in a state of full war efficiency when the critical test came."

This attack in the public press on Italy's leading general was so unprecedented that all Italy vibrated with excitement. It was common gossip that Badoglio had opposed the Greek venture from the beginning, so no one believed Farinacci's contention that the

Marshal had said he had sufficient troops in Albania to carry out the invasion. Besides, the general in charge of Italian forces in Albania at the beginning of the invasion had been Visconte Prasca, an officer-politician who had been military attaché in several capitals of Europe, with practically no war experience, and almost the last man Badoglio would have chosen.

Next day, New York Times correspondent Cianfarra burst into our office and exclaimed: "Gee whiz, do you know the lid's likely to blow off any moment? The professional army is furious over the way Badoglio's been treated, and they say they're ready to revolt if Badoglio will lead them. It's touch and go whether Mussolini can pull through this."

Down in the Stampa Estera, the bar buzzed with rumors. Said a Scandinavian correspondent:

"If there is a revolt, the Germans will take over Italy. They can't afford to let the British move in while the Italians are fighting among themselves." And a Hungarian correspondent observed:

"With a revolution going on in Italy, the British wouldn't have any trouble taking all Libya." (The first British offensive in Libya was just starting.)

Allen Raymond, Herald Tribune correspondent, grinning hugely at the prospect of a whopping big story surpassing anything he had thus far found in Rome, said:

"Looks like I might have a real story to send the boys on Fortieth Street one of these days," and Eleanor, with the bitterness of many years' struggle with the censors, replied:

"Yes, if you can get it out."

Nevertheless, the bare possibility of being able to send a small part of the news — if the revolt occurred — was enough to keep us all in a state of alarm for several days. The correspondents for individual newspapers had less tension — they at least had dead lines, after which they could sleep peacefully. But the agency men, including ourselves, who were responsible for the rapid transmission of news immediately after it happened, twenty-four hours a day, hardly dared to go to bed. For is not the middle of the night the traditional time for revolutionaries to strike — to seize telegraph and telephone centers, police headquarters, government and ministry buildings? And in the upheaval of revolution, there was always the chance that an errant telephone call might get through; that some lucky correspondent might, through somebody's mistake, be able to get the first world-shattering news out. Such things frequently happen, and any correspondent would be willing to risk the consequences for the sake of such a scoop. But the half-expected never occurred. In a few days' time, word got around that Badoglio had retired to a small village, where he was living quietly in a comfortable villa but seeing no one. At the time, we did not know whether it was prudence or patriotism that had determined his course. It did not seem unlikely that prudence was the reason; Badoglio was no longer young and he had always been cautious by nature; his opposition to the Duce's adventures in Ethiopia, Spain, and Greece proved that. And there was no certainty that his revolt, if launched, would prove successful. The army officers might be with him, but many of the rank-and-file soldiers were Fascist-controlled.

On the other hand, he could be certain that if he plunged Italy into civil war, the results would be fatal as far as her powers to resist occupation by Germany or Britain were concerned. To a patriotic, though anti-Fascist, Italian, it probably seemed that the continuance of the Fascist regime was a lesser evil than the loss of Italy's national independence.

Not until three or four weeks later did we learn for certain that it was loyalty to his country that caused Badoglio to make the choice he did between rebellion and retirement. We found out then that Farinacci's unjust editorial had stung him to reply and that certain copies of this reply were going the rounds of anti-Fascist circles to whom Badoglio wished to explain his attitude in the face of the public obloquy into which he had fallen. After much sub-rosa negotiation, we finally managed to procure a copy of this letter and attempted to send it as part of a general review of the Greek campaign, but of course the censors prevented us from doing so. Not only that; the Italian authorities subjected us to a severe cross-examination as to how we obtained a copy of this letter, which they did not attempt to deny was genuine. Had it not been for the Italian habit of regarding foreign journalists as being very nearly in the same privileged class as diplomats, we might have got into serious trouble with the OVRA. Eleanor carefully guarded the document and, when interned, kept it hidden on her person, succeeding, finally, in smuggling it out on the diplomatic train. In this letter Badoglio wrote:

"Signor Farinacci:

"I break the silence which I have imposed on myself because the criticism to which you, Signor Farinacci, have subjected me goes beyond myself and affects the whole Italian General Staff. This criticism, at a moment when discord of any kind should be avoided for the sake of the nation, has undermined, both at home and abroad, the work and reputation of the Italian General Staff. The facts which prove what the Italian General Staff actually did must of necessity be kept secret. I know, however, that someday the light of history will expose certain despicable machinations.

"Above all, I want to state, Signor Farinacci, that I do not consider that you have any right to pose as the supreme critic of the Italian General Staff — nor, for that matter, has any member of the faction which you head and which is so busy propagating un-Italian ideas. You know quite well, Signor Farinacci, that the criticism you have made has nothing whatever to do with the General Staff; and if by chance you do not know it — and I should be exceedingly surprised at such ignorance on your part — you might go to Him Who [obviously meaning Mussolini] is in a position to give you full information about the whole matter. You should also read the contents of my many reports made at the secret sittings of the War Council [presided over by Il Duce]. These reports show beyond the shadow of a doubt what were my plans — fully supported by the whole General Staff — on the strategic and political conduct of the present war."

With regard to Italo-German collaboration, Badoglio frankly wrote, "Without disclosing anything, I may say that all my directives were inspired by the concept of independent action. Collaboration? Yes. Submission? Never."

Charging that Fascist politicians had meddled in military matters that were not their concern, Badoglio continued:

"The General Staff should be left completely free and have full responsibility for its decisions. It should not be hampered by interference of any nature. A General Staff such as ours cannot and must not be tied to any political millstone. In the art of war, the freedom of movement is an essential factor; and you, Signor Farinacci, fully understand to what I refer when I make this statement."

To the anti-Fascist group of Italians who discussed this letter with us, the foregoing sentence referred to Badoglio's stand against political attempts to annex Greece without proper military preparation. He had defied both Mussolini and Ciano, telling them that their scheme to bribe the Greeks was a Ciano chimera and that at least several hundred thousand soldiers should be concentrated in Albania before any such venture be undertaken.

"The General Staff should not be encumbered by people like you, to whom dubious advisory posts have been entrusted," the letter continued, "people who, like you, in the final analysis reveal themselves incompetent because they are ignorant of military matters. The wearing of a uniform of a general, Signor Farinacci, does not make a general [Farinacci was always fond of appearing in the uniform of a Black Shirt general, although in the army his rank would have been that of a captain]. The appropriation of astronomical sums of money which are then doled out with an eyedropper is not enough to win a war. When a nation intends to fight, as Italy did, it is first of all necessary that the industry of the country be slowly and painstakingly converted to war production. A nation which goes to war must foresee as far as humanly possible every possibility of a setback in order to cope with it with her OWN strength. It is not intelligent to count on the help of an ally [Germany] and it is not wise to rely entirely on the aid of this ally. Such a leaning on others can only lead to further tragic consequences for which the nation itself must pay.

"All the rest, Signor Farinacci, is an ignoble plot directed against me — and you know it. My patriotism and my earnest desire to obey an order from my King prevent me from giving you further particulars. This is not the moment to spread discord among our brave people, to whom I wish a splendid future.

[Signed] "Pietro Badoglio."

By going into retirement and refraining from any public declaration, which he knew full well would never be printed in the Fascist press, Badoglio prevented the breach that his resignation had caused between the regular army and the Black Shirt Militia from widening into an armed clash. The regular army, however, continued passively hostile to the Black Shirts.

Despite the crisis they had just been through, the Fascists could not refrain from making political capital out of the Greek war. Once the Greek advance had been halted, and the Fascists got over their panicky fear that they might lose all Albania, they turned the Albanian battlefield into a Roman circus in which some of the leading Fascist politicians performed. In all, nine Cabinet ministers left their desks in Rome to fight in the Greek war. It was part of the histrionics of Fascism. No matter how competent or useful a minister might be at his post, he was supposed to take time out to prove himself a warrior.

The three most important figures to go were Ciano himself, Ettore Muti, Secretary General of the Fascist party, and Farinacci, Minister of State without portfolio. The other six were Alessandro Pavolini, Minister of Popular Culture; Renato Ricci, Minister of Corporations; Giuseppe Gorla, Minister of Public Works; Giuseppe Bottai, Minister of Education; Giovanni Venturi, Minister of Communications; Raffaelo Riccardi, Minister of Trade and Foreign Exchange. Most of them, however, commuted back and forth like suburbanites between their offices in Rome and the Greek front, with the result that they were neither soldiers nor statesmen.

The only one who achieved any glory out of this was Muti, who had already distinguished himself in all of Italy's previous wars. Indeed, Muti owed his political advancement to the fact that he was one of the few genuine Fascist war heroes and was frequently described as a man of "little brains but much liver." Mussolini favored Muti greatly for a while because so far as his war record was concerned he represented all that the Duce wanted Italians to be. But his incapacity as an administrator eventually led to his disappearance from politics. Mussolini once said, "If only Muti and Ciano could be combined into one man."

Muti had a narrow escape in Greece, when his plane was so riddled with bullets from Greek chasers that all three motors were damaged. He managed to fight off his pursuers and make a forced landing in a lonely spot in Greek territory. After twenty-four hours of work, he was able to get one motor sufficiently repaired so that he could take off and finally landed at the airfield in Tirana. Of his crew of five, two were dead and one was wounded.

Ciano also led several bombing expeditions but soon got fed up with the social dullness of airdromes and asked to return to his desk at the Chigi Palace. Mussolini, however, would not let him do so, apparently thinking it good for public morale to have the Duce's son-in-law on the fighting front. Ciano therefore went into a sulk and spent several weeks perfecting his golf strokes, using the airfield at Tirana as a practice links. Finally, he won out and returned permanently to his desk in the Chigi Palace.

In early spring, Italy had redeemed a good deal of the Albanian territory she had lost to Greece, but she still was so far from conquering Greece itself that it was obvious to everyone that she must have help from Germany if she was not to be bogged down indefinitely in the Hellenic peninsula. From all we could hear in Rome, the conquest of Yugoslavia was more or less incidental to the conquest of Greece. When Hitler told the German General Staff that he planned to invade Greece in order to clean up the Grecian war once and for all, the General Staff asserted that they could not conscientiously endorse this plan unless the German flank was protected from a possible assault by Yugoslavia. Hitler and Mussolini then made a political effort to ensure Yugoslavia's noninterference by getting Yugoslavia to become a member of the Tripartite Pact. Political pressure caused the then Yugoslav government to sign the pact, but when the pact was repudiated by the Yugoslav public, particularly the Serbs, the German General Staff decided that the only way to prevent Yugoslavia from remaining a menace to Axis plans of conquest was to occupy it.

The brunt of the attack upon Yugoslavia was borne by the German soldiers, but the Italians quickly moved into those parts on which they had revindications dubiously based on colonization of the Dalmatian coast by traders from the Venetian Republic in centuries gone by. The Italians encountered very little opposition, as the Yugoslavs had mostly retired from these sections into the mountains, where they made their big stand against the Germans, leaving the plains and seacoasts undefended. The Italian army which marched into northern Yugoslavia from the province of Venice suffered, according to official figures, only thirty-four killed, seventy-three wounded, and thirty-one missing. With this minimum loss, Italy was able to annex most of Slovenia and the northern Dalmatian coast. She also occupied part of Croatia, which she did not annex but chose instead to put up as a puppet state. On the Albanian-Yugoslav front, the Italian casualties were somewhat higher, but there was no real opposition to the Italian occupation of Montenegro and Cattaro, where they caught the British Minister to Yugoslavia, Sir Ronald Campbell, and his entire diplomatic staff. Despite their successes in Yugoslavia, however, the Italians still were unable to make any headway against the Greeks and were obliged to swallow the bitter humiliation of seeing their German ally occupy almost the entire country.

As soon as the Greek war ended, the Press Ministry hastily organized a conducted tour aimed at showing foreign correspondents how hard and well the Italian soldiers had fought. Little Capomazza was put in charge, and the party left Rome's Termini Station at ten P.M. The party comprised nineteen foreign correspondents: three Americans, Cianfarra, Massock, and Reynolds; one Jap, one Bulgarian, one Russian, one Spaniard, one Swede, and eleven Germans. Capomazza, who at this time was high in ministerial rank, was nevertheless only a second lieutenant, yet his chief assistant was a regular army major and his other assistant a second lieutenant. We arrived in Brindisi at noon the next day, but instead of embarking immediately for Albania we were taken on a rubberneck tour of Brindisi and didn't go aboard our ship until nearly midnight. We were surprised that fifty young Italian girls were aboard despite the danger of travel in the Adriatic, where British submarines and mines were still playing havoc with Italian shipping. Reynolds asked Capomazza who these girls were. They were too elegantly dressed to be the wives of colonials and yet they did not act like the wives of officers or of government officials. Several of them had guitars and they sang and danced among themselves on the upper deck. Aside from the journalists and these girls, all the other passengers were officers and Black Shirt officials.

"Don't worry about them," Capomazza replied. "You think about the stories you have to write during the next few days. You American correspondents are always asking about things that don't concern you."

By this time the curiosity of Massock, Cianfarra, and Reynolds became acute, and they decided to approach one of the girls. It was quite easy to make her acquaintance, and within five minutes she told us her name was Giuliana and she was looking forward to the big money she expected to make in Greece. She even intimated she wasn't averse to making a little bit extra on the trip. We soon learned from her the whole story. The fifty girls were Fascist prostitutes who had been recruited from different cities in Italy to console the Italian soldiers of occupation who were to remain behind. Giuliana made it quite clear that it wasn't everyone in her profession who was acceptable for such a post.

"Oh, no," she said, "we have to be approved by the party. You know how soldiers talk, and the girls they meet should be trustworthy."

The next morning all the correspondents were on deck early. Even the German correspondents showed their surprise that our ship was part of a convoy. It meant that the British were much stronger in the Adriatic, even after the Greek war had ended, than anybody had supposed. There were at least two destroyers, four torpedo boats, and two observation airplanes overhead. In the harbor of Durazzo a smokestack was all that could be seen of a freighter that had been sunk by a British submarine. The congestion in Durazzo harbor also caused comments among the Germans. To go ashore we had to pass over two other ships being unloaded. The first off were the prostitutes, followed by the journalists.

Capomazza then unwittingly uncovered a news story. He proudly escorted us for breakfast to the best hotel in Durazzo, just recently built. As we passed through the lobby into the dining room, Reynolds was astounded to see thirty-some English people sitting around talking and playing bridge. It was like walking into the Savoy Grill, London. Capomazza became suddenly twitchy and hurried us into the empty dining room.

"Who are those English-speaking people out there?" Reynolds asked Capomazza.

"You American correspondents make me tired," Capomazza said. "This is a tour to show you battlefields, and you keep worrying about other things. Come on, now, and have a cup of coffee."

A few minutes later, Reynolds pretended to go to the lavatory and slipped around through a back hallway into the lobby. He went over to two men who were talking in English and explained that he was an American correspondent and was anxious to find out who they were.

"We aren't permitted to say anything to the press, old man," one of them said. "You'll have to speak to someone else." And they walked away. Reynolds spoke to several other groups, with the same negative result, before Capomazza appeared and ordered him back into the dining room. By this time Capomazza realized that it was no use trying to conceal the facts and he rapped a cup with a spoon for silence.

"I feel I must inform you as a result of the interest shown by the American correspondents that the group of people in the lobby of the hotel whom you saw as you came in are members of the British Legation in Belgrade. They are my enemies and the enemies of the German correspondents. It is not possible, therefore, for the Italian press officers or German correspondents to fraternize with them, but if any of the representatives of neutral or nonbelligerent countries wish to speak to them, I give you permission, but remember it is solely on your own initiative and has nothing whatsoever to do with the Italian Press Bureau."

Massock, Cianfarra, and Reynolds raced to the doorway and tried to find Sir Ronald Campbell. Sir Ronald, however, saw us first and disappeared through a back door into his bedroom upstairs. The English were suspicious of us and refused to say a single word about how they happened to be in Durazzo.

"Were you forced to come over here?" one Embassy Secretary asked us.

We tried to explain to him that we were American newspaper correspondents and that we were anxious to have the British version of their capture rather than the Italian. It was of no use. Nothing we could say would induce them to speak or to take our cards to Sir Ronald. But it was a story; and the three of us were determined to run it down. We probably would never have learned a thing, however, if Cianfarra had not, by chance, run into an Italian acquaintance of his as we were walking down the street to awaiting autobusses. He was one of those strange Italians who had mysterious posts in Albania. Without any hesitancy he told us the inside story, as he had learned it direct from Jacomoni. Briefly it was:

Sir Ronald with a group from the British Legation and members of various British missions in Belgrade had succeeded in fleeing the German onslaught on Yugoslavia and making their way in a heterogeneous column of private automobiles to the Adriatic port of Cattaro, where, by prearrangement, the more important members of the party were to be picked up by a British submarine. But just as they arrived at the Cattaro docks, Italian troops started marching into the town. The British submarine almost simultaneously came to the surface and signaled to Sir Ronald. A young Italian captain, who was in charge of the Italian soldiers, was persuaded by Sir Ronald to carry on negotiations with the submarine commander. By wigwagging back and forth, the submarine and the Italians agreed to make an exchange of officer-hostages. An Italian lieutenant was exchanged for an English mate. Probably Sir Ronald would have achieved the greatest diplomatic victory of his career — convincing his enemies to permit him and a certain number of his colleagues to depart — if at that moment a squadron of German planes had not appeared overhead, threatening to bomb the submarine. The submarine immediately submerged to save itself and disappeared with the Italian officer on board. An Italian general then arrived on the scene, and Sir Ronald and his party were finally taken in Italian autobusses to Durazzo to await an exchange agreement.

The exchange was delayed for almost two months, as we learned later from Foreign Office contacts, because the Italians refused to release Sir Ronald until they got back their lieutenant-hostage who had in the meantime been taken to England and placed in a prison camp.

That evening in Tirana the Albanian Premier, Shevket Verlaci, received the journalists and made an innocuous speech about the ties of amity binding Italy and Albania. There was a chance later, however, to get him off in a corner and talk to him somewhat privately. He told Massock and Reynolds that Greater Albania as he conceived of it, following the Greek-Yugoslav wars, would include parts of Montenegro and southern Serbia as well as large slices of Greece. This obviously conflicted not only with Italian plans regarding Montenegro, but also with Germany's plans for a separate satellite Serbia and with Bulgaria's desires to annex that part of southern Yugoslavia to the east of Albania. Reynolds sent the story that same night, or, rather, he delivered it to Capomazza, who forwarded it, with other stories, by airplane to the Press Ministry in Rome for relay later to the respective offices. The censorship was being done in Rome. Eleanor never received Reynolds' interview with Premier Verlaci; the Rome censors quickly killed it; they did not like their Albanian puppet leader giving out his own ideas about Albanian greatness.

En route to the Greek battlefields, we arrived by nightfall at Port Edda, where troops were being embarked for Corfu, which had just been taken the day before by a band of ten Arditi (Fascist shock troops) who had arrived by airplane. The German correspondents immediately wanted to go to Corfu, and Capomazza arranged for the party to leave with the Italian expeditionary force. We traveled on a small tanker jammed with mules and about one thousand soldiers. The German correspondents immediately occupied in a Blitzkrieg rush the tiny mess saloon, with the result that Massock, Cianfarra, and Reynolds, as well as the other non-German correspondents, found themselves down with the mules. Cianfarra, who was ever the great little fixer of the American group, proceeded to try to ameliorate our condition. Unable to reach the captain himself, he talked to the first mate and convinced him that the first mate's cabin should be turned over to the three American correspondents. The three of us went there and stretched out comfortably on the bunk and two easy chairs, while the mate's cabin boy brought us drinks.

Von Langen, looking in and seeing us comfortable, laughing and drinking, frowned and said, "How did you get a cabin to yourselves?"

"Cianfarra arranged it," Massock laughed.

The cabin boy was talkative as well as willing. He told us that the waters we were sailing through were dotted with mines and that there was a good chance of our hitting one. The three of us had on heavy colonial boots. In view of the conversation, it suddenly occurred to us that if the boat did go down, these boots would fill up with water and cause us to drown almost immediately.

"My boots pinch so I think I'll take them off and give my feet a rest," Reynolds said. Dick and Cianfarra soon thought up other excuses, and before long the three of us were down to our underclothes, ready to swim if need be.

The town of Corfu, once a famous tourist resort, was so battered that in parts it looked like a junk heap. Greek police without weapons were on point duty, and Greek soldiers and officers in uniform, but also unarmed, wandered miserably up and down the streets. Stores were open, but their shopwindows were bare of merchandise. The Greeks, spiritually depressed over their defeat, promenaded the streets like sleepwalkers. The Hotel d'Angleterre, one of the few buildings that had not been hit by bombs, was being used by the ten Italian Arditi. One of them proved to be Enrico Santamaria, the "Tunisian Henlein" whom Reynolds and Eleanor had met in Tunis. He told Reynolds that the airplane he came in first dropped pamphlets telling people on the island of Corfu that the Greek war had come to an end and that they should not resist any longer. They then landed at the airfield without any shots being fired, and the ten of them then took over the town without any trouble. Reynolds asked him why there was such a rush to take Corfu. He hesitated a moment, slightly embarrassed, and then said, "You know how Fascisti Arditi love adventure like that."

There was obviously something behind this foolhardy undertaking. Hiring a horse-drawn carriage, Reynolds set off on a tour of investigation. He went to a number of business establishments that obviously had catered to the tourist trade in bygone days and, introducing himself, talked informally about the war, business prospects, and the Italian bombings of the island. In all cases the Greeks told Reynolds that they were afraid the Italians would never give up Corfu of their own free will. They said the Italians valued Corfu because it was an important fortress guarding the entrance to the Adriatic and claimed it on the basis of Venetian traders who had once, back in the seventeenth century, settled there. Reynolds remembered then that Capomazza had only a few hours before said:

"Most of these Greeks in Corfu speak Italian because Italian for centuries was the commercial language of the Adriatic."

These Greek businessmen revealed that the day before the ten Italians arrived, the Mayor of Corfu, the Greek Orthodox Bishop of Corfu, and an army officer had set off in a small boat with the hope of surrendering the island to the Germans in northern Greece.

"We don't like the Germans," one Greek businessman told Reynolds. "I think we hate them probably worse than the Italians, but they never have had any territorial claims on Corfu, and we thought that if the Germans occupied our island, we would, perhaps, regain our independence from them eventually."

The Italians, through their spies in Corfu, had undoubtedly been informed of the departure of the three Greek delegates and hastened to send at any cost an aerial expedition that would take over the island nominally on behalf of Italy and thus beat the Germans. As a matter of fact, a boat of German naval officers did arrive five hours after ourselves, only to find they had come two days too late because the Italian flag was already flying over the City Hall.

The race between Italians and Germans to occupy sectors of Greek territory was not confined just to Corfu and the other islands in the Ionian Sea. One of the Italian generals who received us in southern Albania toward the end of our trip admitted that he had suffered terrific troop losses because of the speed at which he had been ordered to push ahead into Greece. He said he had received instructions to reach a certain bridgehead before the Germans got there, at no matter what cost in life. He explained that while the main body of his soldiers engaged the main body of the Greeks in that sector, he sent a flying column to fight its way through a more distant mountain pass that also led to the bridgehead. The column barely got there and was still fighting when the Germans arrived.

"But the Italian flag was up on the bridge first," he said grimly. "This mad rush, however, cost us at least two thousand casualties which we would not otherwise have suffered." After the general had taken leave of us and we were drinking coffee with the staff officers, Capomazza quietly whispered to Massock, Cianfarra, and Reynolds, "That speech was off the record. Don't even attempt to send it, I forbid you."

It was certainly the most outspoken criticism of Mussolini any of the correspondents had heard since the resignation of Badoglio. It showed that even despite the final Axis victory over Greece, the generals of the regular army still disapproved of Mussolini's political interference in military matters.

But with all the pressure that Mussolini and Cavallero put on the Italian army, it never succeeded in reaching even Janina, the sore point at which the Greeks began to shove back the Italians in the earlier part of the campaign. That race was won by the Germans. And when a number of correspondents asked Capomazza to take the party to Janina, he ruefully said, "The Germans are there and will permit only the correspondents from Berlin to visit the town."

REYNOLDS, AT AN EARLY HOUR IN THE MORNING, ARRIVED BACK IN Rome from his trip around the Italian battlefields in Greece and Albania and, finding Eleanor just waking up, ordered the maid to bring in the breakfast tea.

"No, *signore*, not tea," the maid protested. "There is a surprise for you. This morning we have coffee."

"It's the story of an ill-wind, I'm afraid," Eleanor said. She explained that our social-climbing cook, Francesca, who had more back-door connections with the *haute monde* in Rome than we had front-door relations, counted among her admirers the Italian chef at the ex-Yugoslav Legation.

"It's a shame, the position those poor Yugoslavs are in," Francesca said, bringing in two cups of coffee for us. She wouldn't trust them to the maid. "They were to be exchanged for the Italian diplomats in Belgrade, but, *Madonna mia*, the war ended so quickly that the exchange was never made and now they have no place to go. They are interned in their Legation with a police guard outside."

"Did you send the story?" Reynolds asked Eleanor.

"Of course I sent it," Eleanor snapped. "As best I could, with Italian censorship."

But Francesca was not to be interrupted, and she continued, "The Italian servants are allowed to go on working for them, but their cook, the one I know, says they cannot buy any more food in the markets because they cannot get their money out of the bank. So they decided to sell their coffee to foreigners, and I was able to buy some for *la signora*."

The truth then came out. Eleanor had bought twenty pounds of coffee at twelve dollars a pound.

"What! two hundred and forty dollars' worth of coffee!" Reynolds gasped.

Eleanor explained that besides helping out our friends, the Yugoslavs, we had actually made a good investment. The price on the Italian black bourse for coffee was fourteen dollars a pound, if it could be found. Coffee had not been sold in stores since the beginning of 1940, and our own carefully hoarded supply had given out more than a month before.

A day or two later we met Radenko Popovich, leading Yugoslav correspondent in Rome, with whom we had always been friendly. He was coming out of a barber shop, where he had been brought by two Italian detectives to have his hair cut. Popovich told us that it had finally been arranged for the members of the Yugoslav Legation to leave in a few days for Lisbon, from where they would continue to London and report to the Yugoslav government that had been set up there. He said that he and the two other Yugoslav correspondents would be permitted to leave with the Legation staff.

"If a Free Yugoslav volunteer army is formed, I'm going to join it," Popovich said in French, scowling defiantly at the two detectives, who, however, were paying no attention but talking to some girl a few yards away. "If not, I am going to try to get a visa for America. We Serbs must fight on alone. The other rats deserted us. My God, what did they want, those Croats and

Slovenes?" cried Popovich, who was himself pure Serb, and his smoldering Slav face darkened. "Do they think Nazi and Fascist rule will be better than what we gave them?"

The question contained the whole Yugoslav tragedy in a nutshell. It explained why Yugoslavia — which was, on paper, larger both as to territory and population and better armed than the Greeks — was not able to resist the German *Blitzkrieg* more than eleven days, while the Greeks, after previously fighting the Italians for over five months, were still battling the Reichswehr at that time in Crete. Greece was a homogeneous nation, while Yugoslavia was a heterogeneous state composed of seven different ethnic groups — Serbs, Slovenes, Croatians, Bosnians, Montenegrins, Herzogovinians, and Dalmatians — besides Italian, German, Hungarian, Rumanian, and Bulgarian minorities; and of this potpourri of nationalities, the Serbs had succeeded in gathering most of the political power of the country and had more or less imposed their rule on the other peoples. Everything was done by parliamentary procedure, but the Serbs usually had a majority in Parliament; also, the King, who had considerable power, was a Serb.

Thus it happened that when the great crisis came for Yugoslavia, her governmental structure fell apart like a mosaic that had come loose, and, though millions of Serbs like Popovich found it difficult to understand, many if not most of her minority populations stood passively by and watched the invaders sweep past them while the Serbs found themselves fighting almost alone. The Serbs then became suspicious of the Croats in Serbian territory and put most of them in concentration camps as possible fifth columnists.

The biggest nationality group next to the Serbs had been the Croats, whose political leader, Vladko Machek, had failed to support the Belgrade government in its rejection of the Tripartite Pact, until the eleventh hour, and then, apparently, he had done so contrary to the advice of his political supporters. At any rate, Machek had gone to Belgrade on the eve of the Axis invasion and thus played right into Axis hands, as he left the Croatian field clear for another and very different sort of leader.

This leader, Ante Pavelich, was a kind of Balkan Jesse James. Probably, like Jesse James, he had started out merely as a violent but fairly honest rebel who balked at certain local injustices, but, again like Jesse James, his life of rebellion had led him from violence to greater violence, until he had become little better than a murderer and assassin. A fierce fighter for Croatian independence, he organized a secret underground organization known as the Ustaschi, membership in which made a Croat liable to a long prison sentence under Yugoslav laws. As leader of this subversive group, Pavelich lived in hiding in Croatia for several years, but finally, to avoid capture, he fled to Italy in 1929. During the next five years, Yugoslav authorities charged him with being responsible for twenty-one political murders in Yugoslavia, and with maintaining, in Hungary and Italy, terrorist "training camps" where fanatical Croat followers were taught shooting, bomb throwing, dynamiting, and other forms of assassination and sabotage. The existence of the Hungarian camp seemed, later on, to have been fairly well proved, but the existence of the Italian one was more doubtful — it was likely that Mussolini was too cunning to expose himself to charges of complicity in permitting such a camp.

It was in November, 1934, that Pavelich, until then an obscure terrorist, suddenly burst into the limelight of world news when he organized and had some of his personally trained followers carry out the assassination of King Alexander of Yugoslavia when the King paraded through the streets of Marseille on an official visit to the French government. The French Sûreté quickly caught the conspirators on French soil and through them learned of Pavelich's authorship of the plot. The French feared the Yugoslavs would consider them guilty of criminal negligence for not having better protected King Alexander, so they made the most pressing demands on Mussolini for Pavelich's extradition. But Il Duce had no intention of surrendering such a resolute terrorist, for whom he was already making plans, and coolly refused the French extradition demands.

Mussolini had never pressed Italian claims on Yugoslavia as he had those on France, but he had long worked quietly to undermine the stability of the kingdom of Yugoslavia, once one of the bulwarks of French hegemony in eastern Europe. It was for this reason that he had sheltered Pavelich and, though he might not have been privy to the plot to murder Alexander, it certainly did not interfere with his plans, since it placed on the throne a child king supported by a weak regency. No opportunity to take advantage of this, however, occurred until the spring of 1941.

When the German war machine started rolling over Yugoslavia, Pavelich, a ruthless opportunist himself, was too astute to wait for Hitler to offer him Croatia; nor did Mussolini want him to wait. Again it was a race between Germans and Italians for war spoils. This time, Mussolini used his cunning. It was to be a contest not between *Blitzkrieg* armies, but between a single man and the German Panzers. Not lacking in courage, Pavelich risked his life to get there before the first German tank. It was a bold stroke, but, on the other hand, he knew better than anyone else how large and far-reaching was his underground Ustaschi organization — far more extensive and more powerful than the Yugoslav government had ever suspected. Consequently, shortly after dawn on April 10, 1941, Pavelich, who had gone part of the way by Italian plane, drove into Zagreb in a bulletproof car with the curtains drawn and went to the house of a well-to-do physician who was one of his Ustaschi lieutenants. With him he brought several thousand proclamations which had been printed in Italy and which his followers quickly pasted up on the walls of the buildings throughout Zagreb. The posters proclaimed Croatia's independence and said that Ante Pavelich was forming a provisional Cabinet. In a few hours, Pavelich then set up a government on Fascist lines and took a title that was the Croatian equivalent of "Duce" — "Poglavnik."

The Pavelich government, blessed by Mussolini, was thus entrenched in Zagreb when the Germans arrived the following day. Pavelich greeted the Nazi commander in the name of the Axis and assured the Germans that his government was capable of maintaining order. Mussolini had scored a point against Hitler. Pavelich had not been a terrorist for most of his life suddenly to change his character at this late date. He immediately organized a new green-shirted Ustaschi organization of youths, many of them only seventeen years of age. Armed with pistols and portable machine guns, these young killers made systematic searches of all the homes in Croatia, to smoke out every Serb opposing the Pavelich rule. It was death to those who took up arms against the new regime. And what deaths these young Ustaschis meted out! Two Italian officers, whom we knew personally, went to Zagreb on a brief mission shortly after the end of the German *Blitzkrieg* through Yugoslavia. On their return to Rome, they told us in the privacy of our home that all the Italians in Croatia were shocked at the atrocities. One of them said:

"I was in Spain and saw a lot of shooting of prisoners there by the Spaniards. But at least that was done without torture. In Zagreb, these young Ustaschis, most of whom have never had a sweetheart to soften them, have become sadists of the worst kind. When they catch a Serb in combat, they delight in torturing him. Slow death by bayonets, crucifixion, and burning are among their methods of revenge. Even castration is used."

The other one said, "But it is the independent Croatia that the Croatians have wanted. It is the Pavelich government that favors Rome more than Berlin. We must let them run their own country. We only fostered and supported the Pavelich government. What can we do? It would have been better had we occupied the country outright and not just sent troops to help out. The Italians have to stand by and watch Yugoslavs murder each other."

"And in the name of God," said the first officer, "never let anyone know that you have heard about these atrocities from us."

The Serbs who did not oppose the Pavelich regime, however, were merely rounded up and put into concentration camps for transfer to Serbia, they said. The Poglavnik's attitude toward the Serbs was similar to Hitler's toward the Jews. Pavelich wanted a Croatia populated one hundred per cent by Croats.

By a prearranged understanding, Mussolini accorded the Poglavnik a recognition of "independence" on April 15, and a month later Pavelich proceeded to fulfill his part of the agreement by begging King Victor Emmanuel to name one of his relatives King of Croatia. The last of the Croatian royal line had died out 850 years before.

The ceremony was held on the morning of May 18, 1941, in the Quirinal Palace. It was, strangely enough, a stag affair without even the Queen or any of the Princesses present. Reynolds was permitted to attend with other male American correspondents, who, in accordance with the stipulation of the press invitation, were all dressed in tails and white tie. Reynolds saw Pavelich, wearing an olive uniform and a green shirt and green tie, lead a procession of Croats down the center aisle of the Throne Room. His followers were dressed in the regional costumes of Croatia and were supposed, as a result of their varied and picturesque attire, to represent all classes of people. They ranged from soldiers in colorful Croat uniforms and bankers and industrialists in business suits to peasants in embroidered jackets, tight-fitting trousers, and clodhopper shoes. As he came near the raised dais on which the King and other members of the royal family were seated, Pavelich gave the Fascist salute. The King, rising, returned the salute.

Speaking in Italian, Pavelich begged King Victor Emmanuel to be so gracious as to name one of his family King of Croatia.

Mussolini was present, but stood to the right and several feet behind the tiny Emperor. Il Duce was not on the dais and took no part in the ceremony except as a prominent spectator. It was very much a royal-family show, in which King Victor Emmanuel played well his Fascist role.

The King thanked the Poglavnik for his tribute to the House of Savoy and named his cousin, the Duke of Spoleto, as the new King of Croatia.

It was Sunday, and there was no afternoon newspaper, but the next day the Italian press was enthusiastic about the part the Duke of Spoleto would have in the building up of the second

Roman Empire. Pictures of the ancient crown of Croatia were
unearthed from museums and encyclopedias, and it was said that
a copy would be made for the great coronation ceremony which
would take place in Banjaluka, which was to become the new
capital. The crown was described as a wreath of gold clover leaves
surmounted by a cross and an apple. Spoleto was going to take
the title of Tomaslav II, after the first Croatian king, Tomaslav I.
Banjaluka was a tiny town, but the new Italian king was to build
an entirely new capital there, with a stately royal palace.

We immediately applied to the Ministry of Unpopular Culture
for permission to travel to Banjaluka to attend the coronation and
asked for reserved seats for the ceremony itself. The ceremony was
planned for a month or two later, but the outbreak of civil war
in Croatia caused it to be postponed indefinitely as it was feared
that the new King might be assassinated. The Duke of Spoleto
himself, who was a great frequenter of what little remained of
Roman night life, confided to friends of ours in a speak-easy
cabaret that he was in no hurry to go to such a dull and boring
place as Croatia, even if it were safe. He is reported to have
told the Pope that he accepted the Croatian throne only under
pressure of Mussolini through Victor Emmanuel, and added
to His Holiness, "It's like a millstone around my neck."

The same day that the Duke of Spoleto accepted kingship of
Croatia, his older brother, the Duke of Aosta, surrendered to the
British at Amba Alagi. The announcement, however, was not
made by the Italian press until forty-eight hours later, in order not
to have bad news detract from official rejoicing. It was the begin
ning of the end of Italy's hopes for the Ethiopian empire. All
Italians knew it, even though a few garrisons were still holding
out in western Ethiopia.

There was no more eloquent testimony to the Duce's initial conviction that the war would be short than the capitulation of the
East African empire. Isolated from the Italian motherland by
thousands of miles of British-controlled land and sea, it was
obvious to anybody that Ethiopia and its flanking colonies of

Eritrea and Italian Somaliland could only defend themselves for a comparatively short time against attack. The colonies were more or less self-sufficient as far as food was concerned, but they were completely dependent on overseas shipments for all kinds of weapons and ammunition, as well as trucks, gasoline, and other war supplies. Not a single bullet could be manufactured in Ethiopia or transported there from Italy, once the Duce declared war on Britain. Ethiopia was very dear to the Duce — it was not only a large and virgin piece of territory that could be made to bloom and prosper by proper application of the energies of hard-working Italian peasants; it was also a symbol to the Duce of his first and flamboyantly successful defiance of the nations that wished to block Italian expansion. We feel sure he would never have gambled on the war if he had thought there was any real chance of losing Ethiopia.

In the summer of 1940 the side-show war in East Africa had begun rather promisingly for Italy. Under the Viceroy for Italian East Africa, the Duke of Aosta, cousin to King Victor Emmanuel, and the Vice-Governor General of East Africa, General Guglielmo Nasi, a talented career army man, the Italian army made its first important move on July 16, when it took the Dolo salient. This was a wedge-shaped bite of British Kenya territory that protruded between the southwestern border of Ethiopia and the northwestern border of Italian Somaliland. Its capture marked a gain of about four hundred square miles of territory and shortened the Italian fighting line by about two hundred miles. More important psychologically, it marked the drawing of first blood against England and therefore mightily elated the Fascist anti-British element in Italy.

General Nasi's next step was much more important. On August 4, right in the middle of the most imaginably unbearable heat of equatorial summer, he launched an offensive on British Somaliland and within sixteen days had captured the whole of it, obliging the British troops to withdraw in a minor Red Sea Dunkirk. General Nasi could easily have taken French Somaliland as well, but the terms of the French armistice forbade it. The capture of French Somaliland was to be left to the diplomats who would be charged with realizing Mussolini's ambition of giving Italian East Africa unbroken control of the African coast from the Eritrean-Sudanese border to Kenya.

In the early fall, General Nasi had advanced as far as one hundred and twenty miles into British Kenya and captured two strategically important towns in the Anglo-Egyptian Sudan. After that he was through. He had carried out his part of the program on the basis of a war that was to end by Christmas of 1940 at the latest. He not only could do no more; he could not defend what he had in a long-drawn-out European war. And he had wasted precious ammunition and other war materials on his offensive.

By the first of the year 1941 the tide had turned — the Italians found themselves ringed around with powerful enemy forces, and the British started taking back not only what they had lost but the rest of Italian-occupied East Africa as well. Ironically enough, the Italian colonies were doomed all the more quickly because of the splendid military roads that the Italians had built during their five years' sovereignty over Ethiopia. The British motorized corps rolled along these roads, and the Italian troops, short on gasoline as well as war materials by then, were quickly beaten in sector after sector. At one time in the spring of 1941, the British had as many as twelve fronts in Ethiopia all going at once. Italy had between sixty and eighty thousand white troops in East Africa at the start of the war, and perhaps twice that many native troops, but these numbers were quickly diminished as the British motorized troops cut off and surrounded detachments sometimes numbering several thousands in various sectors of the front.

The Duke of Aosta and General Nasi, fully realizing the impossibility of defending Ethiopia indefinitely, sought only to hold out as long as possible in a few strong points. They may have hoped that a miracle might eventually save Italian Ethiopia, but they also undoubtedly wished to occupy as many British troops as possible for as long as possible in order to divide English strength. After Addis Ababa and everything south of it had gone and the Italians had been driven from all of Eritrea except Assab, the Duke and General Nasi divided forces, one fortifying himself on the peak of Amba Alagi and its surrounding mountains, and the other preparing to stand siege at Gondar, which was also in a mountainous region. Between them were several garrisons entrenched at other points with natural fortifications.

The British attacked the Duke of Aosta's forces first. The Italian official communiqués on the East African fighting at this time adopted a fatalistic tone designed to break the news gradually to the public that the fight was hopeless, while at the same time painting in heroic colors the tenacity of the garrison's resistance. Because of his graciousness and moderation, the Duke had always been an extremely popular figure in Italy, and without a doubt his stand at Amba Alagi fired the imagination and enthusiasm of the Italian public as it had never been fired before throughout the entire war. When he was forced to surrender on May 18, there were real tears shed in Italy not only for the loss of Ethiopia but also for the Duke himself. The Italian newspapers reported at the time that the Duke, after offering to surrender, asked for twenty-four hours to carry out the wounded before handing over his able-bodied troops. The wounded were said to include more than half the garrison.

By June 21, the British had cleaned up the Italian centers of resistance at the Red Sea port of Assab and in the mountain sectors of Jimma. General Nasi, with five thousand white and five thousand native troops, held out in Gondar for five months more but was finally forced to capitulate on November 27, 1941, thus ending the last vestige of Italian domination in East Africa.

Even though in a British prison camp in Nairobi, Kenya, the Duke of Aosta continued to be a hero and a figure of gallantry to the Italian people, who could always be touched by the sight of an underdog struggling against hopeless odds. More than that, the Duke, whose aloofness from Fascism and all its disciples was

well known, began, as anti-Fascist feeling grew, to be looked on
as a symbol of all that was noble in anti-Fascism in Italy. His
acceptance of a mandate from the Duce to defend East Africa
did not detract from this feeling, since the public view was that
any patriotic Italian in his position would have done the same
thing. If ever there was a popular figure around whom the anti-
Fascist elements in Italy — whose numbers were ever increasing —
could have rallied, it was the Duke of Aosta. So legendary did
he become as a result of his resistance at Amba Alagi that anti-
Fascist Italians were ready to believe almost anything about him.
One report that was discussed for nearly a fortnight — not only
in cafés and on street corners, but also in legations and embassies
— was to the effect that the British had allowed him to return
to Italy with a proposal of peace. A number of the correspondents,
in order to get the reaction of the Press Ministry to this report,
submitted dispatches for censorship. In every case Rocco called
up the correspondent and told him that the message could not be
sent.

"Can we deny the report, then?" Reynolds asked.

"What a silly thing to deny," Rocco said. "It is not in keeping
with the serious character of foreign correspondents to send out a
denial of a rumor in order to spread the rumor itself."

Some of the Scandinavian correspondents believed that Rocco
did not want the report denied from Rome for fear that if the
British had been willing to talk peace, such a denial would have
prevented their doing so. Most of the American correspondents,
including ourselves, were inclined to regard it as another Fascist
trial balloon. Finally, the report, which had originated in Rome,
was published abroad, and the British themselves denied it
officially.

Practically all the non-Axis correspondents in Rome were agreed
at that time that the Duke of Aosta was the only Italian who
might have led an anti-Fascist uprising.

"Maybe the British made a mistake in capturing him," Allen

Raymond said one night. "Otherwise he might eventually have returned to Rome, and who knows what would have happened then? Perhaps revolt."

Aosta enjoyed greater popularity even than Badoglio, whose following was mainly limited to army circles. Also, Badoglio at that time was sixty-four, whereas the Duke was only forty-two. Aosta not only had the following of the titled people of Italy, but he also had the respect of all classes. He was a member of the royal family, yet was fighting for his country and shared his lot with the common soldiers in one of the meanest battlefields of the war. The army also liked him for his military acumen and character, and undoubtedly he would have been supported by Badoglio in the event of an insurrection. And perhaps most important of all, the Fascists themselves respected his qualities as a man and appreciated the co-operation he was giving Mussolini's war plans despite his well-known disapproval of them. They would probably have come around to him in the event of a successful revolution sooner than to Badoglio.

At the time that the Duke of Spoleto was named King of Croatia, rumors were current in quarters close to the Quirinal Palace that Queen Elena would be named Queen of Montenegro, which the Italians had taken under their wing as part of their Yugoslav spoils. The Italian press gave credence to these reports as it stressed for the first time the fact that Queen Elena was the daughter of the last King of Montenegro. Hitherto, little if any mention was ever made of her origin, because the Montenegrin dynasty was considered distinctly inferior to the House of Savoy, the ruling family of Italy. Mussolini, however, appointed Count Quinto Mazzolini as High Commissioner of Montenegro and entrusted him with the job of ruling the country until normal conditions could be restored. Mazzolini's government was not a permanent one, and the way was left open to the eventual setting up of Montenegro as a nominally independent, manikin state with Queen Elena as its ruler when and if the time ever seemed opportune.

Italian military prestige had been so seriously damaged by the campaign on the Greek mainland that Mussolini sought to recoup by having his armed forces play an important part in the German assault on Crete. Owing to the fact that the Germans had no navy in the Mediterranean, they were compelled to rely on the Italian navy, which in this instance acquitted itself very creditably. After the first attack on the island by German parachute troops had succeeded, German infantry was rushed — in small Italian and Greek fishing boats carrying between fifty and sixty soldiers each and convoyed by Italian destroyers and cruisers — to consolidate the Crete positions. Several fleets of these little fishing vessels piloted by Italian sailors were used, and the great majority of them reached their goal safely, even when the escorting warships were engaged in battle by units of the British fleet. Italian planes also took part in bombing and torpedoing operations over Crete ports and military objectives.

During the battle for Crete, the Italian navy also tried out in Suda Bay one of its favorite naval stunts. The Italians employed a weapon conceived by the Japanese, perfected by themselves, and never adopted by any other nation — man piloted torpedoes. Known as "grasshoppers," these huge torpedoes carried a tiny boat wherein two men sat and which was equipped with a powerful outboard motor. Under cover of darkness, Italian destroyers transported these units to within two or three miles of Suda Bay, the closest they could get without the British becoming aware of their presence. Here the torpedoes were lowered into the water and the pilots set their outboard motors going and muffled them down until they approached the entrance to the harbor. Once there, the motors were opened with a roar and set at full speed so that the torpedoes, their noses sticking out of the water, were able to hop over torpedo nets and booms. The outboard propeller would be lifted up as the shell ricocheted over any obstacles. The pilots, who were able to reach within four or five hundred yards of British ships, pointed their torpedoes at the objectives, set the torpedoes' own motors going, and detached their tiny outboard motorboats, in which they tried to escape while their torpedoes blew holes in the sides of one cruiser and two destroyers.

The Italians had used these grasshopper torpedoes with small success twice previously — once at Malta, where they did no damage, and once at Gibraltar, where they only succeeded in reaching the outer harbor and sinking three small freighters. But in the less fortified Suda Bay, these two-men assault units proved extremely successful. The British, who had always jeered at them as being absurd and impractical, never admitted that they had lost any warships through them, but we got the whole Suda Bay story from some Danish sailors whose ship was also anchored there at that time, and who, after the Axis had captured all of Crete, were repatriated through Rome to their own country.

The Duce also threw some hand-picked Italian troops into the Crete operations a week after the German offensive started. The Germans concentrated on the western part of the island while the Italians, who had set sail from the Italian-owned Dodecanese Islands off the coast of Turkey, landed on the eastern tip of Crete, catching its Greek and British defenders in the rear. These troops, besides the help they contributed toward conquering Crete, also served a political purpose since they constituted Mussolini's bid to a share in running Crete after it was taken.

On the anniversary of Italy's entry into the war, June 10, 1941, the Duce made another speech, in which he announced that Germany was turning over the occupation of Greece to Italy, stating that "Greece remains in the Italian sphere of influence in the Mediterranean." What he did not add was that the Nazis had picked the Greek bone clean before handing it over to the Italians. Like a swarm of locusts, the German armies had gone through Greece, requisitioning every single bit of foodstuff they could find, leaving the civilian population on the brink of starvation. The army also took over all the gasoline in Greece and a great deal of the leather, while the individual soldiers using paper marks bought up most of the clothes in the shops to send home to their families in Germany.

The Duce did, however, feel obliged to warn his listeners that they would have to undergo further rationing in order to spare some food for Greece, which had never at the best of times been self-supporting.

The Germans did not give all of Greece to Italy. They gave Bulgaria the long, narrow strip of Greek territory which connected Greece with Turkey and which had formerly separated Bulgaria from the Aegean Sea. For themselves they kept Salonika and a big block of its hinterland stretching to the former Yugoslav border and most of the big islands in the Aegean, including Lemnos, Samothrace, Mytilene, and Samos. They also shared the occupation of Crete and retained control of the important port of Peiraeus, a few miles from Athens. The rest was handed over to Italy, whether as a permanent possession or as merely a wartime occupation neither Hitler nor Mussolini deigned to say.

Conditions in Greece were bearable during the summer of 1941, but when winter arrived, the harassed Italian occupation authorities were at their wits' end over how to keep their Greek subjects from dying of malnutrition by the tens of thousands. As it was, the deaths from starvation during the worst of the winter reached five hundred daily in Athens alone. It would have been a great deal higher except for the work of the International Red Cross, financed with $10,000.000 raised in the United States for Greek relief. With this money the Red Cross, under the direction of a Swiss, Robert Brunel, fed 700,000 Athenians daily. The worst problem was to find some country close by willing to sell food — a far more valuable commodity than money in war-torn Europe. Turkey finally agreed to sell the food for the duration of the winter.

Even so, conditions were appalling and the available food was barely enough to maintain life in healthy bodies; the old and ill quickly died. Besides the Red Cross contributions, the Italians managed to supply a bread ration of eighty grams (about two and

one half ounces) per person per day. For this, bread cards were
issued. The result was that when a member of a family died, the
rest of the family would not report the death but would carry
the body far from the home neighborhood and leave it in the
street. By doing that, the family could keep the extra bread card
which would otherwise be taken away by the Italian authorities.
If the body had not already been stripped by the relatives before
being discarded, the clothes would be stolen during the night by
street scavengers, since there were no clothes left to buy in the
stores. Americans who stayed in Greece doing welfare work until
the Italian declaration of war on the United States put an end
to their activities told us fantastic horror stories reminiscent of the
Black Plague in the Middle Ages. Paul Yphantis, of the Greek-
American Missionary Association of Boston, who was in Athens
during the starvation period, told Eleanor:

"Every day government wagons go around and gather up the
bodies lying in the streets. Doctors apply a stethoscope to these
unclaimed bodies to make sure they are dead. Those that dropped
in the street from hunger but are still breathing are left in the
morgue till they die, because there is no food to keep them alive
— what little food there is must be given to those who have a real
chance for survival. The bodies of those already dead are buried,
without any attempt at identification, in common graves containing the remains of as many as three hundred people. In the poorest
parts of the town, where people have no money to buy a bit of
nourishment on the Black Market, the driver of the public death
wagon knocks on the doors and asks if there are any bodies the
residents want dragged out because the still living are so feeble
from starvation that they cannot carry the bodies out themselves.
Everywhere one sees desperate people hunting through garbage
pails and junk heaps for orange peels, roots of cabbages — anything
that might contain a little nourishment. But there is hardly any
refuse to be found, because the owners of the garbage pails have
nothing to throw away.

"Most of the Italians are kindhearted and hate to see such suffering," Yphantis continued. "The officials do what they can, though there is little to do anything with. But it is not at all an uncommon sight to see an ordinary Italian soldier surreptitiously giving some of his army ration to some hungry Greek child. They are strictly forbidden to do so by their officers, as their ration is supposed to be just sufficient for themselves, but they do it anyway. The most fertile agricultural land in Greece is in the part now occupied by the Germans. But the Germans won't give food to any Greeks except those who have always been residents of the territory the Germans are occupying. And the situation of Italian-occupied Greece is rendered still more acute by the fact that the Bulgarians have been massacring so many Greeks in the territory they've annexed that tens of thousands of refugees have fled from there to Italian Greece, and this flood of refugees makes just so many more mouths to be fed."

Burton Y. Berry, whose official title was "Second Secretary of the United States Embassy in Rome on Special Mission in Italian-occupied Greece," was cornered by Eleanor one afternoon in the United States Embassy during one of his flying trips to Rome. He was reluctant to talk, but she finally pried out of him a few of his observations.

"The Italians have been scrupulously careful about handing over to the Red Cross all the food shipped by Turkey, and the people in America who contributed the money can be assured that every pound of the food their money has bought has gone to the Greeks. Once, when the food ship didn't arrive on time and the Red Cross stocks were exhausted, the Italian commanding officer in Athens gave the Red Cross one million army rations so that the Red Cross could keep its soup kitchens going. But the most important thing the Italians accomplished was to wring from the Germans an agreement that everything grown in Greece in the way of food would henceforth be given to the Greeks, beginning with the 1942 crops."

Eleanor asked him what the Greeks thought of the Italians as compared to the Germans.

"The Greeks certainly hate both of them," Berry replied. "But they started out being contemptuous of the Italians because of the poor showing they had made in the fighting as compared to their awe for the *Blitzkrieg* Germans. But little by little as the Italians took over most of the occupation of Greece, the Greeks began to find the Italians the lesser of the two evils. The Italians were pleasant and understanding, but terribly inefficient, while the Germans were efficient but mean and intolerant. The Germans stripped Greece of everything and made no effort, as the Italians did, to feed the Greeks."

Berry explained that after having obtained the Germans' consent not to requisition or export any more food from Greece, the Italians were organizing an *amasso* system similar to the one in Italy. Under this system, farmers were compelled to hand over all their staple nonperishable crops to the government, which stored them and rationed them out to the whole population.

The Americans who arrived in Rome from Athens all told us incredible stories of the Black Market prices for food. One of the worst scarcities was in fats, which could hardly be bought at any price, so that olive oil was literally worth its weight in gold. Most of the olives were raised in the islands occupied by the Germans, who, during the 1941 season, stored up the oil for themselves from the whole of that year's olive crop.

With all the headaches Greece brought them, the Italians found that the Germans had presented them with a gift horse of very doubtful value when the Nazis turned over to them the occupation of Greece. Here were no rolling miles of fertile land that needed only a little toil to produce rich crops; here, instead, was a rocky and barren land that produced even in normal times scarcely enough food to keep its own population alive; here was a problem, the very solution of which made things worse in Italy. To feed Greece meant to take still more food away from the already tightly rationed Italian people who were grumbling about conditions. The Greek war in which Mussolini had hoped to find so much profit and prestige had brought the Fascists more loss than gain.

# XI

THE LITTLE OLD LADY WITH COTTON-WHITE HAIR BROUGHT
Reynolds a cup of tea. She acted as though she wanted to speak
but did not know how to begin. There were no other customers in
the place, as it had just opened its doors for the late Sunday-after-
noon business. It was a faded, boxlike Russian tearoom on the
Via Babuino, too expensive for most Russians in Rome and not
elegant enough to compete with Rampoldi's and Babington's, both
not far away in the Piazza di Spagna. There were small announcements on the wall advertising bridge lessons, courses in English,
German, French, and Russian, indicating the hard time the White
Russians were having to make a living in Fascist Italy. There were
the usual paintings and water colors for sale, depicting knee-booted
Cossack girls doing wild dances and czarist cavalry making heroic
charges. Finally, as Reynolds, also seeking a conversational opening, asked for a second cup of tea, the old lady broke down her
reserve and said:

"What do you think of the news? Isn't it wonderful?"

It was the afternoon of June 22, 1941. Germany and Italy had declared war on Soviet Russia at 5:30 A.M. that same day. Reynolds told her that he was a newspaperman and had come to her shop, as a matter of fact, to get the reaction, if possible, of the White Russian colony in Rome.

"Would you say that most of the Russians in Italy are as pleased with the news as you seem to be?"

"Oh, yes," she said. "I'm sure we are all pleased. My Russian friends have been on the phone all day telling me how happy they are at the prospect of being able to return to our homes soon."

"Of course," she continued, "only anti-Communist Russians are in Italy. Naturally, we feel that anything which will overthrow the Bolsheviks will be a good thing for Russia as well as ourselves."

As she spoke, four Russians came into the shop and ordered vodka. The old lady apparently told one of them that Reynolds was an American newspaperman. She deduced his nationality as only people in catering work can do — by a combined study of shoes, ties, and accents. One of the Russians came over and told Reynolds that he hoped the American press would be informed how the White Russians supported the Axis war against "the Communist usurpers" in Russia. He said he was a member of the executive committee of the Russian refugees in Italy. He estimated there were several thousand Russians in Italy, all waiting to return to their homeland.

"We have had a hard time trying to make a living as best we can. But why talk of that now, as it is only a matter of months before we will be able to go back. Tonight our Russian organization is drawing up a manifesto declaring its solidarity with the Axis war on Communism."

It seemed to Reynolds, as he slowly sipped his second cup of tea, that the Russians were extremely nervous. Other Russians came in and added to the tensity of the atmosphere. It was obvious that they suddenly regarded the shop, to which they were not in the habit of coming, as a sort of trysting place in time of Russian stress. It struck Reynolds that their protestations of approval of the

Axis invasion of their own country were also connected with their desire to be unmolested by the OVRA. Timely statements of loyalty to the Axis, they thought, would keep them out of concentration camps.

In the meantime, Eleanor was in the bar of the Hotel Excelsior, talking with Russian acquaintances who were frequent habitués of that international meeting place. Prince Volkonsky, son of the last czarist military attaché in Rome, who had continued to reside in Italy after the Bolsheviks took over Moscow, was at the bar. He was buying drinks for everybody and invited most of the convivial gathering to be his guests at his castle as soon as the Russian war was over.

"And it won't be long before I am back there," he said to Eleanor. "Another six months — and that includes postwar settlement. I'm going to join up with a Russian volunteer corps to fight alongside the Axis troops against those Communist buzzards."

The optimism of the White Russians in Rome, as we found out later that night in the Foreign Press Club, was only a reflection of Axis wishful thinking. After we had sent off thousands of words that evening about the Italian angle of the Rome-Berlin declaration of war on Russia, we went down to the press bar, which was blanketed by German correspondents. Romeo, an ex-prize fighter who had turned barman, was kept busy supplying drinks to the Germans with which they were toasting a *Blitzkrieg* victory in Russia. Even Baron von Langen, whom all the American correspondents called "Sourpuss," was making a Prussian simulation of good-fellowship. He even offered to buy us two beers, but when he told him we were drinking whiskies, the invitation was conveniently lost in the hubbub.

"We Germans will be in Moscow before snow falls," von Langen said, "but we won't be leaving again in the middle of winter the way Napoleon did."

Fritz Alwens, of the *Völkischer Beobachter*, said:

"After the way the Finns held the Russians, you can imagine

how our mechanized armies are going to crash through those Soviet moujiks."

The Italian reaction to the new war was less boisterous than the German, but it was nevertheless favorable. Here at last was a war that made sense to the mass of Italian people, much more sense than the conflicts with Britain, France, or Greece had made. Nineteen years of unremitting propaganda against Communism, plus three years of undeclared combat against Russian forces in Spain, had had their effect. Besides, many Italians remembered with aversion the brief period between the end of World War I and the establishment of the Fascist regime, when the Communists had made their bid for power in Italy by using strikes, street riots, and similar devices in their attempts to establish a Soviet state in Italy.

It being Sunday and therefore the cooks' day out in Rome, we found the restaurant where we ate dinner full of people. They were talking loudly and enthusiastically about the "crusade against the Bolsheviks." The consensus seemed to be that the Germans would do most of the fighting (thereby relieving Italy of the duty of sending large numbers of troops); that the Nazi armies would quickly crush the "abominable Reds"; that Russia's vast resources in wheat, petroleum, and iron ore would then be at the disposal of Germany and Italy; and that the British, realizing the folly of trying to continue a war against such a strong team of opponents, would then make peace. The waiters, as usual, freely offered their opinions of the new venture with each dish they served, expressing their convictions that an Axis victory was a foregone conclusion and that it was indeed fortunate that the world was soon to be rid of the "Bolshevik menace," the "Communist scourge," and the "Red plots."

These were the catch phrases that Mussolini had so persistently disseminated in the press for the past nineteen years that they had grown into a part of the average Italian's vocabulary. It was the old advertising principle of "Drink Coca-Cola." Repeat phrases enough and they stick in the mind, influencing people's tastes in politics as well as drinks. And these clichés of Mussolini had stuck.

The news of the war declaration against Russia came too late to be printed in the Italian Sunday-morning papers, and all day Sunday the public knew no more about it than the brief and uneditorialized announcements on the radio. It was not until Monday noon that the first Italian newspapers came out, and with these was launched full blast a thundering propaganda campaign against "Soviet perfidy." According to this, the Soviets, after having received the inestimable boon of a treaty of alliance with Germany, had shown their ingratitude for this favor by carrying on secret negotiations with Britain for the sole purpose of stabbing Germany in the back. Official indignation exuded in the usual flowery Italian phrases over Russian seizure of the Baltic states, Bessarabia, the invasion of Finland; it being conveniently forgotten that all these extensions of Russian frontiers had been carried out with German consent. Italian support of Finland during the Russian-Finnish war was proudly recalled.

"This is a holy crusade, as holy as any ever sent to wrest the birthplace of our Saviour from the heathens," rapturously wrote the ultra-Fascist newspaper, *Il Tevere*. "Stalin's bloody fingers have been at the throat of Europe long enough. It is time to tear them away. The red storm clouds over Europe will be dissolved as our armies smash through to the Volga and then will come the rainbow after the storm, promising the peace and plenty based on the Axis New Order in Europe. This is a war of liberation in which every European country, whether at peace with England or not, ought to join."

The last sentence of *Il Tevere's* outburst sounded a note that was to be greatly developed in the next few days — that the Russo-German conflict was not a war of aggrandizement and conquest by Germany against a former ally, but an ideological war in which every right-minded non-Bolshevik in Europe ought to join. Except for Bulgaria, the smaller signatories of the Tripartite Pact (Hungary, Rumania, Slovakia, and Croatia) all had to join in, and the Italian press announced that the Spanish Falange, as well as the Dutch, Danish, and Norwegian Nazis, were forming volunteer regiments to help Italy and Germany combat Communism.

With the object of representing the Soviets as unscrupulous and bloodthirsty barbarians who could not even be counted on to follow ordinary rules of international conduct, the Italian papers proclaimed that the Fascist government was intensely worried over the fate of its Embassy staff in Moscow and reported that the Duce had warned Stalin that he would take reprisals on the Soviet Embassy in Rome if any harm came to the Italians in the Soviet capital.

"And we have twenty-seven more Bolsheviks in Italy than Stalin has Fascists in Russia," the *Popolo di Roma* pointed out. The Soviet Embassy, situated near the ever-crowded Porta Pia, had immediately been put under heavy guard of several hundred soldiers in full war equipment after the Italian declaration of war. Diplomats who had personal relations with members of the Russian Embassy told us that Ambassador Nikolai Gorelkin and his staff had been completely surprised by the outbreak of war. They had regarded the evidences of tension in Russo-German relations as merely the usual jockeying for position common to dictators when they were about to drive a bargain with somebody. They, therefore, thought that rumors of German and Russian troop concentrations along their mutual frontier were only the stage setting for a new economic accord about to be negotiated whereby German imports of Russian grain and oil would be greatly increased.

Gorelkin, who had once been recalled to Moscow as a protest over Italian expressions of sympathy with Finland, had returned to Rome in June of 1940. A Molotov appointee, he was a product of the Russo-German alliance and had soon found himself out of sympathy with the former Chargé d'Affaires of the Soviet Embassy, Leon Gelfand, who was a Litvinov man; Litvinov as an advocate of Soviet alliance with England and France had been under a shadow in Moscow during the first twenty months of World War II.

Gelfand, who had been in Rome nearly fifteen years and who spoke Italian, French, and English fluently, therefore feared the worst when, during the summer of 1940, the Soviet Ministry of

Foreign Affairs summoned him back to Moscow. He had no relatives in Russia, so there was nothing to compel him to return, and he resolved not to risk going back and possibly being "liquidated" as a Litvinov man.

A good-looking, cultured sportsman who played an excellent game of golf, Gelfand was about as far removed from the popular conception of a Bolshevik as anyone could well be, and he had made many personal friends among Fascist officials at the Foreign Office as well as among the diplomatic colony in Rome. He had no difficulty, therefore, in secretly planning an escape.

He signified to Gorelkin that he would pack up his furniture and personal belongings for his return to Russia. On the day he and his wife and daughter took the train, practically the entire Soviet Embassy was down at the station to see him off. When the train reached a small town near Florence, however, he and his family descended and, with only a suitcase apiece, got into a private car that was waiting for them. The rest of all their vast supply of luggage continued on to Moscow.

The private automobile brought the Gelfand family direct to the Rome airfield, where Gelfand's close personal friend and frequent golfing companion, Count Ciano, had a private plane waiting for them at the end of the field. This plane quickly whisked them to Lisbon, where, armed with American visas provided for them by other friends in the American Embassy, the Gelfands boarded a clipper and were well over the Atlantic before the Russian OGPU ever realized they had left the Rome-Moscow train.

This highly undiplomatic procedure on Ciano's part could not long be kept a secret in a gossipy town like Rome, since all the Italians involved in the plot could not repress their desire to tell about the good joke they had played on Stalin. The whole story soon reached the ears of the Soviet Embassy and caused a distinct frostiness to return to official Italo-Russian relations, and matters did not improve with the passing of time as reports reached Rome that the Russians were not living up to German expectations in the matter of shipping raw materials. In the spring of 1941 — three months before the Axis declared war on Russia — Italian Foreign Office officials told us quite frankly that the Nazis believed the Soviet failure to deliver the amount of oil she had agreed on was deliberate sabotage.

"The Russians, of course, blame the slow deliveries on lack of transportation facilities; but whether their failure to turn over the goods is due to ill-will or mere inefficiency, it can only be cured by having Axis technical experts go into the Ukraine and the Caucasus and organize production themselves," one Foreign Office official told us. "Stalin, of course, doesn't want any foreigners, not even Germans, going into the interior of Russia, where they might find out the truth. They've got a lot of territory for nothing out of this war, and they should expect to have to give a quid pro quo."

Later, some Fascist diplomats also admitted the Hitler-Molotov conversations "had not been a success." It was said that Molotov had asked additional grants of European territory to Russia in return for Russian economic co-operation with Germany and had flatly refused to consider the proposal to have German production experts supervise the shipments of Russian goods to Germany. Hitler retaliated by halting the flow of German armaments and machinery to Russia, and from that point on relations grew more and more tense until they reached the climax of war.

Nevertheless, an indication that Stalin never expected such an abrupt rupture of negotiations could be seen in the fact that he apparently made no effort during this interim to negotiate with the English, although Sir Stafford Cripps was in Moscow for that express purpose. When Cripps went to report to London only about two weeks before the outbreak of the Russo-German war, it was authoritatively stated in London that he had not seen any Soviet official of importance for months and was therefore apparently convinced that the rumors of difficulties in Russo-German relations should be classified as perhaps significant but in the main as unreliable.

Aside from thinking that the invasion of Russia would be comparatively easy, Hitler and Mussolini believed that it was a necessary preliminary to eventual attack on the British Isles. Having come to distrust Stalin because of the encroachments the Soviets had made in the Baltic, Rumania, and Finland — encroachments coinciding with periods during which the Axis was occupied elsewhere — Hitler and Mussolini felt sure that once they became engaged in an all-out attack against England, the Russians would move more deeply into Europe. And Hitler and Mussolini realized there was no chance to make any other than an all-out attack on the British Isles. They had already been disappointed at the result of the mass bombings of London and other big cities in England during the late summer and early fall of 1940.

"But it's amazing that the English don't crack under these bombardments," Baron von Hahn, DNB correspondent, typically said. "Why, they're as tough as we are."

As a result of their inability to crack the morale of the British by air attack, and their distrust of Stalin, Hitler and Mussolini agreed that they first had to secure the eastern door of Europe against any push by the Russians before attacking England. At the time the Russian war started, most of the other American correspondents in Rome agreed with us that Hitler and Mussolini counted on victory before the snows set in. They planned to carry out postwar reconstruction in Russia during the winter, on one hand, and simultaneously prepare for the invasion of England in the west, these preparations to be completed before spring. The operations against England would then start as soon as the weather was favorable for a trans-Channel attack and would be brought to a finish or a near-finish before the usual bad Channel conditions of late September could interfere with Axis plans. It was a roseate picture that the two dictators painted for themselves. The war was to end in only a little more than a year.

The Rome newspaper, Il Tevere, blithely published a war drawing at this time, depicting how the invasion of England might be carried out once the Blitzkrieg in Russia came to a victorious finish. It showed the Channel between Calais and Dover covered for a width of twenty miles with a multilayered ceiling of ten thousand

Axis airplanes, bombers, and chasers. The strip beneath this serial canopy was bordered on each side by heavy margins of Axis navy units ranging from cruisers to submarines. Many hundreds of transport ships made the crossing in the protected lane without any trouble, their landing being simplified by terrific, block-crushing bombardments from airplanes and a screen of shells from coastal batteries on the French shore. Parachute jumpers were also part of the landing operations. It was the sort of optimism that Mussolini served his public whenever he thought it was time to bolster morale.

Although the conquest of Russia was to be mainly the task of the German army, Mussolini hastened to send some token troops to the Russian front. Four days after the declaration of war, he reviewed a motorized division in the Po Valley, prior to its departure a few hours later for the Soviet front. A week later, he reviewed a second motorized division in Rome, and on this occasion correspondents of the signatories of the Tripartite Pact were allowed to be present at the review. This included practically all the correspondents in Rome except the Americans, the Swiss, and the Swedes. But by some oversight — the usual case of the Fascist right hand not knowing what the left hand was doing — the United States Military Attaché, Colonel Norman Fiske, was also invited. Colonel Fiske, in his full American army regalia, stood on the same platform with the Duce, where he had a much better view of the equipment than even the German and Japanese correspondents. And he had a trained eye for sizing up military details. The refusal to admit American correspondents was therefore pointless. Afterward, we talked to Colonel Fiske about the review and asked if there had been anything of interest. He answered:

"Since they were Italians, the most interesting and surprising thing about it was that they had all the equipment they were supposed to have. It was just a standard, modern motorized division, with nothing fancy about it and certainly no secret weapons."

Mussolini's first speech in connection with the Russian war was made on his birthday, July 29, at Mantua. The Italian public, however, was not aware that Il Duce had attained the age of fifty-eight that same day, because, years before, he had ordered the Fascist press never to make any mention whatsoever of his birthdays. He did not want to remind the Italians that even Mussolini grew older the same as other mortals. The speech was in the form of a personal farewell addressed to a small unit of hand-picked Black Shirts departing for the Soviet front. The unit was called the "M" Battalion in his honor. Mussolini said:

"For twenty years, the people of Europe have been agitated by this alternative, this ironclad dilemma, Fascism or Bolshevism, Rome or Moscow. The clash of two worlds which we have willed and which we have instilled in our revolutionary squadrons during years long past has received its epilogue.

"The drama is in the fifth act. The line-up is now complete — on one side, Rome, Berlin, and Tokyo; on the other, London, Washington, and Moscow. We will win because history says that a people who represent the ideas of the past must lose to a people who represent the ideas of the future."

When this speech was released to the press, the German correspondents at the Stampa Estera were more than a little amused at the Duce's saying that "the choice lay between Rome and Moscow," as if Berlin did not exist. "Mussolini is good at fighting a war with words," von Langen said.

German correspondents told us that Hitler had insisted that all Italian troops must be entirely supplied from Italy, including all foodstuffs and blankets as well as arms and munitions. The ostensible reason advanced for this was that the German, Hungarian, Rumanian, and Finnish armies were relying upon the stocks of food close at hand and could not allow their calculations to be upset at this late date. But the implication was that the Germans did not highly value Italian assistance on the field of battle, although it was said they might prove useful as occupation troops.

The German attitude was based partly on the bad showing the Italian chaser squadrons had made during the mass raids on England. At that time, the Italians sent hundreds of planes and a couple of thousand men, including ground crews, mechanics, and repair-shop workers as well as pilots. But when it came to renovating their planes or installing new spare parts, they tried to borrow the necessary materials from the Germans. The Italian air units on the Channel were so badly organized that the Germans found them more of a hindrance than a help. Hitler did not want this Italian lack of foresight to upset his own supply system in Russia.

The German dictum that all Fascist troops on the Russian front must be based on Italy imposed a severely long and complicated supply line on the Italian troops and therefore necessarily limited the numbers that were sent there. After the first three contingents had been dispatched with a great deal of fanfare and publicity, subsequent departures were regarded as military secrets and were not announced. A canvass we made of the military attachés of neutral legations and embassies in Rome, however, indicated that the Italian expeditionary force to Russia during 1941 never exceeded 100,000 men.

The Fascists laid down one novel rule to be followed by all troops that departed for Russia. Practically all Italian men wore religious medallions bearing the figure of the Virgin Mary or Jesus Christ, on chains around their necks. The medallions were usually given them while they were still babies, and they kept the same ones all their lives without being any more conscious of them than of a birthmark. The Italian authorities insisted that all soldiers going to Russia leave these medallions behind, the official explanation being that since the Russians were antireligious they might kill prisoners wearing religious insignia. It was a Fascist attempt to ingraft into the minds of the Italian soldiers that it was better to risk death than to be captured by the Soviets. Being taken prisoner by the British had become all too popular among Italians, and we frequently met Italian families who looked positively happy as they told us that they had just learned their soldier sons were in British prison camps. One Italian father said, "Thank God my son is now safe for the remainder of the war."

Several German correspondents, who had drunk enough *americanos* to be indiscreetly loquacious, whispered to us at the Foreign

Press Club bar one night that Italian soldiers would be all right if they fought under German officers.

"Otherwise, they haven't any fighting spirit," one of them said. "They would rather surrender than die. There have been several cases in Africa where entire units of Italians could have escaped with a few losses and joined the main body of their army, but instead they deliberately allowed themselves to be captured."

During the early part of the Russian campaign, the Italian newspapers were particularly enthusiastic about the Axis advances in the Ukraine, frequently referred to as the "breadbasket of Europe." Italy was beginning to feel the pinch of wheat shortages, and her two staple foods, bread and spaghetti, had so little wheat flour in them that they were a dark-brown color. The thought of millions upon millions of acres of Russian wheat fields, the conquest of which would provide a plentiful supply of white spaghetti and white bread, was enough to make the average Italian believe that the profits to be got from a conquest of Russia were worth while. To reassure the Italian people that Germany would not get all the benefits of the Russian conquest, the Italian newspapers, when the war was about six weeks old, declared that Hitler had promised Mussolini big wheat concessions in the Ukraine once the war was won. The Italians would not acquire this territory as a colony but would have control of it through an enormous stock company which would exploit the Italian concession in Russia in very much the same way the old East India Company used to exploit India in the days of Queen Victoria. The Italian newspapers also said that similar concessions in the oil, coal, and iron producing sections of Russia would be worked out later.

The strength of the Russian resistance was a real shock to the Italian public, which had based its estimate of the Soviet army on what it considered the poor showing the Russians had made in Finland. It was not until after the middle of August, however, that the average Italian began to realize that the war in Russia would not finish that summer.

One of the first warnings was sounded by Ciano's newspaper, *Il*

*Telegrafo* of Leghorn, when its editor, Giovanni Ansaldo, wrote as follows:

"The defenders of the Stalin Line give in only because of the German technical superiority, but even so German divisions have to work hard for their gains.

"Many people expected to see the Bolshevik regime collapse after a few days' fighting, and they are now becoming somewhat disconcerted because of the Russians' military efficiency. These people continually ask how it is possible for the Bolsheviks to resist so well if the Soviet regime is so hated by the masses. Thus the Russian resistance tends to make rife insidious doubts and uncertainties. In order to understand the Russian resistance, the Slavic racial qualities must be taken into consideration. These qualities are fundamentally great physical strength and exceptional psychology for tolerating hardships."

In October, Mussolini's own newspaper, *Popolo d'Italia*, frankly warned the Italian public that the war would probably be long and was likely to develop into an endurance contest. Mario Apelius, chief editorial writer of *Popolo d'Italia*, added that not even the fall of Moscow would end Russian resistance. Apelius wrote:

"The present formidable Axis strategic situation is based on the campaigns in Poland, Norway, Holland, Belgium, France, Yugoslavia, Greece, and Crete, the prolonged resistance in Ethiopia, the military strength in Libya, aero-naval battles in the Mediterranean, the Tripartite Pact, and the friendly attitude of Spain.

"The fulcrum of Axis power is based on the ease with which it can rapidly concentrate its maximum forces by internal routes at any given point in Europe, either for defensive or offensive purposes. . . . In any case, the situation in Europe after the fall of Moscow and the Don basin will be such that the Axis cannot lose the war. Nevertheless, the enemy undoubtedly will not readily recognize defeat and the Anglo-Saxon struggle will be most fierce. This will necessitate on our part great forces of perseverance. We must harden our endurance, knowing that all sacrifices lead to ultimate victory and peace."

With the German failure to win the war in Russia in the course of a single summer, the average Italian began to feel for the first time that perhaps the Germans were not invincible after all. This realization brought a mixed reaction. Unreasonably enough, although the Italians contributed practically nothing toward the winning of the Russian campaign, they began to be angry at the Germans for not winning it singlehanded and became caustic in their criticism — only in private, of course — of German military failures. There was also the fact that they had expected the Germans to win the war against England the previous summer. The Russian campaign was a second disappointment of even greater magnitude than the first because now they had had fifteen months of war instead of three and they had two powerful enemies instead of one. At the same time, the conviction that the Germans were not invincible brought a kind of relief because it meant that the Germans were not supermen and were capable of failures the same as the Italians.

At first, the German *blitz* machine had advanced into Russia with a speed that had almost justified the Fascists' most optimistic forecasts. This was through territory Russia had occupied since 1939 — the Russian half of Poland; Lithuania, Latvia, and Estonia; the areas Finland had been forced to cede to Russia after the brief Russo-Finnish war; Bessarabia and Bukovina, which had been bloodlessly ceded by Rumania. Russia had not yet had time to fortify heavily any of these frontiers, and her armies were unable to halt the German offense tactics in open fighting, either through being unprepared for the blow (which in view of everything we heard seemed the most likely explanation) or through inferior generalship. Also, in the Baltic states of Lithuania, Latvia, and Estonia, the Germans had a native civilian population working actively in their favor. In the areas ceded by Finland and Rumania, on the other hand, there was practically no civilian population at all to support either army, all but a few Russian nationals having withdrawn from these zones before they were handed over to the Soviets.

It was when the Germans tried to crack the old prewar Soviet frontier, where the fortifications had been slowly and painstakingly built and perfected over a span of twenty years, that they ran into real trouble. No single secret intelligence service of any country in the world, including Germany, had ever penetrated very deeply into the secrets of the Stalin Line. It was a veritable hobgoblins' nest. Besides swamps, escarpments, and other obstacles of terrain which had been artificially constructed to supplement the omissions of nature, there were innocent-looking farm villages which were secret military strong points. In these villages every haystack concealed a huge gun, every ramshackle farmhouse was a heavily fortified pill box and every barn an airplane hangar.

The Germans undoubtedly thought they knew more about these secret fortifications than they did. After the advent of the Hitler regime, nearly two thousand leading German Communists had made their way to Russia. Within five years, some eight hundred had changed their ideas about Communism; many were in prison as dissenters, while those who had kept out of trouble were desperately homesick. They wanted to go back to Germany, if they could do so without peril to themselves, and Hitler, with his usual infernal astuteness, saw in them the finest anti-Bolshevik propaganda weapons that had come to his hand in a long time. Through the German Embassy in Moscow, he promised them full pardons and then set about seeking the Soviet government's agreement to their repatriation. This the Führer accomplished by offering to exchange them for about fifty Soviet spies the Gestapo had caught inside Germany. Stalin finally agreed to the deal, and the eight hundred Germans — mostly industrial workers — were strategically spread around factories throughout Germany where they could be counted on to tell their fellow workers everything that was wrong with the Soviets' "Workers' Paradise."

But that was not all. These eight hundred Germans had seen a lot and heard more, and they were not returned to civil life until the German military intelligence service had milked them dry of everything they knew or guessed. On information provided by these ex-Communists and from tidbits gleaned during the Russo-German honeymoon just after the signing of the Russo-German alliance, the German High Command built up a picture of Russian defenses on which it based its campaign. They knew quite a lot, but not nearly enough.

When the Germans thought of finishing the Russian campaign in one summer — i.e., European Russia, for they did not intend to worry about Asiatic Russia — they planned roughly on achieving a front extending from Archangel straight south to the Volga and from there more or less following the course of the Volga until they reached the Caspian Sea. By that time, the Germans believed, the major part of the Soviet armies would have been destroyed and what few remained were not expected to have sufficient industrial resources in Asia to constitute any serious threat.

But the Germans were stalled for nearly a month after they reached the deep, fortified zone the Soviets had built along their old borders. They did not even capture Smolensk, more than one hundred and fifty miles from Moscow, until August 6, which left only about two months until the real Russian-style winter weather began to set in. And besides being one hundred and fifty miles from Moscow, they were another one hundred and fifty miles from their objective — the Volga River around Gorki — in the Moscow sector alone. In other sectors they were much farther from their proposed winter line.

At the same time, the Russians were not retreating the way they were expected to do when their main fortified lines had been passed. Once on their own territory, they gave ground much more slowly than they had in the Soviet-occupied countries. At the farthest point of the German advance before cold weather halted their operations, the Nazi armies achieved only a half-circle around Moscow at a distance about thirty miles from the city. Elsewhere, the Nazi line nearly surrounded Leningrad, slanted southeast to just north of Moscow, where it formed a loop, then bore slightly west, ending in a gentle curve at Rostov, which they held. When they realized they had to dig in for the winter, the Germans retreated distances between twenty-five and one hundred miles, according to where they found the best positions and also according to the fierceness of the Soviet offensive attacks.

One indication that the Fascist government was beginning to realize that the war might drag on for some time could be found in the fact that Italy called up and began to train at least a million new recruits during the late fall and early winter of 1941. What these troops were to be used for when their training was completed was naturally never announced. But many diplomats in Rome understood that Hitler, after the heavy losses the Germans had suffered in Russia, was more disposed to employ Italian troops than he had been at the beginning of the campaign. At any rate, on May 2, 1942, after the United States had been in the war for five months, the Rome radio announced that a considerable number of fresh Italian troops would be sent to the Russian front. A little later, the commander of the Italian expeditionary force, General Guido Messe, made a flying trip to Rome to consult with the Duce on plans for Italian participation in the fighting on the eastern front during the 1942 summer campaign, but Hitler still was adamant in his stand that Italian reinforcements must be used sparingly except as troops of occupation. He did use some divisions, however, to maintain the fiction of Axis solidarity and allowed them to share more credit in victories than hitherto.

The attitude of Hitler toward Italian co-operation from the very beginning of the Russian war did much to make the Italian people, and probably the Fascist hierarchy as well, more angry than ever at the Nazis' patronizing manner. Even though Mussolini started with token regiments on the Soviet front, he expected to get a certain amount of propaganda value out of it for Italy's war effort. It was the one war the Italians liked. And yet the Italians were constantly being relegated in the German communiqués to the same minor ranking as that of Finland, Rumania, Hungary, and even Spain, which officially was not in the war. The Italian communiqués were also forced to make only the briefest mention of Italian participation in Russia. The German point of view that

Italians should be used mainly as troops of occupation, in order to release more German soldiers for the front line, hurt Italian pride. The Russian war, which had started off with such rejoicing in the Italian press, soon became one of the main causes of friction between the Germans and the Italians; not only between the peoples, but between the Fascist and Nazi leaders as well, including both Hitler and Mussolini. Mussolini was finding it harder and harder to play the part of the great dictator on the balcony of the Palazzo Venezia when Hitler was treating him not only as a very junior partner but rather as a spoiled child capable of tantrums, who needed placating from time to time.

The Italian has pride in many things. But above all there are two domains in which he is probably more sensitive than any other national in the world: they are love-making and fighting. In the three years that we spent in Rome, we found nothing that would sooner arouse an Italian to a battling state of mind than the insinuation that perhaps Italian men were not the best lovers in the world and that Italian soldiers were not keen about bullets and shells. Hitler, by his contemptuous attitude toward them in Russia, intensified their natural dislike of Germans into a manifest hatred. We could see this hatred wherever Italians and Germans met in Italy In all the subtle ways of which only the Italian is capable, the Germans were snubbed. The Italian waiters in restaurants would take a long time to wait upon Germans, and the waiters in cafés, which are notorious for their slow service, would pretend that they did not hear the clucking and finger snapping of impatient German soldiers and fifth columnists. On the busy streets in which the Italians loved to meander with slow-motion steps, the hurrying Germans found that no longer would their Latin colleagues move aside when they came marching along in their usual double-quick time. Even in hotels, the Germans found it more and more difficult to obtain rooms. The lodging of Germans became such a problem that Mussolini finally had to set aside a dozen of the larger hotels in Rome in which Germans were given official priority. One of these hotels was the Albergo Ambasciatori, which had long been popular with Americans. Colonel Fiske and Dana Hodgdon, a Second Secretary of the United States Embassy in charge of British interests, were eased out of the hotel on one pretext or another in order to make the hostelry one hundred per cent German. The American Corner, a monthly luncheon club composed of members of the United States Embassy, American correspondents, and prominent American businessmen, which had always held its meetings in one of the private dining rooms of the Ambasciatori, discontinued its sessions there as a sign of protest. Having lived at the Ambasciatori ourselves for the first year of our stay in Rome, we went to the manager, Cavaliere Galante, and told him we wanted to get the facts for a story about discrimination against Americans.

"Why, my dear friends, how can you think such a thing! There is not discrimination against Americans here. This is not a German hotel," Galante said in perfect English. "There is always a room here for you any time, as you'll find if you ever want to stay here again."

A week later, as a result of one of the periodic disinfectings of our house against the perennial Rome bedbugs, we had occasion to go to a hotel for two nights. It was a good chance to check on the story. Eleanor telephoned and asked to reserve a double room and bath for the following two days. The clerk, who knew her, was most profuse in his apologies, but every room was taken. Perhaps if she called back that evening he might be able to arrange something in the meantime. Galante was not to be located, although he lived as well as worked in the hotel. That evening Reynolds telephoned, with the same result: more profuse apologies and no Galante.

The Germans in turn were becoming angry at the Italians because of the way they were being treated. They couldn't put their finger on anything specific, so they demanded, as always, to take over this post or that office as a means to an end, and the Fascist authorities were in no position to object. This friction between Germans and Italians also reached the Foreign Press Club, where Romeo, the bartender, was the victim. Von Langen felt that

Romeo was serving Americans faster and better than Germans. It was probably true, because the American correspondents always gave generous tips, whereas the Germans gave nothing or else the traditional ten per cent service worked out to a decimal point. Von Langen did not want to make an international incident out of it, but the Germans, too, had their pride and were not going to forget that they were the overlords of the Axis. So Romeo was discharged on the basis that he had dirty hands. Reynolds went to von Langen and protested that Romeo was a good bartender and certainly was as clean and neat as most bartenders.

"But you Americans," von Langen said, "do not understand the hidden portent of words. By 'dirty hands' we mean something much worse. And if you try to protect Romeo it will be all the worse for him."

The result was that we took on Romeo as a household factotum — butler, valet, and waiter. Von Langen then had a pro-German Italian installed behind the bar, and henceforth Americans were lucky to get a drink at any time.

The friction between Italians and Germans which grew out of the Russian war paved the way for the creation of a huge group of Italian fifth columnists within Italy, numbering many millions; fifth columnists who were ready to rise up against Germany — and Mussolini, too — once they felt they had any chance of success.

# XII

Before being assigned to Rome permanently, following the expulsion of Bud Ekins, we were sent there in February of 1939 for a period of three months in order to enable Stewart Brown, the bureau manager, and other members of the staff to take overdue vacations. We had been there only a few days when Pius XI, who had been ailing for some months, unexpectedly suffered a setback and died early in the morning of February 10. For the next three weeks we were kept busy almost twenty-four hours a day, covering one of the most difficult stories in our careers. Ostensibly, it was an ecclesiastical story — the death of the head of the Catholic Church; in reality, its political import throughout the world soon became predominant. The choice of a new Pope developed into a part of the struggle between democracy and totalitarianism. The new Pope, who would be the spiritual leader of one sixth of the world's population, was bound to have profound influence on the ideology of the Catholic world. What still impresses us the most in retrospect is the foresight that was shown by most of the sixty-two cardinals who attended the conclave. Day after day during the preconclave period, we interviewed, one after the other, not only American cardinals, but also British, Polish, Spanish, Italian, and German cardinals. More than the European statesmen, they all seemed convinced that the world was reaching a cataclysmic crisis, perhaps war. They almost all spoke of the difficult times the world was going through then as a prelude to still more tragic events in the future. Today, more than ever, it strikes us as incomprehensible that men of religion should have had a more penetrating understanding of what was to come than ambassadors. Perhaps their spiritual aloofness gave them a clearer perspective of the political developments around them, while statesmen were more myopic because of their closeness to the events of the day.

It was evident to the cardinals that the new Pope must be one to cope with the greatest crisis that not only the Catholic Church, but the entire universe as well was to undergo. At first some of them took the view that in time of international stress it would be better to have a pastoral rather than a diplomatic Pope.

But when Eugenio, Cardinal Pacelli was chosen on March 2, after less than twenty-four hours' deliberation in conclave, it meant that the majority of the sixty-two cardinals finally decided that a diplomatist was needed to cope with the coming struggle. Cardinal Pacelli, who mounted the throne of Saint Peter as Pius XII, was the ablest diplomat and statesman the Church could produce. He had been Vatican Secretary of State since December, 1929, and, before that, Apostolic Nuncio to Bavaria and later Apostolic Nuncio to Germany. Speaking eight languages — Italian, English, French, German, Spanish, Hungarian, Polish, and Latin — he was by far the most internationally minded cardinal of the entire Catholic Church. He had also traveled extensively throughout the world, including trips to the United States and Argentina. Never before had there been a Pope with such a background of world affairs.

But no sooner had the triple tiara been placed upon his head as part of the coronation ceremony in Vatican City, and the cries of 'Viva il Papa' died down, than doubts were expressed in Rome that such a capable man would, through his very capability, involve the Church in the political struggle. But Pius XII, by the act of becoming Pope, ceased, in the belief of three hundred million Catholics throughout the world, to have any legal or national relations with any race, nation, or tribe of mankind save that of spiritual father to all humanity. Pacelli the Italian was henceforth the Holy Father of all Catholics. It was this tradition that governed the war policy of the new Pontiff.

The special position of the Pope, however, did not prevent the Axis from bringing pressure to bear upon him in the hope of attaining political advantage. Mussolini, who had personally known the new Pope when the latter was Vatican Secretary of State and the relations between Italy and the Holy See were extremely friendly as a result of the Lateran Accord, undertook to exert this pressure not only for Fascism but also for Hitler and, later, even for Japan. It was an old tale, because for centuries nations had been trying to make political use of the Vatican despite its spiritual character, but never had the effort reached such intensity as it did during World War II.

Italy had the Vatican geographically stuffed into its boot. Only thirteen acres in area, the Vatican, situated near the center of Rome, had neither ingress nor egress except through Italian territory. Considering these conditions, the resistance that this miniature state made against Axis pressure was all the more remarkable. People abroad often did not appreciate the delicate position that the Pope was in, nor did they understand that fine nuance separating the spiritual from the political. In both Great Britain and America there were many who did not appreciate that the Pope's spiritual mission must of necessity embrace all peoples of all countries.

The first of scores of queries that we received about our Vatican dispatches occurred only a few days after the war had started. During one of the weekly public audiences, the Pope received one hundred and fifty Catholics from various parts of Europe, including fifty German soldiers in uniform. An account of this audience was published in the official Vatican newspaper, *Osservatore Romano*. Eleanor picked it up and sent it, as did most of the other American correspondents. Immediately, British Catholics indignantly wired, demanding that we deny the story. The most insistent cables came from Australia, where the Australian Catholics could not believe that the Pope would be capable of receiving their hated enemies, the Germans. The U.P. office in New York also received complaints from a number of American newspapers and wired us to check back on our facts. Reynolds went to the Vatican Secretariat of State and asked for confirmation or denial of the *Osservatore Romano* article. Monsignor Giovanni Montini, one of the foreign-affairs experts of the Secretariat, confirmed the truth of the story and appeared disturbed that it had caused such international repercussions. He explained that the Pope was always disposed to receive all people whenever possible, and that "all people, regardless of their nationality, are beloved by the Holy Father."

Day after day, Italian editors were being embarrassed by the impartiality of the *Osservatore Romano*. The distortions in the Fascist press were exposed by contrast with the Vatican newspaper. The sales of the *Osservatore Romano* reached a new record, with a circulation of three hundred thousand copies daily, as the people of Italy tried to learn the truth about what was taking place. The Vatican was upsetting all Il Duce's propaganda plans to fool the Italian people. Black Shirts armed with clubs soon began to station themselves at all the kiosks in Rome and other principal cities. As Italians paid for the Vatican paper, they were badly beaten up. In some instances, the Fascist ruffians seized the papers as they were delivered at the kiosks and burned them in street bonfires. In order to avoid such rioting, the Pope reluctantly changed the character of the *Osservatore Romano*, and what had long been one of the best newspapers in Europe was transformed into little more than a daily religious bulletin. Even so, the Fascists insisted that its circulation in Italy be reduced to its prewar level of twenty thousand, and new subscriptions within Italy were banned.

Next, the OVRA began to treat all Vatican representatives as though they were enemy aliens. It had many of the Vatican personnel shadowed day and night, and dozens of people connected with the Holy See were questioned by the Italian police. Even the hitherto sacrosanct Vatican mail was opened and read by Italian censors. Since Vatican City, as the spiritual capital of the Catholic world, was easily accessible to the public, Italian secret-service men were introduced inside and checked on the activities of the foreign envoys to the Holy See.

Italy's most flagrant violation of the Lateran Treaty, which Mussolini and Pius XI signed February 11, 1929, and which brought harmony to Italo-Vatican relations for the first time since 1870, occurred in connection with Yugoslavia. Shortly after the conclusion of the Axis *Blitzkrieg* in Yugoslavia, Niko Mirosevich, who had been the Yugoslav Minister to the Holy See for almost two years, was suddenly ordered to leave Italy. As the Vatican Secretariat of State had nearly completed the preparation of the apartment he was to occupy within the extraterritoriality of the Holy See, along with other envoys whose countries were fighting Italy, like Britain, France, and Poland, he replied he would move immediately into Vatican City. The Fascists, nevertheless, informed him that he would not be permitted to enter the Vatican grounds and that he must leave the country. In view of his insistence, uniformed Fascists called for him in an automobile and drove him to the Swiss frontier. Monsignor Luigi Maglione, Papal Secretary of State, immediately addressed a strong protest to Ciano, pointing out that under the terms of the Lateran Treaty Italy was obliged to permit the passage of any envoy to the Holy See through Italian territory and must not place any obstacle in the way of such passage. Ciano replied that the Yugoslav state no longer existed, that the majority of the Catholics in former Yugoslavia were now in Croatia, and that therefore they should be represented by a Croat Minister to the Holy See. Ciano also contended that action had been taken against Mirosevich because of "political propaganda that he was making against Fascism." Monsignor Maglione, refusing to accept the suggestion of Ciano, sent a counterreply in which he stated that the Vatican would continue to regard Mirosevich as the accredited Yugoslav minister to the Holy See. The Vatican yearbook — Annuario Pontificio — of 1942 still listed Mirosevich as being duly accredited at the Vatican Secretariat of State. The word "absent" in parenthesis, however, appears after his name in the Annuario, but it contained the name of no Croat minister.

The most courageous stand the Pope made against Rome-Berlin pressure occurred in July, 1941, when Il Duce suggested that the Vatican come out for the Axis war on the Soviets as a "holy crusade against atheism." The Pope firmly replied that the Vatican attitude toward Russia concerned purely ecclesiastic and spiritual matters and that it was therefore impossible for the Holy See to make any pronouncement or commit any act which might be construed as strengthening any political group. It had been announced more than a week previous to this Fascist démarche that the Pope was to make a world-wide radio broadcast on July 29, 1941. Mussolini was particularly anxious that in this address the Pope should make some remark which might be construed as favorable to the German invasion of Russia. The Italian Ambassador to the Holy See, Bernardo Attolico, called frequently at the Secretariat of State to talk with Maglione about the matter. On the date announced, the Pope spoke on the "Ways of Providence," expressing his sorrow over the loss of life then taking place on European battlefields. But there was not a single word that even the most astute distorters of fact could twist into any possible encouragement to the self-styled crusaders. It was the Pope's categorical answer to the Axis that he would not permit his spiritual leadership to become a part of anyone's temporal ambitions.

The Vatican's attitude toward Soviet Russia had been consistent ever since the Bolshevik revolution of 1917, regardless of who was Pope. It was one of expending every possible effort to persuade the Soviet government to permit the people of Russia to enjoy the boon of religious liberty. And when the Vatican opposed the extension of Russian frontiers to include part of Poland, part of Finland, part of Rumania, and the three Baltic states, it was not a political maneuver against the Russian people but a religious stand aimed at preventing possible extinction of religious institutions.

The Vatican, for the past fifteen years, had been quietly training priests to do missionary work in Russia. On a side street in Rome, a seminary had been opened where priests could study for this work. Besides learning to speak not only Russian, but also Ukrainian and other Slavic languages used in the Soviet republics, they received special instruction in how to combat any heretical ideas that may have been absorbed by the Russian people during the past twenty-five years. This work was carried out as unostentatiously as possible, as the Vatican did not wish to start any political polemics by publicizing the existence of this seminary. We learned that a number of these priests had already gone into those parts of Russia that had been occupied by the German army, and were endeavoring to spread the Catholic religion. One high prelate told us that the Vatican did not regard this as taking any political stand, but simply as a part of its fundamental and permanent policy of sending Catholic missionaries wherever they could go, under any circumstances that happened to exist. The Germans were willing to allow the priests to carry out their duties because they believed many Russians and Ukrainians secretly yearned for religion and, therefore, if the German army was followed by priests, it would help to reconcile the Russians to German occupation.

Mussolini also demanded that the Vatican adopt a rationing system similar to that of the Italians. Il Duce did not want it known by the Italian people that there was still plenty of food in the world outside the Axis countries. The Vatican supplies, after the Italian market had become so meager, were received by way of Portugal from all parts of the world. In order to avoid further friction between Italy and the Holy See, especially since the matter was of minor importance, the Pope agreed, and the Vatican adopted a strict rationing system. Agents of the OVRA did not hestitate to continue searching, however, all people coming out of the Vatican for any food they might have in their possession that was considered contraband by Fascist decree.

An open breach between the Axis and the Holy See was prevented only by the diplomacy of the Pope. Militant in all matters appertaining to the tenets of the faith, the Pope adroitly sidestepped all issues regarding temporal affairs. But by the nature of his position as the head of a state who cannot take a stand in political matters, the Pope was compelled to maintain formal relations with the Axis countries. In this connection, Pius XII instructed Monsignor Cesare Orsenigo, Papal Nuncio to Berlin, on November 10, 1939, to convey the Vatican's congratulations to Adolf Hitler for having escaped death in the bombing that wrecked the Munich beer hall which the Führer had left only twenty minutes before.

In February, 1940, the Pope also sent a message of congratulation to Emperor Hirohito on the occasion of the 2600th anniversary of the founding of the Japanese Empire. Both of these messages, however, were sent purely as part of the protocol required of the head of a neutral state. Axis quarters in Rome explained that had he not sent such congratulations to Hitler and Hirohito, the neutrality of the Vatican would have been gravely compromised, while our Vatican informants assured us that these messages in no way constituted approval of German or Japanese policies.

One of the most fearless attacks that the Pope made against the Nazis for their religious persecution in German-occupied Poland was on January 28, 1940, when the Pontiff issued the text of a memorandum he had received from August Cardinal Hlond, Primate of Poland. The memorandum gave the names of a score of priests who had been killed by the Germans, told of the jailing of priests and the maltreatment of tens of thousands of Catholics in Poland by the Germans. It said that religious groups had been suppressed and churches closed down. The memorandum said:

"At Bydgeszcz, five thousand men were locked in a stable where there was not even room to sit down. There was fixed for their natural needs a corner of the stable, and a priest, Casimiro Stepczynski, was forced, together with a Jew, to carry away with their hands human excrement — work which was fatiguing due to the great number of prisoners.

"Dozens of imprisoned priests are being humiliated, beaten, and maltreated. Certain numbers have been deported to Germany, and no news of them has been received. . . . A group of priests, by hiding themselves among the population, have been able to continue their ecclesiastical function in a region which is without clergy. Imprisonment and arrest are occurring under such conditions that priests have not the possibility of saving the holy Sacraments, which are being profaned. Some priests were closed in a pigsty at night and beaten barbarously and subjected to other tortures. The persecution will soon have achieved its aim — a religion of twenty million Catholics will have become dechristianized while the cradle of the faith in Poland will become its tomb. . . . Germany has begun an extermination of Polish citizens which Hitler foreshadowed in *Mein Kampf* as a capital point of German policy and which was one of the causes and aims of the aggression.

"This extermination is continuing without interruption and takes the shape of perverse sadism."

Another attack on Nazi practices was issued with the approval of the Pope by the Sacred Congregation of the Holy Office, a Vatican institution aimed at protecting faith and morals. This statement contained strong denunciation of euthanasia as a state principle to eliminate the weak merely because they are weak. It implicitly admitted, however, that a criminal may be deserving of death at the hands of the state, as part of the framework of justice. But "mercy killings" were condemned as a government policy.

Pius XII inaugurated his pontificate by making a solemn plea for peace on the very next day after his election by the conclave. From then on until the outbreak of war, September 1, 1939, the Pope made six more appeals for the preservation of peace and during June put out diplomatic feelers to those governments of European countries which were likely to be involved in war. That the Pope was greatly alarmed over the signing of the Russo-German alliance could be seen by the fact that the following morning he received the British Chargé d'Affaires to the Vatican two separate times, and the Italian, French, and Polish Ambassadors once each. On the same day, he made a last supreme appeal that the nations not resort to war. On August 31, he sent messages to the German and Polish governments, entreating them to avoid any incident, and asked the governments of France, Britain, and Italy to give diplomatic support to his request.

The war broke out despite all the Pope's efforts, and the Pope immediately began using his influence to try to humanize the conflict as much as possible. He urged the warring powers to conform to international agreements regarding war rules and expressed the hope that civilian populations would be spared as much as possible and, above all, that gas would not be used. Between the time war broke out and January 1, 1941, the Pope made some thirty peace appeals in speeches, radio broadcasts, homilies, and pastoral letters and actively supported two other peace efforts — one made by President Roosevelt in his Christmas speech of 1939 and the other jointly made by King Leopold III of Belgium and Queen Wilhelmina of Holland. At the same time, Pius XII also made intensive efforts to limit the war and prevent its spread beyond the countries which had been participating in it from the very start.

Of all these peace appeals, the one made on December 24, 1939, in the form of an address to the Sacred College of Cardinals, was probably the most important because it contained the first hint that the Pontiff was already formulating a plan for "a just and honorable peace" which would offer a basis for postwar reconstruction. And on December 24, 1941, while we were interned in Siena, we heard the Pope again refer to his principles for a lasting peace. This time there could be no doubt that he was striking at the totalitarian states when he said:

"In some countries, a godless and anti-Christian conception of the state bound the individual to itself with its vast tentacles in such a way as almost to deprive him of all independence, and this no less in his private than in his public life. Who today can be surprised that this radical opposition to the principles of Christian teaching has finally found its outlet in so intense a clash of internal and external enmities as to lead to the extermination of human lives and the destruction of worldly goods?"

One of the last assignments that Eleanor had in Vatican City, before the entrance of the United States into the war put an abrupt end to our newspaper work in Italy, was to make a survey of the opinions of high Church prelates as to what specific principles were being incorporated in the papal plan for a new world setup. It had long been known that the Pope was working on such a plan, but only vague hints as to its contents had been divulged in his various pronouncements. After a careful study of these opinions and of all the Pope's speeches, including especially the Christmas speech of 1939, Eleanor believes that the following points represent the essentials of the Pope's plan. Eleanor later checked with Cianfarra, who covered most of the Vatican news for The New York Times, and found that they were both in agreement on the general principles involved. Eleanor's conception of the plan follows:

(1) Peace and postwar reconstruction must be in accordance with Christian principles, in which the absence of greed, aggrandizement, selfishness, and intolerance would enable the laying of a foundation of international understanding and comity. "The right to life and independence of all nations, large or small, strong or weak, must be recognized and accepted. One nation's will to live must never be tantamount to a death sentence for another."

(2) Nations must be liberated from the heavy slavery of armaments. The reconstruction must envisage general disarmament on a scale never hitherto attempted. This material disarmament would be worked out progressively in direct proportion to what the Pope described as "spiritual disarmament." Disarmament would result in a more salutary economic condition throughout the world, relieving, first of all, the terrific financial strain on the budgets of all nations. Material that otherwise would be poured

into fighting machines would be used to improve living conditions of the people.

(3) A great international institution would be set up to assure universal security, for without security disarmament would never be more than a theory. The institution would comprise one great council of sovereign states and a score of subsidiary institutions or departments which would be entrusted with the more technical aspects of international problems. Unlike the old League of Nations, this new institution would have supreme jurisdiction over the member states, which in turn would have a direct and democratic part in its administration. The institution thus becomes a legalized family of nations. All states would undertake to accept decisions of the institution as irrevocable. There would be no question of resigning from it. Parties to international disputes would be compelled to submit their disagreements to the arbitration of the established world court, and the rulings of this court would be mandatory. This would render the court much more powerful than the former tribunal at The Hague, which could only decide disputes when the contesting parties agreed in advance to submit their quarrel to its jurisdiction.

The institution would be composed solely of sovereign states which are not subject to the dictates of any other state, in order to prevent any grouping of individual opinion into a political or empire block. It would be the aim of the institution, however, to provide for the granting of independence to vassal states as they proved their capacity for self-rule.

(4) Ethnic minorities must be given every opportunity to develop their own culture within the framework of those states in which they find themselves. They would have the right to speak and write their own languages, but at the same time it would be their duty to learn the language of the larger state of which they form a part. The more conscientiously the state respects the rights of its minorities, the more safely and effectively it can demand their loyalty. There must be no distinction in the rights and freedom of minorities and majorities within a single state.

(5) Economic disturbances are the fundamental causes of wars, and to achieve any lasting peace it is necessary for all nations to have equal access to raw materials. At the same time, measures and expediencies which in the past have contributed to the dislocation of trade should in the future be banned. These include laws forbidding the exportation of goods, the erection of impassable customs barriers, the creation of monopolies, closing of national markets, dumping, and restrictions on the free movement of capital. Free access to raw materials does not mean that they should be internationalized, but rather that the owners, both individual and national, should recognize their responsibility to allow these goods to be used for the general benefit of mankind. Resources in the hands of private ownership must be accessible to all. Ownership of private property in no way eliminates obligation to the community, and all such property must be subordinated to the common good. This principle must be accepted by nations as well as by persons.

(6) Freedom is a natural right, for a man without freedom has no feeling of responsibility. The right of the individual to have personal liberty — including complete religious liberty — in his private life should be recognized by the state and should be embodied in the relations between the individual and the state. Religious freedom is a fundamental condition for a sound peace because the spiritual tendency of the human being toward good rather than evil creates ethical concepts which make for higher standards in national and international relations. Christian principles require that the individual sacrifice his personal benefit to the common good, and recognition of this principle makes for just government within a nation and international justice between nations.

(7) Treaties must be respected by all nations, but this does not mean that there cannot be revisions. On the contrary, revision of treaties when necessary to meet changing conditions in the world would be essential to the maintenance of peace and would prevent the blind perpetuation of a status quo which might become outmoded. All revisions, however, would be carried out by the world

institution. Any unilateral violation of treaties, as committed in the past by the Axis powers, would be outlawed in advance.

(8) Justice would be based on a priori right, and not on the strength of any one nation. Right and wrong would be determined purely as values in themselves, unrelated in any way to power.

The foregoing points, the Pope realized, could never be embodied in a peace resulting from an Axis victory.

Pius XII did not limit himself merely to outlining peace principles which find many parallels with the Atlantic Charter, but also expressed his approval of the United Nations' war aims as contrasted with Axis war aims in other ways. Although it is contrary to Vatican policy to side openly with one or another warring party, German methods and leadership frequently caused him to refer to the German government in terms which were, for the Holy See, exceptionally severe.

The war was only twenty-five days old when the first occasion arose. On that date, the *Osservatore Romano* appealed directly to Hitler to halt the bombing and shelling of Warsaw, saying, "He who said his goal was reached cannot be insensible to a prayer for human generosity." Five days later, the Pope gave further evidence of his indignation over the fate of Poland when he addressed the Polish colony of Rome as his "children of Catholic Poland" and, with tears in his eyes, said, "We hope that despite the many reasons to fear the only too-well-known plans of the enemies of God, Catholic life should continue profound and truthful among you."

In the first encyclical of his pontificate, issued October 27, 1939, the new Pope denounced the totalitarian states in very outspoken terms. Although he mentioned no countries by name, it was plain to which ones he was referring when he said, "To consider the state as something ultimate to which everything else should be subordinated and directed cannot fail to harm the true and lasting prosperity of nations." The encyclical continued:

"The idea which credits the state with unlimited authority is not simply an error harmful to the internal life of nations, but also, in the relations between peoples, robs the law of nations of its foundations and vigor, leads to violations of others' rights, and impedes agreement and peaceful intercourse."

During the winter of 1939–40, the Pope made several uncomplimentary references to Berlin, as when in a speech he blamed the outbreak of the war on "the cult of force," and permitted the Vatican radio to condemn Nazi brutalities to the faithful in German-occupied Poland. His next, more detailed denunciation of totalitarian ideas, however, came during his first post-Lenten public audience. On this occasion, Pius XII said:

"Not a few people today have lost peace because their prophets or rulers have turned away from God and his Christ. Some, followers of an irreligious culture and policy, enclosing themselves in the pride of human reason, have shut the door on the very idea of divinity; moving the image of the divine crucified Master from schools and tribunes, eliminating any mention of the Bible from national, social, and family institutions, although without being able to erase the profound traces."

On the eve of the Nazi invasion of the Low Countries, the Pontiff blamed "excessive human covetousness and thirst for power" for the war in Europe, and on the day after the Reichswehr attacked Belgium and Holland he addressed messages to the monarchs of both nations, expressing the hope that liberty and independence would be re-established in their countries.

On May 15, 1940, the Pope, while addressing some pilgrims, made a statement that was generally accepted as another denunciation of the Nazis, though it was interpreted quite differently in the Axis countries, when he said:

"The world at present is undergoing a threat of dying in violence because too many men are heartless. I address these words, which Saint Paul spoke during his time, to the neopagans and idolizers of gold, pleasures, and pride: 'The heart and courage must serve justice and right and have pity on the weak.'"

Since Germany was foremost of the neopagan countries, these words were everywhere taken as applying to her, except in Rome and Berlin, where the Axis governments insisted that "the idolizers of gold" were Britain, France, and the United States.

Italian Catholics, who had become accustomed to thinking that all the Pope's severe censures of totalitarian states were directed against their Nazi partners, received a jolt soon after Italy entered the war, when the Pope made plain his sympathy and commiseration for fallen France. The Pontiff had brought the full weight of all his Catholic influence to bear upon the Italian Fascist leaders to dissuade them from entering the war — but to no avail. During and immediately after the collapse of France, the Pope pleaded with the governments of Italy and Germany to show leniency toward France and in July he addressed a letter to the French bishops wherein he offended leading Fascists by expressing confidence that France would be reborn to her former greatness. It was repudiation of Mussolini's revindications upon France. The Pope wrote:

"These very misfortunes with which God today visited your people give assurance, we feel certain, through the adorable designs of His Providence, of the conditions for greater spiritual labor favorable to bringing about reawakening of the entire nation. . . . We know the spiritual resources of which France disposes to become tranquil in soul and to make of her misfortunes a believer of the new spiritual ascension which will be an achievement of salvation for her.

"Her resources are so numerous and so powerful that we are sure we will not have to await the conclusion of peace to put them to work, and will give to the world the spectacle of a great people worthy of its secular traditions who find in their faith and infinite charity the strength to face adversity and to resume their march on the path of the future and of Christian justice."

By the end of 1940, the war had spread to such an extent that the Pope despaired of bringing about a peace without victory and more or less resigned himself to the idea that the war would have to run its course until one side or the other had conquered, although at intervals he set aside certain periods to be devoted to peace prayers by Catholics all over the world. It was at this time that Pius began devoting a great deal of time to enlarging and perfecting the kind of peace he intended to urge the victors to adopt — peace terms which His Holiness was well aware would never be adopted by the Axis.

If the Pope's public attacks on Germany later diminished, it was not because he had changed his attitude toward the Nazis but because he had found that German Catholics and Catholics in German-occupied countries were usually the sufferers after one of his public statements. A number of Vatican officials also informed us that the fighting qualities of the German Catholics during the war had done much to relax the opposition of the Nazi government toward the Church, and that the Vatican was making the most of this opportunity. The Nazi government, however, continued to limit the Church's activities to those countries which were Catholic before their occupation — Belgium, France, Czechoslovakia, and, to a much more limited extent, Poland. Vatican officials believed their priests were doing much to alleviate the suffering in those countries; for example, they understood that the Pope's intervention had several times saved French hostages from being shot.

It was in connection with the Holy See's efforts to ameliorate the lot of civilians in occupied countries that the Pope agreed to the establishment of diplomatic relations between the Vatican and Japan, on March 28, 1942, when he appointed Monsignor Paolo Marella, Archbishop of Dioclea, as his Apostolic Nuncio to Japan and assented to the nomination of Ken Harada as Japanese Minister to the Holy See. It was pointed out by Vatican officials at the time that there were eighteen million Catholics in Japanese-occupied territories, including eleven million in the Philippines alone.

Exchange of diplomatic representatives with Japan did not in any way impair the cordiality of the Pontiff's regard for the United States. In fact, the entire Holy See had long regretted that there was no regular exchange of diplomats between the Vatican and the United States, which is one of the largest Catholic countries in the world, numbering more than 22,500,000 Catholics among its citizens. The awkwardness of this diplomatic situation, which left Pius XII and President Roosevelt without any channel of direct communication with each other, was partially remedied by the President when, in February, 1940, he sent Myron Taylor to Rome as his personal representative to the Pope. Taylor was given as his assistant Harold Tittmann, a career diplomatist from the State Department. As soon as the United States entered the conflict, Tittmann took up residence within Vatican territory as United States representative for the duration of the war. He was able to communicate with Washington only by means of the Vatican radio and was compelled to keep within the thirteen acres of the Vatican grounds because he would become an enemy alien the moment he stepped into Italy. The Vatican continued to maintain an Apostolic Delegate, Monsignor Amleto Giovanni Cicognani — an Italian — in Washington even after the United States and Italy were at war, although he had no diplomatic ranking or privilege. For example, he was never permitted to send or receive diplomatic mailbags.

On the Axis side, Vatican relations have been much better with Italy than with Germany. Italy has always been an almost one hundred per cent Catholic country, and even the most fanatic Fascists are at least ostensibly Catholics, whereas most Nazis are not. The result is that there has been no systematic repression of the Church and its influence in Italy as in Germany, although there have been isolated instances of conflict over individual cases, as in the dispute over what should be published in the Osservatore Romano. The Vatican well knew, through its hierarchy, that, with the vast majority of Italians, Fascism could never hope to supplant the Church, and the Pope in return often expressed his affection for his Italian followers by frequently referring publicly to "our beloved Italy."

During the war, the Vatican devoted itself to humanitarian activities, especially in regard to war prisoners. Its peculiarly neutral position, plus its world-wide organization, gave it special advantages for this kind of work. War prisoners were located and identified and the fact that they were alive was reported to their families in their own countries through the Vatican radio. The Vatican also operated an international post office where letters could be relayed between prisoners and their families after having been censored by the country from which they were sent. Major, now Colonel, Michael Buckley, United States army observer with the British forces in Egypt, who was captured by the Italians before the United States went to war, was located first by the Vatican when the United States Embassy in Rome had been vainly searching for him for months.

On July 18, 1940, the *Osservatore Romano* confirmed that the Pope had made *démarches* to all belligerents, requesting that the religious character of Rome be respected by all the warring nations. The newspaper added that both the British and French governments had replied, and from Vatican circles we learned that both Britain and France had acceded to the request, although pointing out that Mussolini must also show the same respect. Throughout our wartime stay in Italy, there was never a single bombardment of Rome, although there were about twelve alarms mainly because of air raids over Naples. At the beginning of the war, the French raided airfields well outside of Rome, but there was never any question of Rome itself being attacked. The Allies were respecting the Pope's request.

Many of us, however, felt that Mussolini was not. As the war went on, and Rome became regarded as the one safe city in warring Europe, Il Duce began to take advantage of the religious character of the city. Mussolini held frequent war councils in the Palazzo Venezia, often attended by representatives of the German High Command. Plans for the Libyan campaign were discussed in the Palazzo Venezia, where Il Duce, on several occasions, received Rommel.

The Germans set up an army headquarters in the Hôtel de Russie, on the Via Babuino. The Italian War Office, as well as all other ministries connected with the Italian war effort, continued in Rome despite the Pope's request that the religious character of the city be respected. The Rome railway station — Termini — was used as the main junction in sending German forces to Africa. The station was heavily placarded with signs in German, giving orders and directions to the Nazi troops. Supplies and war materials of all kinds, intended for Africa, also passed through the Rome station. The population of Rome increased steadily with the bombardments of other towns. Feeling safer in the capital, people left Milan, Naples, and Genoa by the thousands before restrictions were placed on travel.

In Vatican quarters, we were informed that the Pope was distressed that Mussolini had not removed all Axis war activity to beyond the city of Rome. It was reported that during the summers of 1941 and 1942, the Fascist government placed such obstacles in the way of the Pope's usual departure for his vacation at Castel Gondolfo, fifteen miles outside of Rome, that the Pontiff was compelled to spend the hot summer months a virtual prisoner in the Vatican. We know that in the summer of 1941 the Pope suffered so from the heat that he moved out of his papal apartments into the gardener's cottage, where there was more breeze in the late afternoon and evening.

The Vatican built a number of air-raid shelters, the most famous being the one for the Pope and his court. It was located in the Nicholas V Tower. The Pope, however, intimated to his close associates that if Rome were bombed, he would decline to go to the papal shelter and would remain in his private apartment, deep in prayer.

# XIII

There were two stories which went the rounds of the Foreign Press Club. One was about an Italian who entered the Caffè Aragno in Rome and ordered a waiter to bring him all the newspapers. He hurriedly glanced through the front page of each one and then put the paper aside without looking at any of the inside pages. Day after day and week after week, he repeated this same procedure. Finally, one of the habitués of the café, who had been observing him, came over and asked:

"Excuse me, but what have you been looking for all these weeks?"

"A death notice."

"But death notices are always on the inside pages."

"Not the one I'm looking for. It would be on the front page, all right."

The other story concerned a tourist who entered one of the best restaurants in Naples during the time that Mussolini had ordered the Italian people to wage war against flies. Several signs on the walls of the restaurant bore the words, GUERRA CONTRA LA MOSCA, but nevertheless the tourist could hardly eat his spaghetti because of the flies that buzzed about. The tourist turned to the waiter and said:

"But I thought you had a war against flies here."

The waiter replied, with a shrug of indifference: "Oh, we did have one, but we lost."

These two stories are certainly not very funny, but they do illustrate how a people who are indifferent to their surroundings — whether flies or politicians — could accept the continued leadership of a man who at best had only a small minority of support, while millions of Italians wished for his demise. It was this political lethargy of his enemies that enabled Il Duce to remain in power. During our association with Italians, we found them less hot-blooded than any of the other Latins whom we had known — Spaniards, Portuguese, French, and South Americans. They are not capable, like their fellow Latins, of being aroused to revolt. A civil war such as we had witnessed in Spain seemed almost unthinkable in Italy. But the indifference of the Italian public was a two-edged sword, for the Italian would not be whipped up to the pitch of enthusiasm that was necessary for efficient co-operation between fighters and civilians. And this apathy was doubly hard to overcome because of the war's unpopularity. Feeling as they did about Il Duce's territorial ambitions, they refused to put their shoulders to the wheel and, in a way, emulated the civil-disobedience movements in India. Only there was no Gandhi, no leader of any kind. It was blind, almost subconscious, and therefore all the harder to cope with.

As soon as Italy entered the conflict against France and England, Mussolini launched a press campaign to fire the Italians with a war spirit. When word reached him that the people showed little if any interest in official war news, he decreed that all public places having radios, especially cafés and bars, must turn them on at one P.M. and six P.M., when the communiqués were broadcast, and that all people must cease their drinking, eating, or whatever they might be doing, and stand at respectful attention during the reading of the communiqué.

On the radio, the foremost Fascist commentators bored the people with their overwritten, highly adjectival accounts of Fascist daring and victories. The Italians knew that what they were saying was just so much balderdash and did not bother to listen. A trick was needed to arouse interest. For a week, an Italian voice broke into the broadcasts of the Fascist commentators and criticized Mussolini, Fascism, and the Fascist war claims. This ruse excited the people, and by the millions they began listening to the broadcasts, hoping to hear these interruptions by what became known as the "Ghost Voice." Then it was announced that Mario Apelius had been appointed the official Ghost Catcher. Apelius was a curious character. He had run away from home at the age of fifteen to become a sailor and jack-of-all-trades, not settling down to newspaper work until he was thirty-two. We had met Apelius while he was a war correspondent in Ethiopia and Spain. He was a short, fierce-looking fellow whose shock of gray hair stood up like porcupine quills and whose bushy eyebrows flitted about his forehead like beetles when he became excited. He had a squeaky voice for the radio, but that didn't matter, because he knew all the Fascist answers. Every time the intruding voice would interrupt a Fascist harangue, Mario Apelius would come crashing in and give the Ghost a forensic trouncing.

"You're an Italian ass," said the phantom speaking on the Rome radio's wave length.

"That's better than being a British citizen," Apelius replied, becoming the first radio speaker ever to answer back to a heckler.

"But you have sold out," the Ghost said.

"Yes, sold out to my country. But you have sold out to foreigners."

"But victory will be Germany's, not Italy's."

"Yes, victory will be Italy's, too, and you know it. The Axis was never stronger than now."

"I dare you to tell us what is happening in Italy."

"It's raining," chuckled Apelius, "which is good for our crops."

All the Italian newspapers carried lengthy explanations as to how Apelius could both receive and send simultaneously. He was described as wearing special earphones which enabled him to listen in on broadcasts while at the same time he could answer through the microphone in front of him.

The Italian people, however, were not to be fooled. The Ghost was not critical enough to suit them. He wasn't even asking the simple questions that the average man in the street would have asked. He was just a stooge for Apelius, and soon almost all the Italians believed the report that the Ghost and his Ghost Catcher were broadcasting from the same studio. This effort to excite the interest of the people failed so badly that it was abandoned.

But the man the Duce counted on most for disseminating his war propaganda was Virginio Gayda, who was frequently dubbed in the foreign press "Mussolini's mouthpiece."

As editor in chief of the *Giornale d'Italia*, he offered a channel whereby the Fascist government could present its views both inside Italy and abroad, without committing itself to any official utterance. Gayda's articles were read, not only by newspaper correspondents but also by diplomats and foreign offices, with the greatest care and attention for hints of new orientations in Fascist policy. It was true that Gayda was exceedingly close to both Mussolini and Ciano and that his writings often reflected the latest thoughts of the Duce, but he was more than that; he was almost the Fascist conscience. When there were new developments abroad, Gayda often was not able to call on Mussolini before writing an article in time for his newspaper's dead line, yet he seldom failed to react as Mussolini himself would, to news of importance, whether inside or outside of Italy. A shrewd and intelligent man, he had studied Fascist doctrine and policy so thoroughly that he knew reflexively, without waiting to be told by the Duce, what the proper Fascist attitude would be. He was like a skinned frog reacting to a sprinkling of salt. Sometimes he even forecast Fascist policy before Mussolini had made up his own mind, as in the case of Italy's withdrawal from the League of

Nations, which he predicted well in advance of Il Duce's decision, on the basis of the League's attitude toward the Italian campaign in Ethiopia.

Eleanor called on Gayda several times and found him an electrically energetic man of less than medium stature, with iron-gray hair and quick, penetrating eyes. Eleanor found both his French and English extremely fluent, and he told her he also had sufficient knowledge of German, Russian, and Swedish to read newspapers in those languages, which he frequently did. In fact, he always had foreign newspapers lying on the table by his desk, with phrases here and there underlined with red crayon. Despite his evident cleverness, Gayda was a man of vanity. His office was absurdly ostentatious and unbelievably large. It had alcove windows of colored glass with steps leading up to them and was furnished with overstuffed leather chairs, a couch, and massive bookcases. He sat in the center of the room at a giant desk with a long table running at right angles to it. Eleanor noticed on her last visit that he still had in his office a life-sized bronze statue of a wolf suckling Romulus and Remus, although it had been decreed months before that all bronze objects must be turned over to the government metal collectors.

"I can't understand why Americans fail to grasp the real meaning of Fascism," Gayda said to Eleanor, never losing an opportunity for a sales talk. "I am afraid you correspondents here in Rome are not sending the right sort of thing. There is no reason why America and Italy should not have a better understanding."

This was about six months before America entered the war. Eleanor pointed out that the constant attacks of the Italian press against President Roosevelt, his wife, and all things American could certainly not help Americans to understand Fascist philosophy.

"Ah," Gayda replied. "That is for home consumption, for the home front. If you were really helpful, you would not mention these campaigns in your dispatches. You would write about the way Fascism is helping the laborer, the office worker, and people of all classes to improve their standard of living. You would make the people of your country understand Italian revindications on France and her natural desire to take her rightful place in the sun."

"Yes," Eleanor said. "But if I did that I wouldn't be an American journalist. Or, for that matter, an American."

"Yes, yes," Gayda said. "You American correspondents are much more difficult than the European ones. They are all friendly and try to send the things that will improve relations between Italy and their own countries, while you, you are ever the critics and makers of trouble. It is particularly unfortunate because I realize that the American press has a greater world-wide influence than any other press today."

It was an unsatisfactory interview, because Gayda, as a journalist himself, was ever reluctant to divulge a story to another journalist. He would rather write it himself and have it relayed by all the foreign correspondents than give it to just one.

Another important editorial writer was Giovanni Ansaldo, editor in chief of Ciano's newspaper, Il Telegrafo. He had a less racy style than Gayda and was inclined to be more laborious and detailed, and perhaps even more profound, but he did not have Gayda's up-to-the-minute information or his privileged position with Mussolini, being primarily Ciano's protégé. Ansaldo had not arrived at his influential position without difficulty. At one time he had been a Socialist, and when the Fascist regime was first established in Italy, he spent five years in confino (forced domicile in a small town). However, he changed his politics and, owing to his cleverness, the Fascists soon forgave him his former ideology and proceeded to make use of him. Besides his newspaper work, he broadcast every Sunday afternoon to the Italian armed forces, giving pep talks to keep up the morale of the soldiers in training camps as well as at the front. They often contained hints of foreign policy and were therefore always listened to by the American correspondents.

The best the Ministry of Unpopular Culture could do in the

way of getting an American to do Fascist propaganda work was Ezra Pound, of Idaho. He had long been an expatriate, writing most of his poetry in his modest home in Rapallo on the Italian Riviera, where he lived with his English wife and one daughter. He was one of the few American admirers of Fascism, and a personal friend of Mussolini. His letterhead displayed a woodcut of himself, stressing a pointed red beard and an open Byronic collar. It also included a quotation from one of Mussolini's speeches about liberty being a duty as well as a privilege. He had written a number of economic books, subsidized by the Black Shirts, in which he attempted to show that Fascist economy was better than the democratic way of doing business. He was an easy mark for the Fascists, and on January 23, 1941, he adopted a southern accent and began a series of broadcasts against Roosevelt over the Rome radio. The day of Pearl Harbor, Pound unexpectedly came to our house and told us that war between the United States and Italy was inevitable but that he intended to stay on. Reynolds told him that he would be a traitor if he did so, and that now was the time for him to pipe down about the alleged glories of Fascism.

"But I believe in Fascism," Pound said, giving the Fascist salute. "And I want to defend it. I don't see why Fascism is contrary to American philosophy. I have nothing against the United States, quite the contrary. I consider myself a hundred per cent American and a patriot. I am only against Roosevelt and the Jews who influence him."

"What does Pavolini pay you for a broadcast?" Reynolds asked.

"Two hundred lire," Pound said, "for a fifteen-minute one. Otherwise it's less."

"That's only about ten dollars," Eleanor said.

"That's right; it's not much, but you don't think I do it just for the money, do you?" Pound asked, rising indignantly and pacing up and down the room. "I tell you I want to save the American people."

There was no way to reason with him.

We had known him in Paris in the old days of Elliot Paul, when Pound was more poet than politician, more literary than Fascist. There was no doubt in our minds that bitterness had caused him to undergo this queer metamorphosis. He was not interested in money. We decided it was because he had been a failure in his own country. Although he had had forty-one volumes of poetry, essays, stories, and treatises published, they had brought him little in the way of fame or emolument. He was regarded a failure and an eccentric in his own country, and he knew it. But he still had aspirations to be great, somehow or other, and Fascist Italy was interested in his talents, such as they were. He was going to give it a try. We felt that he was suffering from a case of acute inferiority complex.

And when the United States went to war a few days later, Pound opted to continue his broadcasts for Pavolini and thus became the American Lord Haw-Haw of Italy — and a traitor.

The hardest work of the Fascist government was to prevent widespread violation of rationing laws. No Italian we met ever seemed to regard it as his patriotic duty to observe them. Bootlegging and hoarding flourished, and the only people who did not buy contraband goods on the Black Market were those who could not afford them, mainly most of the working-class people who earned very small wages. Quite frequently, Italian inefficiency, combined with transportation difficulties, caused such shortages of food at various times and various places that the workingman was not able to get even the small quotas allotted him by law. When he did get his full amount of food, it was probably adequate to maintain him in fairly good health, but it was never enough to satisfy his appetite. Consequently, there was much grumbling against those who had sufficient money to pay the high Black Market prices and eat well. This privileged group included not only the normally well-to-do classes, such as property owners and the like, but also many men who had made money exclusively through their political positions in the Fascist party. The more difficult the food situation became and the more strict the rationing, the more did the popularity of the Fascist party decline, and the greater the resentment against the new Fascist ruling class became. To make matters worse, the moment there began to be a scarcity in any one food product, so that there was the likelihood that it would be rationed, speculators immediately bought up all they could obtain of it, knowing well that they would be able to bootleg it at four or five times its normal price. For example, just before it was decided to ration chick-peas, which were comparatively plentiful, they suddenly disappeared from the shops. The Fascist speculators had bought them up.

The government did not show any determination about suppressing these speculators. There were numerous arrests, but the arrested ones were only small fry and they were given such light sentences and fines that bootlegging continued to be well worth the risk. The cynical and suffering public quickly came to the conclusion that the reason this outrageous Black Market was permitted to continue to flourish unchecked was that the high Fascist officials were engaging in it and making private fortunes out of the hoarding of essential foodstuffs.

The only common people who were able to live well were those in the army, and that was true only to a relative degree. Mussolini had insisted that soldiers' food should be plentiful and nourishing, as he was well aware that there was nothing that would breed revolution more quickly than an armed but hungry army. The Fascists supplying the army did not dare to go against his orders too much in this respect, because they realized that if Il Duce heard about it they would quickly lose their very lucrative party jobs. In addition, the transportation facilities permitting, the armies at the fighting fronts got better food than the divisions stationed in Italy. However, the stealing and bootlegging of the soldiers' food by army cooks were notorious.

That the war was fundamentally unpopular with the masses was apparently well recognized by the Fascist leaders, since they introduced rationing very gradually, despite the fact that Italy's resources were so limited. A few things had been rationed even before Italy went to war — coffee, sugar, gasoline, coal and laundry soap. In the case of all but sugar and soap, this rationing was owing to the effect of the war on overseas shipping. Of sugar, Italy had far more than she needed, but the Italian government began using a great deal of it to manufacture alcohol for supplementing the limited supplies of gasoline, while increased production of armaments caused a shortage of fats that had been used in making laundry soap. The government also prohibited the sale of beef, veal, pork, and mutton three days weekly.

A few months after Italy entered the war, the Fascist government rationed rice, flour, corn meal, butter, lard, and even spaghetti and olive oil, the two most fundamental ingredients of the Italian cuisine. The spaghetti ration was two kilos (four and a half pounds) a month per person, and if rice, flour, or corn meal were needed, they had to be deducted from the spaghetti quota. Butter and lard could be had only by substituting them for an equivalent amount of the olive-oil allotment, which was fixed at eight hundred grams per person per month but was quickly reduced within a few weeks to four hundred grams, or slightly less than one pound. These measures worried the Italian public, which began to realize for the first time what hardships lay in store for them. And when we left Italy toward the end of May, 1942, the Italian food situation had become immeasurably worse. By that time, the Italian workingman's diet had been reduced to something like this:

Ten ounces of soggy, brownish bread a day; a little more than two ounces of black spaghetti a day; two eggs a week; three or four potatoes a week; enough beef or veal for one meal a week; enough lamb or goat for one meal a week; a quarter of a pound of sugar a week; a quarter of a pound of butter or oil a week; from three to four ounces of cheese made from skimmed milk a week; fish, perhaps once a week (for the most part there was only enough to go around on Fridays); enough rabbit or sausage for one meal a week. Once in a while some beans, lentils, dried peas, or chestnuts, which were still cheap enough for the working-class housewife to buy, could be found, but they were very scarce — partly owing to speculation and hoarding, partly to the fact that flours made out of such vegetables were used in making bread. Chicken had become far too expensive for working-class people, although fairly plentiful. Aside from these staple foods, Italians of the poorer classes had nothing more to eat except green vegetables and fruit, which in Italy gave indication of continuing always abundant. Even the sale of nuts was blocked since they were being used to make a substitute cooking oil. Housewives and children got less bread than their menfolk — about six and a half ounces a day.

We soon learned why the leading bootleggers in the United States during prohibition were of Italian origin. The Italians took to bootlegging rationed products with such aptitude that it showed almost a national characteristic. After a few months of war, when it had been forbidden by decree to serve meat except on Saturday, we went into one of the leading restaurants on a Wednesday night. The menu was vegetarian, but the headwaiter, without any hesitancy, recommended that we have *saltimbocca alla romana*. At a table near us was a bemedaled Black Shirt official in uniform, a red stripe around his left cuff, showing he had participated in the March on Rome. Reynolds pointed out that it might be dangerous for the restaurant to serve us meat in the presence of such an important Fascist official.

"Oh," laughed the headwaiter, "he just ordered a steak himself. That's why he came here — because he knows he can always get meat."

In another restaurant, a week later, we were also served meat on a meatless day. But this time it was cleverly hidden beneath a huge leaf of lettuce which the waiter suggested we use to cover up the contents of our plate whenever a new customer came in.

"We don't think anybody cares, but it's best to be careful. And it's so simple to hide it with a lettuce leaf."

In several de luxe restaurants, it was possible, until the United

States got into the war, to have real coffee, though it had been banned since January, 1940.

Almost every morning, two or three bootleggers would come to our home before we left for the office and offer us legs of lamb, goats, chickens, ducks, eggs by the dozen, and butter. It was just a question of paying more. At first, it was double, but slowly mounted, as the rationing became more and more strict, to as much as five times the legal price. And the strange part was that none of these bootleggers felt he was doing anything wrong or unpatriotic. The war was unpopular, the people were indifferent anyway, and here was a good opportunity to make big profits.

As soon as the OVRA learned of the extent of this house-to-house peddling of contraband produce, it began to search the farm wagons coming into the capital from the country and even to examine the packages and baggage brought into the Rome station by people traveling on suburban trains. The bootleggers soon found the answer to this and would hand their packages of contraband over to soldiers and army officers, who came from the same small town, and had them carried through the station under army protection. Once outside the station, they would get back their contraband and go the round of their customers. The OVRA seldom dared to stop and search men in uniform.

But a limited amount of food was far from being the only wartime hardship the Italians had to suffer. Lack of adequate heating was one of the worst because the winter climate in Italy, though fairly sunny, is far from warm. In Rome, during the winter of 1941-42, heating of apartment buildings, hotels, and houses was permitted only between two P.M. and nine P.M., and that only for one hundred days beginning December 10. Office buildings had even greater restrictions on heat. Owners of apartment houses could only provide hot water for their tenants three times a week for a few hours in the morning. Cooking gas was cut off except for two hours before each meal hour. This was all because of the coal shortage. The million tons of coal a month that Germany was shipping by train to Italy across the Brenner Pass were all needed to keep Italian factories running. The Italians could not begin to pay for all this coal in cash, but Germany was taking everything she could get in kind, and the Italian public ascribed the shortages in many foodstuffs, particularly potatoes, to the belief that a good percentage of Italian crops was going to Germany.

The Italians could not make up for the lack of heat by bundling themselves up in warm clothes, because clothes rationing had already been imposed. Usually, when a new rationing decree was about to be issued, rumors about it got around for several days previously. But the clothes-rationing project came utterly without warning when the Rome radio, during one of its principal broadcasts the evening of September 30, 1941, announced that beginning the next day all clothes, drygoods, and specialty shops and factories supplying them would be closed for a month. The broadcaster stated that during the month's closing, a careful inventory of the stocks would be taken and that when business resumed, clothing could be bought only with coupons.

The closing of the shops marked the inauguration of a bootleg regime of a magnitude far overshadowing anything that had thus far occurred on the food market. People with a little money put away rushed to stock up on clothes for the duration, while the shopkeepers were anxious to sell their goods before they had been inventoried, for fear of establishment of price ceilings.

Clothes rationing was mainly provoked by the activities of the German tourists in Italy. Nazis who, because of party services, had been able to get one of the prized visas for Italy had swarmed over the Italian cities by the thousands, ransacking the shops for the goods they could not buy at home. It was nothing unusual to see a German woman buy five or six dozen pairs of silk stockings at a time. They and the German men bought shoes, suits, dresses, shirts, underwear, ties, and hats in wholesale quantities. The Fascists actually had locked the barn door after the horse was stolen, because when the inventory was taken it was found that the shop shelves were already half bare and many of the textile factories were ready to close down for lack of raw materials. When the rationing cards were issued, it was sadly learned that a man could buy a suit or a pair of shoes in one year, but not both, while if a woman bought a heavy winter coat she could get little else except a few handkerchiefs and some underwear. To check still further the purchase of clothes by German tourists, the government decreed that the stores must demand not only the ration coupons, but also an identity card, before they could sell their goods. As we ourselves soon found, getting identity cards was a long and complicated procedure which only permanent residents would have the time and patience to undertake.

Nearly every day at the press conference, one of the German correspondents or a correspondent from one of the smaller Tripartite countries would raise the question as to when the Press Ministry was going to do something about getting identity cards for the correspondents who were too busy to get them for themselves. Finally, Rocco stated that he had investigated the matter and found that the correspondents' blue press cards were sufficient. Within two or three days, however, a number of the German correspondents stated that they had tried the blue press cards and found they didn't work. Finally, one day a distinctly acrimonious scene took place which was all the more extraordinary when it is remembered that this was less than a month before Italy declared war on the United States. A German correspondent got up in the press conference and demanded to know when this farce was going to cease; that despite his blue card, neither he nor his wife had been able to buy anything, whereas he had positive knowledge that an American woman had gone into a shop he knew of and had bought thirty-five pairs of silk stockings without any kind of identity card or coupon. When he said this, all the correspondents and press officers turned around and looked at Eleanor, who was one of the few American women still in Italy. But before Eleanor had decided whether or not she should say anything, the German correspondent added, "It was not la Signora Packard. It was a lady from the American Embassy." The tension was not lessened by an attempted quip from an Italian journalist, Ermanno

Frankinet, who attended the foreign-press conferences in his capacity as assistant to one of the Japanese correspondents. The Italian said:

"You should feel sorry for the poor *signora americana*. Remember, they do not have any silk in America any more, so probably she wants to take some Italian stockings back home to Mrs. Roosevelt."

"I fail to see the humor," von Langen indignantly interposed. "I can see nothing funny in the fact that any American receives better treatment than Germans from Italian shopkeepers."

Rocco muttered that he would do something about the cards right away, and the incident was closed. But it was an interesting example of how many Italian shopkeepers hated their German allies and felt only the greatest friendliness toward their potential enemies, the Americans.

When we left Italy, the price of a pair of all-leather bootleg shoes — believe it or not — was about forty dollars, and wearing apparel was proportionately exorbitant. This again was another social injustice which was greatly resented by the Italian worker who could not afford to pay such prices. There were other ways of cheating the rationing besides bootlegging. In many reputable shops which were too closely watched by the police to sell goods without receiving clothes coupons, the proprietors would frequently allow their customers to buy twice as many articles for a given number of coupons than they were legally entitled to. Many of the very poor Italians, like servants, sold their clothing tickets to the well to do, not for cash but for old clothes.

Probably one of the worst hardships the population of Italy had to suffer was the inadequate transport. The absolute elimination of private cars and the drastic reduction in the number of taxis swelled the mobs using the already overcrowded public conveyances, like busses and streetcars, to such an extent that a ride in one of them was an ordeal to be dreaded. The busses stopped running at ten o'clock at night, so that all social activities in the evening — even going to the movies — had to be forgone unless one lived in the center of town. Most places of amusement accordingly closed down before ten P.M. Dancing, whether public or private, had been forbidden ever since Italy entered the war. It seemed to us that all this had a very bad effect on Italian morale, since the Italians, instead of being able to forget their troubles in harmless amusements, had nothing to do but go home and grumble to neighbors about how the war was going to turn out and how many more sacrifices they would have to suffer before it was over.

The Ministry of Unpopular Culture set to work to counteract this grumbling. Jokes began to appear in all the newspapers, making fun of the shortage of fuel, food, clothing, and the closing down at early hours of cafés and other amusement places. The comic magazines *Marc' Aurelio*, *Il Travaso*, and *Il Bertoldo*, notorious for their earthy humor, devoted entire pages to witticisms about wartime hardships. A typical cartoon in the *Travaso* showed a man bounding along the street on his head. He explained to a curious friend: "What do you expect? The hat is old, the shoes are new."

In another cartoon, in the *Bertoldo*, two policemen were questioning a man with a basketful of eggs. One policeman asked: "How did you get these eggs?" The man replied: "I laid them myself." The daily newspaper of Turin, *La Stampa*, did its bit with a sketch of a beggar standing in the street with outstretched hands. He was practically nude except for a pair of brand-new shoes. "Why should you beg?" a passer-by asked. "You've been able to buy shoes." The beggar answered: "That's why I'm bankrupt."

Another cartoon portrayed two very ragged hoboes talking together. One of them said: "A taste for alcohol brought about my downfall. What was your weakness?" And the second replied: "A taste for eggs, fried in butter."

The *Marc' Aurelio* used the old Italian custom of men pinching girls to make light of the overcrowded autobusses. It published a caricature of a man in an overflowing autobus, holding his two arms over his head. He was quoted as saying: "I'm not going to be falsely accused any more."

Rocco and Capomazza were very proud of this would-be humor and told the American correspondents that it revealed how much real freedom of speech there was in Italy. But nobody was taken in, least of all the Italians: it was such an obvious effort to make people laugh at their own sufferings.

One evidence of Mussolini's dissatisfaction with the public apathy toward the war was to be seen in his frequent changes of local party leaders. He was constantly trying to find local bosses who could arouse public spirit to a fighting pitch. The Fascist party leadership was also changed three times during the first three years of the war.

The first big shake-up came on October 31, 1939, when Achille Starace, a prominent Briton-baiter, was removed from the Secretary Generalship of the Fascist party, a post which he had held eight years, to make way for the less politically minded but militarily prominent Ettore Muti. It was apparently hoped that Muti — who had started his military career as a sixteen-year-old boy in World War I, had become one of Mussolini's fighting *squadristi* during the internal troubles which preceded the March on Rome, and had later won several medals and considerable distinction as an aviator during the Ethiopian and Spanish wars — would be able to galvanize a marching spirit into the rank and file of the Fascist party. At the same time that Muti came in, other cabinet shake-ups took place. Alessandro Pavolini, who also had a military record and had been a pre-March-on-Rome Fascist, became Minister of Popular Culture, while the Ministers of Agriculture, Communications, Currency and Exchange, Public Works, and Italian Africa were also changed. Most of the new ministers were old-time Fascists, even though young in years, and this *cambio della guardia* was generally interpreted as a sign that Mussolini was battening down the hatches for the European war; that is to say, he was surrounding himself with men whose personal loyalty to himself had been thoroughly tested, even though they might be less able than the ones they replaced. Ciano, Minister of Justice Grandi, Minister of Education Bottai, and Minister of Finance Thaon de Revel kept their posts.

The Muti experiment, however, proved a failure. As Secretary General, he did not prove particularly successful at arousing public hate against the enemies the Fascists had chosen for Italy, while as an administrator he was considerably inferior to past party secretaries. The start of the Greek war permitted Muti to resign gracefully after one year's incumbency, with the explanation that he wished "to give his whole time to war service." He was succeeded by the Vice-Secretary, Adelchi Serrena, a rank-and-file politician and soapbox orator.

Serrena himself was got rid of shortly after the United States entered the war. He was replaced by Aldo Vidussoni, a mere youngster of twenty-seven whose only recommendation was that he had won one of the highest Italian decorations — the Gold Medal — during the Spanish Civil War. The real reason for his elevation was that he was the lover of one of Mussolini's mistresses, who used her amorous influence with the Duce to get him appointed.

These appointments, though more spectacular, were probably less important than the frequent shuffling of the less exalted leaders of the party. During the course of the war, Fascist-party inspectors and provincial secretaries, members of party directorates and of the national council, and heads of national guilds and corporations were frequently changed. In nearly all cases the new appointees were either pre-March-on-Rome Fascists or very young and unknown men who had only recently begun to get ahead in the party mainly because of their Fascist enthusiasm. Also, in nearly every case it was blandly announced that the discharged officials had "resigned in order to serve their country in a military capacity." Mussolini forced all those he fired to join the army so that they could not return to their old precincts and make trouble.

The most puerile campaign that the Fascists launched was the one to stamp out foreign influence. It was aimed at extirpating anything, from words to clothes, that could be traced to British, American, French, or Russian origin. At least once a week the newspapers would print lists of unpatriotic words and give Italian equivalents, generally neologisms, to replace them. For example, "football" was replaced by *calcio*; "cocktail" became *coda di gallo*.

Solemn decrees were also passed ordering, under penalty of imprisonment and fine, elimination of all foreign names for hotels, cabarets, and bars. Italian words, it was stated, must henceforth replace such names as "Metropole," "Beausejour," "Bellevue," or "Majestic." The American Express had to become Espressa Americana. Chez Robert, Café de Paris, and Moulin Rouge under this ruling suddenly became known respectively as Casa Roberto, La Roma, and Mulino Rosso.

The handshake was frowned upon as a foreign importation and un-Roman as compared to the open-hand Fascist salute. Orchestra conductors in the summer were ordered to wear white linen Fascist uniforms instead of the usual tails with stiff-bosomed shirts and collars of "British style."

The Fascist youth took particular delight in the edict against women wearing shorts or long trousers, which were supposed to be a mode imported from Communist Russia and "plutocratic America." The great sport of the Fascist youths was to find a girl so garbed and then chase her down the street or along the beach, trying to remove the offending piece of apparel.

Eleanor had a bad experience one morning when Reynolds was sick and she dashed across the street in her house slacks to buy him some medicine. As she came out of the pharmacy, four Fascist youths in uniform were waiting for her and immediately tried to pull off her trousers. Slapping at them, Eleanor succeeded in defending herself, but only after the key buttons had been torn off. Crowds gathered and impeded her progress. She was nearly taken to a police station. Her explanation that she was an American and therefore entitled to wear American styles saved her from further mauling.

One of the gravest signs of bad morale on the Italian home front was the universal lack of confidence in the lira among the moneyed classes. This was reflected in the soaring inflationary prices of all kinds of property that would presumably have a permanent postwar value. Italians with capital to invest searched frantically for something comparatively safe, but one avenue after another was blocked by various government regulations. Many bought gold and silver ornaments and precious stones until the government put a halt to all such sales, because so much jewelry was being bought by Nazi tourists and taken across the Brenner Pass where its value to Italy would be permanently lost.

For a while, shares in industrial plants were a popular investment, and the stocks of such companies as Breda, Fiat, and Viscosa soared on the Italian bourse until the Fascists slapped high taxes both on the transfers of stock and on the stock itself, and in addition compelled holders to register their title to the stock. The Fascists were trying to find out what people could afford to buy more war-loan bonds. Most people with money were not investing heavily in government bonds, because they feared the bonds would be worthless when the war was over.

Perhaps the most popular wartime investment of all was real estate. A people whose country had been overrun by conquerors as many scores of times as had Italy was apt to turn instinctively to the land in time of crisis. It is something that cannot be picked up and carried away — it is safe from everything except a Communist revolution. Therefore, as soon as Italians generally began to realize that an Axis victory was in doubt, land prices began skyrocketing, since few owners of property had any desire to sell. The government — ever hungry for new sources of revenue — then made owners still more reluctant to sell by decreeing that one quarter of the purchase price was to be paid in government bonds. Since the bonds could not be sold until after the war, this had the effect of reducing the cash value of the land by twenty-five per cent. The situation was further aggravated by the fact that in Italy there was very little property on the market other than city property, even in normal times. The bulk of the agricultural land had been in the same families for generations; in some cases, for centuries.

Yet with all the government price fixing and the close Fascist — and Nazi — supervision of all branches of Italian production, there were plenty of industrialists and big landowners in Italy who were making rich profits out of the war. They couldn't squander it on frivolities or luxuries because there weren't any to be had. There were no jewels, yachts, or automobiles. There were no night clubs, no champagne, whisky, or French brandy. Imported furs had practically disappeared even from the Black Market, and the sale of most furs had been prohibited by government decree on the grounds that fur might be needed for the armed forces fighting in Russia. And these wealthy people hesitated to give lavish entertainments in their homes for fear of drawing unwelcome attention to themselves.

"I am going to give a dinner party as soon as I move into my new apartment, and I want you both to come," one Italian woman said to us in the summer of 1941. "I can't entertain where I am now because a Fascist informer lives in the same building and he would report me for bootlegging food, but in the new place I am moving to even the portiere is anti-Fascist, so I can risk a party now and then."

With most normal spending and investment channels closed to them, people with money turned to the one thing that the government was not likely to requisition — art. Pictures, statues, antique furniture, tapestries, Oriental rugs, even coats of armor were sought after. Prices doubled and redoubled, but even so, these objets d'art were considered good investments since no one knew what the lira was really worth. It was nothing to hear someone say at a cocktail party that he or she had just spent 100,000 lire for a painting by one of the less-known Italian artists.

"I was going to invest in a dozen or so pairs of shoes to last me for the duration," one man told Eleanor, "but my bootlegger tells me he's having such a hard time finding leather that he can only let me have two pairs right now. So I'm buying some tapestries instead. They'll still be worth quite a lot after the war and in the meantime they'll look very nice in my study."

During the year preceding the United States' entry into the war, we were besieged by well-to-do Italians who wanted to sell us lire for dollars at a rate considerably higher than the official

one. They offered twenty-four lire to the dollar as against the
official exchange of seventeen. Since Italian-American financial
transactions had been "frozen," they did not want or expect to be
paid for their lire until after the war was over. What they hoped
for was to have a stake with which they could start life again no
matter how badly Italy was beaten. It was insurance against a
terribly rainy day. They always seemed to be disappointed when
we explained that our very delicate position as correspondents
under constant surveillance of the OVRA made it impossible for
us to enter into any such transactions, besides all the other reasons.

Some idea of the Italian public's lack of confidence in the
Axis' chances of winning may be gathered from the fact that the
rate on dollars went up after the United States entered the war!
While we were interned in Siena we could have bought lire
cheaper than at any time during the previous year. The rate offered to us while we were interned was twenty-five lire to the dollar — a whole lira more than before America became involved in
the conflict. It was economic evidence that even Italians favored
America against the Axis as the winner in the final outcome.

XIV

The Italian as a fighter has long been the butt of jokes abroad and in general has the reputation of being one of the world's worst combatants, whether on land or sea or in the air. Actually, we found that the Italians were not half so bad as they were generally believed to be by others, and not half so good as they thought they were themselves. Our association with Italian fighting units in Ethiopia, Spain, and the present war gave us the impression that the men themselves would make a better showing if they had better training, equipment, generalship, and, even more important, good captains and majors to lead them. Also, we discovered that the three armed branches were of three different calibers.

The navy was the least Fascist of all and, because of that, the best. Mussolini once said, "I don't know anything about naval matters, so I let the navy look after itself."

The army, a hybrid organization comprising both regular soldiers and Black Shirt Militia, should rank next in effectiveness and efficiency.

The aviation, which is virtually one hundred per cent Fascist, was always the worst. And frequently, because of its lack of co-operation, was the cause of many disasters suffered by the other two armed branches.

Probably the greatest deficiency of all three of the services was Italy's lack of fighting tradition. Even before the fall of the Roman Empire in the year 476, the Italians had begun to count almost exclusively on mercenaries. In the intercity wars that followed between rival capitals like Florence and Milan, the Italians used foreign troops to do the fighting. Venice alone developed a renown for the warring prowess of its own people and that was exclusively in the domain of the sea. And the Venetian navy was smashed by Napoleon, who then burned all its ships. In 1870, when the city-states united into a single kingdom, one of the most pressing problems was building up an Italian army and navy. Today, the Italian forces are still young and devoid of background as compared to those of other nations like the United States, England, France, Germany, and Poland.

The Italian navy, probably because it was associated with the British as an ally for so many years, developed the first semblance of a pride in itself. It also had as officers, from the first, members of the Italian aristocracy, many of whom had been educated in England and spoke English fluently. They grafted on the Italian navy much of English ways and thought. We were always impressed whenever aboard an Italian ship, whether a fighting unit or a freighter, by the Bristol fashion in which everything was kept, compared to the sloppiness of the Italian army and aviation. The Italian navy had become extremely proud of itself and therefore was deeply hurt when the BBC made fun of it by broadcasting:

"While the United States navy drinks whisky and the British navy prefers rum, the Italian navy sticks to port."

It was a grand joke and certainly did much to upset Fascist morale. Mussolini was so furious that he wanted the fleet to steam right out and engage in combat with the British, but not daring to meddle in navy matters of which he knew absolutely nothing, he acceded to the more prudent policy of his admirals, and the navy was permitted to continue with its hide-and-seek strategy. But actually, despite wisecracks by BBC broadcasters, the British, alone, were never able to prevent the Italian navy from fulfilling, with a considerable degree of success, its chief war task — the keeping open of communications between Italy and Libya so that the Axis armies in North Africa could be properly supplied. The Italian navy, being considerably smaller than the British Mediterranean fleet, consistently sought to evade any large-scale engagements. Such naval battles as did occur while we were in Italy nearly all took place as a result of the British catching the Italian warships by surprise, usually while they were protecting convoys, which it would have been disastrous to lose.

Since units of the German navy could never pass Gibraltar, the Italian navy has been almost entirely unassisted by the Germans, who have been able to contribute only a number of submarines which were sent overland by rail to Italy piecemeal and then assembled in Italian ports. Unable to do more themselves, the Germans were forced to rely entirely on the Italian navy for conveying supplies to their Afrika Korps under command of Field Marshal Rommel, whose victories in Africa would never have been possible without plentiful supplies and reinforcements.

Although the German submarines came to the Mediterranean by an overland route, the Italian submarines went to the Atlantic underwater via Gibraltar during the earlier part of the Axis Atlantic blockade. The British, with all their vigilance, did not catch on to the Italian navy's trick until after ten submarines had slipped through the Straits. From then on, Fascist underwater craft were bottled in the Mediterranean. The Italian method used to cope with the British detectors at Gibraltar was cunningly simple. It was merely this: the submarine would pass through the Straits directly beneath the keel of a neutral or nonbelligerent ship, generally Spanish. The detector could register only the presence of a single craft at a single spot, and the British naturally assumed that it was the ship on the surface. Once through the Straits, the Italian submarine would speed up and leave its protective covering and head for a German base on the French coast. Italians assured us that the captains of the surface ships were never aware of the service they were performing the Italian navy, but we took this *cum grano salis*. The British ended this ruse by having all ships passing through Gibraltar anchor for a short time in shallow water.

We met two Italian naval officers at a cocktail party one night and, getting them off in a corner, asked them why it was that the Italian navy appeared to be afraid of a big battle with the British.

"But you don't understand the setup, when you ask a question like that," one of the officers, a commander of a destroyer, said to us. "In the first place, the Italian navy is not a self-contained fighting force in itself. When it was developed before the last war, and for that matter for many years after the last war, it was intended to fight alongside the British navy. Consequently, it is only a complement of the British navy."

"Yes," the other officer said, "you could hardly expect a complement to attack the main body of which it was once supposed to be a part. We are remedying the situation gradually, but ships cannot be built at the same speed as airplanes."

This struck us as a rather farfetched excuse, and we checked with five or six naval attachés in Rome, including Captain Lawrence McNair, of our own Embassy, and confirmed, nevertheless, that it was true. Reynolds wrote a dispatch on this subject and half an hour later was called up by Capomazza and reprimanded for trying to send a naval secret.

"But everybody knows it," Reynolds said.

"Then it's not news," Capomazzo suavely replied, "and I wouldn't want you to get a bad reputation with your office for sending old stuff."

The news story never left Rome.

Aside from the fact that the Italian navy was unbalanced, it suffered from shortage of fuel and lack of repair material. The fuel shortage was especially serious because it prevented proper training of the crews. In order not to waste any more oil than necessary, the sailors were trained ashore on imitation ships made of wood. It was impossible to give recruits even coastal cruises so that they could accustom themselves to sea conditions before becoming full-fledged sailors. It was estimated by most naval attachés in Rome that the Italian navy was receiving only about thirty thousand tons of fuel a month, most of which was allotted to its submarines.

The first decisive British victory over the Italian fleet was a victory of naval torpedo planes and secret service. Five months after Italy had entered the war, nearly half the Italian fleet, based at Taranto, was preparing to put to sea. It was to leave at dawn, and since it was difficult to raise torpedo nets during darkness, they were removed a little while before sundown on the previous day — November 11, 1940. Just at sunset — barely an hour after the torpedo nets had been raised — a fleet of British bombers and Swordfish torpedo-carrying planes appeared in the darkening sky, and before the Italians could organize their defense a score of torpedoes were launched and found their marks on the hulls of three Italian battleships. When the battle was over, it was established that one of Italy's six battleships — either the *Conte di Cavour* or the *Doria* — had been sunk so that only its masts remained sticking out of the water. Another battleship of the same class had suffered one or two hits but had been beached so that it could be repaired. The *Littorio*, one of Italy's two newest 35,000-ton battleships, was very seriously damaged but not sunk. This left Italy with only three battleship able to put to sea — the 35,000-ton *Vittorio Veneto*, which had been commissioned only a few months before, and two pre-World War I battleships of 23,600 tons each, the *Duilio* and the *Giulio Cesare*, which had been remodeled by Mussolini. It was so obvious, because of the perfect timing of the attack, that the British had information that an immediate investigation was ordered and eventually twenty-five Italians were brought to trial charged with spying for the

British. The proceedings were secret but the verdicts were published — four were acquitted and twenty-one found guilty. But the astonishing part was that out of the twenty-one found guilty, only two were sentenced to death.

Two of the battleships torpedoed at Taranto have apparently been repaired since, as they were stated by the United States War Department to have been in a battle between United States planes and Italian ships in the Mediterranean, June 16, 1942. The two repaired ships were the *Littorio* and the *Conte di Cavour*, giving Italy, at the time, a total of five battleships — the *Duilio*, *Vittorio Veneto*, and *Giulio Cesare* being the other three ships.

Italy has been even less fortunate with her 10,000-ton heavy cruisers of which she originally had seven: *Trento*, *Trieste*, *Zara*, *Fiume*, *Pola*, *Gorizia*, and *Bolzano* — all named after cities which Italy acquired as a result of its victory in World War I.

In the disastrous battle of Cape Matapan, southwest of Crete, the British claimed, and the Italians confirmed, that the Fascists lost three of these 10,000-ton cruisers — *Zara*, *Fiume*, and *Pola*. The United Nations believe they have sunk at least three more of these heavy cruisers on three different occasions; the *Gorizia*, reported torpedoed by the British submarine *Utmost* in June, 1941; an unnamed one accounted for by another British submarine on April 9, 1942; and a third sunk by Anglo-American planes on June 15, 1942. This third sinking was confirmed by Italian official communiqués. This left only one 10,000-ton cruiser still in the Italian service, probably the *Bolzano*, which had the heaviest armament.

The Italians also had the two fastest light cruisers in the world, the *Bartolomeo Colleoni* and the *Giovanni dalle Bande Nere*, both named after famous Italian *condottieri* of Renaissance times. They were of five thousand tons, but in order to achieve their great speed their armoring was very light, so that one well-placed shell would be enough to sink one of them. Such a fate overtook the *Colleoni* when she was cornered and bombarded by the guns of the Australian cruiser *Sydney* in July, 1940. From all we could find out when we left Italy, the *Giovanni dalle Bande Nere*, was still operating.

Italy also had twelve other light cruisers, varying in size from three thousand to eight thousand tons, whereof at least three were sunk and two others badly damaged. We estimated that Italy has lost twenty-eight destroyers, leaving only thirty-nine in service, and eighteen torpedo boats sunk, leaving fifty-one in service, and lost half of its one hundred and twenty submarines. We compiled these figures on the diplomatic train out.

When we left Italy in May, 1942, two more 35,000-ton battleships, to be named the *Impero* and the *Roma*, were being rushed to completion. The keels of these ships had been laid before Italy went to war. She was also building at least twelve more light cruisers. One merchant ship was reported in drydock for the purpose of being converted into a tender-aircraft carrier. We also learned just before departure that the navy had embarked on a gigantic submarine-building program which was to specialize in submarines of one thousand tons and over. According to some reports, the Italians were even planning 5000-ton submarines which would be used as underwater tankers, freighters, and possibly aircraft carriers.

We frequently saw in Rome German naval officers whose presence confirmed, at least to our satisfaction, the report that the Italian admirals were being advised in Mediterranean strategy by their Nazi colleagues, and that many of the Italian submarines had German officers aboard.

Owing to the fact that the Italian navy was Mediterranean-bound with little hope of egress by either Gibraltar or the Suez Canal, their warships were mainly of light construction which could not withstand heavy sea pounding such as encountered in the Atlantic. Their cruising radius was also short, seldom exceeding four thousand miles. Most of the neutral observers with whom we talked interpreted this as indicating that the Italians never thought of really finding an outlet to the Atlantic during the present war except for their submarines. This was also the reason why the Italian navy developed small Mas boats which were purely for Mediterranean use, and why they experimented with two-man torpedoes. They also used against British convoys, on several occasions, torpedoes that traveled in a circular instead of a straight course, the idea being that in blind firing they would be more likely to find a target.

Eleanor had an opportunity to look over two of the Italians' battleships and six of their heavy cruisers when with eighteen other correspondents she visited the naval bases at Naples and Messina under the chaperonage of three press officers during the first week of December, 1940. Once aboard these ships, she found the difference between the navy and the other armed forces immediately apparent.

Everything both above and below decks was clean and orderly. The crews' uniforms were also spick and span, and the sailors saluted smartly, avoiding both the shambling indifference of the Italian soldiers and the exaggerated ostentation of the Fascist fliers. The kitchens were as well scrubbed as the decks.

Naples was one of Italy's chief naval bases because of its fine harbor, plus its strategically convenient geographical location. In an older day it had been extensively equipped with all kinds of installations, repair shops, drydocks, and wharves, all impossible to move. But with the coming of modern war weapons, Naples had one terrific drawback, as a naval officer explained to Eleanor when he ruefully told her:

"We don't like to have our ships linger long in Naples — too much chance of having them hit. The British planes can't possibly miss us, no matter how dark the night, because of Mount Vesuvius, which always sends up a red glow that can be seen for miles. We can black out the town, but we can't black out the volcano. We now call it the 'British lighthouse.'"

In Messina, Eleanor met Admiral Luigi Sansonetti, who talked to the correspondents about a naval battle he had had with the British a few days before. The Admiral revealed that the commander of the British squadron, Vice-Admiral Sir James Somerville, had been his personal friend in prewar days. Many Italian naval officers have English blood in their veins, and Admiral Sansonetti, with his blue eyes, ruddy face, and bluff manner, looked as though he might be one of them. He discussed with us the account of the battle which had been put out by the London radio, and it was evident that he considered all propagandists — of whatever nationality — a lot of bounders.

"I am sure my old English friend with whom I had many drinks in days gone by never made the report that has been put out by the BBC," Sansonetti said. "I feel certain Sir James' uncolored technical version of the battle would agree with mine. He would never have claimed a victory when there wasn't one. The engagement began, developed, and ended in a logical manner, which I am sure Sir James would be the first to admit.

"When our cruisers made contact with the British ships, they immediately maneuvered to bring the British cruisers and the Battleship *Renown* within range of the big guns of the *Vittorio Veneto* and the *Giulio Cesare*. Our scouting planes had reported to us that the British had only one battleship whereas we had two.

"The maneuver succeeded, and our two battleships opened fire. When the *Renown* realized she was outnumbered two to one, she immediately withdrew according to normal naval strategy. That was all there was to it. We made direct shell hits on two British cruisers, one of the *Kent* class and the other of the *Birmingham* class. Sir James showed good sense by withdrawing in view of the fact that he was outnumbered — for once."

In contrast to the navy, the army was constantly a victim of the political whims of Mussolini, who tried to make the army fit into his foreign policy rather than adapt his foreign policy to the military capacity of the country. The regular army and the Black Shirt Militia distrusted and hated each other. The regular army officers resented that a man who was a captain in the regular army reserve would suddenly become a colonel or even a general when he joined the Black Shirt Militia. Also, the old army officers never

really approved of Mussolini as a strategist and down deep in their
hearts objected to receiving orders from a man who before becoming dictator never had held a rank higher than corporal. The
army sided with Badoglio in the scandal of the Greek campaign,
and this overt split did much to shake the morale not only of
the higher officers but also of the humblest soldiers. In fact, the
Fascist army, whether Black Shirt or regular, was from the very
start undermined by politics. Not once did the Italian soldier have
the feeling that he was risking his life for his country half so much
as that he was merely being a pawn, and a damn fool one at that,
for somebody else's political gambit. We are inclined to think that
if the average Italian soldier had an honest conviction that he was
really fighting for something worth while, he might not be deserving of the bad reputation he has abroad today. He has also been
let down by bad strategy, bad tactics, bad organization behind the
lines, and just general inefficiency running all the way back from
the front-line trench to the Palazzo Venezia.

Both in Ethiopia and in Spain, we found the Italian soldiers
patient and long suffering. They put up with deprivation, lack of
amusement, food, water, cigarettes, with the greatest forbearance.
But in both wars, most of them felt that they were victims of
some political game. Many times in Ethiopia, soldiers would say
to us when we were alone with them, "What does Il Duce want
with all these mountains and rocks, anyway?"

In Spain, we frequently were asked by the Italian soldiers, "Why
can't the Spanish fight their own pig war without bringing us into
it?" Or, "We don't like the Spaniards and they don't like us,
so why should we be risking our lives for them?"

When Mussolini ordered the attack on France, again the Italian
soldiers felt let down. Here he was attacking a major power without even proper artillery and aerial preparation. Almost every
Italian who survived the fighting on the French Riviera came back
convinced that there was something "rotten in the Palazzo
Venezia."

In Greece, the Italian soldier was at first bewildered at the political whirlpool into which he had been thrown. Pavolini glorified the resistance of the Italian army throughout the bitter winter that they were beaten back halfway through Albania by the Greek advance, and apotheosized the suffering of the Italian soldiers, thousands of whom died or had hands or feet amputated because of being frozen. But the Italian soldier could not understand why he or his comrades in arms should have suffered from the cold. He failed to see why he was not given warm gloves, socks, boots, and underwear to protect him against the elements. He also revolted inwardly that Mussolini should have started the campaign with such flimsy material as just happened to be on hand in Albania. How could anyone be expected to show real fighting spirit under such conditions?

In Libya it was not much better. After the first setback that the Italians suffered at the hands of the English toward the end of 1940, Graziani came out with his famous report to the Duce in which he declared that the Italian defeat was due to inadequate equipment, especially lack of tanks and motorized vehicles. But the Italian soldier out in the desert had already known long before the fight even got underway that he was not receiving the right support. Such a feeling did not make for a bloodthirsty desire to stand up and take it.

The appointment of General Ugo Cavallero to replace Badoglio as Chief of the General Staff, on December 6, 1940, shattered Italian fighting spirit still more. When the announcement of his appointment was made, one of our Italian office boys exclaimed: "What! That crook."

For the next few days, circles of all classes buzzed with indignation. Everybody knew the background of Cavallero. It was true that he had been a distinguished soldier, having won a bronze medal for valor during Italy's war against the Turks in Libya in 1912; that he had been chief of operations under General Diaz at the time of the Piave and Vittorio Veneto victories in World War I; and that he had done commendable work for two years as a member of the Versailles Inter-Allied Military Committee.

Ma — when he resigned from public office in 1928 he became manager of the Ansaldo Shipbuilding Company of Genoa, which supplied the Italian navy with ships. Then navy inspectors suddenly discovered that two 10,000-ton cruisers, *Il Trento* and *Il Trieste*, had been constructed of ordinary steel instead of shellproof steel as had been contracted for and specified by the navy. One of these ships was constructed under the supervision of Cavallero. Cavallero would have gone to jail had it not been for the intervention of Costanzo Ciano — the Foreign Minister's father — who interested himself in the case. Even the Duke of Aosta came to Cavallero's rescue simply because Cavallero once held a high position in the royal household. But the scandal was never hushed up, and Cavallero withdrew from all activities and did not make any public appearances until Mussolini surprisingly gave him the place of the distinguished Badoglio.

Probably no people in the world are given such long military training — at least on paper — as the Italians. It theoretically begins in the cradle, because every male child, as soon as he is born, is regarded by the Fascist government as being a member of the Figli della Lupa — Sons of the Wolf. When the tiny tots enter kindergarten they don uniforms, consisting of grayish-green shorts, black shirt, and trench cap. They practice marching and learn all the elements of parade formation. They also receive special instruction with emphasis placed on developing hatred of the English and Americans.

At the age of six the child is promoted to membership in the Balilla, in which he remains until the age of twelve. He is then given a wooden gun and put through mock field maneuvers. He is made military-minded as much as possible. Crippled children and sons of Jews and Anglo-Saxon foreigners who attend Italian schools are not permitted to belong and are made miserable by this ostracism.

At the age of twelve the Balilla boys become Avanguardisti and are given small-caliber rifles ranging from B-B guns to .22's. The training is progressively stiffer and more advanced. The boys also begin to study Fascist theories and doctrines as applied to modern history.

At the age of sixteen, the schoolboys become Giovani Fascisti and are given real guns and more warlike uniforms. They are taught to use firearms, bayonets, knives, and daggers, and the more promising ones are assigned to instruct the younger Avanguardisti and Balilla.

At the age of eighteen, the premilitary period starts, and all boys, whether at school or working, must devote their Saturday afternoons to this training, and no absences are excused without punishment except in the case of sickness, and all sickness must be attested to by a doctor's certificate. In the U.P., where we used many messengers to carry dispatches, we had to have old men as substitutes on Saturday afternoons.

At the age of twenty, the regular military training starts and, in peacetime, continues for a year. During this year, the boy leads the life of a soldier, living in barracks or under canvas. Long marches and field maneuvers are part of his daily program. He is pigeonholed into the branch of service for which he is considered to be best suited, having the opportunity, however, to go into aviation if he shows the proper Fascist qualifications.

College students, known as the Gruppo Universitario Fascista, were permitted to do their premilitary training along with their studies and on graduation had always been automatically considered eligible to become officers. In the spring of 1941, a regular campus revolution took place in Rome University when the graduating student body which had "volunteered" en masse (on the instructions of the Fascist party) staged demonstrations to demand that they be automatically given their degrees without having to pass examinations. The Fascist government resisted these demands and punished the students by giving them the rank of sergeants instead of second lieutenants as was customary.

With all these years of training, both physical and mental, that the average Italian had forced upon him, it seemed strange that every Italian youth did not develop into an ardent Fascist.

But the fact was that the so-called Fascist ideals ran counter to the Italian character. Fundamentally, the Italian is nonmilitaristic by nature and he loathes all forms of regimentation. All the uniforms and Fascist regalia with which Mussolini bedecked Italian boys could never change this; so that as soon as Fascist precepts were hard to follow — that is, when they involved hardships and sacrifices as in wartime — the average Italian instinctively turned against them. When the Italian boy was called up to serve in the army he went with a hodgepodge of Fascist ideas in his head; but by the time the average recruit had been in the army a year or so, he had generally rejected most of these ideas and in their place had a kind of political vacuum because, always having been isolated from other ideals, he had nothing to substitute for his erstwhile Fascist principles. Unless, paradoxically enough, it was a bit of American philosophy.

There was hardly an Italian family that did not have at least one member in the United States. These overseas relatives frequently sent money and always wrote of the greatness of America. In many cases they may even have exaggerated their own prosperity and the fine time they were having, in order to impress the people back home, but they did do one thing, consciously or unconsciously, and that was to sell the United States to the Italians. We were constantly meeting, in our workaday lives, people of all classes, from office boys to editors in chief of newspapers and members of the Italian government, who proudly told us that they had a brother, a cousin, or an uncle who "was doing splendidly" somewhere in the U.S.A. — New York, San Francisco, Chicago, or even smaller cities. In almost every case, the Italo-American had fared much better than the stay-at-home members of his family. It was a propaganda that Mussolini could not combat.

Long before World War II started, Il Duce had bragged that he could place eight million bayonets in the field. But when Italy entered the war, it was soon found that neither literally nor metaphorically could he fulfill such a threat. Not only were there not enough bayonets for such a mighty army, but there were not enough rifles, cloth for uniforms, leather for shoes, or vehicles for transport. At best, they could only form a ragtag, unequipped force, if he could produce so many men, but most military observers agreed that he exceeded by several millions the number of men who would actually be fit for fighting. So many men in the field would also have meant complete disruption of Italian production, which even in peacetime was not sufficient to supply the needs of the country.

During the winter of Italy's nonbelligerency period, when Germany, England, and France were at war but Italy was not, the Italian government announced that it had nearly a million men (960,000) under arms as a defensive measure. During the months immediately after Italy entered the war, approximately another million were mobilized, and during the fall and winter of 1941, just before and after the United States' entry into the war, the Fascists began calling up and training nearly a million more. Many of these last were reservists who had already done their regular military training but needed considerable additional instruction in modern weapons.

Thus, in 1942 Italy probably possessed an active army of about three million men, less the losses she had suffered. Her losses in prisoners had been between 150,000 and 200,000, including the entire Ethiopian army and about 90,000 prisoners captured by the British in their first North African drive. Probably her killed and wounded in battle did not exceed 200,000. This left Italy with well over two and a half million men. She had an estimated 400,000 in Libya, where the Italians did all the routine work of garrisoning, policing, supply services, and so on, leaving to the German forces only the work of forming the spearheads of attacks and the brunt of defense. Another 100,000 were actively engaged on the Russian front, leaving over two million in nonfighting sectors. Of these, around three quarters of a million were used in occupation work in Greece, Yugoslavia, and France. The remainder were in Italy either completing their training or guarding Italy's coastline against possible invasion. It was estimated by neutral observers in Rome in the spring of 1942 that Italy had between half a million and one million men under arms for which she had no immediate use, and there was consequently great speculation as to what Italy planned to do with these troops. Some believed they were to be sent to the Russian front, while others thought Italy planned to wrest her revindications from France by force or make a deal with Franco whereby Italy would aid Spain in seizing Gibraltar.

Besides the three million men who had been taken out of Italian civil life by enrollment in the army, another half million men were working at industry, mining, and agriculture in Germany, thus further decreasing the number of men for Italy's own civilian needs.

The strain of outfitting and equipping an army of three million men taxed Italy's industrial output tremendously and was in a large measure responsible for the severe rationing of clothes, shoes, and other civilian necessities. The shortage of wool for soldiers' uniforms was so severe that the Fascists instituted a house-to-house canvass for old wool in the form of mattresses and blankets and underclothes. They also gave benefit opera performances to which admittance was paid in wool, so many kilos according to the value of the seat — one kilo of wool for an orchestra seat, four kilos for a box.

As the war progressed, the Black Shirt Militia was merged more and more with the regular army. The militia had originally been organized by Italo Balbo in the early days of Fascism more or less as a means to find something for the rowdy *squadristi* who, before the March on Rome, distinguished themselves as street fighters. Later, these same *squadristi* were the ones who administered castor oil to recalcitrant anti-Fascists. Under the training of Balbo, they became the official storm troopers of the party, whose main function was to take part in parades on national holidays. Their ranks were increased by thousands of volunteers, however, during the Ethiopian war, and they soon became a formidable number of combatants. As a result of the good showing they made against the ill-equipped Ethiopians, they enjoyed a reputation far above their actual merit. In the Spanish Civil War they were the first to take part in the fighting, but after Guadalajara it was decided that they must be put in battle only with regular army soldiers. In World War II, Mussolini always sandwiched regiments of Black Shirts in between regiments of regulars. Although General Enzo Galbiati replaced Achille Starace on May 25, 1941, as nominal head of the Black Shirt Militia, nevertheless it had already become an integral part of the army and under army direction. The regular army itself, on the other hand, became more than ever subordinated to Mussolini and his own personal appointees such as Cavallero. Thus, what power Mussolini lost in one way, he regained in another.

Aviation always remained exclusively Fascist and as such was the most corrupt and inefficient of the three armed branches. It was used as a political playground in which party leaders could show off their talents for war without coming under the discipline of the army or the navy. It offered an opportunity to politicians like Ciano and Pavolini to perform a few spectacular stunts and then return with war records to their ministerial desks. Mussolini, who was always one of the world's worst fliers, regarded Italian aviation as his pet service and uninterruptedly held the portfolio of Minister of Air since 1933. Flying was modern — therefore, it had to be Fascist. As the leader of Fascism, Il Duce, therefore, posed as a great pilot. While his followers quaked, the dictator would take off in an airplane and land unexpectedly at any airfield. There was no telling when he was coming or, for that matter, how he would land. There was always another pilot at the controls, but even so it was extremely dangerous because Mussolini insisted on playing to the gallery. He had to be seen doing the actual taking off and landing. His landings were described to us by one flier who was frequently a member of his crew as "modern-day miracles." He said there was nothing more harrowing than to be in the same plane which Mussolini insisted on running in the same dictatorial manner as he ran the state. Hitler was supposed to have told Mussolini in 1941:

"With the war on, it is necessary for the good of the Axis that you do not needlessly imperil your life by piloting your own plane. In fact, I think we should both stay on the ground as much as possible during these critical times."

The Duce forced his sons, Vittorio and Bruno, to become fliers at early ages. Vittorio took up aviation in 1934 and was given his pilot's license the same year. He was eighteen at the time and for many months afterward held the distinction of being the youngest aviator in Italy. His younger brother, Bruno, broke this record by becoming an army pilot in 1935 when he was only seventeen years of age. We met them both in Ethiopia, where they were stationed at the Enda Jesus airport near Makale. We sat at the same luncheon table with them on our return from one of our flights over Ethiopian lines. They were dressed in singlets, khaki shorts, and native sandals. Both had long, curly beards which were surprisingly blond.

Eleanor found Vittorio fat and arrogant and not very intelligent, while she rather liked Bruno, who had a sweet smile which from time to time lightened his serious face. Neither of them showed any sense of humor. Reynolds didn't like either of them. They were both only second lieutenants at the time, and it must be admitted that they received, as far as we could see, no special treatment from their superior officers. We learned later that the Duce, who was disappointed in his two sons because they showed no aptitude at leadership and certainly gave no promise of ever being able, one or the other, to take his place, had ordered that they be given the same treatment as any other subalterns.

Eleanor asked Vittorio if he was doing much bombing.

"Yes," he said, "I go out almost every day and drop a few eggs on Ethiopian concentrations, but it is dull work. There are no air battles. I should like to have a chance to shoot down some planes. There is more thrill in that."

Reynolds, without much result, tried to engage Bruno in conversation, but he was reluctant to talk and made only laconic answers.

"My father warned me," he said naïvely, "not to talk to newspapermen." And then, as if quoting from a lesson he had learned, he continued:

"I can only say that I am doing my duty the same as all Italians and I am sure we are going to win quickly and decisively."

The superior officers at the table did all they could to prevent us from talking to the Mussolini brothers, as though they were afraid that the two youngsters might say the wrong thing.

We saw them later in Italy, where they showed much more interest in soccer and boxing than in aviation or things Fascist. They also played around in the Spanish Civil War, where, as far as we could learn, they did not distinguish themselves particularly.

On August 7, 1941, Bruno, who had meanwhile volunteered as a test pilot, was trying out a new type of four-engine bomber at the San Giusto airport near Pisa when something went wrong. At an altitude of about three hundred feet, the plane slid sideways and crashed to the ground, killing Bruno and two others and injuring five, including two workmen on the field. A communiqué was issued explaining the disaster in the most favorable light. It attempted to exonerate Bruno — as the dictator's own son — of all blame and at the same time tried to show that there was nothing wrong with the plane, for that would have been a reflection on Fascist aircraft construction. The general impression, however, was bad. Some people were convinced that the accident was due to graft in Fascist airplane factories and that the plane had not been constructed according to specifications, while others contended that Bruno was too inexperienced for the delicate post of test pilot, and it had only been given him through his father's favoritism. Up to the time we left Italy, no further attempts were made to use this type of plane.

Bruno's death revealed more than anything else how the people felt about Mussolini. It was the kind of tragedy that should have aroused public sympathy for Il Duce. Instead of feeling sorry for him, the people used the accident as an argument against him. The situation was not improved any when three weeks later Il Duce published a book entitled *I Talk with Bruno*. Actually, he was only showing the normal grief of a father for the loss of a favorite son. But to put such grief between the covers of a book shocked many of the die-hard Fascists who themselves had lost sons and brothers in the war and who, because of Mussolini's dictates, had shown no outward signs of grief. He had even decreed that women were not to wear mourning for their loved ones killed in action. Yet Mussolini publicized his loss in an un-Fascist way. One Italian, who was still prominent in the party, despite his change of views since the entrance of Italy into the war, told us:

"It's a weird thing for a dictator to do — take time out from a world war to write an emotionally hysterical book about the loss of his son. Many of us have suffered greater losses, yet he was the one who told us not to mourn. And then, *Dio mio*, the book indicates he thinks he is having spiritualistic conversations with Bruno's soul. He has become quite unbalanced."

The greatest loss to Italian flying, however, occurred at Tobruk on June 28, 1940. Italo Balbo, known as "the father of Fascist aviation," was returning to his headquarters after an aerial inspection tour of the Egyptian front. As he arrived over his airfield, he was greeted with a barrage of antiaircraft fire. The plane was hit and plummeted to the ground. Balbo and all the occupants were killed. The Press Ministry at first tried to give credit for "the kill" to the British, but the British Air Ministry announced that on that particular day their airplanes had not engaged in any combat in North Africa and therefore could not have shot down Balbo. Consequently, rumors were current in Rome for a time that he had been deliberately assassinated because Mussolini was jealous of his ever-growing popularity since his famous mass flight from Rome to Chicago and back. Balbo was not only a great aviator and flight commander, as attested by several other mass flights which he headed, but was also an able statesman. At the age of twenty-nine he became Undersecretary of National Economy — the youngest member of the Cabinet. Three years later, he became an aviation general, and in September, 1929, he was appointed Minister of Air at the age of thirty-three, and for a time ranked as the second leading Fascist. But when Mussolini decided to line up with Germany against the advice of Balbo, who was always friendly to the English and the Americans, he was summarily shelved by being made Governor of Libya.

Italian officers who were in Tobruk at the time and whom we knew quite well convinced us later that the death of Balbo was a pure accident.

"It was almost the first airplane that the Tobruk antiaircraft brought down," one of the officers said. "And I can assure you the boys were certainly sick when they learned it was Balbo. It was the old story of shooting first and checking afterward."

The most spectacular achievement of Fascist aviation in the early part of the war was the bombardment of the British-owned Bahrein Islands in the Persian Gulf. It represented a round-trip flight of several thousand miles from the nearest Italian base in North Africa. We learned from fliers, who were extremely proud of the stunt, that the flight was led by Muti and that the planes were refueled by submarine tankers in the Red Sea on their return. They told us that seaplanes had been used in order to make possible a refueling at sea. It was the sort of spectacular performance that Fascists were enthusiastic about — even though there were no practical results. It was typical of Italian aviation, which boasted of a few aces who were marvels at individual exploits, but could not carry out the day-by-day routine essential to winning a modern war. Three times Italians had won the Schneider Cup races — twice, however, in 1920 and 1921, before the March on Rome and only once, 1926, since the advent of Fascism. At the outbreak of World War II, the Italians held seven international aviation records. The Fascist planes resembled their pilots in the sense that there were only a few good ones and mass production was slow and faulty. We traveled in Italian planes on numerous occasions and every time we landed we would rush to the bar of the airport and toast our luck.

The planes which composed the bulk of the Italian air force when Italy went to war were certainly far from modern. The Savoia-Marchetti 79 was a three-engined monoplane bomber which had been used throughout the Spanish war and had even seen service toward the end of the Ethiopian war. The only modification that had been made in this bomber since World War II started had been an increase in speed owing to improvements in the three 750-horsepower engines. For a long time, the Italians also used the same Fiat single-seater fighter plane that they had flown in the Spanish war. This plane was very maneuverable, but the position of the machine guns, of which there were only two, was bad and its armoring was too light for modern air fighting. Italian pilots who flew it against British Hurricanes and Spitfires were at a great disadvantage from the start, as it was neither so fast nor so rapid-firing as the British planes. It was not even on a level with the British Gloucesters, which the British themselves considered outmoded.

Since the war started, the Italians have tried out a number of new models, the details of which have been closely guarded military secrets. Besides the four-engine bomber of the type in which Bruno Mussolini met his death, and which apparently was a failure, there were also a fast, light, twin-engine bomber and several new types of chasers, but none of them have been produced in any great quantity. The most successful Italian planes have been the naval planes. Naval bombers have had a moderate success, while Italian torpedo-carrying planes have undoubtedly been the most successful of all. But Italy has very few of them because at the time the Fascists first started making them, their Nazi allies deemed torpedo planes impracticable and discouraged Italy's continued manufacture of them.

At one time the Italians tried dive-bombers copied after the Stukas, which were called Picchiatelli, meaning pixillated. The experiment was not a success, however, and production soon stopped. Italian dive-bomber pilots co-operating in North Africa later used regular German Stukas. At Italy's entrance into the conflict, Italian aviation was generally estimated by American correspondents in Rome at about eight hundred bombers, including more than three hundred seaplanes of which only about one tenth were torpedo-bearing; one thousand fighters; four hundred scouting planes; seven thousand pilots and ground crews numbering nearly forty thousand. We estimated their replacement capacity at about four hundred planes a month, which possibly since has been speeded up to five hundred.

In accordance with Fascist autarchy, Italian aviation experimented with new types of planes. One of the most publicized experiments was made by Constantio Mozza in a Breda plane which derived its power from a charcoal-burning engine. It was written about on all the front pages of the Italian press but never appeared in any battle skies.

Another Fascist invention that flitted across the headlines of the Italian press and then was forgotten was a propellerless rocket plane. After making a secret flight from Milan to Rome, it was announced that it would fly over Rome at five P.M. one afternoon in the fall of 1941. The housetops were crowded. But all anyone could see was a speck flitting through the air at terrific speed. We couldn't tell whether it had a propeller or not, but all the Italian newspapers, including the *Popolo di Roma*, gave a detailed description of it the following day. According to these propaganda accounts, it was propelled by gases which emanated from a combustion chamber and, passing through a turbine, were ejected through a nozzle in the tail of the plane with such force that they kicked the craft forward. That was the last we heard of that experiment.

Aside from politicians, the aviation attracted to it many of the younger members of Italian aristocracy who wanted to avoid the discipline of the army or navy. Many of these aristocrats proved brilliant individualists in the sky but were frequently being put in the guardhouse because they thought nothing, when they became bored with airfield monotony, of hopping off in a plane and flying to Rome for a couple of days' vacation — AWOL.

Fascist aviation was not only undisciplined in its personnel, but also failed to collaborate with the other two armed branches. Both the navy and the army blamed most of their major disasters on the bad co-operation they received from the air. The Germans considered Italian aviation so weak that they set up their own airfields in Sicily and Sardinia in order to support Nazi units in North Africa.

Party politics, inefficiency, and ineptitude have been responsible for much of the poor showing made by the Italians in World War II. But another cause was exhaustion. Italy had already been worn out by two previous wars — Ethiopia and Spain. The Abyssinian adventure, including its postwar reconstruction and the supplying of the army of occupation, cost Italy 19,000,000,000 lire. The Fascist participation in Spain cost another 7,500,000,000, of which 5,500,000,000 was to be repaid by Franco in twenty-four annual installments. Despite all his saber rattling before stabbing France in the back, Mussolini, during the Greek war, was compelled to admit how depleted the Italians' war strength was as a result of Ethiopia and Spain. Speaking in the Adriano Theater — where he read his speech for the first time instead of delivering it extemporaneously as was his custom — he said:

"With the outbreak of hostilities on September 1, 1939, we had just finished two wars which imposed relatively modest sacrifices in human life, but had forced us to make an enormous logistic and financial effort. . . .

"But developments in history, which sometimes are speeded up, cannot be halted any more than the fleeting moment of Faust could be halted. History takes one by the throat and forces a decision. If we had been one hundred per cent ready we would have entered the war in September, 1939, and not in June, 1940."

The Duce neglected to add, however, that Italy had not been ready in June, 1940, either — and that Italian production since that period had never been able to keep pace with the critical needs of Italy's armed forces.

WHEN THE GRAZIANI ARMY FIRST BEGAN TO LOSE IN LIBYA AND the British pushed it back beyond Benghazi, many Italians whom we knew complained that the Germans were not helping out in Africa. Their opinion was that Italy alone was fighting the British. Where were the Germans? Why couldn't they come to Italy's assistance in Libya?

"The Germans haven't taken any constructive war action whatever since they stopped their large-scale air raids over England," one Italian newspaperman said to us. "Their forces are not engaged elsewhere, so why don't they send us some of their armored divisions?"

But these very same Italians were the first to protest against the Germans as soon as Nazi forces began to win in Libya. The same Italian newspaperman by that time had done a complete mental somersault and, retracting some of his previous words, said:

"Rommel didn't need to move in on us in Libya. We wanted help, not subjugation. Now he's trying to run everything and we make a *brutta figura*."

We heard similar remarks from all our Italian acquaintances, ranging from our servants to high Fascist officials. In a way, the Libyan campaign was the entirety of Axis relations in microcosm. All the dislike that the Italians and Germans felt for each other could be seen in this one phase of the war. The unwillingness of the Italians to call on help from the Germans was shown, as was the Nazi technique of stepping in to help and then taking over completely. It brought out the weakness of Mussolini in his relations with Hitler by the way Il Duce consented to German control of military operations in Italian territory.

The German correspondents often openly criticized the bad showing of the Italians. One night we heard them, at the bar of the Foreign Press Club, laughing over the latest story they had heard at their Rome Embassy. There were at least six correspondents there, including the omnipresent von Langen, as well as Alwens, von Hahn, Wiebel. They were talking loudly and obviously didn't care whether or not we heard. The gist of their joke was that Rommel had asked Berlin direct for twenty thousand reinforcements. The German High Command, so their story went, wired in reply:

"Twenty thousand Italian infantrymen are being rushed over from southern Italy."

Rommel snapped back: "I said I want soldiers, not ditchdiggers."

The Nazi usurpation of power in Libya particularly annoyed the Italians because, among many other things, it undermined their prestige with the Arabs. Mussolini had long been proud of his self-styled title, "The Defender of Islam." Just before Italy entered the war against England and France, Reynolds flew to Tripoli and Benghazi as part of a general survey of the Middle East that he was making for the U.P. He found the Italians had done extremely well in consolidating themselves with the Arabs. After the first bad period, immediately following World War I, when the strong-arm killer methods of Graziani had been called upon to quell all revolt, the Italians made friends with the Arabs by a score of ruses and tricks and entered upon good terms, comparatively speaking, with these subject people. While in Tripoli and Benghazi, Reynolds had a chance to see how the Italians strove to win over the natives. The Italians had successfully merged their administration into the atmosphere and background of Islam. Italian government buildings, for example, were of Moslem architecture. There were daily propaganda broadcasts over the radio in Arabic. Italian films, carefully chosen for Africa, were dubbed in Arabic. The Libyan chieftains were permitted to share in Fascist graft; they were awarded impressive decorations and titles and were given posts that were lucrative but devoid of any authority. The Libyan soldiers were outfitted with colorful uniforms which appealed to their native love of display. Italian aviation, as bad as it was, also helped in impressing the Arabs with Italian superiority. Reynolds had never seen in English or French colonies so much use made of airplanes. Dozens of Italian aircraft were every day to be seen in the skies over almost all the large cities of Libya, profoundly impressing the Arabs, who had not gone beyond the camel as a means of travel. Reynolds was convinced that Mussolini had succeeded much more with his "Sword of Islam" propaganda in Libya, where there were no rival countries to interfere, than in Tunisia, where the French ably undermined Italian prestige.

Reynolds was amazed in both Tripoli and Benghazi at the extent to which the Italians had militarized the natives. They had put into uniform not only the Arabs, who were famous for their fighting qualities, but also the Negroes, who formed forty percent of the population. Scores of thousands of natives had been trained as foot soldiers, artillerymen, mounted spahis, ground crews for Italian aviation, and even parachutists. This dependence on native soldiers was one of the factors that caused the Italians, before the Germans came to their aid, to make such a bad showing against the English. Whether it was Mussolini's or Graziani's idea was never clear; but the Italians did try at first to fight the war in Libya and Egypt on a colonial basis. The British beat back the Italians by merely bringing into play European methods and weapons, and the Germans in turn threw back the British by using the most modern of *Blitzkrieg* tactics and tanks. The Libyan fighting soon proved that the desert offers an even better terrain for mechanized warfare than the battlefields of Europe and that native troops were of negligible value. Gasoline had stripped desert warfare of its old-fashioned romance.

The German correspondents bragged that Rommel was the first to recognize that a desert was like an ocean and that therefore desert tank tactics should be similar to naval battles. One of the quarrels Rommel and Graziani had concerned this point. Rommel was supposed to have said:

"I give no more importance to gaining or losing so many hundreds of square miles of Libyan terrain than an admiral does to gaining so many square miles of the sea. The admiral only worries about the number of enemy ships he destroys, and all I worry about are the number of British armored forces I can smash."

Graziani made the mistake of thinking of the campaign in North Africa in terms of the past, just as the French General Staff had based its plans for World War II on what had happened in World War I. Graziani therefore had accumulated vast stores of equipment and a large amount of infantry with a view to fighting a colonial campaign such as had always been fought in Africa.

The Germans always thought the Italians committed a colossal blunder when they did not follow up their initial advantage in Libya and use Nazi *Blitzkrieg* methods against Egypt before the British had a chance to accumulate superior armaments there. After the Italian declaration of war, Graziani started an offensive against Egypt as soon as weather conditions permitted. On September 14, 1940, he took Solum and, two days later, Sidi Barrani. Although his forces at that time were numerically vastly superior to the British, he halted at Sidi Barrani and failed to follow up his advantage. Later, when the tide of war turned against Italy, he justified his failure on the grounds that the water supplies at Sidi Barrani and beyond were so inadequate that he could not continue until he had constructed an aqueduct that would assure his troops of a fixed and continuous supply. He also did not consider that the communications between the Italo-Egyptian frontier and Sidi Barrani were sufficiently good to supply an army taking the offensive, so he paused to build a military road. Some idea of the unmechanized condition of the Italian army could be gained from the fact that many Italian regiments had walked from Libya to Sidi Barrani because there were no trucks or other transportation available. There were only enough vehicles to transport supplies.

While he was building his road and his aqueduct, Graziani was also concentrating large numbers of troops and great reserves of food and war materials of all kinds at Sidi Barrani, with the intention of pushing forward to Marsa Matruh as soon as he had made what he considered the necessary preparations. But what Graziani forgot was that the British were not remaining idle during this period. Also, the British had learned a severe lesson in France. By this time they fully appreciated the possibilities of a war of movement fought with tanks, mechanized troops, and other modern weapons. While Graziani was concentrating his old-fashioned war materials in preparation for an outmoded colonial campaign, the British were gathering together in Suez, Port Said, and Alexandria, and then forwarding to Marsa Matruh, the kind of weapons with which they had seen the Germans crush the French army and their own expeditionary force in France.

Graziani admitted in his report that his scouting planes had noted the British preparations in Marsa Matruh and other defensive points, including the large oasis of Siwa, but said that he was not sure whether it heralded a British offensive or whether it was of a purely defensive character. Rommel later contended that Graziani had been much too prudent — if he had forgotten his aqueduct and his road, he might have struck a telling blow at Egypt when Britain was almost completely unprepared. Instead, the British, not content with defending Egypt, saw a chance of wiping out the Axis bridgehead in Africa and on December 9, 1940, launched their most successful offensive. The British attacked first

an Italian encampment at Nibeiwa, fifteen miles south of Sidi
Barrani, which was held by the Maletti column. Seeing themselves
outmechanized, the Maletti troops began to withdraw and wired
for reinforcements. The Second Libyan Division was sent to their
aid, but both were overcome and those who were not annihilated
surrendered. General Maletti himself was killed in the battle.

To excuse himself for the defeats that the British were adminis-
tering to his army, Graziani sent his famous apologia of December
21, 1940, to Il Duce — which was in reality a protest against
behind-the-lines corruption as well as an alibi for himself. Many
Italians read between the lines and considered it a subtle criticism
of Mussolini. Graziani wrote:

"Against strongholds occupied by our troops in flat desert terrain,
and without any possibility of tactics, the enemy had an opportunity of employing masses of armored units, armored cars, medium
and heavy tanks, supported by mobile artillery, and with the
effective co-operation of air forces.

"As soon as the massacring air bombardment had ceased,
armored units struck from every direction against our troops. Thus,
despite the fiercest resistance, our strongholds within a few hours
were taken one by one."

The Italian defenders probably outnumbered their British attackers at this point, but the British armament was immeasurably
better. The Italians were completely unprepared for defending
themselves against an armored and motorized offensive in the European style. Sidi Barrani was soon cut off and was able to hold out
for only three days. Other Italian forces on the Egyptian side of
the frontier were forced either to surrender or, at best, to fight a
costly rearguard action to cover the retreat to Libya. The Graziani
report implied that there was something seriously wrong with the
Italian antitank guns when it said:

"Against an armored mass operating concentrically on a large
front, our antitank arms and artillery were forced to waste shots on
numerous mobile targets which interminably came forward, and
therefore had little effect.

"The essential reason for the enemy's lightninglike initial success must be attributed to the crushing superiority of the enemy's armored units."

Three other insinuations were seen by almost every Italian when he read the following three paragraphs of the report:

"We lacked a complement of motor vehicles which, as you know, were pouring in from the mainland. . . .

"Episodes of epic greatness occurred in the unequal battle between soldiers of Italy and the British Empire's armored divisions. . . .

"The British aviation, evidently reinforced by new units, continually attacked our troops, back areas, our supply bases and aviation fields and ports at Tobruk and Bardia. Owing to fatal adverse atmospheric conditions — first, sandstorms, then floods caused by exceptional rains — our air force could not make all its weight felt in battle."

To the Italian mind, accustomed to look for inner meanings as a result of Fascist censorship, it was clear:

(1) Motor vehicles were just beginning to arrive in Africa, but Graziani had not received them in time. There had been an inexplicable delay.

(2) The juxtaposition of the phrase "Italian soldiers" and "the British Empire's armored divisions" was significant. It could only mean that Italians without tanks were fighting British mechanized forces. Why?

(3) There was something wrong with Fascist aviation. The sandstorms and floods had not interfered with the British fliers.

After the fall of Sidi Barrani the Italians attempted to make a stand in the quadrilateral formed by Solum, Fort Capuzzo, Sidi Omar, and Halfaya, where vigorous fighting went on for three days. The Italian troops here were under the command of the now famous *Barba Elettrica*, General Annibale ("Electric Whiskers") Bergonzoli, who was to slip through the British fingers three separate times before the Imperial Army of the Nile finally nabbed him. The British forces attempted to encircle Bergonzoli's troops and cut them off from Bardia, and when Bergonzoli saw that there was danger of their succeeding, he decided to forgo the defense of Solum and Capuzzo and make a stand in the highly fortified seaport of Bardia. The Italian force defending Bardia consisted of between 40,000 and 45,000 men, manning a complicated system of fortifications, equipped with large-caliber stationary guns which protected it on both the land and sea sides. The roads leading from Egypt to Tobruk were only lightly defended by the Italians with small patrols which could not have resisted any advance by the large British mechanized forces. But the British did not dare to advance along these roads so long as Bardia remained in Italian hands. To bypass Bardia would have been exceptionally dangerous since it would have exposed any British column to being cut off from its base.

Confronted with the possibility of its offensive in Libya being held up indefinitely by Italian resistance at Bardia, the British High Command turned to the navy. A number of British battleships having sixteen-inch guns were brought up and the shells released from these cannon soon silenced all the Italian coastal artillery. In fact, the concussion from these sixteen-inch guns was so shattering that it loosened the whole side of the cliff overlooking the sea, and all the guns and other fortifications perched on this cliff were swept into the Mediterranean by a landslide.

Bardia surrendered on January 5, after a three-week siege, but when the British looked around for Electric Whiskers he was not to be found. Apparently deciding that the fall of Bardia was inevitable, he had left the doomed city with two of his staff officers during the preceding night.

The loss of Bardia caused the greatest consternation in Italy, since it was generally believed to have been the most strongly fortified town in Cyrenaica and the point which had always been designed to bear the brunt of any attack from the east. Besides this, the Italian public had, for some reason or other, great faith in the powers of Bergonzoli, whose exploits in Ethopia and Spain had been recounted in the Italian press.

During the southern campaign of the Ethiopian war, Bergonzoli had taken the strategically important towns of Neghelli and Wadara. He had earned the nickname of Electric Whiskers because of his extraordinary energy and activity and his fits of excitable temper, during which he would yell and gesticulate, causing his bristling black beard to wag up and down as if it were receiving a series of magnetic shocks. Instead of relaxing comfortably in his headquarters tent when there was nothing doing, he would grab a musket and go out on one-man raids. Sometimes he would return with two or three native prisoners. When leading his troops, he was always himself among the vanguard, fighting like an ordinary soldier.

In Spain, Bergonzoli's military standing had become somewhat impaired because he was involved in the Guadalajara catastrophe. But he soon retrieved his personal reputation on other Spanish fronts. His followers acquired an almost superstitious awe of him because he seemed to be so lucky. Although his staff car was a pepperpot of rifle and machine-gun bulletholes, he himself was only once wounded during two years' fighting in Spain, when, on the Aragon front, his right thigh was pierced by a bullet.

When Italians realized that neither the powerful fortifications of Bardia nor the magic luck of Electric Whiskers had been able to stop the British, they feared that the whole of Libya would soon be lost. The Italian High Command, however, issued some soothing and reassuring communiqués to the effect that during the three weeks the British had been halted before Bardia, the Fascists had succeeded in strongly fortifying Tobruk and that the real Italian stand was to be made there. The superstitious Italians' hopes were further revived by the news that the British, who at first had claimed capture of Electric Whiskers, now admitted that he had escaped. While British scouting planes combed the desert and scanned the seas for him, Bergonzoli walked from Bardia to Tobruk in five nights. During the daytime he hid under a patch of thorn bushes or beneath a rocky ledge, according to what he could find. Although rumors that he was safe soon got about Italy, the Italian General

Staff, for what reason we never discovered, refused to issue any official communiqué about his successful escape. Possibly Graziani thought Electric Whiskers was already getting too much publicity in the world press.

Seventeen days after the fall of Bardia, the Italian people's hopes crashed again when Tobruk surrendered. At Tobruk, as at Bardia, the British captured many thousands of prisoners, and there was another similarity in the fact that Bergonzoli eluded them once again. Electric Whiskers made his third and last escape twenty-four days later, when the British captured Derna. From Derna he went to Benghazi, where Graziani handed him the thankless task of trying to defend what remained of Cyrenaica. The Italian forces were considerably demoralized by this time, and they had only a fraction of the arms and equipment with which they started the North African war. The remainder had already fallen into British hands. The civilian population in Italy was demoralized too, and it was then that a loud public clamor — not printed in the newspapers, of course — began demanding that Germany do something to help Italy before all Libya was lost.

The British did not give the hard-pressed Bergonzoli any time to organize his defenses. Within a week, they advanced upon Benghazi in two directions, and this time they got him as well as a majority of the other defenders. He did not surrender tamely, however. He had about one hundred and fifty tanks, most of them light, and the remainder only medium, which he hurled at the British armored columns south of Benghazi in an attempt to force a break-through so that the bulk of his army could retreat into Tripolitania. When the British did lay hands on him, they had quickly to rush him by plane to a Cairo hospital because he was suffering from appendicitis.

The British raced on until they captured El Agheila, the last city of any size in Cyrenaica, on February 9. Here they paused. Before them stretched three hundred miles of the worst desert along all the North African seacoast — a broad natural barrier which was a more effective defense for Tripolitania than anything the Italians themselves could have constructed. To go forward with forces of any size meant organizing a big-scale water-supply system. This was far from impossible, of course, but it did mean waiting for a certain length of time, and in the meantime, events were taking place elsewhere which apparently caused the British High Command to have some uncertainty as to what move they should next undertake.

The Axis was pressuring Yugoslavia to sign the Tripartite Pact, and to the British this could mean one thing only — that Germany was preparing to intervene in the Italo-Greek war. The British apparently did not have sufficient troops to send aid to Greece and at the same time continue their offensive in Libya. They had to make a decision between the two. It must have represented a battle between the statesmen and the soldiers. The statesmen argued that since Greece was an ally and Britain had a treaty guaranteeing her, Britain must send Greece military aid — even if it could not be effective. The generals insisted that the number of troops Britain could send Greece would not be sufficient to withstand a full-dress German invasion, while at the same time, by pressing forward in Libya, they had a chance to clean up the Axis foothold in North Africa once and for all and effect a juncture with the French Army in North Africa which was wavering in its fealty to Vichy France.

The statesmen won. From a military point of view, the decision probably represented a strategic blunder as great or even greater than Graziani's failure to strike into Egypt while it was still comparatively unarmed. The sending of British reinforcements to Greece was not officially announced until April 6, but they actually left Alexandria on March 10. The blunders in Libya were even: Italy, one; England, one.

The British leisurely finished their mopping up. The isolated Italian garrison on the oasis of Giarabub, a great Arab commercial center and seat of Senusi learning, held out until March 21, while the sixty Italians holding the oasis of Kufra, nearly three hundred miles south of the seacoast, had surrendered to the Free French only a short time before. Giarabub had been cut off more than two months before it was captured, and its resistance was greatly publicized by the Italian press. But we accidentally fell into conversation with an Italian whose three sons were among the garrison, and his only desire seemed to be that it surrender quickly, before any of his sons got killed. Shaking his head anxiously, he said:

"Is this a war or a printing press? Two of my three sons in Giarabub have been promoted to officers. It is terrible. There is no military point in their holding out. It is just mock heroics. Just so the Fascist newspapers will have something to write about."

"But you should be proud that your sons distinguished themselves like that," Reynolds said, seeking to console him.

"No, no. I do not wish them to distinguish themselves. I only want this pig war to end. They have only been made officers because the man on the balcony needs something that resembles a victory in Libya."

The exact date of the arrival of German troops in Libya is not known, but it is certain that they had been there for some considerable time before they first put in an appearance on the battlefields.

We were surprised to see German troops pass through Rome, who, because of their nut-brown tan, looked as though they were veterans of tropical warfare. We would have thought that they were returning from Africa, except for the directions of the trains on which they came and left. We also knew that they could not be returning from Libya, because there had been no Nazi contingents there. It seemed a possible news story, so we checked with friendly military attachés in Rome. At first they were skeptical of what we told them — about the soldiers being so tanned. Nevertheless, several of them checked and learned that it was more of the methodical way the Germans prepared for individual campaigns. These soldiers, most of whom had never seen a desert, had been trained in artificial Libyas back in Germany. They had been subjected to toasting by machine light, electrical heat, and even imitation sandstorms for several months. They were acclimatized to Libya before they even reached there.

Around the first of March, they began trying out their desert tactics by clashing with the British in patrol encounters. And when they felt they had got the hang of it, they started out on a steamroller push that startled their slow-moving Italian allies. The timetable followed was:

The Germans captured El Agheila March 24; Benghazi, April 4; Derna, April 7; Bardia, April 12; Solum, April 14. In other words, they took back in twenty-one days everything it had taken the British three months to capture, with the exception of Tobruk, which they bypassed and which remained in British hands until the summer of 1942.

The Italian public had wanted German aid to save Libya, and when they got it, they were astonished at the speed with which the Nazis rolled the British war machine back into Egypt. At first they were gratified and enthusiastic, and not for some time did stories begin to sift back from Libya to Italy about how Marshal Erwin Rommel was treating the Italian commanders. In the relief the Italians felt over the German capture of El Agheila, the resignation of Marshal Rodolfo Graziani next day went almost unnoticed. He had held three posts and he gave up all of them. His positions as commander of the Italian army in Africa and Governor of Libya were taken over by General Italo Gariboldi, and his post as Chief of Staff of the army was assumed by General Mario Roatta. Graziani's ostensible reason for resignation was illness, but the right name for that illness was acute Germanophobia. On the other hand, Rommel complained to Mussolini that Graziani was constantly interfering with his plans and was generally recalcitrant. Graziani followed Badoglio and went into retirement in a small Italian town. The Marshal had never been such a hero to the Italian man in the street as had Badoglio, but there was nevertheless considerable indignation over his peremptory shelving. Inevitably, national pride was hurt that the Italian Commander in Chief in North Africa — no matter how bad he may have been — had been fired from his job like an office boy by a superior and arrogant ally. Other tales were heard in Italy of how the German army openly sneered at the

ineffectiveness of the Italian aviators, not even permitting the
Italian pursuit pilots to escort the German bombers, as had been
done in Spain.

Meanwhile, German air units established themselves in great
numbers in Sicily, Sardinia, and Calabria, as well as in North Africa
itself. The official German reason for this was logical enough —
they wished to protect their own Afrika Korps and to assist the
Italians in attacking the British navy in the Mediterranean. But
they were so numerous that everyone suspected an ulterior reason
— to be on the spot to quash any Italian movement to break away
from the Axis. At first the Italian population was inclined to welcome them and to make an effort to get along with them. But soon
their Teutonic unyieldingness and their methodical requisitioning
of everything they needed aroused great antagonism. And within a
few months, any attempts at fraternization between Germans and
Italians were practically unknown. A frigid politeness was the most
they accorded each other.

A Swiss friend of ours who lived in Sicily told us that the German
fliers there pulled up vineyard stakes and fence palings whenever
they wanted to make fires for cooking. This was particularly serious
in Sicily, where wood was scarce and expensive.

"I am sure the Sicilians would welcome any invasion which would
get rid of the Germans," he said. "They hate them."

Very quietly and little by little, the Germans in the course of the
following ten months brought seven divisions of troops into Italy,
which they stationed at strategic points — officially to help guard
the Italian coastline. There were also great numbers of German
civilians in Italy, on one task or another. Some of them were advising various Italian ministries. Others were advising the direction of
Italian industry. What was happening was that under the guise of
"advice," the Germans, gradually and with firm tactfulness, practically took over the running of Italy. In every government department Fascists would be doing the cigar smoking and the handshak-
ing, but there were always a couple of Nazis in the back room to
tell them what to do and how to do it. The German assumption of

control of Italian industry was also smoothly accomplished. It was done by the exchange of German and Italian missions of economic and industrial experts. The so-called Italian experts, however, when they got to Germany were merely given apprentice positions where they could be instructed in German methods of mass production. On the other hand, when the German experts came to Italy, they soon found everything wrong with the way Italian factories were being operated, and the Italian industrialists, who had an inferiority complex anyway about their own efficiency as compared with the Germans', usually retired on a long vacation while the German experts put the factories in new running order. The Italian owners were generally permitted to continue drawing all the profits from the business and were thus placated.

For seven months after the first Rommel counteroffensive ended, only minor battles took place on the North African front. A few bits of territory were exchanged along the Egyptian-Libyan frontier, and a few minor assaults were made on British outposts around Tobruk. But in general, no large-scale activity was attempted on either side. On November 18, 1941, the British launched their second big offensive on Libya, using quite different tactics from those of their first drive. This time, instead of pausing before each Axis stronghold until they took it, they passed south of Solum and Bardia and also struck northward from caravan trails deep in the desert. The strategy was to effect a juncture with the Tobruk garrison whereby the Axis forces to the east would be encircled and would therefore ultimately have to surrender when their supplies ran out. Furious tank battles between German and British forces took place in the vicinity of Sidi Rezegh, southeast of Tobruk, as the British fought to join forces with their garrison and the German Afrika Korps fought equally furiously to prevent them. For days the battle pendulumed back and forth until the Germans finally withdrew westward to prevent being cut in two.

Going on Rommel's principle that battles between highly armored and mechanized forces on a desert terrain are similar to naval battles, the Axis forces made no reckless stands to defend cities but instead concentrated only on keeping their armored forces intact, even at the expense of losing important centers. The British pushed forward and speedily took many towns, including Derna, Benghazi, and Agedabia. For some reason, Rommel felt that he was not sufficiently prepared to meet them in a full-scale direct engagement.

In the course of this confused desert fighting, the Germans, on November 26, made a haul of British correspondents, mainly South Africans, who were captured along with the British Field Battalion Headquarters. One lone American was among them — Harold Denny, of *The New York Times* — whose fate immediately became one of the main preoccupations of the American Embassy in Rome. The Embassy could not find him for six months because the Italian Ministry of War did not wish him to talk to Americans until any information he might have gained from his experience had become too old to be of any use. Every so often, the American Embassy heard rumors that he was in such and such a place. But whenever discreet inquiries were made, it was found that if he had been there, he had been meanwhile transferred. Later we learned that he was shifted about from one place to another, once even being sent to Berlin, where he was questioned at length by the Gestapo. Denny told us he didn't know the reason why he was such a much-traveled prisoner. But then Denny, when we finally all met in Rome to take the diplomatic train out, frankly said to the assembled newspapermen who were bombarding him with questions:

"Listen, this is my story and I'm not giving it to a lot of competition. I'm going to write it myself, and if you're really interested you can buy the book."

The British Royal Dragoons walked into Benghazi for the second time on December 24, 1941, when their offensive was thirty-six days old. Chasing the elusive Rommel, they pushed quickly on to Agedabia and were halfway to El Agheila by January 21, when they were halted by a sandstorm. Next day, the Germans, who by now had received their long-awaited supplies and reinforcements, turned and struck back. Much more slowly this time, but nevertheless relentlessly, the Nazi armored divisions pushed the British back, retaking most of the ground they had lost west of Tobruk and establishing a line slightly east of Tmimi and El Mekili. Here they halted for nearly two months.

From the point of view of the number of armored units involved on both sides, the biggest battle of the Libyan war began May 27, 1942, when Rommel, starting from positions south and southwest of El Gazala, sent his tanks south of the strong point at Bir Hacheim and engaged the major part of the British forces. For days the all-out struggle went on until Rommel had won a tactical advantage which enabled him to reoccupy all of Libya, including Tobruk, which he entered on June 20, capturing about twenty-eight thousand British troops. Without pausing to rest or reorganize his troops, he pushed on into Egypt, capturing Sidi Barrani, Marsa Matruh, and Fuka, and was finally halted seventy-five miles from Alexandria at El Alamein.

Although Rommel used two Italian divisions in his last drive, he himself was completely in command, and the Italian head of operations in Africa, General Ettore Bastico, had very little to say in the decisions. Bastico had replaced General Gariboldi on March 25, 1941. General Roatta, who, with Gariboldi, had succeeded to Graziani's various commands, was also replaced January 19, 1942, by General Vittorio Ambrosio, who became Chief of Staff. Roatta was demoted to command of the Second Army on the Adriatic. These changes all represented efforts on the part of Mussolini to find competent men who would be willing to co-operate with Rommel and accept German commands in an Italian sector.

But if Italian soldiers did not make a brilliant showing in the North African fighting, Italian agitators were more successful in the field of intrigue. Not until March 10, 1937, did Italo Balbo, then Governor of Libya, induce the Libyan Arabs to hail Mussolini as the "Grand Protector of Islam." But Mussolini had been conducting clandestine negotiations in the Arab world for some time before that. The Mohammedan chieftains of Tripoli fell in with Balbo's plans and on March 17, 1937, they cheered the Duce as he

"New Caesar" and presented him with a bejeweled sword, symbolic of the Sword of Islam.

Most of the governments in Europe considered Mussolini's assumption of the role of Protector of Islam a ridiculous pretension, but they vastly underestimated his influence with the Moslems. There were seventy thousand Italians in Egypt, comprising the largest single European national group outside of the British. Many of these Italians were harmless, law-abiding people, but there were a great many who, either from conviction or for gain, were constantly trying to spread Fascist ideas and to undermine the British position in Egypt. These agents, working underground and exploiting the Egyptians yearning for independence, were constantly fomenting anti-British feeling, which led to riots, anti-British demonstrations, and the aggravation of the already strained relations between England and Egypt. Under the terms of the Anglo-Egyptian Treaty of Alliance, the Egyptian government had been compelled to break off diplomatic relations with Italy after Mussolini declared war on Britain, but while we were in Rome we were informed that the Duce still had secret channels of communication with several pro-Italian members of the Egyptian government, with whom he frequently exchanged messages.

That the Italian propaganda in Egypt was not completely unsuccessful was proved by the fact that despite the Axis invasions of their territory, the Egyptians did not allow their own troops to be used by the British against the Axis. The Egyptian army was small and its contribution could never be anything but a token one, but the Egyptian government did not permit even that much of a display of hostility toward the Axis. The Italian propaganda since the outbreak of Italo-British hostilities had been that Axis troops were invading Egypt only in order to smash the British forces there and that once this had been accomplished, the Axis would restore Egypt to full independence and sovereignty. Apparently some of the Egyptian leaders were credulous enough to believe this.

Mussolini did not confine his fishing in troubled Moslem waters to Egypt. He was also active in Iraq, which was restless under its

British mandate. At the start of World War II, the Iraqi government had consented to the British request that it break off diplomatic relations with Germany, but when Italy entered the war nine months later, three successive Iraqi Premiers resisted all British pressure to break with Mussolini, and the Italian Legation in Bagdad became the headquarters of Axis activities in Iraq. The Italian Minister, Luigi Gabrielli, made the most of his opportunities. One of Iraq's former Premiers, Rashid Ali El-Gailani, was pro-Axis, and in collaboration with him Gabrielli organized a *coup d'état* whereby Rashid Ali seized power on April 4, 1941.

As soon as this plot had been successfully carried out, the German Arabian expert, Dr. Fritz Grobba, who had formerly been minister to Iraq and Saudi Arabia, returned secretly to Bagdad and, together with the Italian Minister, laid plans to bring Iraq, with its great treasure of petroleum, into the Axis orbit. It was undoubtedly with Axis approval that Rashid Ali, two days after his successful *coup d'état*, publicly announced his intention to fulfill the Anglo-Iraq treaty. The Axis had no wish to make Iraq a battleground, especially at that time, and they were anxious to lull the British into thinking everything was all right. However, the British distrusted the new government and soon started landing troops at the Iraqi port of Basra, on the Persian Gulf. London was especially concerned over the fact that Rashid Ali had dismissed the regent of the six-year-old King Feisal. When fighting between British and Iraqi started on May 2, Rashid Ali immediately appealed to the Axis for aid. Some German and Italian planes were quickly sent to Bagdad, where the pilots donned Iraqi uniforms. The Germans also sent munitions and other war supplies by plane via French Syria and the Italians sent some high army officers to give the Iraqi generals advice on military operations. The Italian military attaché at Ankara also went to Bagdad.

The Axis, however, was at that time very busy with the invasion of Crete, and since the German High Command decided that the Crete and Iraqi ventures could not be carried out successfully simultaneously, the Nazis, with their characteristic singleness of purpose, decided to forget about Rashid Ali and stopped sending him supplies. As a result, he was soon unable to continue the fight against the British, and on the twenty-ninth day of the war he fled to Iran with his chief general, Dr. Grobba, the Italian Minister, and seven of his favorite wives. Thus years of Mussolini's labors and intrigues were wasted through bad timing of a *coup d'état*.

As a result of the British getting control of Iraq and later of Iran, one of the Moslem world's most notorious troublemakers, Haj Amin El Husscini, the Grand Mufti of Jerusalem, was forced to seek asylum in Italy. The British had been chasing the Grand Mufti all over western Asia and, according to Italian newspapers, had offered a reward of $100,000 for his capture. For more than a decade, he had fomented trouble between Jews and Arabs in Palestine, but he was so well hidden by his followers that he was never caught.

After years of this hide-and-seek with the British police, first in Palestine and then in Iraq and Iran, and hiding out for a time in Afghanistan, he suddenly arrived in Albania aboard a private airplane during October, 1941. At first he showed a disposition to stay in Albania, which is a Moslem country, but this did not suit Mussolini, who wished to employ him in making propaganda amongst the Arabs against the English. After a few days, he was induced to come to Rome, where he was quickly put to work broadcasting over the Bari radio station, which was specially beamed on the Near East. A number of El Husseini's lieutenants also came to Rome to talk with him, and conferences were held at which Italians with long experience in Arab countries were present. The Fascists made no secret of the fact that new plans were being made for further fifth-columnist activity in Mohammedan countries. In a statement to Italian newspapermen, the Mufti said:

"I thank Il Duce and the Italian government for my reception in Italy. Arabs and Moslems extend their trust and friendship to all who are targets of British propaganda. Our only answer to England's possible actions will be continuance of our efforts in the struggle for the cause to which we have consecrated our entire existence."

El Husseini also made a visit to Berlin, where he had conversations with Hitler and von Ribbentrop.

Mussolini also carried on extensive negotiations with Ibn Saud in Saudi Arabia and with the Imam of the Yemen. In September, 1937, he signed a twenty-five-year treaty of friendship with the Imam, the importance of which, however, diminished considerably as a result of the British capture of Ethiopia. Ibn Saud was more noncommittal in his dealings with the Duce, but Italo-Arabian relations were always most friendly. In fact, the only prominent Arab leader who had been militantly anti-Axis was the Emir of Transjordan, who was frequently blasted in the Fascist press as a "British stooge."

What the grand objective of Mussolini's Arab policy had been all these years it was difficult to ascertain, but it seems likely that the Duce aspired to overthrow British dominion in the Near East and Egypt. It seems likely that he had planned a large-scale fifth-column action to take place at the first big military success of the Italians in North Africa. Had Graziani's first offensive, in September, 1940, got under way with the speed intended, such a fifth-column action might very well have been tried, since Italian prestige would then have been high and many Arabs were weary of British rule. During the past three years, however, the British counterespionage service has had plenty of time to track down the chief Arab conspirators in pro-Axis secret organizations. Those conspirators who remained at large, however, probably deserted Italy for Germany, whose exploits on the desert battlefields greatly overshadowed anything accomplished by the Fascists. Mussolini's toy sword of Islam was soon lost sight of by the Arabs in the dust kicked up by Rommel's spectacular tanks, and again Mussolini lost out to Hitler in one of Italy's traditional spheres of influence — this time Libya.

# XVI

By the spring of 1941, all the American correspondents in Rome were convinced that war was inevitable between Italy and the United States. No one specific event or date accounted for this conviction, but, rather, an accumulation of many things added up to mean war. For decades Italy had been, after France, the most popular country on the European continent with American expatriates. It had become a combined playground, finishing school, and old ladies' home. Americans by the thousands not only visited Italy as tourists, but took up permanent residence in such charming places as Florence, Capri, Sorrento, Rapallo, San Remo, Venice, and Rome. Somehow, this queer conglomeration of divergent types — gray-haired spinsters with incomes, title-hunting divorcées, students of music and art, and retired bankers, industrialists, and diplomats — found what they were looking for on the Italian peninsula and, settling down, took root. The Italians were pleasant, easy to get along with, and extremely understanding of those personal peculiarities which made these people want to live abroad.

By the hundreds these Americans began to return to the United

States, and at the beginning of June, 1941, the ultrasophisticated American colony of Rome had dwindled down to a Main Street of diplomats, consuls, newspapermen, and incorrigible Italophiles who were willing to risk invalidation of their passports rather than leave *la bella Italia*. These expatriates, as we found on investigation, did not leave of their own volition, but, rather, were squeezed out by the State Department, which refused to issue them new passports except in the rare cases of occupational necessity.

In a way, we were surprised at the unofficial reasons given by the consuls in some of the cases. One girl who had been divorced several times asked Eleanor to intercede at the U. S. Consulate on her behalf.

"The United States is not at war," she said, "and I don't see why I shouldn't be entitled as a free American to stay over here until it starts."

Not wishing to make a special call at the Consulate about this matter, Eleanor waited until she had occasion at a bridge game to ask one of the consuls why this girl could not stay on.

"She only stays over here because she likes Italian men," he replied. "It's about time that she returns to the United States and learns that American men aren't so bad."

Actually, what the United States Consulates were doing was trying to get out of Italy all unofficial Americans, so that when the break did come, the task of repatriation would be simplified. To us, this was tacit admission on the part of the administration that it was expecting a war with Italy.

On the Italian side, we think it could be said that the Fascists did not abandon hope, until March 30, 1941, that America would keep out of the war. But the United States' seizure of Italian ships on that date brought home to the Fascists a realization, as nothing else had ever done, of the fundamental hostility of Washington to the Axis cause. Until that time, the Fascist government officials had been inclined to dismiss American antagonism as nothing serious and as only a natural manifestation of sympathy toward the mother country of England.

Relations between the two countries became even more acrimonious when the State Department sent a note to the Italian government requesting the recall of the Italian Naval Attaché in Washington, Admiral Alberto Lais, and accusing him of "acts and violations of the laws of the United States." At a press conference, Secretary Hull said these acts were the giving of orders to sabotage Italian ships in American ports. In accordance with international protocol, which gives any nation the right to request the withdrawal of a foreign envoy, the Italians had no grounds for protesting the branding of Admiral Lais as *persona non grata*, and they did not do so. On the contrary, they said they would remove him at once, but they requested the recall from Rome of the United States Assistant Military Attaché for Air, Major William C. Bentley. The brusque dismissal of Major Bentley provoked a comment from Secretary Hull in press conference in which he remarked that governments intent on activities outside the law do not hesitate to resent the activities of foreign representatives who faithfully observe the law.

Secretary Hull's statement stung the Italian government to the first hostile declaration against the United States since the beginning of World War II that could be considered official. It could not be so dubbed by the correspondents, because the Ministry of Unpopular Culture would never permit its statements to be so described; but the answer to the State Department was put out in mimeographed form by the Italian Press Ministry, obviously acting under instructions from the Foreign Office. The statement, firstly, denied that Admiral Lais had in any way exceeded the legitimate functions of his office; secondly, declared that the dismissal of Major Bentley "was not a reprisal — though that would have been justified — but because of activities which exceeded his task and neglected his duty as a guest of a country at war"; and, thirdly, said that "the gratuitous insults against so-called 'nations without law' could very easily be applied to that government which, after carrying out acts of robbery against merchant ships not belonging to it, claims these ships should be consigned to it, decked with flags as for a holiday." This declaration marked a fundamental change of policy on the part of the Fascist government toward the United States; in diplomatic procedure, these were strong words to utter about a nominally neutral country, and from then on Fascist officials spoke harshly of America or kept silent.

Mussolini himself was the most outspoken of all and in an uncalled-for attack on the United States during an otherwise conventional speech before the Chamber of Fasces and Corporations, June 10, 1941, on the occasion of the anniversary of his declaration of war against France and England, he bluntly declared that the United States could be considered as already at war, and that American intervention could make no difference in the outcome. He said:

"There is a state across the ocean which expects to enter the conflict. It is well to make it known that American intervention does not disturb us excessively. An explicit declaration of war would not modify the present situation, which is already one of de facto war, if not de jure. American intervention, even if it becomes complete, will be too late, and even if it were not too late, it would not alter the terms of the problem.

"American intervention will not give victory to Great Britain, but will prolong the war. American intervention will not limit the war in space but will extend it to other oceans. American intervention will transform the United States' form of government into an authoritarian and totalitarian regime which will greatly surpass and improve on its European precursors — Fascism and National Socialism.

"When one wants to remember a dictator, in pure classic expression, one cites Sulla. Well, Sulla seems to us a modest amateur compared to Delano Roosevelt."

He pronounced the name Delano in a way that gave it a scurrilous Latin meaning every Italian understood. It was probably the filthiest schoolboy pun, comparable to writing dirty words in a lavatory, that the head of any state had ever used about another chief of state in modern times. Mussolini's pronunciation of Roosevelt's middle name was a Roman epithet so foul that it cannot be translated here.

An Italo-American war seemed even closer when, on June 14, 1941, President Roosevelt announced the freezing of Axis funds in the United States. Owing to the difference in time between Rome and Washington, Roosevelt's announcement did not reach Mussolini until after all his ministers had left for Roman week ends at Ostia and other resorts. He was so enraged, however, that he did not even try to get in touch with the various ministers, such as those of Foreign Affairs, Finance and Foreign Exchange, under whose jurisdiction this action came. He picked up a pen and in his large, bold handwriting wrote out a reprisal decree. He ordered it to be issued by the Press Ministry the following morning, which was a Sunday. He wanted to make sure Americans would have no chance to withdraw any funds from the American Express early Monday morning before his ministers returned. The decree, whose wording revealed the hasty manner in which it had been drawn up and which contained no hint as to its practical application, read textually as follows:

"Following the freezing of Italian and German funds and the evaluation of foreign property ordered by the President of the United States, the Fascist government, besides having ordered similar measures in retaliation, has ordered the immediate evaluation of all property belonging to the United States existing in Italy."

We were caught short with only a few hundred lire in cash on hand as a result of this week-end economic battle. On Monday, Reynolds was informed at the American Express, where we had our personal account, that it was impossible for us to make even the smallest withdrawal, pending specific instructions from the Ministero di Scambi e Valuta. Owing to Italian inefficiency rather than to the actual measure itself, it was weeks before we could receive any of the $500 a month per person that we were entitled to under the decree. This sudden placklessness had one bright facet. It revealed how many Italians liked and trusted Americans. Not only did our servants willingly forgo their pay and lend us money, but the neighborhood shopkeepers extended us unlimited credit. In restaurants where we were known, waiters who were aware of the decree kindly suggested that we pay the check when we had become "unfrozen." As a matter of fact, we had always found it much easier to obtain credit or borrow money in Italy than in the United States. The Italian (in Italy) has a greater confidence in an American than Americans (in the United States) have in each other.

Permission to draw money from the U.P. account in order to pay Italian members of our staff and to pay bills which the United Press owed Italian firms was, oddly enough, much more difficult to obtain than in the case of drawing money for our personal needs. At the Ministero di Scambi e Valuta, Reynolds had a long conference with *Dottore* Leone, who was in charge of the freezing of American business interests. Reynolds pointed out that the blocking of the U.P. account was harming the Italian employees more than the United Press. Leone interrupted saying:

"It serves them right for working for an American organization. If they were good Fascists they wouldn't do it."

The carrying out of the defreezing regulations was slow and cumbersome, showing a lack of co-ordination in policy among the various Fascist ministries. The Ministry of Unpopular Culture was anxious for us to withdraw sufficient funds so we could send news dispatches about Italy, while the ministries concerned with finance did everything possible to prevent us from sending even a Fascist communiqué. At the same time, our biggest creditors were the government-owned telephone company and the government-owned Ital-Cable and the government-owned radio station at Pisa, yet the Ministero di Scambi e Valuta wouldn't release us funds to pay them. It was one government department strangling another. The only possible explanation of this confusion was that the Italian government was trying to force us to bring in more American dollars instead of letting us use any of the large reserves of lire which the U.P. had in Italian banks.

In connection with the freezing of Italian funds, the State Department also laid down a rule that persons of Italian nationality could not leave the United States without special permission. The Fascists immediately retaliated by requiring that all Americans leaving Italy must be supplied with exit visas. As in the case of the freezing itself, the ruling was very similar on paper to the American one, but in practical application it was entirely different. In the United States, permission to depart was refused to hardly anyone once United States officials had ascertained the departing Italian had complied with freezing regulations. In Italy, on the other hand, exit visas were maliciously and deliberately held up with the purpose of intimidating the American Embassy and State Department with the large number of Americans who were more or less prisoners in Italy. It was Mussolini himself who was holding up the visas. There was no use in Embassy representatives taking up these cases at the Chigi Palace or police headquarters, because no official could do anything until Il Duce had issued the orders. And the Duce was not in a hurry to issue any — he was angry over the turn Italo-American relations were taking, and if Americans were worried over not being able to leave Italy, why that pleased him immensely. George Jordan of the Associated Press bureau in Rome, who had just received instructions to return to his New York office the day before the exit-visa ruling was announced, asked every day at the press conference what progress was being made. This daily question annoyed Rocco and Capomazza intensely; they did not know the answer any better than anyone else did. Mussolini did not set up the machinery for granting these visas for nearly a month after he had issued the general ruling that Americans could not leave without them.

Still another sign of impending Italo-American war was the Italian government order on June 19, 1941, closing down the American Consulates within the next twenty-six days as a gesture of Axis solidarity. It was in reprisal for the Washington decision to close down all German Consulates in the United States. The official Rome communiqué did not, however, refer to reprisals but went further and hinted at espionage, saying:

"The attitude and activities of the American consular officers in Italy have given rise to grave developments."

The State Department reacted quickly and two days later ordered Italy to shut all its consulates in the United States by July 15.

The departure of the consular train from Rome was the biggest social event of the summer season among the American colony, and there were a lot of farewell bottle parties on the station platform, which had been carefully roped off so that only Americans and foreign officials, watched by detectives, could be present. Scores of unofficial Italians who wished to say good-by to their American friends were not permitted to pass the cordon.

The train's departure was delayed forty minutes while an American-born clerk in the Rome Consulate, Mrs. Emilia Rosano, struggled with her emotions. Her decision was finally made for her by two *carabinieri* who went to her house and forcibly brought her to the train. She arrived in tears, unknowing which she wanted to do — return to the land of her citizenship or remain behind to await the arrival of her husband, a captain in the Italian army, who had been wounded in Libya. Actually, Mrs. Rosano had no choice in the matter, as her name was included in the list, agreed upon by the American consular service and the Italian authorities, of those ordered to leave. She jumped the train, however, when it was held up at San Remo three days, and the Italian government finally consented to let her stay. Ambassador Phillips, who was at the station to bid farewell to his departing colleagues, was pained at the incident, especially when a Chigi Palace official said to him, with a Gioconda smile:

"You see how charming Americans find Italy."

With the departure of the U. S. Consulate staffs, the American colony in Rome became smaller than ever, and we were more and more dependent socially upon each other. Fascists, especially those in important positions, were afraid to invite us to their homes and were also unwilling to accept invitations from us. Anti-Fascist Italians had to be careful not to draw attention to themselves by association with Americans. Even Swiss, Swedes, Spaniards, and

Danes, who had formerly been friendly with us, saw less and less of us for fear of compromising themselves or their legations with the Axis. Tipsters who had worked for the U.P. for the past ten years or more resigned or else just ceased giving us any information. Secret police hung around the American Embassy and quietly followed all people coming out of it, generally accosting them several blocks away. They demanded to see identity papers in all cases and carefully wrote down the names and addresses of these people. If they were not Americans, it meant that they would be investigated further by the OVRA on suspicion of espionage activity. Few Italians dared to go to the Embassy after this.

The State Department further emphasized its view that war was inevitable by giving all its employees in Rome — whether or not they had families — until the end of September to pack up and ship home their furniture at the State Department's expense. The Department stated that it would not assume the responsibility of looking after their furniture in case of an emergency and, by setting a time limit on the free transportation offer, intimated that it did not think the emergency was far off. After that, members of the Embassy staff who had not rented furnished apartments had to bear the expense of living in hotels.

All Embassy wives except five had departed by the end of summer, as a result of State Department pressure, and they were followed shortly thereafter by all the wives of the American correspondents except Eleanor, who was herself a working journalist, and Mrs. Cianfarra, who was not an American. Many of the departing women had small children whom they were taking home with them, and this added to the arduous, nightmarish trip through Italy, Switzerland, France, Spain, and Portugal — six days and nights without sleeper or dining car, so that the travelers had to provide their own food and blankets. It was also wise to bring drinking water, as there was typhoid in many sections of war-torn France and Spain. To add to the other miseries, the women and children had to change trains several times, and in most of the stations there were no porters to carry the luggage. It probably constituted one of the worst travel hardships American women had put up with since the days of the covered wagon. Women who had always been afraid of airplanes preferred to risk their own and their children's lives on the Italian passenger plane to Lisbon, but these planes were always so crowded that it was difficult to find accommodation for even a single person and almost impossible for a whole family. As the international train departed only once weekly, however, there was usually a group of Americans traveling together and they would team up and pool their resources.

Long before we had come to Italy, all international phone calls were recorded by official Fascist eavesdroppers, but listening in on all local calls made or received by Americans was inaugurated in the summer of 1941. The first we knew of this was during a conversation Eleanor had with Mrs. Charles Livengood, wife of the United States Commercial Attaché. It was one of those rare feminine conversations that Eleanor seldom had time to indulge in. She and Mrs. Livengood were talking about a bridge party, who was to be invited, how the various people played, and what clothes should be worn — the kind of conversation guaranteed to bore a man excruciatingly. Finally Eleanor and Mrs. Livengood, after talking over a number of items in each other's wardrobes, decided to wear daytime dresses with hats instead of dinner dresses without hats. As they prepared to say good-by to each other, a voice on the phone said, in perfect English, "Thank God you've made up your minds at last!"

Several friends of ours had similar experiences in which the listener-in would interrupt to make some comment about the subject being discussed. Livingstone Pomeroy, one of the U.P. staffers in Rome, was talking to an Italian flier friend about the latter's departure for the front.

"I'm leaving tomorrow . . . " the flier began, when a voice interrupted, saying:

"You must not give away military movements." The line went dead.

As a result of this isolation of the American colony, we became dependent almost entirely upon the Embassy for news, although the Embassy itself knew little more than the American correspondents. Actually, the Embassy became a sort of clearinghouse in which Embassy information and newspapermen's information were pieced together, checked one against the other, and interpreted. We made it a point, as did all the other American correspondents, to call on Wadsworth at least twice a day, once in the morning and once in the afternoon.

George Wadsworth for many years had been Consul General in Jerusalem and had established a name for himself at the State Department as an expert on Middle Eastern affairs, but for some unknown reason he was suddenly transferred to Rome as Counselor to replace Harold Tittmann, who had been appointed assistant to Myron Taylor, the President's personal representative to the Pope. With the departure of Ambassador Phillips on one of his periodical trips to the United States, Wadsworth, as Chargé d'Affaires, and his wife became the leaders of what remained of American social life in Rome.

Wadsworth immediately endeared himself to American newspapermen by his understanding attitude toward the press. He was more informal than Ambassador Phillips, who, because of his reserve, precluded journalistic chitchat which often could lead to ideas helpful to interpreting the news of the day. Tall, thin, and distinguished in appearance and dress, Phillips was always polite, cordial, and friendly, but uninformative. Most of the correspondents respected him, but only Herbert Matthews and John Whitaker were able to break down his barrier and really talk to him. And then it would be in such strict confidence that they were unable to send as much as the other correspondents who had not talked to him.

Phillips was so unapproachable that when his major-domo, Mario, put Italian ersatz whisky in White Horse bottles and served it to guests at his palatial Villa Taverna, no one dared to tell the Ambassador, who did not himself drink whisky. We were not afraid, however, to mention it to Wadsworth, who immediately sampled it but also decided he would not saying anything to his superior. It was a minor point, but it was part of the reason why correspondents went with their troubles to Wadsworth, which they never felt free to do with Phillips.

Phillips had the distinction in 1941 of being the only Ambassador, or for that matter envoy of any kind, accredited merely to the King of Italy and not, as were all other foreign diplomats, to "The Emperor of Ethiopia and King of Albania." This was because Phillips had presented his credentials to Victor Emmanuel before Mussolini started empire hunting. Any Ambassador sent to replace him, however, would not have been accepted by the Fascist government unless his letters of credence were addressed to the King with all his newly acquired empire titles, which would have been tantamount to recognition by the State Department of the Fascist occupation of Ethiopia and annexation of Albania. It was laughingly said, therefore, by members of the foreign diplomatic corps, that Phillips was sure of his job as Ambassador to Rome as long as Italy and the United States continued diplomatic relations.

Phillips was a diplomat's diplomat, and what he may have missed in his contacts with the correspondents he more than gained from his good relations with many of the other ambassadors and ministers in Rome. Almost every day, four or five diplomats would call on him to consult on international affairs. Despite the tension between the United States and Italy, Phillips also was always able to see Ciano because of the latter's high personal regard for him.

Wadsworth took the attitude that American correspondents knew much about what was going on in Italy and encouraged us to relate to him the odd bits of gossip, rumor, and information that we picked up at the Foreign Press Club and elsewhere. He became a sort of father confessor to whom correspondents might go for advice. When Reynolds, for example, was nominated for an executive post in the Foreign Press Club, he went to Wadsworth and asked what to do about it, as the organization was dominated by Germans.

"Let them elect you and then immediately resign," he said.

"That will let everybody know that Americans will have nothing to do with Nazi maneuvering in Italy and will also show that the Germans are trying to make a play for the Americans."

Reynolds was duly voted into office and embarrassed the entire Foreign Press Club by being the first member to turn down a post after being elected.

Although Wadsworth was ever helpful, his wife, Norma, was the real source of Embassy news. She told us much more than the Press Attaché, Elbridge Durbrow, who had been transferred from the Moscow Embassy to Rome. "Derby," as we all called him, was an amusing and likable fellow, but he disapproved of the way in which newspapermen would often send stories that did not fit in with State Department policy. We jokingly called him "the Press Attaché who hates the press."

Mrs. Wadsworth had quite the opposite point of view. She was a daughter of a newspaper owner, the late Norman Mack, of Buffalo, and had a great respect for the power of the press. In reality, she soon became, as far as the American correspondents were concerned, the real Press Attaché of the American Embassy. Correspondents did everything they could to be invited to her bridge parties, at which one was certain to pick up a good front-page story. She had an uncanny sense of news, combined with an understanding of Washington's foreign policy. When Matthews, of The New York Times, moved into the Grand Hotel where the Wadsworths lived, Allen Raymond, his direct competition as the Herald Tribune correspondent, remarked:

"He's just trying to get an inside news track with Mrs. W."

It was the first time that we, in our fifteen years of international journalism, had found bridge games an imperative newspaper assignment. But there was no doubt that we were worried whenever Matthews, Raymond, or Massock was invited to Mrs. Wadsworth's suite and we were not. It meant that we might be beaten on some exclusive angle of an international story. Among ourselves, we correspondents called it "boudoir bridge," but actually it was Culbertson with a news beat.

It was while Eleanor was playing with Mrs. Wadsworth that we learned the inside story on Padre Woolf. In contrast to the close-mouthed Durbrow, with whom Eleanor had spoken just before going to the Grand Hotel, Mrs. Wadsworth gave all the details about the case to Eleanor.

"I think you should know all about it," Mrs. Wadsworth said to Eleanor. "It's another Fascist trick that should be exposed. I see no reason why it shouldn't be published."

When Eleanor was dummy, she excused herself and phoned Reynolds the entire story at least an hour before Wadsworth called in the press to announce it. The scoop was purely theoretical, however, since Italian censorship would not pass any dispatch about the Woolf arrest for the next twenty-four hours.

Woolf was arrested at 9:30 on the morning of November 18, 1941, by two agents of the secret police who came to the rectory of St. Paul's Protestant Episcopal Church on the Via Nazionale while he was discussing hymns with his organist for the Thanksgiving Day service. He was taken off in an automobile and was held incommunicado. Wadsworth's efforts to see him were unavailing, and the officials at the Foreign Office could only tell him that Woolf was being held "on suspicion of intelligence activity." They explained that under Italian law, persons held on such a charge could not see anyone from outside until the examination of the case had been completed. Although both police and Foreign Office officials refused to divulge the specific things he was supposed to have done in the line of espionage, Italians whom we regarded as official gossipmongers spread wild tales about him. According to one of these stories, he had taken over a mausoleum in the Protestant Cemetery in Rome and converted it into a radio sending station, utilizing the cross on the top to disguise an antenna for his transmitting set. They also spread false rumors about his moral conduct. Even Rocco and Capomazza told us that they knew nothing officially about his case, but that they had heard — not for publication, of course — that two Italian officers with whom he had been in league had already been found guilty and executed by a firing squad. All these stories and falsifications soon reached Wadsworth, as the Foreign Ministry wanted them to do. It was the old Florentine trick. The purpose was to magnify the importance of Woolf and give the Italian government the upper hand in the ensuing bargaining about his release.

"They are trying to make a blue chip out of him," Wadsworth told Reynolds. "Dear knows how many white chips he will cost."

He actually cost thirteen white chips — the number of Italians who were finally released from jail in the United States in exchange for him. It was good Italian bargaining — one man for thirteen.

All this time, the Italian press grew nastier and nastier in its attacks upon the United States. The Fascist newspapers printed horrifying cartoons of Mrs. Roosevelt and the President and were ingenious in the distortions of fact that they used to discredit Americanism among the Italian people. Gayda even cited Father Divine as a reason for Axis unwillingness to be friendly with the United States. In a front-page article in *Il Giornale d'Italia*, Gayda wrote:

"The United States is a mixed race which has not yet created internal spiritual unity. There are twenty million Negroes in the United States who are followers of Father Divine from whom Europe cannot obtain any spiritual or social inspiration whatsoever. Europe may respect the United States but cannot tolerate the efforts of the United States to install its own mixed civilization abroad."

The official Stefani news agency issued a vile description of Mrs. Roosevelt, saying:

"The President's wife suffers from a bellicose frenzy which is a real surprise in Europe, where the conception of femininity is based on kindliness and sweetness in conformity with the social functions of women as mothers, wives, and daughters. Mrs. Roosevelt's extremely nervous manifestations remind Europe of La Pasionaria during the Spanish war."

Ciano's newspaper, *Il Telegrafo*, also tried to make American women look ridiculous. An editorial in it said:

"Undoubtedly, uniforms such as those worn by the Massachusetts Women's Defense Corps are very, very cute, but in reality they serve the United States government's war propaganda. This female war craze, so widespread in the United States, which is being used to make war popular, particularly shocks and offends our European mentality. War is a manly business and must be willed, decided upon, and fought by men."

Even Roosevelt's fishing trip was presented to the Italian public as a ghoulish act by Rome's leading morning newspaper, *Il Messaggero*, which said:

"While the President himself enjoys fishing, millions of men are fighting with munitions furnished by Roosevelt. Other millions are suffering the consequences of Roosevelt's intrigues and still other millions are preparing to fight in new sectors of the world as the result of his provocative policy. Such is plutocratic morality."

*Il Tevere* was blatant in its charge that America was run by Jews, and said:

"Roosevelt hopes to repeat the *pax judaica* of Woodrow Wilson, who led America into World War I on behalf of Morgenthau, Warburg, Jacob Schiff, Brandeis, Kuhn, Loeb & Co., all Jewish bankers of New York and rulers of the United States."

The newspaper then went on to contend that the President was a Jew himself.

"One of his forebears, who was named Rosenfelt, migrated to Holland from Spain at the time that Spinoza and other Jews were forced to leave Spain. The name soon became changed to Roosevelt."

These were just a few of the hundreds of pinpricks published by the Fascist newspapers in an effort to undermine the prestige of America and its leaders. Serious, documented editorials against the United States gave way to this low mud slinging so that it would be easier, Mussolini thought, to make the masses of the Italian people accept an eventual declaration of war.

War was so inevitable by the fall of 1941 that many of the American newspaper organizations began systematic withdrawals of their correspondents. Percy Winner and Mike Chinigo, the two Americans on the I.N.S. staff, were the first to leave and were replaced by an English-speaking Italian who had an American mother, Prince Rospigliosi, and by Ernest de Wirth, of mixed nationality. Allen Raymond left late in November for an assignment in Africa and closed down the *Herald Tribune* bureau in Rome. The Associated Press withdrew all of its American correspondents, including, besides Jordan, Charlie Guptil, who was transferred to Buenos Aires, and Frank Bruto, who was sent to Switzerland, leaving only the bureau manager, Dick Massock, who replaced his staff as best he could with Swedes and Italians. In the United Press, Italo-Americans of American citizenship were given an opportunity to be transferred, as it was not known whether such persons of dual nationality might be judged Italians in case of war. Aldo Forte availed himself of this offer and joined the U.P. Zurich staff. Earl Johnson, U.P. Vice-President in charge of news, cheered us up with a letter saying that the State Department had agreed that American correspondents should leave on the diplomatic train in the event of war.

"That's fine," Eleanor said, "if only the Italians agree to it when the war breaks."

*The New York Times* decided that its news staff of Matthews and Cianfarra would continue on in Rome. That was fine: misery always wants company.

All the other correspondents of Rome fame, like John Whitaker, Cecil Brown, and Charlie Lanius, had left months before. The rest of us stayed behind and nervously waited to be engulfed by the war.

Just before the attack on Pearl Harbor, December 7, the Japanese in Rome made extremely friendly overtures to members of the American colony. The Japanese Ambassador had invited practically all the members of the American Embassy staff to a tea to be given December 9. The Japanese Counselor, Ando, gave a lavish cocktail party and buffet supper at his new home in honor of American and Japanese correspondents on December 4. It was attended by Matthews, Cianfarra, Massock, Reynolds and Eleanor, and about eight Japanese newspapermen whose names for the most part we never could remember. In view of the fact that it was only three days before the attack on Pearl Harbor, we believe, more than ever now, that it was done deliberately to create a false impression of Nipponese friendliness toward America. It was a small part of a world-wide plot which later we learned took place in every capital in the world where there were Japanese and American colonies. Similar parties, we confirmed later, were given at about the same time in Berne, Berlin, Madrid, and Lisbon. Despite the difficulties in obtaining in wartime Rome large quantities of food and liquor for such a party, Ando produced a gourmet's array of good things to eat and drink, including Scotch whisky, which the Japanese consumed enthusiastically. Ando raised a glass of straight Scotch and solemnly said:

"Here's to the continued friendship of America and Japan."

We sat around and talked for nearly two hours, during which all the Japanese repeatedly assured us that Japan would never go to war against America for any one of a number of reasons, ranging from Japan's lack of oil to the fondness of both Americans and Japanese for baseball. One grim note, however, slipped out — probably as a result of the whisky. Reynolds received a call from the office informing him that the Albanian government had just been reshuffled. Although Reynolds tried not to let the other correspondents hear the context of the conversation, Massock and Cianfarra, on one pretext or another, found occasion to come into the telephone room and heard Reynolds telling Eddie Laura what follow-ups to send. The party quickly broke up as the Americans dashed off to their offices to deal with the story. The Japanese correspondents, however, didn't budge, but continued with their swilling. Maida said to Reynolds:

"Resignation of Albanian cabinet is no new. You no consider that important, do you? In few days you have big new."

Reynolds is still wondering if he was not extremely stupid to have put it down as the silly chatter of just another Jap in his cups.

When the attack on Pearl Harbor came, the entire American colony realized it meant war between the United States and Italy, as well as with Japan. The first news of the attack was received by the U.P. in an urgent cable from New York. Eleanor was in the office at the time and immediately telephoned Wadsworth, Colonel Fiske, and Captain McNair. None of them had heard the news before, and a war council was immediately set up in the Wadsworths' hotel suite, where they listened to the radio and received Eleanor's relaying of U.P. messages from New York and, much later, the reports which we got from Stefani.

The next day, Monday, the American colony went to work to prepare for war. There was no way to leave hurriedly because the issuance of exit visas to Americans had again ceased. We were all prisoners in Italy. The Embassy immediately started burning their most secret documents, which they did not wish to have fall into Italian hands, and prepared for a later wholesale bonfire of thousands of papers, pamphlets, and books, including secret codes. Wadsworth told us that same Monday that the Axis might even declare war that evening, although it was more likely that Hitler and Mussolini would require a few days to prepare the stage setting for their declarations.

Eleanor attended the press conference as usual on Monday and asked Rocco if there was any Italian comment on Pearl Harbor.

"Pending official confirmation of the events of yesterday," Rocco said, reading from a slip of paper in front of him, "there can be no official or semiofficial reaction to the newspaper accounts. There is nothing more to be said at the moment."

The Italian newspapers that day were also noncommittal about the Italian attitude to America, and even Gayda did not dare to go further than to pay tribute to "Japanese heroism and ability."

We heard from Italian sources in Rome that both Hitler and Mussolini had been informed in advance of the attack and that German generals had drawn up the general strategy of the Japanese battle plan, including the surprise attacks on Pearl Harbor, Manila, and Hong Kong. The delay in Axis reaction was owing to

Hitler's and Mussolini's desire to make sure that the Japanese had attained an initial success in the undertaking. As soon as they were satisfied of that, they agreed on the Axis declarations of war against the United States, which were made on Thursday, December 11, four days after the Japanese hostilities had started. We were convinced that had the Japanese failed, Italy and Germany would not have backed them up.

When, on the afternoon of December 11, 1941, we crashed through the cordon of police and detectives that surrounded the American Embassy and got inside its portals, we had our first view of America at war. Colonel Fiske almost knocked us down the steps as he tore out of the Embassy with a dispatch to the State Department. Wadsworth was still at the Chigi Palace, where he had been summoned by Ciano, and everybody was awaiting his return. There was an odor of smoke as documents were burned in the different offices. An American Jew was ruefully sending up in flames a check for fifty thousand lire, for fear that he would compromise an Italian business associate if it were found upon him later by the OVRA. A number of the Italian clerks, both men and women, were crying. Some of the staff were laughing with nervous relief that the war had finally come after all the months of expectancy. Six American priests who planned to reside in the Vatican for the duration of the war were having their passports renewed. We joined them, as our own passports had already expired. As usual, we had no extra pictures with us and had to tear off the photographs on our various press cards to meet the necessary requirements.

After we had our passports fixed up, Reynolds telephoned Matthews because we were amazed that we were the only correspondents who had come to the Embassy. Reynolds told Matthews that it might be a good idea for himself and Cianfarra to join us.

Matthews pooh-poohed the idea and said he and Cianfarra had to clean out their desks. Suddenly he changed his tone and said: "I have to hang up now. Call me later."

Reynolds called back in fifteen minutes, and Herbert said in his usual calm way: "I had to hang up because two detectives came in while we were talking and took Cianfarra away with them."

"Don't you think you'd better try to come to the Embassy?" Reynolds asked. "You could probably crash the cordon of police the same as we did."

"No," Herbert replied with exasperating aloofness, "I must finish sorting out my papers. Since they didn't arrest me along with Cianfarra, I guess I'm all right here."

Half an hour later, however, following Wadsworth's return, Herbert succeeded in phoning Wadsworth one brief sentence: "They've come for me, too."

David Colin, who had some sort of connection with the National Broadcasting Company but who had not been accredited as a correspondent by the Embassy or the Ministry of Unpopular Culture, phoned Derby to say that Dick Massock had just been arrested.

We phoned our house to tell our cook that we would not be home for dinner. The cook was clever enough to warn us by saying, "That is too bad. There are two gentlemen here waiting to see you . . . " before the receiver was banged down.

We next tried to phone our office, but by that time, about seven P.M., the OVRA had finally overcome its inefficiency and cut off the third and last Embassy phone so that it was impossible to make any further calls except with special permission of the Foreign Office. All the Embassy phones were supposed to have been cut off at three P.M.

Meanwhile Michele, Counselor of the Swiss Legation, was conferring with Wadsworth about taking over American interests in Italy by Switzerland as had been prearranged months before. After Michele's departure, Wadsworth held a series of conferences, first with the Embassy officers, second with the Embassy clerks, and third with the American press as represented by Reynolds and Eleanor. Wadsworth received us about eight P.M. in his private office. We had expected to find him looking fatigued and anxious, but instead he was thriving on the excitement. We had never found him more chipper. Taking advantage of his mood, Eleanor asked him about his visit to the Chigi Palace.

"I've just written a memorandum," he said, "about this visit — while it was still fresh in my mind. I received a summons this morning from the Foreign Office saying that Count Ciano wanted to see me at 2:30 P.M. about a most urgent matter. Of course, I knew what it was going to be. Count Ciano received me most brusquely, so unlike his usual, promiscuously friendly manner. When I walked into his office he halted me halfway to his desk by rising, making it quite clear that I was not to sit down. With a scowl on his face he recited his piece as though he had learned it by heart, saying in one sentence that he must inform me that Italy considered herself at war with the United States. I bowed my head and said, 'I'm very sorry to hear it.' "

Eleanor asked, "Well, why did you say that?"

"Protocol, my dear lady, protocol. One is always sorry when war is declared on one."

"And then?" asked Reynolds.

"I then said, despite his forbidding manner, 'May I give you a message before I take leave of you?' Ciano replied coldly, 'I don't think there is anything more to be said.' I then told him that it was a message from Ambassador Phillips. Ciano said, 'In that case I should like to hear it.' I told him that the Ambassador wished to convey at this time his appreciation of the collaboration that he had received in the past and the personal kindness that the Foreign Office had always shown him while he was in Italy. Count Ciano then relaxed somewhat in his manner and said with the suspicion of a friendly smile, 'Thank you.'

"I then asked him if I might discuss exchange arrangements with members of his cabinet and he answered that della Rosa and Montanari would be at my disposal.

"There is a real scoop for you two, because you are the first to learn how Italy delivered its war declaration to the United States, but you'll have to wait until you leave Italy to write it."

Wadsworth added that as soon as he left Ciano he talked with della Rosa and asked for permission to send direct from the Foreign Office to the State Department a message in clear about Italy's declaration of war. Permission was accorded him, and Wadsworth to this day claims he scooped all journalists as well as the Italian Ambassador to the United States, Prince Colonna, who, we learned later, called on the State Department that same day in complete ignorance of Mussolini's action. He was informed, on the basis of Wadsworth's telegram, that Italy was already at war with the United States. He retired, considerably embarrassed.

We then got down to brass tacks with regard to ourselves and asked Wadsworth what we should do. Stay in the Embassy indefinitely — if he would permit that — or go out and be arrested? He thought awhile, scratching his head with his gray-and-black fountain pen, and then said:

"I suggest you get a good meal here and then leave sometime during the night. It is better to get into the concrete mixer early rather than late. There is sure to be an arrangement made for all American correspondents, and it is better that you don't make yourselves special cases by avoiding arrest."

It was undoubtedly sound advice, but we were at heart a bit hurt that he did not offer us indefinite shelter in the Embassy, as at that time we expected an exchange would be worked out within a fortnight's time. How wrong we were! When we left his office, Derby opened a can of tongue, a can of corn, and a can of salmon for us. We stayed on, chatting and talking with members of the Embassy staff. By this time the OVRA had arranged a system whereby members of the Embassy could leave escorted by an Italian detective. As journalists, no detective had been assigned to us, and the police in charge of the gate were unwilling to allow us to go out. Finally, word came through to us that the Packards had received permission to leave. At one A.M. Derby took us to the stone gateway and said, "Good luck." We walked exactly five yards in the tarry blackness of a moonless Rome blackout when two men joined us and said:

"We have orders to take you to the Questura."

# XVII

WE HAD GONE ONLY A FEW STEPS WITH THE TWO SECRET AGENTS when a police car drove up and we were ordered to get into it. The two policemen, whose faces we couldn't see in the blackout, politely tried to reassure us that we were merely being apprehended as a part of war routine and that there was nothing to worry about. At the Questura we encountered the usual Fascist inefficiency. Nobody seemed to know what to do with us. It was too late to call up Cavaliere Aguesci, head of the Foreigners Department of the Rome Questura. We sat on a bench and watched police bring in two drunks, a disorderly character, and a sneak thief. In between these cases we could hear the detectives and night chief discussing what to do with us. The chief said he had received written instructions to send Reynolds to the Regina Coeli prison but that this couldn't be done now as the prison was closed for the night and that Eleanor was to be booked and permitted to go home under police surveillance. Two new detectives came in, and we soon learned from the conversation that they had been waiting at our house in the Corso Umberto all afternoon and evening to arrest us.

The two detectives who had taken us into custody were most apologetic to their two colleagues. One of them said:

"Sorry we copped these two birds. They were your catch. But there was no way to get you on the phone so you could bring them in."

We felt this was carrying the police etiquette even to Italian extremes. At four A.M. it was decided to take Eleanor to our apartment, and four detectives got in the same police car with her after assuring Reynolds that they would behave themselves. They were quite proper and, as far as Eleanor could make out, two of them merely went along to get a ride part of the way home. Eleanor was handed over to still another detective, who was stationed in the porter's lodge. He permitted Eleanor to go to our apartment on the top floor, where she found the cook and maid still up and in a fine state as a result of the frequent visits of the police, who had insisted on repeated searches of the apartment to make sure that we had not somehow sneaked in. The servants insisted, however, on cooking some of our hoarded spaghetti and eggs for Eleanor in order to show their sympathy.

Hours later, Reynolds was taken to the Regina Coeli prison, the detectives asking him whether he wanted to go by autobus or taxi.

"What's the difference?" Reynolds asked.

"If you go by taxi you have to pay for it yourself," one of them answered, "but you get a free ride in the autobus at the expense of the state."

The trip was made by taxi, as Reynolds did not relish the idea of being escorted by police in public. Once in Regina Coeli, things became so pointless and complicated that Reynolds wrote them down in the form of a prison diary the day after his release.

From Reynolds' prison diary:

December 12 — I arrived at Regina Coeli about ten A.M. Was immediately fingerprinted and then for some unknown reason was locked up in a smelly toilet which kept flushing automatically. Through keyhole saw prisoners, handcuffed with huge wooden blocks and legs chained, go clanking by. An hour later was taken before another official who took my passport and locked me in another toilet for half-hour. Next found myself in big office where two wardens ordered me to strip naked. Shivered cold while contents my pockets including money were wrapped in package and my trouser cuffs and coat lining carefully examined. Clothes were returned to me except for belt, tie, and scarf. Received two pieces of bread and was handed over to guard who marched me through endless corridors. My unbelted pants kept falling down, tripping me like a hobble. Was placed in cold cell with concrete walls, one heavy wooden door and a barred window facing a dark courtyard. Gray-haired Italian who had two weeks' beard was shoved in. He told me he was arrested for safecracking but this time was innocent.

"Just because I was caught cracking a safe once, am arrested now every time a safe is cracked."

Old lag taught me tricks of prison life. How to pile up our iron beds so we could walk in a straight line. He suggested removing my coat, saying, "It will be colder tonight, then you put on your coat and you feel warmer." There was one wooden bucket in the cell for our corporal needs, but he warned against using it except just before six P.M. and seven A.M., when trustees came to empty it. Later we were each given a bowl of soup, which I was unable to stomach, but the old lag consumed both. We were also given thin wooden spoons and forks. "So we cannot kill each other or commit suicide," the old lag explained. Late afternoon. Warden took me out of cell, through labyrinth of fire-escape-like corridors to bare room where two other wardens told me to strip to the waist. They then ordered me to drop my trousers. Livingstone Pomeroy, one of the Rome United Press staff, was brought in. He laughed while two wardens frisked me for hidden objects.

"What's so funny?" I snapped.

"I always wanted to catch my boss with his pants down."

After we redressed, were led out. Passed Matthews and Massock in the corridor. Before guards could intervene, Matthews said:

"I think the Embassy has gotten us paid cells."

This proved correct, and Pomeroy and myself found ourselves

in cell small as ever, but with sheets, better mattresses, and cleaner blankets. We heard tapping on concrete wall. Finally caught on. Next door cellmates were talking to us by using taps for letters of alphabet. One tap stood for A, for example, and four taps meant letter D. They asked us why we were in jail and I replied, pounding my fist against the wall, bruising the flesh:

"Because we are Americans and at war with Italy."

Neighbors, who had told us they were political prisoners, replied:

"Not heard that before. Sorry."

Tonight permitted to buy against money taken from us some extra food — can of bully beef and glass of wine each. Went to bed early as only tiny blue bulb in cell for light and Pomeroy still chattering about a salary increase.

December 13 — During night, guards entered cell three times, flashed electric torches over our faces, and ran iron stick across window bars, producing sound like sour xylophone. Were making sure we hadn't sawed bars. Had to make own beds. Were so badly made warden sent in trusty to show us how.

Lunch. More bad soup. When Pomeroy told warden through peephole in door he thought we were entitled to extra food, warden answered, "That's right, but the guard last night forgot to take your order."

Warden said he had a brother in Chicago and liked Americans. Hinted if we could find our way to pay him he could get us bootleg food "that will make you forget you are in prison." Early afternoon warden returned, his face beaming, and whispered in half English, half Italian, "You leave carcello."

Later he returned and ordered us to follow him. We trudged through steel corridors to office where all our possessions had been docketed. Here all other American male correspondents were gathered. Detectives were also there. Laughed and joked with us. After putting on ties and belts, we were led out by detectives, who asked us if we had taxi fare. We all said yes and asked where we were going, but detectives refused to say. Pomeroy, myself, and two detectives squeezed into one taxi and rode through Rome, down the Corso Umberto, past my apartment, to a third-rate boardinghouse, the Pensione Suquet, which had once been a brothel. There were three rooms for the six correspondents who had been arrested. The bedroom of Pomeroy and myself was also the dining room and lounge, but it seemed de luxe after prison. Detectives sat in the hallway guarding us. The six were: Matthews, Cianfarra, Massock, Pomeroy, Allen-Tuska, and myself.

(End of prison diary.)

Robert Allen-Tuska, an American who had lived in Como for many years, was taken on by Reynolds, just six weeks before Mussolini's declaration of war, to replace Aldo Forte, who had been transferred to Zurich. He was not a newspaperman, but his knowledge of Italy and the Italian language made him a useful adjunct to the office. His wife, who was Italian, was the first visitor at the Pensione Suquet. She promised to deliver a message to Eleanor from Reynolds.

Eleanor, meanwhile, had been going through a lot of waste motion. Not knowing how long Reynolds might be detained in prison, she had endeavored to send him warm clothes, toothbrush, books, and so on, which, owing to the molasses-in-January-like slowness of Italian prison routine, never reached him. On December 12, Eleanor was visited by a different set of detectives from those who had carried out the arrests and was told that she would be sent to Perugia, a small mountain city, on December 21, to be interned for the duration of the war.

"But I believe we are leaving with the Embassy staff," Eleanor protested, aghast at the prospect of remaining in Italy for the duration.

"I doubt it. We have seen the Foreign Office list, and no journalists are on it," one of the detectives insisted, then added consolingly, "You might be able to go to Montecatini instead of Perugia. Some Americans are being sent there."

That was the first intimation Eleanor had about the disaccord between the United States and Italy over the status of newspaper correspondents, and it continued up until the time we left, with the State Department using one set of words and the Chigi Palace another. Eleanor finally received permission to visit Reynolds and soon arranged a home-meal service for the inmates of the Pensione Suquet. The Italian detectives, who liked the looks of our cook and maid, permitted them to accompany Eleanor as food bearers. The Suquet food, curiously enough, was quite good for wartime Italy, so between the two meals, which were combined into one, everybody ate extremely well. Eleanor was also permitted to receive the Wadsworths at lunch on December 14 and learned that the snag in the negotiations about correspondents was that the Italians did not have enough of them for bargaining and wanted to include newspaper people in a general group to be known as "notables," who would be permitted to leave with the diplomatic party. The Italians had one hundred and twenty-seven notables to Wadsworth's twenty-one.

On our third day at the Pensione, we were surprised when suddenly the glamorous Teddy Lynch, who had given up singing at the Stork Club to study opera in Rome, came popping in. She was still out of breath with the excitement of her experience. She had been arrested on December 11, suspected of intelligence activity, and had been held in the Women's Prison of Rome for five days in the same cell with an abortionist and an Austrian Jewess accused of espionage. Tall and red-haired, she still had allure despite her bedraggled appearance. Everybody called her Teddy Lynch, although she was the wife of Paul Getty, millionaire oil magnate of California.

"I hope this prison life hasn't ruined my voice," Teddy said.

She soon had the detectives running errands for her, and by the next day an amazing amount of luggage and clothes, all kinds of games, and a collection of stuffed Donald Ducks and teddy-bears filled her room, which was on the same floor as the other three, but separated by a long hallway.

"I do hope you don't mind my staying in your room, which is really a sort of clubroom," she said to Reynolds, "but I don't feel safe with those detectives who keep knocking on my door all the time and asking the stupidest questions."

If the correspondents were worried about their status on the exchange list, she was even more so because the Embassy was nettled at her refusal to leave Italy during the general American exodus. The Embassy took the attitude that she could have studied opera just as well in the United States as in Italy. The fact that she had been arrested on suspicion of intelligence activity also gave her a certain amount of preoccupation.

The first official visit at the Pensione Suquet was made by a delegation of three from the Ministry of Unpopular Culture, headed by one of the lesser ranking officials, Count di Sorbello. Sorbello, speaking as always with an Oxford accent, was most apologetic about the arrest of the six male correspondents. He tried to tell us that we were quite comfortable where we were at the moment and that soon we would be interned in a small town where we would have greater liberty.

"You see, you were put in such unpleasant cells only because we heard, I think it was over the Swedish radio, that Italians had been arrested and treated as criminals in the United States. So we felt we had to do the same thing."

"But you might have confirmed it officially first," Matthews said.

Sorbello muttered something about the difficulty of confirming things in a country at war with his own, and then flitted on to say:

"And you see we did not put Mrs. Packard in jail because it is our policy to treat ladies, even if they are journalists, with the proper respect for their sex."

"What about Teddy Lynch?" Pomeroy asked.

"That is a different case," Sorbello replied. "It has nothing to do with the Press Ministry."

Next day, Wadsworth visited us and explained in a rather formal, cold way that he was doing the best he could for the newspaper people and hoped they would all be able to leave on the diplomatic train.

"Whenever that may be," he added with diplomatic caution. As he left the room, Teddy Lynch stopped him and asked about herself.

"Sit tight," he said, and walked out.

Everybody felt rather depressed, disappointed at the unusually formal and noninformative way in which he acted. He had always been so expansive before.

Two days later, Aguesci came to the Suquet and announced that the correspondents would all be interned in Siena pending negotiations for our repatriation. We were to leave within two days, and permission would be granted to those who still had personal affairs to liquidate to go to their homes for a few hours under police escort. Reynolds was allowed to visit the Embassy in order to take up with Wadsworth various problems of the correspondents. The detective who escorted Reynolds had also guarded the Yugoslavs.

"They were such generous fellows, and constantly gave us whole cartons of American cigarettes," he said. "Legation stuff. I certainly appreciated it. Italian cigarettes are impossible."

Close to the Embassy, he said that the visit was only supposed to last an hour but he would be glad to wait much longer, especially if Reynolds remembered about the American cigarettes.

What surprised Reynolds the most was that the Embassy was still functioning as usual. All members of the staff were keeping regular office hours and drawing up reports of all kinds for Wadsworth. Derby was making daily trips to the Foreign Office where, though he was not received by Ciano, he was able to discuss the exchange problems with Count Celesia di Vegliasco, one of the Foreign Minister's first assistants. Merritt Coots made daily visits to the Swiss Legation in regard to problems of all the American internees in Italy. Wadsworth was in conference with the Panamanian Minister, but Reynolds had to wait only a few minutes before being received. Reynolds told Wadsworth that everyone had been upset in the Pensione Suquet as a result of his visit, that everybody felt he had been decidedly distant and, instead of giving us encouragement, had caused us even greater anxiety than before.

"Why can't you fellows stop being just newspapermen?" Wadsworth said, with the first show of irritation that Reynolds had ever seen him display. "I was in no position to talk freely, with at least eight detectives outside the door — every one of whom probably understands English perfectly — and the likelihood that there was a gur-gur in the room to record everything I said. You journalists have nothing more to worry about than the diplomats. But I am not going to jeopardize the exchange negotiations by talking where I am sure everything I say is going to be relayed immediately to the Chigi Palace. Whether you go out of here as notables or correspondents, you can be sure that I am doing my utmost to see that you're on the same diplomatic train with me. I can't say more."

Reynolds then told Wadsworth that the correspondents, including Eleanor, had received orders to prepare for internment in Siena within forty-eight hours, as that had been decided upon as the place of internment for the correspondents, instead of Perugia, but that Teddy Lynch was to be left behind. Reynolds asked Wadsworth to use his influence to have her transferred to Siena as was her desire, and added now that she was to be left alone in the Pensione Suquet, she would prefer women to men guards. Wadsworth at that time, December 20, believed that the diplomatic train would leave possibly within a fortnight or, at most, before the end of January.

Reynolds learned from members of the Embassy staff that the Foreign Office officials were extremely friendly in an effort to obtain things American. Derby's negotiations regarding the diplomatic exchange, as a case at hand, were interspersed with bargaining by the Italians for frigidaires, automobiles, electric phonographs, radios, electric heaters, furniture, and apartments. In fact, Derby was more welcome at the Foreign Office after Mussolini had declared war on the United States than before.

All the Suquet correspondents were permitted to visit their homes for several hours under police guard to pack up for Siena. Massock said he had a grand time burning up anti-Fascist material

in his apartment in front of his detective, who was completely indifferent to what was occurring.

We arrived in Siena under police escort in the late afternoon of
December 22. There were seven of us — Matthews, Cianfarra, Massock, Pomeroy, Allen-Tuska, Eleanor, and Reynolds. We went to
the best hotel in town, the Excelsior, which was practically deserted except for a few other internees, and took our pick of all
available rooms. The seven of us agreed to split the expense of
one large room which we could convert into a sort of clubroom.
We later christened it "The Suquet Sporting and Debating Society." From then on, it was a plot out of a Dostoevski novel. Here
were seven of us who had never got along particularly well in Rome,
suddenly isolated in an insular group in the small town of Siena,
where we were not supposed to have contact with Italians. We
could walk around the town, go into stores, restaurants, cinemas,
generally followed by detectives, but unable to speak, except on
business, to the thousands of Italians around us. We were dependent on each other's society. Outside of Eleanor and Reynolds,
there were no two people who were really congenial. The Packards
and Massock had been journalistically cutting each other's throats
for nearly three years; Massock and Matthews had also been competition because Matthews and Cianfarra had collaborated with
the Packards. Yet, on the other hand, the Packards and Matthews
had recently fallen out over a personal matter. Matthews and
Cianfarra had their own intraoffice differences. Pomeroy, as a
cub in the U.P., followed the ups and downs of the Packards'
relations and at the same time felt Reynolds worked him too hard
and did not increase his salary as often as he should have. Allen-
Tuska, who all of his adult life had associated with the haute
monde of Europe, felt that he was slumming to be with a lot of
newspaper people. At the same time, the attitudes of Pomeroy and
Allen-Tuska irritated Eleanor and Reynolds. Furthermore, Massock
regarded himself as the dean of the American correspondents because he had been in Rome some months more than the other two
bureau managers, but Wadsworth insisted always on addressing

group communications to Matthews, while Reynolds, heading a bloc of four Unipressers, controlled the voting. And on top of this, there was the gloomy thought that all of us might be stuck in this small provincial town for the rest of the war. It was a psychological test of just how much the human mind could stand in the way of constant friction.

Just before New Year's, Teddy Lynch was brought to Siena and moved into the Excelsior. Not being of the newspaper ilk, she had a hard time to keep up with the psychological counterplays going on around her. In mid-February, David Colin, who had been appointed NBC representative in Rome just a short time before Mussolini declared war on the United States, but had not made a broadcast from Rome, also was interned in Siena. The delay was due to his quasi-journalistic standing. He completed the group and contributed to further disarrangement of neuron patterns by consistently winning at bridge.

Nevertheless, the whole group determined to get along somehow or other, if only to make a show of American solidarity in front of the Italians. It was a great effort, and we think that, at least outwardly, it succeeded.

To cope with the boredom of internment, the group of nine took up one hobby after another. First, it was visiting the historic monuments of Siena, including the zebra-striped Siena Cathedral, the fourteenth-century Palazzo Pubblico, art galleries, various churches, the home of Saint Catherine, and mounting the many spires of the town. Many of the group became collectors of antiques and spent hours poking around in dusty, rubbishy antique shops, hoping to find genuine Renaissance masters. A number of spurious paintings were purchased at great expense by the more enthusiastic shoppers. Next, there was a bicycling craze, and to everyone's astonishment no objection was made by the police to long, cross-country excursions during which contraband eggs, butter, and flour were bought from farmers.

The third craze was drawing with charcoal and crayon, and for weeks everybody acted as each other's models and some of the worst atrocities of art were perpetrated. This was followed by a beard-growing contest in which all the male correspondents vied with each other in the luxuriance of hirsute growth. There was also a camera rage and, later, a bird-raising contest, in which the Packards and Teddy Lynch were the main contestants. Teddy won out with the largest number of hatched eggs, but the Packards, who allowed their birds to fly around their room for five hours every day, claimed superiority in the art of taming feathered pets.

Woven through all these evanescent fancies was a steadfastness for bridge. Every night in the Suquet Club room there was at least one, if not two, bridge games. It was the one thing besides reading which continued unfailingly to hold our interest and make us forget our plight. The stakes were incredibly high. Only freedom mattered, and it was impossible to get excited about small sums. We are ashamed to say how high the stakes were, but an indication can be gained from the fact that Eleanor and Reynolds, as a team, lost twelve hundred lire in one night's play — about seventy-five dollars. Fortunately, we also won sometimes.

We also went to the movies regularly and frequently saw old American films dubbed in Italian. Another permanent institution was the Saturday-night burlesque show at the Impero, which was so bawdy that neither Teddy nor Eleanor dared go again after their first visit. Russian billiards in a small caffè was also popular in the early evening, despite the fact that Italians would crowd around and gape at these strange Americans. Ping-pong in the wintertime was replaced in the spring by regular tennis on the courts of another hotel. When a group of tennis players consisting of Matthews, Cianfarra, Teddy, and Pomeroy appeared on the courts with new tennis balls received from the Embassy, an Italian lieutenant among the score of spectators cried out:

"Signori e signore, a minute of silence, please, out of respect for these ghosts of the past."

Italians had not been able to buy new tennis balls for nearly two years.

What impressed us the most about our stay in Siena was the

friendliness of the Italian people to us whenever we had the few contacts ever permitted. The clerks in stores were extremely friendly and were always giving us more than we were entitled to under rationing laws. Reynolds had to cease going to one of the cinemas because the ticket seller there insisted on giving him a free pass.

"My fiancé is in America," she said, "and I won't let any American pay money to see these old pictures."

It seemed to all of us that wherever we went, we were given preferred treatment, whether in barbershops, at bars, tearooms, millinery shops, or grocery stores, just as in the old days of peace. Twice we received anonymous presents of champagne from Italian businessmen passing through Siena who merely signed themselves "friends." The only trouble we encountered was from Fascist leaders who passed by and resented the fact that we seemed to be enjoying ourselves so much and were on such friendly terms with the hotel employees. Several protests were registered with the police about our conduct, but only once was the Questore nasty, and then he ended his harangue by saying:

"I don't think you've done anything seriously wrong, but you must realize that it is bad for Fascist morale when the Italian people see interned enemies living so much better than themselves."

During the beginning of March, 1942, Reynolds was permitted to go to Rome under police escort to take up with the Embassy and the Swiss Legation outstanding problems of the Siena group. Arriving in Rome, Reynolds was surprised to find that the Embassy was still functioning the same as in peacetime. Derby was still making his daily calls on the Foreign Office and Coots his daily visits to the Swiss Legation. The entire staff was working on regular hours, with the exception of the Military and Naval Attachés, who reported, however, both in the morning and afternoon for consultation with Wadsworth regarding problems that came under their jurisdiction. Wadsworth was especially busy with drawing up dossiers of all the exceptional cases that did not fit into exchange pigeonholes, such as those of Denny, Woolf, Teddy Lynch, Buckley, and innumerable others.

One great tragedy had occurred since our departure for Siena. Sally Cole, the youngest of the Embassy wives, had died. She was the wife of William Cole, a Third Secretary. As far as Reynolds could learn, her death was due to the Fascist inefficiency of handling the Americans guarded in Rome. The Coles continued to live in their apartment, being guarded constantly by detectives. Their phone had been cut off. Sally was stricken with acute appendicitis in the middle of the night, and when Bill tried to get a doctor he was delayed by detectives, who would not permit him to telephone. Almost an hour was lost before he could finally arrange for a call to be made to his doctor from the porter's lodge. Later, on the rush to the hospital, the ambulance ran out of gasoline and it was nearly another hour before fuel could be had. By the time Sally reached the operating table her appendix had burst and a few days later she died of peritonitis.

Reynolds remarked to Wadsworth that it was most amazing that the Embassy was still functioning despite the war that existed between Italy and America, and that relations were still maintained between the Embassy and the Chigi Palace. Already the war between the two countries was three months old. Wadsworth admitted that this was probably the first time in history that such a thing had ever occurred, and appeared extremely proud of it. The Foreign Office permitted Wadsworth to wire to the State Department in clear over Ital-Radio, an Italian government-owned company.

During his stay in Rome, Reynolds heard gossip that this keeping open of the Embassy in a country at war with the United States was perhaps not the diplomatic achievement it seemed. Why did the Fascists permit it? Their Embassy was not allowed to function in Washington. In fact, Prince Colonna and his entire staff had all been interned far from the American capital. One proffered explanation was: Ciano was able to read Wadsworth's messages, which were never permitted to be sent in code. Wadsworth, however, confined his dispatches to reporting on the difficulties he was encountering with the Italians in connection with the exchange negotiations and the counterdemands they were making for the release of Woolf, Buckley, and Denny. The Swiss did not particularly like the arrangement, as they felt they should be in complete charge of American interests and that all such messages should be sent through them in code. Nevertheless, Wadsworth kept the Embassy functioning up until the day of the departure of the diplomatic train — a period of five months and two days.

The Embassy staff lived for the most part in the Grand Hotel, except for a small group which stayed in the Albergo Maestoso on the Via Veneto. The Embassy staffers were no doubt worse off than the group in Siena. The Embassy people, including wives, were escorted by detectives wherever they went. Even while they slept, detectives sat in the hallway outside their bedrooms. They were under an 11:30 P.M. curfew. They were not permitted to eat in public restaurants or to go to the theater or cinema. In the Grand Hotel, all of them ate in their own rooms, but in the Maestoso there was a small, isolated dining room for Americans.

Mrs. Wadsworth continued with her bridge parties, which now were important as sustainers of morale. Despite the coventry imposed upon Americans, she received visits from time to time of other foreign diplomats, including the Danish Minister, Wadstedt, who had formerly been Minister in Washington, members of his staff, and foreign prelates from Vatican City, such as Monsignor O'Flaherty of Ireland, all of whom had only to obtain permission from the Questore.

Interrupting the bidding during a game of "boudoir bridge" in her suite, Mrs. Wadsworth said to Reynolds, "You're so much better off in Siena than we are here. We cannot move without a shadow following us wherever we go. You cannot imagine how detestable that is. You tell me that in Siena you run around quite freely. Well, I hope you can see what the Fascists are doing."

Reynolds said, quite dumbly, that he did not see.

"Well, it's quite clear, to me at least, that the Italians are trying to make the lives of the diplomats in Rome miserable in order to pressure them for concessions in the exchange negotiations, while they treat you journalists so much better, hoping you won't write too unfavorably about them when you get away. If you fall for that Florentine trick, I'll never forgive you."

We think that Mrs. Wadsworth, in her trenchant way, was undoubtedly right. The correspondents in Siena were treated decidedly better than the diplomats in Rome, and there must have been some explanation for it. We cannot think of a better one than that offered by the wife of the Chargé d'Affaires.

Although Reynolds' permission to visit Rome was only for three days, Wadsworth succeeded in having it extended twice so that altogether Reynolds spent nine days in Rome with the Embassy group. These extensions were connected with the negotiations between Wadsworth and Celesia at the Foreign Office for the transferring of Denny from wherever he was being held prisoner — it was an Italian army secret — to be with the other correspondents in Siena, where Wadsworth thought he would be happier and, more important, stand a better chance of being with the diplomatic party, once he was got away from the army's clutches.

While Reynolds was in Rome, Wadsworth put him to work writing detailed reports about the treatment of the seven internees in Siena, reports on United Press problems, memoranda about the special cases of Teddy Lynch and David Colin, and an addendum to the petition which Reynolds brought from Siena requesting the admission into the United States of Mrs. Cianfarra, who had an Albanian passport. When Reynolds returned to Siena, he said, "I never worked that hard in the U.P."

Massock and then Matthews also made visits to Rome under police escort, just as Reynolds had done. While in Rome, neither Massock, Matthews, nor Reynolds could make any telephone calls without special permission from the police or the Foreign Office, as such was the ruling applying to diplomats. But all the time we were in Siena, we had no difficulty whatsoever in making even long-distance phone calls to all parts of Italy, including Rome. Teddy Lynch, for example, would talk to friends in Rome as often as three times a day, and Allen-Tuska frequently telephoned his family in Como and relatives in Milan. Although in Rome it was possible only with special police permission to receive visits from friends, no such restrictions were applied in Siena. We had our maid come up on two separate occasions to do some sewing and mending for us, while Teddy had several visits from her maestro, who kept tabs on her voice, and Matthews received a visit from an Italian friend. Queerly enough, the attitude of the Siena police seemed to be that it was all right for us to receive callers from outside so long as we did not have contact with the local gentry. Count Chigi was reprimanded by the Siena Questore when he permitted us as a group to visit the private art gallery in his palace. On the other hand, there was never any complaint when we attended Chigi's concerts of chamber music.

All in all, the Siena group was treated quite well. The worst feature of our internment was the uncertainty of our departure. There were times when we all thought we might be held in Italy for the duration of the war. It was also unpleasant to read the claims of great Axis and Japanese victories over the United States which were printed in the Italian papers. Matthews did yeoman work, however, in keeping the group informed of all the high spots in the news broadcast by BBC and American stations, which he picked up on a rented radio he had in his room. He wrote out summaries of these newscasts and handed them around the clubroom. He ran a one-man, one-copy newspaper, devoted to British and American war news.

Massock and Reynolds were playing Russian billiards in the neighboring caffè one Sunday evening when a detective came in and said that the Questore wanted to receive the Americans at eight P.M.

"It is good news for you," he said. "I cannot tell you what it is, but it is the one thing you have been waiting for."

He was all smiles and pleased at being the bearer of such

tidings. At eight P.M. the Questore received the group and confirmed in a few brief words that we were to leave for Rome on the
following Tuesday morning. He was officially stern and tried to
talk to us as to enemy aliens. His reserve was broken down, however, when Massock let out a loud cheer. Then he smilingly said:
"I'm as relieved to get rid of you as you are to go."

That night we kept the entire hotel awake with our own special
form of celebration. Massock, who had developed into a comedian
during his internment, auctioned off the weird drawings that had
resulted from the artistic phase of the Suquet Club and then
proceeded to imitate the Returned-War-Correspondent lectures
that he imagined each one of the group would eventually have
to make. He also performed his trained-seal act. The next day was
spent in packing, and our last night, which we had always imagined
would be the gayest of all, was anticlimactic. Everybody was too
tired from the celebrations of the night before and the ensuing
daylong packing to stay up late. Also, there was the prospect of
catching a 6:50 A.M. train.

On our trip to Rome we changed at Chiusi, where we saw an
entire train filled with German sailors waiting on a siding. They
were undoubtedly headed for the Mediterranean to man Italian
submarines, or perhaps German submarines which had already
been sent overland in sections and reassembled in one of the
Italian ports. Escorted by only four detectives, we found our trip
otherwise uneventful. We installed ourselves in the Grand Hotel
in Rome, where the Italians had organized a detective service
for us so that we could be escorted around town. The police, this
time, were much more lax than when Reynolds was there last and
made amazing exceptions with regard to our liberty of action.
Allen-Tuska, for example, was permitted to go out in the custody
of his Italian wife, and Pomeroy in the custody of his sister, who
was married to an Italian baron. We made the most of the eight
days we spent in Rome and, although we were always accompanied
by an Italian detective, went to all the best restaurants and even
to the gayer underground cafés where there were music and

singing. On all sides we were treated with great friendliness. The only expressions of disapproval we encountered were from a few professional Fascists in party uniform who scowled when they heard us talking English.

The Siena group left on the fourth and last diplomatic train, May 13, 1942. The other three trains had left at intervals of two days apart, beginning May 7. The first two trains carried mainly Latin American diplomats and their families. Denny was delivered to the Embassy the day of our arrival in Rome from Siena. He was white-haired and had a long white beard, looking at least twenty years older than when we had last seen him in Rome two years before. Major Michael Buckley was handed over to the Embassy a few days later, but Padre Woolf, who had been tried and sentenced to thirty years' imprisonment, May 11, on a charge of espionage, was not released until the evening of May 12, less than twenty-four hours before he was to take the train.

Actually, all the fears of Americans that they would not be permitted to leave because they weren't either diplomats or correspondents turned out to be needless. For in the end Wadsworth could not get enough Americans to fill his quota, which was equal to the large number of Italians whom the State Department finally permitted the Italian Embassy in Washington to take out of America.

We correspondents were never officially informed as to why we had been assigned to the last train, but as we all knew our organizations would expect us to send news stories from Lisbon — or even before if it were possible — we assumed it was because Wadsworth wanted to get the whole official party safely out of Axis territory before the correspondents let lose their broadside of cables against Fascism. At any rate, outside of ourselves, the last train was almost exclusively filled with the important members of the Embassy and the three most prominent "notables" — Woolf, Buckley, and Denny — whose release had taken many months of negotiation. Because no one knew what state of health Woolf might be in when he was released, he was given a whole sleeping compartment to himself next door to the doctor's compartment. Actually, however, though he had lost considerable weight during his six months in prison, he was otherwise quite fit and cheerful when he was released. He said that he had received no physical maltreatment while in prison, but had resigned himself to facing a firing squad, as the prison officials had told him that the American Embassy had already gone months before, leaving him behind.

Probably to make our leave-taking as unobtrusive as possible, the Foreign Office had arranged for our departure to take place at the siesta hour, and at 2:45 P.M. on May 13, a big red autobus slipped away from the side street beside the Grand Hotel and took us on a half-hour ride to the rarely used Ostiense station on the outskirts of Rome. The station had been specially built to receive Hitler when he made his 1938 visit to Italy.

Even at the station we continued to find evidences of Italian regard for America. Right in front of Foreign Office officials, a number of the *carabinieri* who were on guard at the railway platform asked us to look up their relatives in the United States. One, who gave us the address of his brother, said:

"Tell him I will join him in Brooklyn as soon as this war's over."

As a result of Wadsworth's postwar negotiations with the Chigi Palace, we had better accommodations than the departing British. As far as the Italian cars went, which was to the French-Spanish border, everyone aboard had a sleeper. Although a few of the party who had lived in Italy many, many years may have felt grieved over what the war might bring to the orderly and lovely countryside of Italy before they saw it again, to the great majority of us the imminence of freedom was so wonderful that we became quite giddy and, frankly, not quite normal. The train jerked forward and started moving out of the station at 4:30 P.M. Mrs. John Evans, wife of the Embassy Disbursement Officer, immediately produced a small American flag and waved it out the window at the Fascist officials. As many as could possibly be jammed into one wagon-lit (in other words, about ten) gathered in the compartment of that eminent guitarist, Douglas Flood, Third Secretary of the Embassy, and between sips of brandy and soda sang to the accompaniment of Doug's guitar such songs as Carry Me Back to Ole Virginny, Old Black Joe, Home on the Range, Susannah, Ole Man River, and many others until we were in a state of mellow but noisy sentimentalism. Speeding north-ward along the seacoast we occasionally glanced out of the window to look at an ineffectively camouflaged coastal battery. We saw several, but they were so far apart that we concluded the Fascists didn't think there was any danger of a landing party along this part of the Italian seacoast.

Next morning at six A.M., the train halted in Menton. Although we were still very sleepy, we threw on our clothes and hurried to get onto the platform, for it was the first time we had been in France since the war started. As old Parisians who had often vacationed on the French Riviera, we were anxious to see for our-selves what the effects of the war on France had been. Menton was Italian-occupied, and most of the soldiers and guards around the station were Italian, while the few French to be seen were not communicative, but it was another story when we arrived in Nice, which was in unoccupied France. Ignoring the worried looks of our Italian guards, the French — porters, travelers, railroad em-ployees, and newspaper vendors — gathered around us and talked quite freely. The substance of their remarks was: that living con-ditions were unbearable; that they hated the Germans but had to try to get along with them because "a man must live, n'est-ce pas?"

"Come back," they pleaded. "When Americans come back it will mean we are rid of les boches. When American troops land in France you will see that we mean what we say."

From the windows of the train, we caught glimpses of how the Riviera — once the playground of the rich of all countries — had fallen into decay. Tennis courts and golf courses were over-grown with weeds; the big hotels were shut up and falling into dis-repair. People were walking or bicycling — along the whole stretch of French seacoast we saw not a single automobile and only one truck. People carried knapsacks on their backs, in which they would put any fruit or bits of wood they might find along the highway. Everybody was shabbily dressed, though some of the women preserved a faint air of French chic despite their much-mended clothes.

Reynolds talked to one of the French detectives who was detailed to the train during its passage across France. A good-looking young man, he exhibited a biting Gallic cynicism about the war and its outcome for France. Reynolds asked him about an insignia he was wearing in his buttonhole. With a gesture of disgust he replied that it was his army service button:

"It's to show I was a combatant in a combat that ended without a combat."

When Reynolds tried to sound him out about France's position in the international situation, the Frenchman shrugged.

"Nous sommes des victimes. What can he do, le pauvre Pétain? Do you think in America that we take pleasure in the company of les boches? We only try to defend ourselves as best we can. If we are to be still alive when liberation comes, why in the meantime we must eat."

Reynolds asked him what he and his friends thought of Laval, and he did not conceal his disdain for that Germanophile, but added in a disillusioned way:

"Of course Laval has sold us out to the Germans, but de Gaulle has sold us out to the English."

We got the distinct impression that Americans were looked up to much more by the French than the English, and that, in fact, the French thought their only hope of the salvation the English had not been able to give them was now in America. Perhaps it was only flattery, but after six years of living in France we have yet to experience flattery from the French — outside the realm of amorous byplay.

We reached Cerbère on the French side of the Spanish border late in the afternoon of May 14, and there we had to change trains because the Spanish and Portuguese railroad gauge is wider than in the rest of Europe. As a result of the Civil War, Spain was short of sleeping cars, so compartments were provided only for the diplomats. The rest had to sleep in a day coach, which, however, was not unduly uncomfortable as there were only two to a compartment.

As soon as we had walked across the border into Port Bou, Spain, we telephoned our Madrid office and gave them a detailed story about the departure of the diplomatic party from Italy. When we went to pay for the call we offered the café proprietor some lire we wanted to get rid of. We thought that in view of the close diplomatic relations between Spain and Italy, lire would be acceptable in Spain. The proprietor laughed in our faces and said we could only buy pesetas with dollars. Even dollars he could not accept, as it was contrary to law, but there was a government exchange office in the station. The government official also said the lire were no good and gave us a Shylock's rate for the dollars.

At Barcelona, which we reached around midnight, Spanish newspapermen came down to meet the train. Eleanor and Reynolds knew most of them from the Civil War days. They avoided any discussion of internal politics but said most Spaniards hoped Spain could keep out of the present war. One said:

"Of course, if the Germans decide they want to try to take Gibraltar, I suppose we will have to let them come through Spain. But we hope we can stay out of it. We are in no condition to fight — hardly enough food, and our guns and planes were all used up and worn out in the *Guerra Civil.*"

But if the popular feeling toward the Axis was lukewarm, the official attitude was extremely pro-Italian. When we arrived in Madrid the next afternoon, May 15, the U.P. bureau manager, Ralph Forte, told us that the Spanish censor had killed practically everything we had sent from Port Bou and Barcelona, for fear it might offend the Italians. Actually, there had been nothing in our dispatches that an Italian censor would not have passed readily, because we were waiting for the more liberal censorship of Portugal. We had worked in Spain long enough to know the uselessness of trying to pass anything that might be construed as a criticism of totalitarianism — but the Spanish censor was taking no chances. However, Ralph Forte had brought two bottles of the best sherry down to the station to console us for the loss of our stories.

Around dinnertime, as we were halfway between Madrid and the Portuguese border, the train stopped in a small town about half an hour, and we got a glimpse of how bad conditions in Spain were. Children gathered round the dining-car windows, begging for bread, and when the diners gave them some, pandemonium ensued. The shrieking and yelling brought other children and adults, and within a few moments nearly everyone in the town was there in hope of getting in on the bounty. Some of the more tenderhearted diplomats went to their compartments and got boxes of biscuits they had brought with them, which they passed around the crowd. Begging in Spain had always been commonplace, but this was quite different because even respectable citizens took part in it.

When we got to the Portuguese frontier late that night, the train was not allowed to cross, for the Swedish diplomatic ship, Drottningholm, had not yet docked in Lisbon with the official Italian and German parties. Not until seven A.M. were we permitted to continue. We dashed into the café of the Portuguese frontier station and had our first real coffee in many months. Here we sent, at long last, the dispatches we had been trying to send all across Spain.

Outside of talking to people at the various stations, the main diversion of most of the members of the diplomatic party during the trip was bridge. Although we were out of Italy, we were not yet free; six Fascist detectives guarded us and two Chigi Palace officials were in charge of us. At any time — up to the Portuguese frontier, at least — we could have been halted, or even turned back if something had gone wrong with the Drottningholm and the Axis diplomatic staff she was carrying. In the Lisbon railroad station we suddenly realized that at last we were free; British and Yugoslav correspondents we had previously known rushed up and shook our hands, while at the same time the Fascist detectives politely said good-by and then, leaving us behind, hurried out of the station to shop for all those articles no longer to be found in Italy.

We were really free at last. To be sure, a wide ocean lay between us and America, but at least we were safely delivered out of the hands of the enemy.

# XVIII

We never realized how miserable we had been in warring Italy, before as well as during internment, until we arrived in Lisbon, where the gaiety, plenty, and brilliant lights made the somberness of the blacked-out, half-starved Europe we had left seem all the more dismal by comparison. To eat what one wanted, to dance, to walk on brightly lighted streets at night, to drink real coffee, to smoke American cigarettes — all trivial things in themselves, but in their sum total they went a long way toward representing the difference between comfort and hardship. The Portuguese complained of a shortage of gasoline, but there were many taxis, and we thought that if the Portuguese had nothing more than that to worry about they were indeed lucky.

But our own reactions raised a psychological question; if we had not ourselves realized the extent of our deprivations while in Italy, was it not probable that the Italians themselves did not feel them so much as might be supposed in lands of abundance?

It seemed to us that the American people, accustomed to a cornucopian standard of living, were placing altogether too much reliance on the belief that the Axis peoples must eventually crack because they could no longer endure the conditions under which they lived. To Americans reading of the shortages of food, clothes, fuel, soap, transportation facilities, and a dozen other seeming necessities, it was easy to believe that the Axis peoples would revolt against their leaders because they could not stand such hardships indefinitely. But we believed that unless things got much worse than when we left Italy in the middle of May, 1942, the Italian and German civilian could and would endure them for years more. To be sure, some individuals got sick and even died from malnutrition, but the great mass of able-bodied people accustomed themselves to privation.

The reason was that rationing was imposed gradually, particularly in Italy. The population generally had time to get used to one restriction before another was imposed. At first it was easy to do with less spaghetti and sugar because there was plenty of everything else. Little by little, as rationing increased, housewives found new substitute foods which they would never have used in peacetime — beans instead of spaghetti, "almond butter" instead of olive oil — only to have them rationed in turn until, at last, they abandoned all idea of trying to make meals that would please the palate and were relieved if they could find sufficient food of any kind to satisfy halfway their families' appetites.

The Italians ate and enjoyed food which many Americans would regard as unappetizing: brains, kidneys, sweetbreads, tripe, heart, lungs, and coxcombs. They liked goat meat and rabbit, which they served in a dozen different ways. Such omnivorousness, of course, helped to make the most of every animal slaughtered and gave a semblance of variety.

Naturally, there is always the possibility that the Italian people might crack from other causes, but they are not likely to be defeated by privations and food shortage alone. We were not the only ones of this opinion; the energetic and technically minded young acting assistant Commercial Attaché of the American Embassy in Rome, John Goshie, who had made a thorough study of economic and living conditions in Italy, held the same view.

The life of plenty in Portugal, however, was complicated by the problem of neutrality. The war had boomed business, particularly what might be termed the "tourist trade," to a terrific extent. Hotels, restaurants, movies, cafés, gambling casinos in Lisbon and the beach resorts near by were crowded and lively. Portugal only admitted poor refugees on transit visas; they had to have a permanent visa to another country and their transportation there paid before they could step upon Portuguese soil. Otherwise the government feared the country would be flooded with charity cases which it would have been impossible to care for. Even refugees with money had a hard time entering. Nevertheless, the really rich usually managed to wangle it one way or another, and there were hundreds of wealthy but homeless people from all parts of Europe and even the Orient, enjoying themselves at pleasure resorts simply because they had nothing more worth while to do. In these places we saw meet, but not speak, hundreds of representatives of the warring sides: Americans and British; Germans and Italians. There were large staffs of intelligence officers of all nations working in this crossroads of Europe, because in World War II Portugal, by virtue of its geographic position, assumed the role played by Switzerland in World War I — the espionage clearinghouse of the belligerent powers. This didn't please the Portuguese, but they could not very well prevent it except by enclosing their country in a Chinese Wall and not letting in foreigners of any kind. In their anxiety to remain neutral, the Portuguese people of all classes had become exceedingly chary of expressing any political opinions that could be interpreted as indicating they favored either warring side. We noticed that whenever we entered into conversation in Spanish or French with strange Portuguese, such as at bullfights, in streetcars, cafés, and restaurants, they were always careful to ask immediately: "What nationality are you?" They were not going to offend anyone — American, British, German, or Italian.

The censorship worked the same way. The first two days of our stay in Lisbon we were permitted to send really good broadsides at the Axis, but on the third day the corrugated-iron shutters were dropped. Rome and Berlin had protested. We had lunch with the chief censor and asked him about the change in censorship, and he replied:

"You sent your best material, didn't you? Now we have to placate the Axis. Remember, we are trying to be neutral."

After several changes of sailing date, the exchange ship *Drottningholm* finally weighed anchor at six P.M., May 22, after one dramatic incident just before the gangplank was pulled up. Horrell, of the I.N.S. Paris bureau, suddenly yelled:

"I'm not going to leave my wife and kids behind," and he dashed down the gangplank and through the customs shed before the surprised Portuguese police could stop him. He left his passport and all his luggage aboard ship. His friends explained that he had been debating with himself for weeks whether to return to the United States or to join his French wife and four children in occupied France, where he had been stationed before being transferred to Berlin.

Aboard the *Drottningholm* the staterooms were so tiny, crowded, and uncomfortable that we all spent most of our waking hours on deck and in the salons. When we weren't playing bridge, talk among the Rome group inevitably turned to Italy and her role in the war. We formulated then some of the ideas that had been swimming through our heads during the past two years. As the prow of the overcrowded Swedish liner plowed through the sunlit Atlantic with never a single submarine in sight, we talked, thought, argued. We can't say that all our fellow debaters always agreed with us.

One thing we did all agree on was this: that Italians cordially disliked the Germans and that this dislike was no temporary disagreement arising out of the strain of the present war, but inherent, deep-rooted in the past, when waves of German conquerors periodically swept over the Italian peninsula; and intensified by the dissimilarity of the German and Italian temperaments.

The political and diplomatic need for each other that had

caused the Nazis and Fascists to join forces during the political maneuvering that preceded World War II could not smooth over their old antagonism which was again brought to the surface and accentuated by the emotional upheavals of war. Even most of the Fascists bitterly resented the way the Nazis had moved in and taken control of all of Italy, including key posts in all civilian occupations as well as the direction of military affairs. And every Italian knew that the seven divisions of German troops (in addition to German air-force units) which were in Italy when we left were not there solely to assist Mussolini against invasion, but also to put down any revolution against the regime or even to prevent a turn-about-face on the part of the Duce himself.

Fascist dreams of large territorial expansion after the war were fading. Party leaders already realized that the inability to win decisive victories without German aid was going to weigh against Italy in any division of Axis spoils. The Nazis were not noted for their generosity and even though they would probably be more openhanded with Italy than any other country, in recognition of her having given friendly support from the beginning, they were not likely to abandon their newly established position in Africa, let alone hand out any territorial plums.

Mussolini himself was reputed to be worried about this aspect of the situation: that Italy would have ruined herself economically and spilled much blood only to have very little reward for her efforts in the end, because his armed forces had not been equal to the plans he had conceived for them. Most of all, Il Duce was worried about Laval and what sort of bargain he might drive with Hitler. If Laval could cajole or coerce the French people into any considerable collaboration with Germany, Mussolini well knew that Italian claims on France would quickly be dropped by the Führer. Despite all Hitler was getting from France then in the way of foodstuffs, iron ore, coal, factories, and so on, he still wanted more French munitions workers to go to Germany, French volunteers to fight in Russia, and, above all, that portion of the French fleet anchored in the Mediterranean. If he could get these,

Italian soldiers would never be allowed to set foot on Corsica, Nice, or Tunisia. Mussolini, therefore, stood opposed to Franco-German reconciliation. The closer Vichy and Berlin become, the more likelihood is there of a breach between Rome and Berlin.

Another cause of disagreement between the two Axis dictators was the forced subservience of the Italian army in Libya to Rommel and his staff. An idea of how Mussolini felt about Rommel was reflected in the lack of publicity accorded the German marshal in Italy. To jump slightly ahead of our narrative, we were surprised to see on arrival in New York that the American press gave more prominence to Rommel than the Italian newspapers, which always mentioned him briefly and as seldom as possible. They never glorified him as a collaborator one twenty-fifth as much as our own newspapers did as an enemy.

The same things that worried and antagonized Mussolini about the Germans also disturbed the Italian public, but they placed the onus for them all on Il Duce. In the past three years Mussolini's prestige and popularity with the Italian people had declined with sensational rapidity. The loss of Italian East Africa and the complete German control of Libya were blamed on him. He was accused in whispering campaigns of not having had the foresight to make these colonies sufficiently strong to defend themselves before engaging in a war with England. The ill-prepared and almost inconceivably ill-managed attack on Greece greatly undermined his position at home as well as abroad. Had it been well planned, the Italian people might have accepted it as a necessary and practical move to consolidate Italy's power in the Mediterranean and to give her greater striking power in the unpopular war against England. The whole campaign was so badly done, however, that the quick-witted Italians sensed something was wrong even before the Greeks took the offensive and made their rapid advance into Albania; and when stories of the real situation came trickling back by word of mouth, the public was indignant and began to wonder if the Duce was losing his grip. From the start of the campaign, the Italian newspapers had blamed the bad weather for the slowness of the advance, but since the attack had begun in bad weather, this hardly seemed a plausible alibi. While Reynolds was in Albania, Eleanor went to a cocktail party where she talked to a young Foreign Office official who seemed very gloomy about the whole affair. When Eleanor asked him why the Italians had started a campaign while the weather was unfavorable, he replied: "Well, we had to invade Greece sometime, so we thought we might as well start on the anniversary of the March on Rome."

Military considerations had been ignored. A war was started to make a Roman holiday for the great Fascist date of October 28.

Mussolini's personal popularity suffered further owing to the general unpopularity of his allies — the Germans and the Japanese. The Germans were personally and actively disliked; the Japanese, being individually unknown to most Italians, were distrusted on principle because they were Asiatic and sinister. The Italians, like most Europeans, were suspicious of Orientals mixing in European affairs. Because they didn't like either their allies or the Fascist setup, the Italian civilian population greatly resented making the war sacrifices demanded of them by the Duce. Had they been enthusiastic about the war they would have indulged only in the normal amount of grumbling — such as the English do — but, hating the cause of the restrictions almost as much as the restrictions themselves, they became filled with smoldering rebellion.

On top of all these other grievances came the declaration of war against the United States, and Il Duce's unpopularity reached a new high. Quite aside from personal ties with America represented by blood kinship with the millions of Italo-Americans, most of whom maintained correspondence with their Italian relatives, the Italian public could not see that any sufficiently important dispute between Italy and the United States warranted Mussolini's striking at the United States. The war against England was scarcely popular, but at least there was the issue of Italy's need of an exit from the Mediterranean through either Suez or Gibraltar; but in the case of America there was no clash of interests whatsoever — so the Italians thought. The ideological aim of the war against America as expounded by the Fascist press — the crushing of "pluto-democracy" — did not appeal to them.

Thus the Duce's hold on the Italian people diminished almost to zero and stories began to get around that he was failing mentally. We ourselves felt, on the rare occasions when he made public speeches, that he did not have his old fire, and the Italians took this as an indication that his control of affairs was slipping. The obvious disorder and anarchy in the Fascist war effort, the constant German penetration, and the Duce's obvious inability to maintain himself on an equal footing with Hitler in his diplomatic dealing with Germany, all were ascribed to the rumors that Mussolini was getting sick and old and that his mind had lost its keen edge. Rumor went that he spent fewer hours at his desk than formerly. But even when nearly sixty, he was still blatantly active in amorous intrigues. The Duce had always had a lot of love affairs and was proud of them as a sign of his lusty virility. He believed that the masses liked and admired a colorful Casanova more than a prude in such matters, and made promiscuity a Fascist principle. When a woman correspondent once asked him:

"What do you do when you wake up in the morning?" he replied:

"I jump right out of bed, no matter how beautiful the face beside me."

He set the pace in multiple amours, and his example was followed by his own son-in-law and most of the other party leaders.

For the past six years the Duce, in addition to his transient passions, had a permanent mistress, Clara Petacci, daughter of a doctor. A pretty blonde, she was quiet and serious, rather a home body. She was said to have borne him at least one child, but apparently he tired of her, for, since we reached the United States, word has reached us that she had been married off to a wealthy Milan industrialist named Broggi, whom the King, at Mussolini's request, made a marchese.

From one cause or another, the Duce probably commanded the undivided loyalty of less than ten per cent of the country by the time we left Italy. The remaining ninety per cent were filled with discontent over the present and anxiety as to the future. And the discontented ones included millions who were themselves members of the Fascist party. Unlike the Nazis in Germany, the original Fascists never tried to keep their party exclusive; they made it easier to join than not. There was always, therefore, a large body of the Italian public who wore the Fascist emblem as a matter of convenience and not from any deep-rooted conviction.

Yet despite the widespread antagonism to Mussolini's rule, there was, we decided after prolonged discussion and analysis of the matter, little chance of a popular uprising in Italy. For one thing, the Italians had never shown themselves to be a revolutionary people by nature. Contrary to popular American conception, they did not impress us as hot-blooded or inclined to take the long chances such as would be necessary for a revolt against Mussolini. Between the OVRA and the Gestapo, it was nearly impossible for anti-Fascists to plan and carry out the overthrow of the Duce regime. The tentacles of the OVRA spread to every farm, village, and city block, obtaining its information mainly from local gossip, of which there has always been an abundance in Italy. It was almost impossible for a meeting of potential revolutionaries to take place anywhere in Italy without an OVRA agent getting to hear about it and then checking up as to whether it was a social gathering or something more serious. The OVRA seldom resorted to the terroristic methods of the Gestapo, but in its haphazard Italian way it was quite thorough.

We saw an example of OVRA work when a Fascist acquaintance in good standing with the party went out to a musical caffè with an American friend of ours. After much winebibbing, the American wanted to sing and proceeded to render Tipperary, in which the Italian, being also far from sober, joined. Afterward, the Italian realized he had been rather indiscreet but did not worry about it as he had never been in the caffè before and was consequently not known to the management. Within a week, however, the OVRA had identified him and called him up for questioning. Sentenced to *confino*, he appealed to some of his influential friends, and the judgment was set aside. The OVRA, however, was convinced that anyone who would sing a British war song in his cups was secretly pro-British and they kept watch on him. About two months later they arrested him on some other pretext and this time he stayed arrested. The last we heard of him, he was still in jail.

Italy was also full of Gestapo agents, ostensibly there to watch over Germans in Italy, but also keeping an eye on everything else that went on. They worked independently of the OVRA, but when they discovered evidence against Italians they turned the information over to the Italian police, who made the arrests.

All this constant watching precludes the hatching of any conspiracies. On the other hand, an unplanned, spontaneous revolt is nearly impossible because of the absence of any popular leader. The two men who stood the best chance of igniting a spontaneous revolution have both died since the war began. They were Italo Balbo, who, though a Fascist, did not see eye to eye with Mussolini about the German alliance, and the Duke of Aosta, who devoted himself to the army and held aloof from politics.

Badoglio, the only prominent man who was publicly anti-Fascist and got away with it for a time, is too old and too cautious. He would never risk such an undertaking unless he had at least an eighty per cent chance of success, and that he will never have without an Anglo-Saxon invasion of Italy. The only other well-known military man who is not working with the regime is Graziani, and he could not succeed in leading a revolution because, owing to his reputation for cruelty and brutality, he does not have either the affection or the trust of most Italians.

The only kind of *coup d'état* that would have a good chance of success in Italy would be a "palace revolution" — that is, an agreement among the most prominent Fascists to remove Mussolini and put another Fascist in his place. In an event of this kind, the Nazis would be uncertain what attitude to take and probably would not use their troops stationed in Italy as they would in the case of a popular revolt. The practical results would depend entirely on the character of the successor. The three likeliest men would be Farinacci, Grandi, and Ciano.

Farinacci, who was the castor-oil administrator in the early days of Fascism, is not popular in Italy generally, but very strong in his own district of Cremona. In internal politics he is a Fascist extremist and in foreign policies violently pro-German.

Ciano would probably never consent to such a coup d'état unless Mussolini were genuinely failing in mind — more than usual. Being a very wealthy man, Ciano is inclined to be conservative in regard to domestic policies, while in the foreign field he is interested solely in extending the power and influence of Italy. In his social life he dislikes most Germans and likes most Anglo-Saxons, but this would not prevent his continuing the alliance with Germany if that might seem most profitable to Italy. His ambitions, however, are apt to outrun Italy's potentialities as a military power, as in the case of the ill-starred invasion of Greece. Furthermore, despite his prominence, his abilities are not such as to make it likely that his fellow Fascists would choose him as the new Duce. Ciano's strongest claim is that Mussolini wishes him as a successor, but the public would never have confidence in him.

Grandi is a mystery man so far as his views on Italian foreign policy are concerned. During the Ethiopian and Spanish wars, when he was Italian Ambassador to London, he very ably presented and promoted the Fascist cause in many a rough-and-tumble conference of the powers. In the present war he has occupied a rather obscure position, but whether that was from choice or because he had incurred the displeasure of the Duce is uncertain. He could not have been too much out of favor because Mussolini appointed him Minister of Justice to speed up the completion of the new Fascist law code which was finished in the fall of 1941, after which Mussolini took over the Ministry of Justice and Grandi was assigned to war service. In regard to Fascist internal policies he is known to be moderate. He is reputed to be both intellectual and a levelheaded, shrewd politician who has a large following among thoughtful Italians.

Perhaps Giuseppe Bottai, Minister of Education, should be mentioned as a possible "dark horse." Too colorless to be a popular leader, he is a die-hard Fascist who spends a great deal of time and thought writing essays on the principles of Fascism. Although not violent as Farinacci is, he is almost as much of an extremist and, being something of a scholar, tries to co-ordinate sound principles of economics and statecraft with Fascist fantasies, merging the two into a logical-whimsical hodge-podge of political science. His bold criticisms of Fascist policies published in his own magazine sometimes made Italians gasp; but his comments were generally based on the fact that principles had been sacrificed to expediency and were never criticisms of Fascism *per se*. It would be hard to predict what he would do if a freak of fate were ever to make him the head of Italy.

A list of possible Italian revolutionary leaders would not be complete without mentioning the royal family. Both Americans and English vastly overestimate the personal standing and influence of the royal family in Italy. Perhaps it is easier to understand the English making this mistake, since they so greatly revere their own royalty, but the truth is that Victor Emmanuel and his wife and children occupy nothing like so prominent a place in their people's lives as do George VI and his family. Not that the King is disliked in Italy — on the contrary, he is very popular — but he is regarded as a kindly, patriotic, but not too brilliant old gentleman who could never in the world guide Italy through the dangerous shoals of contemporary history.

The King enjoys the affection of the Italian people, but he himself is not without the taint of Fascism. It was his refusal to allow martial law to be imposed which made the success of Mussolini's March on Rome possible. Also, there is good reason to believe he welcomed the March; he in company with many others was worried over the social unrest in Italy as manifested by the hundreds of strikes and the apparent inability of the government ministers to deal with the situation. Many Italians who did not subscribe to the principles of Fascism welcomed Mussolini's accession to power as promising a strong, stable government. During the first weeks of the Ethiopian war, the King was reported to have said:

"No matter what the result, it will strengthen my position. If we win, I shall become Emperor of Ethiopia. If we lose, I shall really be King."

The heir to the throne, Umberto, Prince of Piedmont, also is not sufficiently a leader to head a rebellion. Handsome and hot-headed, as a young man he was restrained only by the urgings of his father from taking a publicly anti-Fascist stand, and he held aloof from the Fascist campaigns in Ethiopia and Spain. But the passing years appear to have cooled his ardor, as he is now co-operating with the Fascists and holds the post of Inspector of Infantry with the rank of full general. He was nominally in charge of the Italian offensive against France, which had as one of its objectives the recovery of French Savoy, the land from which his royal line, the House of Savoy, sprang. This objective was not attained.

The naming of Amadeo, Duke of Spoleto, as King of Croatia was another outstanding example of co-operation between the House of Savoy and Mussolini. The royal family is now definitely committed to a policy of Italian imperialism, which means they are committed to Fascism and must continue to support Il Duce. A royalist-led revolution, therefore, should be dismissed as not being within the range of practical possibilities.

Yet the fact remains that there is a huge Anglo-American fifth column in Italy, many millions strong, a great potential source of aid to us if we can only find a way to use it. It would be a blunder not to try to harness it up, as to employ it might shorten the war and save the lives of many British and American soldiers. And these fifth columnists would be willing to work for us if we were to give them help, but they are not going to rise up and risk being killed in a revolt that does not have at least a seventy-five per cent chance of success.

How then can these potential allies be used, and what inducement do they need to work actively on our side? We believe our theory about this is a sound one because it makes allowance for the fundamental Italian aversion to taking big risks.

Capomazza once remarked to Reynolds, "Italian babies are born with old eyes." It was just a catch phrase, but it struck us as being extremely true and it explained much in the Italian character which was difficult for foreigners to understand.

The Italians are an extremely old and disillusioned race which has already lived through every known phase of human development, including triumphs, decadence, and disappointments. They passed their most decadent period soon after they reached the peak of their Renaissance development. Now they have returned to and prefer the simple life. They work hard, go to bed early, drink very little, smoke very little, come home for dinner, go to church on Sunday mornings, and take a stroll in the park on Sunday afternoons. Their greatest dissipations in the overwhelming majority of cases is to go to the movies or have their relatives in for a family *festa*, where everyone sings and drinks red wine. Even in Rome, the night clubs were always wholly dependent on foreign customers for their existence — Italians just didn't care for them.

But because Italians prefer the simple life does not mean they are simple-minded. On the contrary, they are historically over-sophisticated and ultracynical. Fourteen hundred years of living under various conquerors of one race or another has rubbed away much of their idealism. Such fighting words as "liberty" and "democracy," which so stir American blood, leave Italians unmoved. They are inclined to look out first and foremost for their own skins and worry about moral principles afterward.

Now they are not going to spill their blood for liberty and democracy unless they see a seventy-five per cent chance of material success. They have become political opportunists. Exhortations from America and Britain that the Italians should overthrow the Fascist yoke in order to achieve freedom and independence fall upon skeptical ears. They want to know just what they are sure of, specifically, in return. They are bargaining horse dealers. We believe, however, that the great mass of discontented Italians, despite the lethargy of their political passions, would rise up if Anglo-American troops (with accent on the American) should make a landing in force, but really in force, in an all-out invasion attempt.

Why not make our second front in Italy? If the attempt were timed to the psychological moment, it would be sensationally successful, and the conquest of the peninsula would probably be achieved within a few weeks with the help of the local population.

The advantages of invading Italy rather than some other point in Europe are many. For one thing, many parts of the long Italian coastline are not nearly so heavily fortified as the German-occupied coasts of France, the Low Countries, and Norway. It would end the war in Africa at a stroke, since the Axis armies there would be cut off from their base of supplies. It would mean landing in a country where the population was friendly and there would be no civilian resistance; where there is even a strong possibility of an army revolt in favor of the invaders if the political ground is correctly prepared in advance.

The northern half of Italy would probably offer the most favorable landing spots. Southern Italy and Sicily were already quite heavily fortified because before Greece and Crete were conquered, the Fascists feared a British landing attempt in the south. The bulk of the mechanized troops, tanks, and airplanes that were not sent to Libya were concentrated in the south when we left. Most of the units of the Italian fleet were also in southern waters, where they were constantly engaged in convoy work between Libya and Italy.

But Mussolini didn't have enough armament to go around, so he was obliged to gamble by leaving the northern coast more or less exposed. We believe that up to the summer of 1942, he had here only a few coastal batteries, pill boxes, and a few outmoded fighting planes. Most of the soldiers were of second-grade caliber, being ordinary infantry without specialist training. Some idea of how unprepared the Italians have been for a surprise attack in this region can be gained from the fact that a British cruiser once shelled Genoa for nearly twenty minutes without opposition from a single Italian airplane or naval unit. All during the summer of 1941 we heard in Rome stories of British submarine crews landing on Italian beaches to stretch their legs or get a breath of fresh air. Italian fishermen reported their presence to authorities, who, however, failed to act in time to capture them.

In general, the region between Genoa and Viareggio presents the best strategic advantages to an invading force. The mountains are narrower here and, once over them, Anglo-American troops would be able to swarm down the valley of the Po River to the Adriatic. Another advantage of striking in the north would be that a wedge of Anglo-American occupied territory across the breadth of Italy would cut Italy off from Germany, greatly weakening any further Italian resistance. Without the Germans to prod them on, the Italian soldiers would not be inclined to fight very hard against a friendly enemy, and the Anglo-American fifth columnists would not be afraid to revolt against the Fascist regime.

Such an invading force would, of course, have to be prepared to resist a terrific German assault from the direction of the Brenner Pass, but that would certainly be no worse than trying to land on German-held territory. The number of German divisions already in Italy would not be enough to stem a large invading force.

Once Italy was in Anglo-American hands, the French and Yugoslavs would probably facilitate our entrance into their countries and thus would begin the reconquest of Europe.

The only possible objection to Italy as a second front is its distance from Anglo-American bases. Convoying the troops and equipment to Italian shores would require using a big fleet of naval units in order to give them adequate protection. We believe the numerous advantages offset this disadvantage. Once a small piece of territory could be seized, transport planes could be used to bring up fresh troops. If Libya could be occupied first it would, of course, greatly simplify the invasion of Italy, but it seems likely that waiting for that means waiting too long.

If Italy should be chosen for the second front, it would be desirable to change American propaganda beamed on Italy, somewhat before the attack is launched. We frankly don't think the present angle is a good one either for Italy or for the occupied European countries. Without changing our ideals or goals in any way, we can present them differently. Quite a lot of what we say eventually reaches Italian ears — it is amazing how much Anglo-American news gets passed around by word of mouth in Italy.

One thing that we think America should do is to lay more emphasis on the role of America and Britain — but particularly America — in this war. To the long-suffering people in the Axis-occupied countries, the phrase "United Nations" calls up, however unjustly, a picture of countryless governments whose members, after fleeing their homelands, are comfortably sitting around in London or America, planning to return to power when America and Britain win the war for them. Anti-Fascists in Italy, we know, do not take these "ghost governments" seriously, and a revolt in their favor is unthinkable. But they would revolt, we believe, in the name of America and Britain, who represent tangible and real fighting forces. The Italian fifth columnists know that the fighting in Europe is being done by America, Britain, and Russia, but what they do not know is whether, in case of an Anglo-American invasion, they can with confidence throw themselves on the mercy of the Americans and the English without being afraid that their fate is going to be decided by the Russians, Czechs, Poles, Yugoslavs, Norwegians, Dutch, and so on. If the Italians think there is the slightest chance of this happening, they will not abandon the Duce or the Germans.

Although Americans at home may not realize it, America is the one major power in the world today with a reputation for trying always to be both just and humane. The worst Europeans can say for us is that we sometimes take wrong attitudes and make a mess of things because we do not understand the overseas problems involved, and this is sometimes a fair criticism. But despite the abuse that has been heaped on America by the controlled Axis press of various countries, European people in general give America credit for at least trying to do the right thing. This is a precious reputation which should be exploited, and its effectiveness should not be diminished by our giving too much prominence to the war roles of exiled governments.

The same feeling that the Italians have about this is shared also by many of our smaller allies and enemies. They trust us much more than they trust each other, for when it comes time to write the peace there are a thousand vexing problems which only the utmost good will and patience of America can solve. To name just a few of them: Who is going to draw the boundary between Russia and Poland? Should Lithuania be reconstituted? If so, what should her boundaries with Russia and Poland be? Should the Croats be compelled to become a part of Yugoslavia again, whether or not they like it? As between two enemy countries, Hungary and Rumania, what should the frontier be when both sides claim Transylvania? All these countries, friend and foe alike, would feel surer of getting a square deal if America had a dominant voice in the matter. The psychological effect of this might be a factor in shortening the war, which otherwise bids fair to endure for years and years.

As regards our active allies, Britain and Russia, Britain has a reputation for fairness second only to America's. She is generally credited with being just where such a course does not directly conflict with her own interests, and certainly all peoples know she can be trusted not to exact any mass vengeance or to set up a reign of terror in conquered territory.

Russia is quite a different case. Without in any way depreciating the magnificence of the Russian resistance or the inestimable value it has had in giving the Anglo-Americans a breathing space in which to make their preparations, there is no use closing our eyes to the fact that the Soviets are profoundly distrusted throughout Europe. It is a waste of breath to tell enemy countries like Finland, Hungary, Rumania, and Italy, or friendly countries like Denmark and France, that Nazi occupation is worse than Soviet occupation. They do not believe it. The Bolsheviks have built up their reputation for terror during twenty years, and we cannot expect them to be washed clean of it in a few months just because they happen to be on the side of the democracies. Our Italian fifth column will certainly never revolt if they think Russia will have anything whatsoever to do with the occupation. The same is true of the peoples of all the smaller countries allied to the Axis.

It is even true of the Germans themselves. We believe that a second front will never divert a serious number of troops from the Russian front on this account. The Germans have an almost morbid dread of the Soviets and think that if the Bolshevists ever occupy Germany they will wipe out everyone — civilians as well as soldiers. If the Germans ever believe they are hopelessly beaten, they will try to hold the Russian line at all costs and let the Americans and English occupy their country.

Besides taking an ineffective line in talking of the United Nations rather than of the United States, we think the American publicists should also go warily in the importance and support they give to personalities in the exiled governments. Several rulers and leaders who are today being lionized by the American public are far from being considered heroes at home. The attitude of the people of the occupied countries toward their overseas governments is bound to be affected by human nature. These people are enduring terrible oppression and privation and are inclined, therefore, to resent that their leaders were able to escape and that they were left behind. Their preferred leaders are the ones on the spot, leading subversive movements against their conquerors and sharing the hardships of their fellow citizens. Their names are not known to the American and British publics, maybe are not known even to the American and British governments. Their only protection lies in complete anonymity. But Americans should realize that when the war is over these leaders will be difficult to brush aside in favor of those who are now enjoying the hospitality of England and America.

Following the example of the exiled allied governments, non-Fascist Italians in North and South America have held some meetings and have endeavored to set up a sort of committee to work for a liberated Italy. It is obvious that such a movement, if organized on a sound basis, might prove most useful to the American

Government as forming a liaison body between America and potential revolutionaries in Italy. The sincerity of most of these Italians in their adherence to the democratic cause is beyond doubt since many of them chose self-imposed exile rather than living under Mussolini's regime. Naturally they are interested in trying to save Italy from suffering too greatly after the military defeat she is slated to receive at the hands of America and America's allies, but that does not mean that they will work for our cause any less whole-heartedly.

Organizing this anti-Fascist Italian movement on a sound basis, however, does not mean setting up a puppet Italian Government which will be ready to move into Italy with American troops. Indeed, to encourage the creation of any such government would mean to encourage the founders of the movement to engage in internal politics instead of attending to the business at hand — the winning of the war and the part they should play in it. Furthermore, the setting up of such a post-war Italian Government to be imposed upon Italy by her conquerors is not going to encourage our Italian Fifth Columnists in Italy to work for us. They will not revolt if they think they will not be allowed to choose their own rulers.

There is also, of course, the possibility that Mussolini himself will want to break away from Germany, taking the whole nation with him. Such a course seems outside the realm of political probabilities, however, because Mussolini himself initiated the pro-German policy and has since insisted that it be followed with one hundred per cent thoroughness. He has risked everything on a single throw of the dice, and to retract would mean admitting that he had made a gigantic error in judgment that has cost Italy tens of thousands of lives and threatens to ruin her economically. He could never turn such a diplomatic somersault and hope to continue as dictator of Italy.

In the midst of the emotional upheavals of war, it is hard to assess what Mussolini's place in history will be when research workers centuries hence make a cold and impartial appraisal of him.

They will certainly divide his dictatorship into two parts. The first period of about twelve years was marked by his collaboration with the democratic powers of Europe, including France and England, who had been Italy's allies in World War I. Although he stifled all internal opposition during this period, he did carry out a social program that was good: it included child and maternity welfare, social security for workers, housing and reclamation schemes, general improvement of sanitation, water-power projects and agrarian reforms of all kinds. Much of his program had already been adopted by democratic countries in 1922, and the remainder of them are now in force in democratic countries today.

The second part of his regime began in 1934, when he planned the invasion of Abyssinia the following year. From then on he became a menace to world peace. He dropped his domestic reforms and concentrated on building up a war machine for conquest. He abandoned Italy's former allies and joined up with Hitler, with whom he founded the Rome-Berlin Axis in the hope of extending Italy's frontiers in Europe and Africa. But the Axis proved a boomerang, and Mussolini has since found that collaboration with the Germans meant loss of Italian independence and a diminishing of his own power in his own country.

The people in Italy today are against him. They are anxious to overthrow him. They accuse him of two grave crimes: first, he crushed democracy in Italy; and second, he lined up Italy with Nazi Germany.

The Italian people are right, and we should encourage them to revolt at the opportune time and join our side, but not with the ·inducement of complete forgiveness. As Secretary of State Hull has said, democracy is something that must be worked for and struggled for. This the Italian people failed to do, and this failure must stand as a black mark against them. But one thing is clear in this confused situation: the Italian people have more to hope for by coming over to the side of America and Britain than they have by continuing their alliance with Germany, and many of them realize it.

We had formulated all these ideas aboard the *Drottningholm*, and it was as well we did, for we had little time for rumination after we arrived in America! We had been away from the United States long enough to have forgotten the whirlwind pace of these shores.

We had planned to take a vacation and get the full savor of our homeland again, but the moment we stepped off the exchange ship in Jersey City on June 1, 1942, we were swept up into a round of activity which included radio broadcasts, lectures, after-dinner speeches, and interviews both with the press and with government representatives.

After three weeks, the whirlwind died down and we had a chance to look about us. We were surprised to see practically no changes in the American way of living since we had left New York six years before. The war effort had not cost us the freedom of speech and liberty that the Axis press had always said it would. We found that America at war was much the same as it was at peace. We were shocked at first at the lightness of attitude that many people took toward the grim future in store for this country, but we realized that, without hearing the guns shooting and bombs falling, it is difficult to be realistic. In fact, we have since concluded that too much grimness at this early stage of the war would be theatrical. We believe that if the American people just carry on as they are now doing, adapting themselves to every new sacrifice that must be borne, there is no need to worry about the outcome of the war. America is bound to win if it just remains American.

Ideals are not so much ballast to be tossed overboard in a storm. After seeing how that was done in Axis Europe, we have only one modest word of advice: cling to the American way of life and American democratic principles as far as it is possible to do so without impairing the war effort.

If we hold to our ideals of liberty and democracy, we believe that the greatest fifth column in the history of the world will rise up to revolt against their masters in Europe and welcome our invasion. But let's make that invasion as American as possible.